C000044871

Through the lens of legal experimentalism this compelling book analyzes immigration and minority policies and the European Convention of Human Rights. Law emerges from a transnational process of continuous contestation and learning of international legal institutions and local and national actors. Because it offers an instructive contrast to the experimentation movement in the social sciences, this highly original and carefully developed application of the experimentalist turn appeals to readers interested in both European law and general legal and social analysis.

Peter J. Katzenstein, Walter S. Carpenter, Jr. Professor of International Studies,
Cornell University

This is an innovative and impressive book which analyzes the functioning and effectiveness of the European Court of Human Rights in the area of minorities and migrants' rights from an "experimentalist" perspective, and with particular focus on civil society mobilization. During a time of populist and nationalist illiberalism, the author presents a compelling theory of the effectiveness of strategic litigation before the ECtHR in these two important fields. The book should be of great interest to lawyers and political scientists who want to understand the role of courts and litigation in social change, and particularly to those interested in examining the effectiveness of regional and international human rights systems.

Gráinne de Búrca, Florence Ellinwood Allen Professor of Law, New York
University School of Law

The European Convention of Human Rights Regime

Prompted by an unprecedented rise of litigation since the 1990s, this book examines how the European Convention of Human Rights (ECHR) system and the Strasbourg Court interact with states and non-governmental actors to influence domestic change. Focusing on European Court of Human Rights litigation and state implementation of judgments related to minority discrimination and asylum/migration, it argues that a fundamental transformation of the Convention system has been under way. Repeat and strategic litigation, shifting methods of supervision and state implementation to remedy systemic violations, and above all the growing engagement of civil society and non-governmental actors, have prompted a distinctive trend of human rights experimentalism. The emergence of experimentalism has profound implications for the legitimacy, effectiveness and further reform of the ECHR system. This study provides an original constitutive account of regional human rights regimes and how they are activated by societal actors to claim rights, advance case law, and pressure for domestic legal and policy change. It will be of interest to international law and international relations scholars, political scientists, specialists on the ECHR, the Strasbourg Court, as well as to scholars interested in the human rights of immigrants and minorities.

Dia Anagnostou is Associate Professor, Panteion University of Social Sciences, Athens, Greece, and Senior Research Fellow, Hellenic Foundation for European and Foreign Policy (ELIAMEP), Greece.

Routledge Research in Human Rights Law

For more information about this series, please visit:
www.routledge.com/Routledge-Research-in-Human-Rights-Law/book-series/
HUMRIGHTSLAW

The European Convention of Human Rights Regime

Reform of Immigration and Minority Policies from Afar

Dia Anagnostou

Routledge
Taylor & Francis Group

LONDON AND NEW YORK

First published 2023
by Routledge
4 Park Square, Milton Park, Abingdon, Oxon OX14 4RN

and by Routledge
605 Third Avenue, New York, NY 10158

Routledge is an imprint of the Taylor & Francis Group, an informa business

British Library Cataloguing-in-Publication Data
A catalogue record for this book is available from the British Library

Library of Congress Cataloging-in-Publication Data
A catalog record has been requested for this book

ISBN: 978-1-032-18830-0 (hbk)
ISBN: 978-1-032-18836-2 (pbk)
ISBN: 978-1-003-25648-9 (ebk)

DOI: 10.4324/9781003256489

Typeset in Galliard
by Taylor & Francis Books

Contents

Illustrations

Figures

Tables

Acknowledgments

This book was very long in the making and progressed slowly with several stops and detours along the way. It started off with an idea and purpose quite different from the one it ended up being about. Originally, I wanted to write a book about the causes of rising litigation and legal mobilization in the ECHR. I stayed on this path and worked on it for a couple of years only to realize that a study on litigation and legal mobilization would be limp and pointless without a broader theory of internationally induced domestic change that would be applicable to the European multi-level setting. It became all too clear how the release of a Court judgment – victorious or unsuccessful – was not the end of efforts by individuals and other non-state actors to advance rights before an international tribunal. It was only a moment – an important and even critical one – in the continuous struggles and efforts of individuals and organizational entities to uphold and strengthen rights protection in state policies and practices.

It was in search of a theory to understand how international rights litigation and legal mobilization – as valuable and key tools – could effectively promote rights enhancing reform and domestic change, that I discovered transnational experimentalist governance. The basic characteristics of the experimentalist governance model seemed to bear close resemblance to the ECHR regime transformed by tectonic developments over the past twenty-five years. This was a turning point in the writing of this book and took me in a direction that was intellectually and timewise far more demanding than I had anticipated. It opened though for me a new terrain of knowledge and thinking about international human rights law and courts, socio-legal activism and domestic change.

The original idea for this book was planted with a Marie Curie Fellowship at the Law Department of the European University Institute in Florence in 2010–2012. The basis for it though was established even further back when a three-year long project funded by the 6th Framework Program of the European Commission (JURISTRAS project, FP6 contract no. 028398) enabled me to learn about the ECHR and cross over to a field of study which at the time was exclusively the domain of legal scholars.

During my fellowship at the EUI, but also well before and after it, Bruno De Witte inspired and constantly supported my inter-disciplinary research on the ECHR and on human rights law more broadly, in times and ways too many to mention. Over the following years, I conducted interviews in London, Strasbourg and Athens, as well as remotely, with many individuals who generously shared with me their time, experience and knowledge of the ECHR.

A number of people provided me with critical and substantive assistance in taking this book forward. Mathilde Chatzipanagiotou, Maria Xiari, Elli Pallaiolo-gou and Christiana Antonoudiou, all talented and incredibly capable young researchers and scholars, helped me put together and update the large ECtHR case law data set on which this study is in large part based. Bruno De Witte, Peter Katzenstein, Grainne De Búrca and Stephanos Stavros read and provided me with substantive and constructive comments on some of the chapters, as well as with fresh ideas that pushed the book in new and exciting directions that I had not originally envisioned. I am thankful for their support in what was otherwise a solitary and challenging intellectual journey. I would also like to thank the Hellenic Foundation for European and Foreign Policy (ELIAMEP) in Athens that for over fifteen years now has provided me with a hospitable place and the space to pursue my independent research interests too.

Last but not least, I would like to thank my husband Giorgos Kaminis, who is my "rock" and my "star". With a uniquely rich perspective of a constitutional law scholar who is at the same time immersed into real life politics, he read closely several chapters of this book more than once. He gave me unconditional and steady support throughout the years, in good but also in difficult times, and made me believe that I can complete this project. Our daughters Katerina and Angelina grew fast along with it, and they are more excited than I am to see this book nearing to fruition. I dedicate this book to all three of them with infinite love and gratitude.

1 Minorities and migrants in the Strasbourg Court

International human rights courts are prominent global institutions and central pillars of regional human rights regimes. In response to complaints brought by individuals, they issue rulings that expose systemic problems and necessitate domestic structural and policy reforms. In the past decades, the remit of international judicial review has extended to issues and disputes that are linked to traditionally core state prerogatives, such as national security, migration and border control. As human rights courts grew more autonomous vis-à-vis states and expanded their authority, they became both well-entrenched in international governance, but also profoundly challenged by national governments.[1] The European Court of Human Rights (hereby ECtHR or the Court) – admittedly the world's most successful human rights judiciary – is a case in point. An unprecedent docket crisis, the Court's increasing engagement with sensitive national issues like minorities and immigration, the growth of structural human rights violations have all posed strong challenges to its legitimacy and effectiveness.[2]

Prompted by a notable rise of litigation in the Strasbourg Court, this book examines how the ECHR regime interacts with states and non-governmental actors to influence domestic human rights change. Since the 1990s, large numbers of marginalized individuals belonging to minorities and migrants, and lacking voice or real access in the domestic political arenas, took recourse to the ECtHR to claim rights protection from state action. A key upshot of rising human rights claims is the emergence of structural reform litigation (hereby SRL). It is a form of strategic legal action that challenges and seeks to tackle systemic human rights problems besetting state institutions and large administrative organizations.[3] Transnational litigation is a key mechanism through which individual and non-governmental actors seek to enforce state conformity with human rights.[4] It also stands at the heart of processes through which international human rights regimes evolve and are reconstituted.

Why and how have vulnerable and marginalized persons from minorities and migrants increasingly taken recourse to the ECtHR and to what extent is litigation strategic? What effects do the relevant judgments that expose structural human rights problems have on states' policies and practices, and on the nature and functioning of the ECHR regime? In addressing these empirical questions, this book is more broadly interested in how regional human rights courts and regimes

DOI: 10.4324/9781003256489-1

evolve amidst conflicting pressures to effectively enforce conformity with human rights while also deferring to states' sovereign powers. In examining ECtHR litigation and state implementation of judgments related to minorities and migrants, it argues that a fundamental transformation of the Convention system has been under way. Repeat and strategic litigation, shifting methods of supervision and state implementation to remedy systemic violations, and above all the growing engagement of civil society and non-governmental actors, have prompted a distinctive trend of human rights experimentalism.

Human rights experimentalism is a theory about how international legal institutions can bring about domestic reform and rights-enhancing policy change. It grows in a multilevel system where participating states have agreed to implement a shared framework of norms embedded in a treaty.[5] States have wide discretion as to how to apply broad and inherently ambiguous human rights principles across diverse national and local contexts. Transnational experimentalism proposes that related social and political changes can come about not through prescriptive orders from above, but incrementally, through continuous interaction, contestation and learning between local-national actors and international legal institutions.[6]

What is distinctive about experimentalist settings is that a series of stakeholders and non-state actors engage in articulating and enforcing broad norms, such as the prohibition of inhuman treatment and discrimination, or the protection of freedom and security, as well as in monitoring state actions to implement them. In the ECHR, growing civil society mobilization since the 1990s and the use of transnational litigation to redress structural human rights problems, as this study shows, fundamentally opened up the system. They paved the way for changes in its institutional rules and practices that pushed the ECHR in an experimentalist direction.

The experimentalist understanding laid out in this book advances a constitutive account of regional human rights courts and regimes that departs from legalist assumptions often permeating the study of these regimes. Legalism assumes that codified international legal rules are reinforced from above; and that state decision-makers align their behaviors with human rights simply because these have become law through obligation, judicial rule making and delegation.[7] From the constitutive perspective that this book advances on the other hand, human rights law is forged through and in turn reinforces political and social struggles. These are often waged between vulnerable individuals and groups and powerful states. Individuals, civil society and non-governmental actors have a constitutive role in the functioning and evolution of international human rights regimes. The emergence of experimentalism has profound implications for debates about the legitimacy, effectiveness and continuing reform of the ECHR system.[8]

Human rights litigation is often embedded in broader national and transnational mobilization strategies. It prompts and enables the Strasbourg Court to intervene in particular areas of state action and in many cases, to pronounce violations of the Convention. International human rights rulings can act as catalysts and other times as "focal points" in ongoing processes of rights litigation, adjudication, state implementation and follow-on action.[9] The remaining parts of this chapter analyze the basic characteristics of experimentalism in human rights courts (section 1), define and discuss international rights litigation (2), review existing explanations for the rise in ECtHR litigation (3), provide an overview of the domestic implementation of ECtHR rulings (4), present the approach, research and argument of this book (5), and lay out the chapters that follow (6).

1.1 Experimentalism and international human rights courts

In transnational experimentalism, states agree to give practical effect to common framework goals across diverse national-local settings in a multilevel system.[10] National authorities interact with international treaty bodies and with a variety of non-state actors in seeking to implement broadly defined and inherently ambiguous normative standards. A central treaty body reviews and monitors the implementing measures and deliberates with governments who readjust the means and the goals if necessary. In this recursive process, all actors learn from prior experience (including from that of other states) and from international organizations.[11] Experimentalist governance arrangements have been shown to emerge in the European Union[12], in areas such as the anti-discrimination legislation[13], and in international regimes of environmental protection, the rights of persons with disabilities[14], and forest sustainability[15], among others. As a mode of policy implementation in multi-level governance, experimentalism unfolds in a pragmatic and mid-way ground between integrated and state-centered regimes on the one hand, and non-hierarchical and loosely coupled, pluralist arrangements, on the other.[16]

In the human rights field, experimentalist arrangements have emerged in the frame of treaties like the Convention on the Elimination of all Forms of Discrimination Against Women (CEDAW), the Convention of the Rights of the Child (CRC), and the Convention on the Rights of Persons with Disabilities (CRPD). These regimes a) are premised on a consensus among signatory states to promote human rights protection, b) they articulate a set of rights and principles that are broad, flexible and general, c) they allow for significant discretion on the part of states as to how to implement the agreed norms, d) they establish a system of periodic reporting, monitoring and feedback, under which states are obliged to report regularly on their compliance with treaty obligations, and e) they involve iterative processes of deliberation, periodic reconsideration and revision of goals by international treaty bodies and national-local actors and institutions.[17] A key feature of experimentalist arrangements is openness to a wide variety of stakeholders and civil society. These actors pressure governments to implement the relevant norms, monitor the adopted measures, provide input to the treaty body, and participate in consultations.

While experimentalism has so far been ascertained in human rights treaties based on periodic reporting, litigation, courts and judicial intervention can be central features of experimentalist arrangements. This may at first seem counter-intuitive as courts' intervention is traditionally conceived as a kind of top-down enforcement that is incompatible with the decentralized and pluralist thrust of experimentalist premises.[18] Studies though compellingly expound how the shifting nature of judicial intervention in US public law in the 1960s-1970s set the basis for the rise of experimentalism. In his classic analysis on the subject, Abraham Chayes showed how civil rights litigation radically departed from the traditional lawsuit that involved two private parties' dispute over a past wrong. It raised claims and led to court rulings that implicated the operations of large public organizations such as schools, prisons and police departments, and required long-term restructuring and institutional reform.[19]

In areas of such complexity, judicial intervention stumbled over the difficulty of determining appropriate measures to tackle structural discrimination in different local conditions. In racial segregation in public schools in the USA, for example, highly detailed regulatory orders issued by courts in the 1970s failed to enforce desegregation. As command-and-control regulation stumbled and more litigation followed suit, the nature of judicial intervention in the USA transformed. Instead of directing specific action through detailed rules, judicial decrees invoked rights and elaborated broad goals and standards, with only vague implications about the appropriate remedies. Their implementation relied on substantial local discretion and on the participation of different actors to determine how to achieve those goals.[20] It involved semi-permanent processes of setting and revising goals, and monitoring their achievement, rather than to one-time policy adjustments.[21] Defendants alongside interested stakeholders, including NGOs, actively engaged in determining and putting to practice such broad norms and standards in different contexts.

Thus, civil rights litigation prompted a new species of public law intervention exerting its impact primarily through "destabilization rights": it primarily pronounced norms that unsettled well-established but illegitimate or unfair rules and practices in public institutions.[22] In situations of normative uncertainty and administrative complexity, courts began to act as catalysts or facilitators. They spurred government efforts to realize in practice particular values and principles and made space for the participation of non-governmental stakeholders in the implementing processes.[23]

Human rights courts like the ECtHR partake in many of the features defining the shifting nature of judicial intervention in civil rights struggles in the USA and its experimentalist turn. In the first place, the Convention was always structured as a decentralized system that is subsidiary to national rights protection. Subsidiarity permeates the way ECtHR judges adjudicate cases: they pronounce violations of human rights but refrain from prescribing specific remedies and implementing measures. Far-reaching discretion is allotted to national authorities in implementing ECtHR judgments and remedying violations. The Strasbourg Court relies on precedent, but at times it also departs from it to advance new interpretations in response to litigation, and in the light of changing conditions and societal values within states – a dynamic approach rendering the Convention a "living instrument".[24]

Litigation in the ECtHR has increasingly challenged structural human rights problems within states, prompting the Court to intervene in entire areas of state action and administration. Driven by strategic goals and often embedded in broader campaigns for rights, this structural reform litigation (SRL) is the first phase of a judicially enforced human rights regime with experimentalist characteristics, as elaborated in the next section.

2 Individuals, civil society and litigation in international courts

Human rights litigation is a distinctive feature of "new style" international courts, such as the Inter-American Court of Human Rights and the African Court on Human and People's Rights, that allow for individuals and other private actors to bring claims against states.[25] Public law and politics studies have for a long time now explored the role of courts as venues for individuals and groups to claim rights and seek social change, mostly in the context of national political and legal systems.[26] Legal action before courts tends to take place where traditional avenues of electoral politics and interest group representation are restricted or closed. In the second half of the 20th century, various kinds of minorities in the USA used the law to claim rights before courts and to pursue social reform goals.[27] In their seminal study of the early 1990s on the use of law by pressure groups, Harlow and Rawlings for the first time included a section on transnational legal action with a focus on the ECtHR.[28] The protection of fundamental rights though was still considered to predominantly lie within the purview of constitutional law and national courts.

Over the past few decades, various kinds of minorities and marginalized individuals in Europe have also resorted to national and European courts and legal processes.[29] Individual actors and organizational entities committed to various social causes have variably deployed national and transnational litigation among their repertoires of action. In the 1960s and 1970s, the Court of Justice of the European Union (CJEU, formerly European Court of Justice, ECJ) pronounced the principles of supremacy and direct effect that formed the seedbed for new rights emanating from EC law. Since then, disadvantaged individuals and social groups have used EU litigation to claim rights, to pressure governments or to challenge state laws and policies for their compatibility with EU law. They have pursued EU litigation in areas as diverse as environmental protection,[30] Roma rights,[31] gender equality and violence against women,[32] gay rights,[33] access to employment and social benefits,[34] ethnic and racial discrimination[35] and disability rights.[36] Supranational litigation is an increasingly important form of public participation in the EU's highly decentralized, quasi-federal polity. Unsurprisingly, rights litigation in the Strasbourg Court has been far more voluminous and systematic than in the CJEU.[37]

In transnational rights' litigation, individuals or collective actors resort to international courts or quasi-judicial bodies to challenge state action (less frequently action by private parties) and to seek justice. They contest state action on grounds of breaching fundamental rights, in reference to substantive or procedural norms enshrined in international conventions. Besides seeking an individual remedy, international legal action may also intend to challenge particular state laws, policies and practices. In leading to an authoritative court decision, legal action has been seen as a form of public participation that regulates and delimits relations between citizens and the state. Unlike the organization of group interests to pressure the government, litigation, as rightly noted, is not hampered by collective action problems.[38] Individual and collective actors resort to law and courts in the place of, or alongside political and social mobilization strategies.[39]

Human rights' litigation before international courts may be self-interested, discreet and isolated, involving aggrieved individuals who seek a remedy in a particular case or dispute. They engage in international or supranational litigation to seek a legal remedy that is not available in national courts and legal systems.[40] Alternatively, human rights litigation may be strategic when legal action before an international court is significantly driven by broader legal, policy or social reform goals. While it may have the form of an individual complaint, strategic litigation often involves the initiative of, or support by civil society and other non-governmental organizations. It also tends to be part of broader mobilization and advocacy campaigns, lobbying or other, aimed at achieving legal, policy or social change, and/or at raising awareness around an issue. As part of such broader social struggles, international rights litigation may be pursued for its "boomerang effect" – occurring when domestic social actors, such as NGOs, reach out to international allies, including international courts, in order to bring pressure to bear on their states from the outside.[41]

Regardless of whether or not it is an explicitly strategic form of action, human rights litigation may have a significant policy dimension when it prompts an international court to decide an issue that will affect a significant number or class of people. It may also be aimed at or lead to advancements in human rights law when a court decision provides an innovative perspective on an issue, and/or expands the boundaries of treaty law.

Since the 1990s, the ECtHR saw a rapidly increasing trend of minority- and migrant-related litigation originating from different countries in West, East and Southeast Europe. The relevant complaints invoked Convention principles to frame various issues and disputes as human rights claims against states, and they were often linked to or driven by strategic – political as well as policy goals. Individuals from ethnic minorities challenged states' restrictions to establish and operate minority political parties and associations, as breaches of their freedom of expression and freedom of association. Arrests of members of minorities and abuses by the police or the military in the name of the fight against internal terrorism or militant secessionism, allegedly breached the prohibition of inhuman and degrading treatment. Complaints in the ECtHR also challenged ethnic discrimination against the Roma, in cases involving racially motivated treatment by the police, or school segregation. Large numbers of immigrants and asylum seekers in different European countries also invoked their right to a family life or the risk of inhuman and degrading treatment, in order to prevent their removal to another country.

In response, the Strasbourg Court has adjudicated and variably embraced a wide range of relevant claims, at times expanding and at others restricting the nature and scope of Convention provisions.[42] While, for example, it was reluctant to endorse rights claims related to cultural identity, the Court in numerous cases upheld the right to life (Article 2 ECHR) and the prohibition of inhuman and degrading treatment (Article 3 ECHR) of minority individuals. It also indicated time and again that general references to state integrity and national security are not sufficient grounds for banning minority-friendly political parties or the publication of books and newspaper articles expressing minority-friendly views. Regarding immigrants and asylum-seekers, the ECtHR has upheld in a large body of case law the *non-refoulement* principle: according to it, returning a person to his/her country of origin, where he/she is likely to face death or other harm, amounts to inhuman and degrading treatment (Article 3 ECHR).[43] Even though minority- and migrant-related claims do not make up the bulk of cases in the ECtHR, they have acquired a substantial weight on its agenda, while the relevant case law is crucial for defining the boundaries of the Convention.

Related to the rise in migrant- and minority-related litigation is the growing weight of structural reform litigation (SRL). An increasing volume of minority- and migrant-related claims reviewed by the ECtHR has brought to light systemic rights violations. SRL is a particular kind of strategic legal action that challenges state policies and practices that systematically give rise to human rights breaches. SRL may be intentionally orchestrated by individual, legal and organizational actors, often through the selection of a test case with particular characteristics that allows them to expose a situation or area of state action that is problematic from a human rights point of view. Alternatively, SRL can also take the form of a large number of repeat individual claims leading to several court decisions that find recurring human rights violations in a particular area of state activity.

Irrespective of the form it takes, SRL paves the way for the ECtHR intervention in domestic law, policy and state administration. It thus gives rise to a profoundly significant albeit strongly controversial facet of international judicial rights review in domestic decision-making that has received scant attention by researchers. In fact, it is this kind of review that arouses most uneasiness and is at the heart of the discontent with, and resistance against international courts.[44]

In a decentralized and judicially enforced treaty like the Convention, litigation, whether of the individual or strategic kind, provides the chief mechanism for enforcing broad human rights principles across states. Strategic litigation, specifically that aimed at structural reform, can be seen as the first phase that sets in a cycle of human rights experimentalism: in bringing a complaint before the Strasbourg Court, a variety of legal and non-governmental actors help individuals frame particular issues, state (in)actions, practices and administrative structures in different national and local contexts, as contrary to human rights. Minority- and migrant-related litigation in the ECtHR though is not necessarily strategic or driven by reform goals, but it has variable causes and forms. The next section reviews and discusses different arguments regarding the factors that underpin the rise in human rights litigation in these areas since the 1990s.

3 The causes of rising litigation in the ECtHR

From its inception in the 1950s and up until the 1990s, the ECtHR had admitted for review a relatively small number of petitions related to migrants and minorities. The ECHR, as it is well-known, safeguards basic civil and political rights of individuals against state abuses, and not rights specifically for migrants and refugees, or special rights of minority communities.[45] Attempts in the early 1990s to adopt an additional protocol to the ECHR specifically addressing the protection of minorities failed due to strong opposition from states.[46] Despite the lack of a clear legal basis in the text of the ECHR – an important precondition for advancing a claim in front of a court[47] – minority- and migrant-related litigation flourished and diversified since the 1990s. The overall rise in ECtHR litigation witnessed since the 1990s has been attributed to a) the geopolitical expansion of the ECHR to East Europe and the former Soviet Union, and b) the institutional reform of the Convention system. A less plausible factor posited for explaining the rise in ECtHR claims is the Convention's expanding scope through a series of additional protocols that added further rights and liberties.[48]

The overall growth of litigation in the ECtHR has been viewed as an unsurprising consequence of the accession of former communist states from Central-East Europe (CEE) and the former Soviet Union to the ECHR.[49] In the course of the 1990s, twenty-five new states acceded to the Council of Europe and ratified the Convention, increasing its total membership from 22 to 47 contracting states.[50] Its eastward enlargement nearly doubled the population that came under the Court's jurisdiction, greatly expanding the pool of prospective litigants in it (from 451 to 800 million).[51] This expansion also paved the way for human rights problems that were qualitatively different from the good-faith, occasional rights limitations that the Convention system had dealt with in established west European democracies.[52] The entry of newly democratized states from Central-East Europe and the former Soviet Union that lacked a rule of law tradition brought into the system human rights issues of a systemic nature. Large numbers of complaints involved repeat violations in the justice system, prisons, or the regulation of private property, among others, that were especially difficult to remedy.[53]

The ECHR's enlargement to East Europe and the former Soviet Union and the resulting expansion of the Court's jurisdiction are a significant backdrop for understanding the overall rise of human rights litigation. They did not though cause the rise of ECtHR litigation. The Court still delivers most of its judgments against the established democracies of west and south Europe that are long-standing members of the Convention (based on the number of its judgments per one million citizens).[54] Eastern enlargement also does not explain why large numbers of litigants from ethnic-religious minorities, immigrants and asylum seekers, bring complaints to the ECtHR. A large amount of minority-related litigation originated from new states like Russia and Bulgaria. Large numbers of complaints related to ethnic-religious minorities though also came from states like Greece and Turkey, which had accepted the right to individual petition already in the 1980s.

The rise in litigation related to immigrants and asylum-seekers on the other hand, is apparently unrelated to the Convention's eastward expansion. Relevant claims have mostly originated from old contracting states like the United Kingdom, France and the Netherlands, Belgium, Greece and Italy, which had accepted the right to individual petition much earlier – in the 1960s, 1970s and early 1980s – and always renewed it afterwards.[55]

A second explanation views the growth of human rights litigation as the direct result of the institutional-structural reforms that expanded individual access to the

ECHR system. In the 1990s, a fundamental overhaul of the Convention system culminated with the entry into force of Protocol 11 (P-11) to the ECHR. Significantly, it rendered the previously optional right to individual petition mandatory for all Contracting States, "old" and "new", which would no longer withhold or renew it at will. P-11 also abolished the European Commission of Human Rights (ECommHR), the first body to examine petitions and decide which ones to refer to the Court. It thus created a single court that petitioners could directly access. By removing all institutional barriers to access for individuals and non-state actors, P-11 facilitated litigation in the Strasbourg Court. Individuals throughout Europe "… did not hesitate to use this new opportunity to participate in enforcing Convention provisions, claiming rights and demanding greater protection."[56] The opening up of structural access, alongside the massive expansion of the ECtHR jurisdiction to twenty-two new states from CESE and the former Soviet Union, arguably paved the way for a sharp rise in human rights litigation overall.

Rules shaping individual access and standing are part of a broader legal opportunity structure that influences levels of litigation in international human rights courts. The underlying assumption of approaches that emphasize international legal opportunities is that litigation is driven by the rules and institutional make up of international judicial bodies. By facilitating recourse of individual and other non-state actors, structural access and standing can be expected to attract increasing numbers of complaints in a human rights court.[57]

The decisions of individuals and organizations to engage in human rights litigation though are shaped by a broader constellation of structural possibilities and constraints, many of which are linked to national legal and political conditions. The expansion of individual access in the ECtHR is only one component of a broader, multi-level structure of legal and political opportunities and constraints shaping international rights litigation, as it is elaborated in chapter 2. Filtered through different legal and political systems and national contexts, individuals, minorities and non-state actors delineate distinct sets of possibilities and constraints to litigate. How they view their opportunities to litigate is not solely or even predominantly shaped by the extent of structural access to the ECtHR.

The expansion of structural access undoubtedly facilitated the recourse of individuals to the ECtHR overall since the 1990s. Why and how, though, increasing numbers of migrants and individuals from minorities were both willing and able to utilize this opportunity and bring claims before the ECtHR? The present study traces the growth of ECtHR litigation in this area since the 1980s, when milestone rulings broke new legal ground and paved the way for more minority- and migrant-related petitions to be lodged. Drawing from rich case law data and case study research, this book shows that increasing numbers of human rights lawyers, minority and migrants' rights organizations, and a variety of non-governmental organizations (NGOs) provided indispensable support to petitioners to bring claims before the ECtHR. Not infrequently, they were motivated by broader strategic or collective goals. In some countries and issue areas, legal and civil society actors pursued structural reform litigation (SRL) to challenge state structures and administrative practices that disadvantaged minorities and systematically breached the rights of migrants.

In response to such kind of strategic litigation related to migrants and minorities, a large number of ECtHR judgments find violations of a structural kind. State implementation of Strasbourg Court judgments takes place under the supervision of the Council of Europe Committee of Ministers (CoM). Judgments involving complex and structural problems often necessitate reform of state laws, policies and administrative practices, regarding asylum procedures, detention conditions, police treatment of minorities, or discrimination in education, in order to prevent the recurrence of rights abuses.

From the perspective employed in this book, structural reform litigation and state implementation of ECtHR rulings are distinct but closely interdependent phases of a regional, judicially enforced human rights regime with increasingly experimentalist features. Besides engaging in identifying and framing state policies and practices as alleged violations of human rights law, lawyers, NGOs, human rights institutions, and international organizations have also increasingly mobilized in the post-adjudication phase. The next section discusses state implementation of human rights rulings and the ECHR supervisory mechanism to enforce it.

4 State implementation of Court judgments

Once the ECtHR pronounces a violation of the Convention, national authorities of the respondent state must take measures to redress these. Judgment implementation is integral to regional human rights regimes[58], and profoundly consequential for their legitimacy and effectiveness. Litigation and implementation are closely inter-linked and inter-dependent phases of the ECHR regime and its enforcement machinery (as other judicially enforced human rights systems for that matter). Litigation raises claims that prompt the Court's intervention in areas of state action that present human rights problems. In turn, the failure of states to give effect to the Court's judgments and to remedy shortcomings in rights protection, generate more violations. As long as the root causes of domestic rights abuse persist, and as newly emerging issues and conditions present new human rights problems, legal recourse to the ECtHR is likely to recur.

By institutional design and legal-judicial practice, the Convention system leaves a wide margin of appreciation to national authorities, both at the adjudication and the implementation phase. The ECtHR, as it is well-known, limits itself to declaring violations, while it does not order remedial measures, except for just satisfaction. Judgments that specify remedial measures are a small fraction of the ECtHR's case law and their number has not grown.[59] When the Court (exceptionally) intervenes expressly in matters of legislative reform, it is to clarify benchmarks, or set specific time frames for implementation.[60] In its rare issuing of prescriptive judgments, it primarily targets states that fail for a long time to resolve specific human rights problems. At the implementation phase too, state authorities are primarily responsible and have far-reaching discretion over how to remedy human rights violations pronounced in Court judgments. Over the past decade, subsidiarity has been reinforced in response to challenges to the ECtHR legitimacy, supporting further the margin of appreciation and discretion of national authorities.

In order to redress violations pronounced in ECtHR judgments, states must introduce not only individual remedies, but also broader legal and policy measures to prevent recurrence of violations.[61] In each state, an institution or office under the executive is commonly assigned responsibility for coordinating the actions of national authorities in different sectors to give effect to ECtHR judgments. National authorities may amend legislation, change administrative practice, or reform policies, in areas that come under the Court's purview in the context of examining individual cases.[62] Such kinds of general measures encapsulate the potential of the Strasbourg Court's rulings to influence national policies and human rights practices. Besides the government and administration, domestic courts play a key role by aligning their approach with that of the ECtHR.[63]

State authorities' efforts to give effect to the Court's judgments are overseen by the Committee of Ministers (CoM) of the Council of Europe, a body comprised of state delegates. Through its government representative, the respondent state reports to and discusses with the CoM and the Department for the Execution of Judgments the implementing measures connected to adverse judgments. The Committee terminates its supervision when it considers the instituted measures adequate. In practice, most of the work is carried out bilaterally between the respondent state's authorities and the Department for the Execution of Judgments (a secretariat body of the CoM), whose role has been reinforced.[64] Prior to the 2000s, state implementation of ECtHR rulings was entirely at the discretion of national authorities of the respondent states.[65] Their discretion was amplified by the fact that they submitted remedial measures to the ECHR supervisory bodies in confidential exchanges. These bodies engaged in a lax and often cursory kind of control. They commonly accepted any kind of state measures as sufficient to terminate their supervision, regardless of how appropriate or relevant they were to remedy the violations pronounced by the Court.[66]

A voluminous international law and political science scholarship has explored state compliance and implementation of ECtHR judgments and international law more broadly.[67] *Compliance* with such judgments refers to state observance of particular legal rules that presumably directly follow from a ruling issued by an international court. It may be accomplished even without any state action if those legal rules reflect pre-existing standards in a country.[68] In the ECHR, the CoM grants its formal approval of compliance when a respondent state enacts individual and general measures that are deemed sufficient to tackle the violation pronounced in a judgment.

Studies show that evasive and partial state compliance with human rights rulings is widespread.[69] Not infrequently, governments tend to adopt minimalist measures or remedial measures that are only ostensibly related to the Court's findings. They meet the basic requirements of the supervisory body (approval by the CoM) but fall short of redressing the actual causes of rights infringements.[70] Thus, a human rights judgment may be formally complied with but the state's enacted measures may be unrelated to the underlying problem or do not tackle the causes of a violation.[71] International relations and political science studies have critically appraised this gap between formal compliance on the one hand, and lack of actual

domestic change on the other. This incongruity is at the heart of a broader challenge of the concept of compliance as a yardstick for assessing whether international law promotes domestic rights protection.[72]

This book shifts attention to the *domestic implementation* of ECtHR judgments, and it is specifically interested in their potential to stimulate rights-enhancing changes in state policies and practices. Implementation refers to the efforts of
national authorities and non-state actors to put into law, policy and practice the
normative prescriptions that follow from a judgment. Legislative reform, its systematic enforcement, the establishment of new structures and institutions, and
changes in administrative practice and judicial approaches, among others, are all
part of human rights implementation.[73] The case studies in this book specifically
focus on areas involving structural human rights problems that are characterized
by multiple causes and administrative complexity. In such areas, implementing
human rights rulings into domestic policy and practice is far from a straightforward task, but it involves considerable uncertainty and political contestation.

Over the past fifteen years, the ECHR bodies have recognized the weight that
structural violations have in the Convention system and the distinctive challenges
that they pose for its effectiveness. Changes that the CoM has introduced to more
effectively handle such violations shift the focal point of its supervision from individual judgments to groups of similar or related cases. Since 2010, the CoM
supervision directs its attention on leading cases involving complex and systemic
human rights problems that are subject to enhanced supervision. By grouping
together similar cases under a smaller number of leading judgments, the ECHR
supervisory bodies effectively extend their oversight to entire domains of state
policy and administrative practice that generate repeat human rights violations.

Besides the increased emphasis on structural problems, the supervisory system
was also reformed in the direction of opening itself up to the participation of non-
governmental actors. Prior to the 2000s, the CoM exclusively communicated with
the government authorities of the respondent state and reviewed their submissions. A 2006 change in working methods for the first time allowed non-state
actors to also submit to the supervisory bodies their views and analyses of the
measures enacted by national authorities. NGOs, academic entities, equality
bodies and international bodies could now intervene in the supervisory mechanism
and provide independent input and documentation on the measures enacted by
the respondent state. Since then, they have increasingly engaged in the implementation process, often as an extension of their involvement in litigation before
the Strasbourg Court, and as part of broader mobilization strategies. The participation of non-governmental actors has profound consequences for the workings of
the Convention as a regional human rights system, as this book shows.

The focus of external supervision on entire areas of state policy and administration and the opening up of the ECHR enforcement machinery to non-governmental actors are aspects of a human rights regime that are conducive to
transnational experimentalism. Where human rights violations arise in the functioning of large and complex administrative systems or emanate from entrenched
prejudicial attitudes, implementing remedial measures is a largely undetermined

and inherently provisional task. Removing the causes of human rights violations in such cases is rarely accomplished in the frame of a single judgment or with a change of a legal rule, but it requires systematic, longer-term and multifaceted action. Political resistance but also plain uncertainty hamper efforts to give effect to broad principles pronounced in Court judgments. There may be multiple sets of remedial and reform measures that are viewed as equally compatible with the ECHR and Court judgments.[74] Pre-existing domestic conditions often shape perceptions of which remedies are feasible and politically attainable.[75] State implementation of ECtHR judgments in such cases is often part of a broader context of struggles and repeated reform efforts – a quintessentially dynamic process, in which non-governmental actors, besides government authorities, are variably involved.

5 Approach, research and argument of the book

ECtHR litigation is the first step and a recursive phase in a broader process of rights claiming, judicial intervention and domestic implementation with increasingly experimentalist characteristics.[76] The first part of this book explores the patterns and causes of rising minority- and migrant-related litigation, and the actors involved in it. It draws from a large body of sociolegal scholarship on international law and European courts that view litigation as a form of mobilization to achieve goals of social and policy change, including on behalf of vulnerable and minority groups.[77] Litigation and civil society mobilization are key mechanisms through which international treaties and courts enforce states' conformity with human rights.[78]

ECHR minority- and migrant-related litigation grew rapidly but unevenly since the 1990s. Individuals from minorities such as Muslims and Turks in Greece and Bulgaria, Kurds in Turkey, Chechens in Russia, Gypsies and Travellers in the UK, the Roma in Central-East and Southeast Europe (CESE), began to systematically bring cases in the Strasbourg Court. Migrant-related litigation on the other hand, primarily targeted the "old" states of the CoE from West Europe, such as the United Kingdom, the Netherlands, France, and Belgium, but also south European states like Greece and Italy.

Drawing on a large case law data set (of 491 judgments and decisions issued by the ECtHR bodies in 1960–2012 for minorities, and 605 ECtHR migrant-related judgments issued in 1960–2020), the first part of the book unravels the critical role of lawyers and a wide range of non-governmental and civil society actors in the growth of minority- and migrant-related litigation in the ECtHR (chapters 4–5). Through a process tracing approach, it shows how their legal action both drew on and in turn helped advance the Court's case law in certain critical junctures, making it relevant for minority and migrants issues. The growth of human rights lawyering and support by a variety of non-governmental organizations (NGOs) enabled increasing numbers of individuals from minorities and migrants to seize international legal opportunities to bring complaints before the ECtHR. In some countries and issue areas, they were instrumental in advancing structural reform litigation (SRL) to challenge state policies and practices that systematically disadvantaged minorities and breached the rights of migrants.

The second part of the book shifts attention to the domestic implementation of ECtHR judgments (specifically of general measures) entailing structural human rights breaches related to migrants and minorities (chapters 6 and 7). In areas of organizational complexity and systemic discrimination, ECtHR rulings can be seen to pronounce what has been called "destabilization rights": the finding of a violation signals that an entrenched situation of power and hierarchy is illegitimate and calls on national public and interested non-state actors to redress it.[79] More so than in any other area of rights violations, those rulings do not prescribe or impose specific rules or measures to states. How are domestic measures to redress violations determined, and what is the impact of judgment implementation on states' laws, policies and practices? Under the growing weight of structural human rights problems, the grouping together of repeat violations under leading cases amounts to the CoM overseeing domestic reforms in entire areas of the state that breed human rights violations, as mentioned earlier.

In exploring state implementation of ECtHR rulings two cases are selected for study: a) discrimination against the Roma in education in the Czech Republic, Hungary, Croatia and Greece, and b) immigration and asylum reform in Greece. These cases are selected, first, because they are characterized by repeat and mostly strategic litigation and civil society mobilization, and secondly, they exemplify areas of recurring human rights violations stemming from system-wide deficiencies in large administrative organizations (education, immigration and asylum management). Case study analysis relies on a large body of legal and policy documents, particularly from the Committee of Ministers (CoM) and the Council of Europe Department for the Execution of Judgments; reports issued by governments, NGOs and international organizations on judgments' implementation; and thirty interviews with lawyers, NGO representatives, state and CoE officials.

The empirical analysis of the case studies shows that state implementation of ECtHR judgments is not externally mandated by the Court or by CoE bodies, but it is not solely determined by national authorities either. Instead, human rights implementation in complex and systemic violations is determined by the continuous and often protracted interactions between ECHR bodies, respondent state authorities, and increasingly by an array of non-governmental actors. Through these interactions, provisional and often evasive, state measures are enacted, assessed, revised and monitored, variably resulting in domestic policy and human rights change, and prompting further follow-on action. The opening up of the ECHR enforcement system to the participation of civil society and other non-governmental actors has been critical in rendering judgment implementation – at least at the ECHR level – a more participatory and transparent process. Their growing engagement also in the phase of judgment implementation both reflects and reinforces a profound transformation of the ECHR system in an experimentalist direction.

In state domains marred by structural human rights problems, growing civil society involvement in litigation and increasingly also in implementation, and new practices of supervision over the latter both reflect and reinforce an experimentalist turn in the ECHR system. Experimentalism is a broad principle that has increasingly shaped the functioning of the Convention system since the 1990s. It is also a specific approach pursued (unintendedly) in the ECHR supervisory system of judgment implementation since the 2000s. While not eliminating structural discrimination and systemic deficiencies, this book argues that experimentalism is better suited for redressing structural breaches and more conducive to rights-enhancing reform. In unravelling the experimentalist features of the ECHR, this book makes an original contribution to the study of the Convention and of international human rights regimes more broadly. It expands our understanding of the effects of international human rights rulings beyond the notion of compliance understood as state conformity and obedience to rules enforced from above.

Experimentalism counterbalances conflicting pressures confronting the ECHR and international human rights regimes more broadly, of how to effectively enforce human rights while also deferring to states' sovereign powers. It navigates between support for strong authority, legal precision and scrutiny of international judicial institutions over state action, on the one hand; and demands for far-reaching subsidiarity and decentralized human rights enforcement, on the other hand. While the former is generally advanced as a way to bolster the effectiveness of international human rights institutions, the latter is embraced on grounds of enhancing their legitimacy (by limiting interference with democratic decision-making, and not imposing uniform normative standards across countries with diverse social values and legal traditions). As a mode of functioning of human rights regimes, experimentalism charts a middle ground between these two: it shows that their strength and distinctive potential lies in the recurring interaction and dialogue between external review and domestic, bottom-up state efforts to advance rights-enhancing policies and practices.

6 Overview of chapters

Chapter 2 lays out the conceptual frame for this study. It expounds on the theory of transnational experimentalism and how it can be adapted to the study of international human courts and their potential to influence domestic change. Drawing from law and society scholarship, the first two sections discuss the role of legal opportunity structures, legal support structures and civil society for understanding the factors driving the growth of international rights litigation. This chapter also analyzes how the growth of international rights litigation and civil society mobilization can transform a judicially enforced human rights treaty into a regime of transnational experimentalist governance – at least in areas involving structural deficiencies.

Chapter 3 sets the legal and institutional context in which human rights litigation and judgment implementation take place. It provides an overview of the ECHR institutional structures and rules, and the reforms that took place from the 1960s and through the 2000s that promoted and consolidated the legalization of the ECHR system. A critical aspect of the ECHR structural transformation was that it expanded access and standing of individual petitioners to the Court. From the 1980s onwards, it also gradually increased legal opportunities for the participation of non-governmental actors in ECHR litigation and later on (in the 2000s) in judgment implementation.

Chapters 4 and 5 examine the causes behind the rapid growth of ECtHR minority- and migrant-related complaints since the 1990s. Drawing on aggregate data generated from two case law data sets of over 1000 decisions and judgments,[80] and from 30 interviews with lawyers and NGOs, they describe and analyze patterns of migrant- and minority-related litigation in the ECtHR over time: the countries from which the relevant petitions most frequently originated, the issues that they raised, the judicial responses, and the actors involved in litigation before the Strasbourg Court. The analysis shows that the litigation growth in these areas was driven by the proliferation of legal and civil society actors, and by mobilized ethnic-religious groups in different European countries. Possessing expertise and the necessary resources, they supported individuals to mount an international legal challenge against the state with a variety of motives – to pursue group demands, to advance human rights law, or to attract international attention to issues of their concern. Supporting or intervening in ECtHR litigation was incorporated in broader organizational and collective strategies and struggles for rights.

Chapters 6 and 7 shift attention to ECHR implementation of Court judgments and how they influence areas of state action marred by structural human rights problems. They focus on school segregation and discrimination against the Roma in Central-East and Southeast Europe (chapter 6), and on immigration detention and asylum reform in Greece (chapter 7) – all cases of systematic and strategic litigation. The increasing, albeit variable engagement of non-governmental actors, as these chapter show, fundamentally transform the ECHR supervision and judgment implementation in an experimentalist direction. In recurrent cycles of external review of remedial measures by the respondent states, non-governmental actors provide feedback, critical analysis and context-specific information to the supervisory bodies, and they engage in follow-on legal action and mobilization. The emergent experimentalist dynamics, this study argues, over time promote rights-enhancing changes domestically, even if they fall far short from eradicating ethnic discrimination and state abuses against immigrants.

The last chapter 8 summarizes the findings and the main argument of this book. It also analyzes experimentalism in redressing structural human rights problems, as an approach that is distinct from the model of pilot judgments. This chapter further elaborates on the ECHR as a regime of transnational experimentalist governance, and juxtaposes this account to the individual justice, constitutional, and pluralist models of the ECHR. Experimentalism is best placed to address concerns related to the legitimacy and effectiveness of the ECtHR. Promoting and developing further the participation of and dialogue with non-governmental and civil society actors, both at the ECHR and at the national level, will strengthen it. While experimentalism does not necessarily expand rights protection, it is more likely to be impactful in areas of structural and complex human rights problems, and it can powerfully promote the embeddedness of the ECHR domestically.

Notes

1 Robert Keohane, Andrew Moravscik and A.-M. Slaughter, "Legalized Dispute Resolution: Interstate and Transnational," *International Organization* 54, no. 3 (2000): 482.

2 Questioning of the Court's legitimacy was all too evident in the draft Copenhagen Declaration that had called upon the ECtHR to avoid intervening in asylum and migration cases except in the most exceptional circumstances. The relevant paragraph though was not carried on in the final version of it. See Andreas Follesdal and Geir Ulfstein, "The Draft Copenhagen Declaration: Whose Responsibility and Dialogue?" *EJIL Talk* (blog), 22 February 2018, ejiltalk.org/the-draft-copenhagen-declaration-whose-responsibility-and-dialogue/.

3 Leora Bilsky, Rodger D. Citron and Natalie R. Davidson, "From *Kiobel* Back to Structural Reform: The Hidden Legacy of Holocaust Restitution Litigation," *Stanford Journal of Complex Litigation* 2, no. 1 (2014): 156.

4 Beth A. Simmons, *Mobilizing for Human Rights – International Law in Domestic Politics* (New York: Cambridge University Press, 2009); Rachel A. Cichowski, *The European Court and Civil Society – Litigation, Mobilization and Governance* (Cambridge: Cambridge University Press, 2007).

5 Gráinne De Búrca, "Human Rights Experimentalism," *American Journal of International Law* 111, no. 2 (2017): 277–316, 281.

6 Gráinne De Búrca, *Reframing Human Rights in a Turbulent Era* (Oxford: Oxford University Press, 2021), 38.

7 Geoff Dancy and Christopher J. Fariss, "Rescuing Human Rights Law from International Legalism and its Critics," *Human Rights Quarterly* 39, no. 1 (2017): 12–13.

8 See the debate around the Copenhagen Declaration in Philip Leach and Alice Donald, "Copenhagen: Keeping on Keeping on. A Reply to Mikael Rask Madsen and Jonas Christoffersen on the Draft Copenhagen Declaration," *European Journal of International Law* (blog), 24 February 2018.

9 Susan Sturm, "Second Generation Employment Discrimination: A Structural Approach," *Columbia Law Review* 101 (2001): 557.

10 Gráinne De Búrca, "Human Rights Experimentalism," 281; see also Gráinne De Búrca, Robert O. Keohane and Charles Sabel, "Global Experimentalist Governance," *British Journal of Political Science* 44, no. 3 (2014): 477–486.

11 Charles F. Sabel and Jonathan Zeitlin, "Experimentalist Governance," in *The Oxford Handbook of Governance*, ed. David Levi-Faur (Oxford: Oxford University Press, 2012), 170.

12 Charles F. Sabel and Jonathan Zeitlin, "Learning From Difference: The New Architecture of Experimentalist Governance in the EU," in *Experimentalist Governance in the European Union: Towards a New Architecture*, eds. Charles F. Sabel, and Jonathan Zeitlin (Oxford: Oxford University Press, 2010), 1–28.

13 Gráinne de Búrca, "Stumbling into Experimentalism: The EU Anti-Discrimination Regime," in *Experimentalist Governance in the European Union: Towards a New Architecture*, eds. Charles F. Sabel and Jonathan Zeitlin (Oxford: Oxford University Press, 2010), 215–235.

14 See Gráinne de Búrca, Robert Keohane, and Charles Sabel, "New Modes of Pluralist Global Governance," *International Law and Politics* 45 (2013): 723–786.

15 Christine Overdevest and Jonathan Zeitlin, "Experimentalism in transnational forest governance: Implementing European Union Forest Law Enforcement, Governance and Trade (FLEGT) Voluntary Partnership Agreements in Indonesia and Ghana," *Regulation & Governance* 12, no.1 (2018): 64–87.

16 De Búrca, Keohane and Sabel, "New Modes of Pluralist Global Governance".

17 De Búrca, "Human Rights Experimentalism," 285.

18 Joanne Scott and Susan Sturm, "Courts as Catalysts: Re-thinking the Judicial Role in New Governance," *Columbia Journal of European Law* 13 (2007): 566.

19 Abraham Chayes, "The Role of the Judge in Public Law Litigation," *Harvard Law Review* 89, no. 7 (1976): 1281–1386.
20 Charles F. Sabel and William H. Simon, "Destabilization Rights: How Public Law Litigation Succeeds," *Harvard Law Review* 117, no. 4 (2004): 1026.
21 Sabel and Simon, "Destabilization Rights," 1020.
22 Sabel and Simon, "Destabilization Rights," 1020, 1032.
23 Scott and Sturm, "Courts as Catalysts: Rethinking the Judicial Role in New Governance."
24 *Tyrer v UK*, no. 5856/72, 25 April 1978, § 31. For a detailed discussion of the Convention as a "living instrument" see Alastair Mowbray, "The Creativity of the European Court of Human Rights," *Human Rights Law Review* 5, no. 1 (2005): 57–79.
25 Karen Alter, *The New Terrain of International Law – Courts, Politics, Rights* (Princeton: Princeton University Press, 2014).
26 Stuart A. Scheingold, *The Politics of Rights – Lawyers, Public Policy and Political Change* (Ann Arbor: The University of Michigan Press, 2007).
27 See William N. Jr. Eskridge, "Some Effects of Identity-Based Social Movements on Constitutional Law in the Twentieth Century," *Michigan Law Review* 100, no. 8 (2002): 2062–2407.
28 Carol Harlow and Richard Rawlings, *Pressure Through Law* (London: Routledge, 1992), see especially chapter 6.
29 See Carlo Guarnieri, "Courts and marginalized groups: Perspectives from Continental Europe," *International Journal of Constitutional Law* 5, no. 2 (2007): 187–210; Dia Anagnostou, ed., *Rights in Pursuit of Social Change* (Oxford: Hart Publishers, 2014).
30 Tanja A. Börzel, "Participation Through Law Enforcement The Case of the European Union," *Comparative Political Studies* 39, no. 1 (2006): 128–152.
31 Mark Dawson and Elise Muir, "Individual, Institutional and Collective Vigilance in Protecting Fundamental Rights in the EU: Lessons from the Roma," *Common Market Law Review* 48, no.3 (2011): 751; Sophie Jacquot and Tommaso Vitale, "Law as a weapon of the weak? A comparative analysis of legal mobilization by Roma and women's groups at the European level," *Journal of European Public Policy* 21, no. 4 (2014): 587–604.
32 Karen J. Alter and Jeannette Vargas, "Explaining Variation in the Use of European Litigation Strategies," *Comparative Political Studies* 33, no. 4 (2000): 452–482; Rachel Cichowski, "The European Court of Human Rights, Amicus Curiae, and Violence against Women," *Law and Society Review* 50, no. 4 (2016): 890–919.
33 Marion Guerrero, "Activating the Courtrooms: Opportunities for Strategic Same Sex Rights Litigation before the European Court of Human Rights and the Court of Justice of the European Union" (Presentation, LSE Conference on Social Justice in the Next Century, 2014).
34 Lisa Conant, "Individuals, Courts and the Development of European Social Rights," *Comparative Political Studies* 39, no. 1 (2006): 76–100; Lisa Conant, *Justice Contained* (Ithaca: Cornell University Press, 2002).
35 Rhonda Evans Case and Terri E Givens, "Re-engineering Legal Opportunity Structures in the European Union? The Starting Line Group and the Politics of the Racial Equality Directive," *Journal of Common Market Studies* 48, no. 2 (2010): 222.
36 Lisa Vanhala, *Making Rights a Reality? Disability Rights Activists and Legal Mobilization* (Cambridge: Cambridge University Press, 2011).
37 Even though Convention law, unlike EU law, lacks supremacy and direct effect, the ECHR has been incorporated in the domestic legal orders of nearly all Contracting States and national judges must interpret state laws in conformity with its provisions and the ECtHR case law.
38 Frances Kahn Zemans, "Legal Mobilization: The Neglected Role of the Law in the Political System," *American Political Science Review* 77, no. 3 (1983): 691–93; Joel

Grossman and Austin Sarat, "Litigation in the Federal Courts: A Comparative Perspective," *Law and Society Review* 9, no. 2 (1975): 321, 375.

39 Grossman and Sarat, "Litigation in the Federal Courts," 325; Zemans, "Legal Mobilization: The Neglected Role of the Law in the Political System," 700.

40 Alter, *The New Terrain of International Law – Courts, Politics, Rights* (Princeton: Princeton University Press, 2014), 49.

41 Margaret Keck and Kathryn Sikkink, *Activists Beyond Borders – Advocacy Networks in International Politics* (Ithaca: Cornell University Press, 1998), 12–13; Karen J. Alter and Jeannette Vargas, "Explaining Variation in the Use of European Litigation Strategies," *Comparative Political Studies* 33, no. 4 (2000): 452–482. See also Kathryn Sikkink, "Patterns of Dynamic Multilevel Governance and the Insider-Outsider Coalition," in *Transnational Protest and Global Activism*, eds. Donatella della Porta and Sidney Tarrow (Oxford: Rowman & Littlefield Publishers, Inc., 2005), 157–8; Harlow and Rawlings, *Pressure Through Law*.

42 Patrick Thornberry and Maria Amor Martin Estebanez, *Minority Rights in Europe* (Strasbourg: Council of Europe Publishing, 2004), 68.

43 The Court has done so even if in strict contractual terms, the harm that the individual will presumably suffer lies outside of the jurisdiction of the Convention, in a state that is not a party to it. Colin Harvey, "Dissident Voices: Refugees, Human Rights and Asylum in Europe," *Social and Legal Studies* 9, no. 3 (2000): 385.

44 Alexandra Huneeus, "Reforming the State from Afar: Structural Reform Litigation at the Human Rights Courts," *Yale Journal of International Law* 40, no. 1 (2015): 1–40.

45 Stefan Trechsel, "Human rights and minority rights – Two sides of the same coin? A sketch," in *Protecting Human Rights: The European Perspective*, eds. Paul Mahoney, Franz Matscher, Herbert Petzold and Luzius Wildhaber (Berlin: Carl Heymanns Verlag KG, 2000), 1443–1453.

46 In the light of strong disagreement among states, the CoE instead opted for a Framework Convention for the Protection of National Minorities (FCPNM) that established a reporting and monitoring mechanism. See Florence Benoit-Rohmer, *The Minority Question in Europe – texts and commentary* (Strasbourg: Council of Europe publishing, 1996.)

47 Conant, "Individuals, Courts and the Development of European Social Rights," 79.

48 Christina G. Hioureas, "Behind the Scenes of Protocol No. 14: Politics in Reforming the European Court of Human Rights," *Berkeley Journal of International Law* 24, no. 2 (2006): 724.

49 Robert Harmsen, "The Reform of the Convention System: Institutional Restructuring and the (Geo-) Politics of Human Rights," in *The ECtHR between Law and Politics*, eds. Jans Christoffersen and Mikael Rask Madsen (Oxford: Oxford University Press, 2011), 119–143; Steven Greer, *The European Convention of Human Rights – Achievements, Problems and Prospects* (Cambridge: Cambridge University Press, 2006), 36–37.

50 In 1998, when Protocol 11 of the ECHR [P-11] entered into force, 35 states had acceded to the ECHR. Over the next five years, seven more states would join the Convention and ratify P-11, with the last ones being Serbia (2003), Montenegro (2003) and Monaco (2004).

51 Greer, *The European Convention of Human Rights*, 30; Leo F. Swaak and Therese Cachia, "The European Court of Human Rights: A Success Story?" *Human Rights Brief* 11, no. 3 (2004): 32.

52 Mikael Rask Madsen, "The Challenging Authority of the European Court of Human Rights: From Cold War Legal Diplomacy to the Brighton Declaration and Backlash," *Law and Contemporary Problems* 79, no. 1 (2016): 143–144.

53 Greer, *The European Convention of Human Rights*, 30–40.

54 Petra Guasti, David S. Siroky and Daniel Stockemer, "Judgment without justice: on the efficacy of the European human rights regime," *Democratization* 24, no. 2 (2016):

226–243; Madsen, "The Challenging Authority of the European Court of Human Rights," 141.

55 When the Court became operational in 1959, ten countries (Sweden, Ireland, Denmark, Germany, Iceland, Belgium, Austria, Netherlands, and Luxembourg) accepted its jurisdiction and the right to individual petition. By 1966, the UK finally accepted the ECtHR's jurisdiction and individual petition, albeit for a limited three-year long period and then up for renewal (like most countries at the time). With Switzerland and Italy following suit in 1973, France remained a latecomer that finally accepted the right to individual petition in 1981, Greece in 1985, and Turkey in 1987.

56 Rachel A. Cichowski, "Courts, Rights and Democratic Participation," *Comparative Political Studies* 39, no. 1 (2006b): 67.

57 Conant, "Individuals, Courts and the Development of European Social Rights," 76–100.

58 Rachel Murray, "Addressing the Implementation Crisis: Securing Reparation and Righting Wrongs," *Journal of Human Rights Practice* 12, no. 1 (2020): 10.

59 Alice Donald and Anne-Katrin Speck, "The European Court of Human Rights' Remedial Practice and its Impact on the Execution of Judgments," *Human Rights Law Review* 19, no. 1 (2019): 92.

60 Nino Tsereteli, "The Role of the European Court of Human Rights in Facilitating Legislative Change in Cases of Long-Term Delays in Implementation," in *The International Human Rights Judiciary and National Parliaments*, eds. Matthew Saul, Andreas Follesdal, Geir Ulfstein (Cambridge: Cambridge University Press, 2017), 226, 230.

61 Council of Europe, *European Convention for the Protection of Human Rights and Fundamental Freedoms, as amended by Protocols Nos. 11 and 14*, 4 November 1950, ETS 5 ("ECHR"). Article 46 of the ECHR provides for the binding force and execution of judgments, and Article 39 ECHR (paragraph 4) also foresees supervision of execution for friendly settlements.

62 Elisabeth Lambert-Abdelgawad, *The Execution of Judgments of the European Court of Human Rights* (Strasbourg: Council of Europe Publishing, 2008); Laurence R. Helfer and Erik Voeten, "International Courts as Agents of Legal Change: Evidence from LGBT Rights in Europe," *International Organization* 68, no.1 (2014): 77–110.

63 See Helfer and Voeten, "International Courts as Agents of Legal Change," 89.

64 Elisabeth Lambert Abdelgawad, "Dialogue and the Implementation of the European Court of Human Rights Judgments," *Netherlands Quarterly of Human Rights* 34, no.4 (2016): 346.

65 This may appear as a paradox considering that the term used by the ECHR is "execution" of judgments – denoting the carrying out of a top-down order, plan or course of action.

66 Dia Anagnostou, "Untangling the domestic impact of the European Court of Human Rights: Institutional make-up, conceptual issues and mediating factors," in *The European Court of Human Rights: Implementing the Strasbourg's Judgments into Domestic Policy*, ed. Dia Anagnostou (Edinburgh: Edinburgh University Press, 2013), 1–25.

67 Dia Anagnostou and Alina Mungiu-Pippidi, "Domestic Implementation of Human Rights Judgments in Europe: Legal Infrastructure and Government Effectiveness Matter," *European Journal of International Law* 25, no.1 (2014): 205–27; Andreas von Staden, *Strategies of Compliance with the European Court of Human Rights* (Pennsylvania: University of Pennsylvania Press, 2018); Courtney Hillebrecht, *Domestic Politics and International Human Rights Tribunals* (Cambridge: Cambridge University Press, 2015); Helfer and Voeten, "International Courts as Agents of Legal Change."

68 See Kal Raustiala and Anne-Marie Slaughter, "International Law, International Relations and Compliance," in *Handbook of International Relations*, eds. Walter Carlsnaes, Thomas Risse and Beth A. Simmons (London: Sage Publications, 2002), 538–558.

69 Darren Hawkings and Wade Jacoby, "Partial Compliance: A Comparison of the European and Inter-American Courts for Human Rights," *Journal of International Law and International Relations* 6, no.1 (2010): 35–85.

70 See Andreas von Staden, *Strategies of Compliance with the European Court of Human Rights.*

71 Rachel Murray, "Addressing the Implementation Crisis," 9.

72 Lisa Martin, "Against Compliance," in *International Law and International Relations: Interdisciplinary-perspectives-international-law-and-international-relations*, eds. JL Dunoff and M Pollack (Cambridge: Cambridge University Press 2012); Alexandra Huneeus, "Compliance with Judgments and Decisions," in *The Oxford Handbook of International Adjudication*, eds. Cesare P. R. Romano, Karen J. Alter, and Yuval Shany (Oxford University Press, 2013), 438–460; Robert Howse and Ruti Teitel, "Beyond Compliance: Rethinking Why International Law Really Matters," *Global Policy* 1, no. 2 (2010): 127–136.

73 Dinah Shelton, "Law, Non-Law and the Problem of 'Soft Law'," in *Commitment and Compliance – The Role of Non-Binding Norms in the International Legal System*, ed. Dinah Shelton (Oxford: Oxford University Press 2000), 1–18.

74 Alice Donald and Anne-Katrin Speck, "The Dynamics of Domestic Human Rights Implementation: Lessons from Qualitative Research in Europe," *Journal of Human Rights Practice* 12, no.1 (2020): 67.

75 Donald and Speck, "The Dynamics of Domestic Human Rights Implementation," 54.

76 This line of analysis is pursued in Chiara Georgetti, "What Happens after a Judgment is Given? Judgment Compliance and the Performance of International Courts and Tribunals," in *The Performance of International Courts and Tribunals*, eds. Theresa Squatrito, Oran R. Young, Andreas Follesdal and Geir Ulfstein (Cambridge: Cambridge University Press, 2018), 324–350.

77 Jacquot and Vitale, "Law as a weapon of the weak?"; Alter and Vargas, "Explaining Variation in the Use of European Litigation Strategies"; Evans and E. Givens, "Re-engineering Legal Opportunity Structures in the European Union?"; Guerrero, "Activating the Courtrooms: Opportunities for Strategic Same Sex Rights Litigation."

78 Alter, *The New Terrain of International Law – Courts, Politics, Rights*; Simmons, *Mobilizing for Human Rights – International Law in Domestic Politics*; See also Rachel Cichowski, "Civil Society and the European Court of Human Rights," in *The European Court of Human Rights between Law and Politics*, eds. Jonas Christoffersen and Mikael Rask Madsen (Oxford: Oxford University Press, 2011), 77–97.

79 Sabel and Simon, "Destabilization Rights," 1066–1068; Scott and Sturm, "Courts as Catalysts," 571–572.

80 The data sets include 492 minority-related decisions and judgments covering the period 1960–2015, and 605 migrant-related judgments issued in 1970–2020.

2 Transnational litigation and human rights experimentalism

This chapter applies the theory of transnational experimentalism to the study of international human rights courts and their potential to influence domestic structural reform. Experimentalism proceeds from the premise that "translating" broad rights principles into concrete state policy and practice across diverse national-local contexts is a long-term undertaking. It envisages a decentralized system where state authorities and non-state stakeholders actively engage in putting into practice broadly agreed norms embedded in an international treaty agreed by states. National authorities are in continuous interaction with an international body (an external accountability "center") that reviews claims and oversees domestic implementation and reform efforts.[1] Human rights treaties and international courts rely on decentralized enforcement. Their power to intervene domestically becomes activated in response to bottom-up rights claiming by individuals and non-governmental actors. They also regularly interact with state authorities who typically have far-reaching discretion in putting into practice international human rights rulings.

International treaties like the ECHR embody the signatory states' broadly shared perception that a set of human rights entitlements must be protected, and their commitment to pursue this through international judicial review. Human rights norms and principles, such as those contained in the Convention, are broad, flexible and open-ended. They become relevant and acquire content and meaning through their application and interpretation by the ECtHR in response to individual claims from different countries. The Strasbourg Court, as it is well-known, reviews such claims and pronounces whether there is a violation of the Convention. It rarely though indicates the measures that national authorities must adopt to remedy violations. As the Court makes clear, "it is primarily for the State concerned to choose, subject to supervision by the Committee of Ministers, the means to be used in order to discharge its legal obligation under Article 46 of the Convention, provided that those means are compatible with the conclusions contained in the Court's judgment".[2]

Transnational experimentalism can emerge in the context of a judicially enforced human rights treaty, in areas where legal action is strategic, systematic, and specifically aimed at structural change. In this context, litigation is the first step and a critical step that sets into motion the experimentalist dynamics.

DOI: 10.4324/9781003256489-2

Through litigation, individual and non-state actors frame state (in)actions and local or national conditions as human rights breaches, and channel them to an international tribunal for review. International rights litigation, it could be countered, involves disputes with states that are primarily of an individual nature, in which human rights courts rule. An increasing amount of claims that are raised before these courts though, are connected with broader social struggles. They potentially affect different aspects of public policy and even state structures. Individual complaints that have such broader implications, are often initiated or supported by organizational actors with strategic goals. They form an important subset of cases that have been brought before the ECtHR since the 1990s.

This book expounds the idea that the growth and diversification of international rights litigation as a strategic form of action can, in certain areas of rights claims, transform a judicial human rights regime into one that is akin to transnational experimentalism. Drawing from law and society scholarship, the first part of this chapter reviews and discusses perspectives on the factors that promote the growth of international rights litigation, as well as the actors involved in it. The rise of human rights litigation cannot be understood outside of the treaty-specific rules and structures that define who has access to an international court and the procedural requirements for such an access. These rules, alongside the content and scope of treaty norms and other factors, shape the international legal opportunities and constraints for human rights litigation. The first section of this chapter elaborates on the formal rules, structures and norms that shape the legal opportunity structures (LOS) for individuals and other social and non-state actors who seek to bring claims before an international human rights court.

International legal opportunities set the context for an overall rise in human rights litigation. Yet, they do not shed light on why individual, social and associational actors variably make use of such opportunities to bring rights claims against states. International legal opportunities and constraints, as a longstanding social movement scholarship shows, are shaped by a multiplicity of structural factors and conditions. Whether an international treaty's rules and structures are enabling or constraining is largely determined by the perceptions of individuals and other social actors who are situated in different national contexts. The extent to which these actors turn to an international legal strategy also critically depends on the resources (legal, financial) that they possess or can access, and often on organizational initiative and support. The second part of this chapter discusses the role of lawyers, non-state actors and resources that form the basis for the growth of national and transnational legal support structures and networks.

Systematic and strategic litigation that aims to tackle structural human rights problems is initiated by actors knowledgeable of local and national context. It highlights injustices, it raises rights claims, and it also provides an essential feedback loop for bringing to the attention of an international court new or ongoing human rights problems. Thus, the court applies and interprets broad human rights principles to local and national problems and disputes, and it decides whether there is a human rights violation. This cycle of interaction between national and local actors and the human rights regime though does not end with a court ruling.

If there is a violation, It continues past adjudication with the ruling's domestic implementation. In this phase, national authorities, who, typically enjoy wide discretion, seek to put into practice appropriate measures that give effect to the ruling and to remedy the violations.

The implementation process involves repeat exchanges of the treaty bodies with state authorities, but also with a wide array of non-state actors who pressure for domestic reform and change. The participation of domestic and transnational non-governmental organizations (NGOs), advocates and various other non-governmental actors are critical for the emergence of transnational experimentalism. Besides engaging in human rights litigation, they also mobilize for the domestic implementation of adverse rulings: they independently monitor government measures, and they pursue follow-on action and mobilization (follow-on litigation, reporting to the treaty bodies responsible for overseeing implementation, and other kinds of action). The third part of this chapter lays out and discusses each phase of a judicially-enforced human rights regime with experimentalist features: a) transnational litigation, mobilization and judicial review, b) judgment implementation and external review, and c) continuous revision of domestic measures and follow-on action.

1 Human rights litigation and legal opportunities

Human rights courts embody the advent of a new model of international adjudication that extends to individuals and civil society actors the right to bring claims against states.[3] This model radically departs from traditional inter-state adjudication in which states were the only subjects of international law that could bring a dispute to an international court. States and governments are no longer gate-keepers and do not control who has access to international judicial institutions. Allowing for private access, as well as compulsory jurisdiction are the most distinctive characteristics of the new-style international courts, including human rights tribunals.[4] Individuals and other non-state actors invoke norms and rules to bring a variety of claims against states that often have public policy implications. In this sense, international rights litigation can be viewed as a distinctive form of public participation in multi-level governance structures.[5]

At the crossroads of law, politics, and sociology, a sizeable body of scholarship of primarily Anglo-American origin has explored litigation and legal mobilization as tools for social change through courts, mostly at the national level. Studies have explored the use of litigation by national minorities, persons with disabilities[6], gays and lesbians[7], or gender equality and equal pay activists[8], and the legal opportunities and constraints that influence their mobilization strategies in different countries.[9] Over the past fifteen years, a number of studies have also probed into the patterns and causes of litigation in international and supranational courts in Europe and elsewhere.[10] Despite such growing interest, theoretically informed accounts about the factors that lead individuals, lawyers and civil society entities to engage in international rights litigation, are still few.

Legal opportunity structure (LOS) is a central concept advanced to explain why individuals and social groups decide to pursue a legal battle in court. Conceptualized by analogy to the political opportunity structure (POS) in the study of social movements[11], LOS refers to the relatively stable set of formal rules, institutions and legal norms that enable or conversely constrain individual and other social actors to go to court. Established institutional structures and rules may render a legal system relatively open or closed to different kinds of actors (individual, organizational), and litigation an easily attainable or conversely cumbersome course of action. They create incentives or present constraints for individual and organizational actors who contemplate bringing a case to court. Access is a key component of the LOS in a national or an international legal-judicial system: established rules determine who can petition a court, the specific admissibility requirements, and the ability of a petitioner to demonstrate to the court sufficient connection to, and harm from the state action challenged (locus standi).[12]

The ECtHR is a prominent – indeed archetypal – example of a new-style court that allows for direct access of individuals and civil society actors. It gives individuals the right to bring a complaint, as long as a person is able to show that she is the direct or indirect victim of an alleged infringement of the Convention. The right to petition also applies to groups of individuals and to organizations, under the same precondition, namely that they show to be directly affected by an alleged violation.[13] In fact, the ECtHR is hailed – rightly so – for its unusually broad accessibility to individuals, unlike supreme or constitutional courts in countries like the USA and Canada, which are highly selective in the cases that they review. Anyone can submit a complaint without cost or the requirement for legal representation, while the Court and its Registry are obliged to consider every single petition. The presumably unrestricted access to the ECtHR though, is countered by important constraints: a) a highly restrictive admissibility process in the Convention system: only a fraction of petitions submitted to the ECtHR are actually retained for a review on the merits, and b) the requirement for individuals to exhaust all domestic remedies in order to lodge a petition in Strasbourg.

Besides rules of access and standing, the existence (or absence thereof) of a sufficient and pertinent legal basis that can be invoked to construe an issue or grievance into a justiciable claim further shapes LOS. Sociolegal scholars refer to this as legal stock, namely, the content of existing legal norms deriving from constitutional and international law or established case law.[14] These may present an opportunity, or conversely a constraint for those contemplating legal action before an international court. For example, the higher levels of social rights litigation in the CJEU as opposed to the ECtHR are attributed to the stronger legal provisions that explicitly address social rights in the EU system.[15] Over the past twenty years, EU law has expanded the scope of equality and non-discrimination rights, thereby liberalizing legal opportunities to litigate equality claims.[16]

The existence of legal stock that petitioners can invoke to construct a human rights claim before an international court must be qualified as a factor shaping legal opportunities for litigation. Human rights treaties like the ECHR, comprise a set of highly abstract and general principles that only provide broad normative guidance. Their content and scope is malleable and open-ended; it is thoroughly contingent on the creative framing of claims, and the power of judicial interpretation that furnishes human rights with meaning and policy relevance.

The lack of a clear and explicit legal basis in the Convention does not necessarily prevent or deter individuals and other social actors from bringing claims in the Strasbourg Court. In fact, the broad and open-ended nature of Convention principles has allowed individual and social actors to construe a wide array of issues as human rights claims before the Court. In response to litigation, the ECtHR has at times applied human rights principles in an expansive fashion. It has broadened the relevance and scope of these principles through its evolving case law by applying these in an increasing array of issues and contexts. For example, even though the Convention does not enshrine a right to a healthy environment as such, the Strasbourg Court has creatively and expansively interpreted rights principles as to recognize breaches stemming from exposure to environmental risks.[17] At other times, though, the Court provides more restrictive interpretations of Convention rights that may dissuade prospective petitioners from pursuing international litigation.

Innovative judicial interpretations and advances in the evolving human rights case law may open up new directions for lawyers and petitioners to frame claims, thus expanding opportunities for international litigation. To illustrate this, in its breakthrough judgment in *Soering v United Kingdom* (1989), the ECtHR for the first time established that a State Party to the ECHR could be held responsible for violating human rights, if it sent an individual back to a state outside of the Convention's jurisdiction, where she was likely to be subjected to inhuman treatment. By establishing the principle of non-refoulement, the *Soering* judgment paved the way for growing numbers of legal claims by migrants and asylum-seekers faced with deportation back to their country of origin. Such advances in international human rights jurisprudence occur in an incremental, but also at times in a sudden and unanticipated way. Judicial interpretations of human rights influence legal opportunities for international litigation. They are more malleable (than legal-institutional structures), and thus amenable to short- and medium-term change in response to litigation by determined social and legal actors.[18]

Last but not least, judicial receptivity has been posited as another factor shaping legal opportunities for international rights litigation. *Judicial receptivity* refers to how favourable, or conversely reluctant and unsympathetic, prevailing judicial preferences and approaches to particular rights claims are.[19] Legal doctrine, comparative law, and the priorities of international judges related to the authority and independence of the court, in which they sit, arguably shape their preferences, rather than their national or geopolitical interests.[20] Judicial receptivity can be inferred from the decisions issued by an international court and its evolving case law. It can also be gleaned from dissenting opinions, non-admissibility decisions, as well as extra-judicial statements and communications. These communicate the extent to which judges at a particular point in time are open to considering novel claims and arguments that depart from precedent.[21] Prevailing judicial approaches may motivate potential litigants and activists to pursue a court-oriented strategy, or conversely dissuade them from doing so. At the same time, disagreements among judges sitting in a court are a sign that particular principles are contested and prone to reinterpretation and change.[22] Litigants respond to such signals by bringing particular kinds of cases, or by crafting legal arguments in specific ways.[23]

Pursuing human rights litigation though is a two-level game, in which opportunities and constraints are not solely influenced by international legal norms, structures, and rules. The decision of individual and collective actors to engage in international rights litigation is also a response to opportunities and constraints arising at the national level, where these actors are situated. Individual, collective and organizational actors may resort to courts as an ancillary strategy at the same time that they engage in political action (lobbying, campaigning). Alternatively, they may pursue a legal strategy to outflank the political constraints they face in advancing rights protection through electoral politics, i.e. due to lack of support by decision-makers.[24] When domestic law or judicial practice is at odds with international norms, those whose rights are as a result curtailed, may bring a challenge and seek a remedy before an international court or quasi-judicial body. Limits in accessing and influencing domestic channels of participation – legal or political – arguably prompt disadvantaged groups, such as minorities and migrants, to turn to international or supranational litigation as an alternative strategy.[25]

2 Actors, resources and legal support structures

International legal opportunities and domestic constraints set the backdrop for the rise in human rights litigation overall but do not explain the growth in minority- and migrant-related claims in the Strasbourg Court. Why minorities and migrants variably seize opportunities to bring international court proceedings against states cannot solely be attributed to structural opportunities and constraints – legal or political – at the national and international level. Domestic disadvantages may render ECHR litigation a possible, alternative course of action. Generally, it has been argued that socially marginalized individuals or groups are allured by the possibility for legal action in court, where in principle at least everyone is equal before the law.[26] Many others though counter that they are unlikely to initiate international legal action on their own.[27] They are reluctant to do so due to lack of rights consciousness and financial resources,[28] and an ethic of survival that militates against publicly exposing a situation of oppression and discrimination.[29]

Irrespective of any individual predisposition, a longstanding social movements scholarship shows that whether legal and political structures (domestic or international) present opportunities or constraints is, at least in part, socially constructed: it is contingent on the actors' perceptions, their organizational identity and how they frame issues and grievances. Furthermore, it critically depends on their ability to access and mobilize particular types of resources.[30] Issue framing refers to "the conscious strategic efforts by groups of people to fashion shared understandings of the world that legitimate and motivate collective action".[31] In an important study on disability rights, Vanhala argues that the resort to a litigation strategy was primarily a consequence of the ways in which non-governmental organizations and activists started to frame disability through a social, rather than a medical perspective. Their reconceptualization of disadvantage as discrimination led them to redefine their mission as the pursuit of rights and equality, and to prioritize law reform and litigation in their mobilization strategy.[32]

Besides organizational identity and issue framing, which may be conducive to a court strategy, access to resources – such as funding, legal expertise and organizational support – are critical for utilizing opportunities for rights litigation especially at the international level. The availability of resources is particularly vital for the more vulnerable individuals and disadvantaged ethnic-social groups, as law and society scholars have since long ago recognized.[33] Drawing on the intertwined role of social agency, organizational identity and support, as well as resource mobilization, law and society scholars have highlighted the impact of legal support structures for sustained rights litigation. An influential study attributed the increased judicial attention to rights claims in the UK since the 1970s -1980s to pressures from below. These were channeled to courts through robust legal support structures, comprising government-sponsored legal aid programs, able and committed lawyers, equality bodies, and the mobilization of rights advocacy groups, and community law centers.

Legal support structures enabled widespread recourse to courts to advance diverse rights claims that were often driven by public interest goals.[34] In response to a steady supply of cases, judges in the UK began to embrace a wide variety of rights claims, including those raised on behalf of minorities.[35] It must be noted that the growth of a legal support structure is not a stable characteristic of the political, legal or judicial system, but it is instead contingent on social mobilization, learning, and political strategy. It is arguably more likely to emerge in common law systems where rights advocacy lawyers can strategically cultivate and build on judicial precedents.[36] With a robust legal support structure domestically, it is not coincidental that a large volume of ECtHR minority- and migrant-related litigation from the 1970s-1980s onwards originated from the UK.

Human rights lawyering and legal support structures also grew variably in other European countries such as France[37] and the Netherlands.[38] From the 1970s onwards, lawyers, activists and civil society actors in these countries increasingly embraced and mobilized human rights law before domestic and international courts, including on behalf of minorities and immigrants. Growing legal mobilization around migrants' rights in France has been attributed to the growth of professional lawyering and legal expertise on rights and immigration law, shaped by distinct national dynamics.[39] In the ECHR too, the increasing recourse of asylum seekers to the Strasbourg Court to seek protection arguably cannot be understood independently from the "support from a range of civil society organizations, legal professionals, [who] help them to substantiate their legal claims and litigate through multiple hierarchies of appeals".[40]

In Europe's multi-level system, legal support structures comprise specialized lawyers, and a variety of loosely coupled, organizational and civil society actors, who actively engage in rights litigation before domestic and international courts as a mobilization strategy. They provide support to individual claimants and pursue social, legal or public policy goals, with varying degrees of connection to broader campaigns and political strategies. What they have in common is that they use human rights law as a "master frame" to articulate a wide variety of grievances, issues, disputes, and state practices as rights violations, in reference to broad treaty norms and evolving international case law. Their systematic engagement in international rights litigation is contingent on being able to access or generate the necessary resources, such as funding, expertise and networking, from public or private sources. Different types of human rights cases and international legal strategies have varying resource requirements.[41]

The existence of a robust legal support structure at the domestic and transnational level is critical to sustained international rights litigation as a strategic form of action on behalf of disadvantaged individuals and groups. Migrants and minority individuals often have limited access to resources and lack the organizational capacity to benefit from increased opportunities to resort to an international court. Asylum seekers in most European countries face numerous obstacles, such as lack of rights consciousness, language barriers, limited financial means, and lack of support. These hinder effective access to justice and the ability to navigate through the complex legal and asylum procedures.[42] Individuals facing discrimination or exclusion in the domestic sphere lack the resources that are required for a possibly protracted international legal battle with uncertain results.

International litigation, as scholars acknowledge, "...is long, costly, and uncertain, even in this permissive environment [as the ECHR establishes]; the process can take six to eight years and requires substantial legal expertise."[43] Even though filing a claim in the ECtHR is low-cost, and legal aid is also available for covering lawyer fees, the requirement to exhaust all domestic remedies means that petitioners must first go through all the levels of the domestic judicial system – usually a costly and time-consuming process. In view of the very low admissibility rate of petitions (less than 5%), specialized legal expertise and other needed resources are critical for constructing a grievance into a defensible human rights claim that can pass the stringent admissibility threshold in the Strasbourg Court. Assistance and support by civil society and legal actors with the necessary expertise and resources enables marginalized individuals and minorities to surmount resource-related constraints and to make use of the structural opportunities to litigate in an international court.[44] Litigating European human rights law on behalf of religious and ethnic minorities is arguably more likely when supported by a civil society organization or when an expert lawyer is involved.[45]

Over the past decades, the involvement of civil society organizations – many of them based at the national level and driven by domestic interests[46] – in international and supranational rights litigation has grown.[47] At the same time, dense transnational networks of lawyers and human rights activists have also emerged and flourished in Europe, lobbying or litigating before EU and international institutions, including the ECHR. In the area of gender equality, for example, transnational contacts among women's groups, experts and civil society organizations were instrumental in the expansion of anti-discrimination litigation in the Court of Justice of the European Union (CJEU). Litigation became a focal point for networking and mobilization, as well as a stimulus for lobbying and other policy-related activities targeting the European Commission. Individual, civil society and organizational actors do not only seize international legal opportunities. They also contribute to further expanding those opportunities through legal action. In response to litigation, CJEU rulings progressively redefined rules of access and standing. They thus opened up space for the participation of previously excluded actors such as feminists and environmental activists in the EU governance structures.[48]

To be sure, international rights litigation is not necessarily strategic or part of broader social and political mobilization campaigns, and this study does not make such an assumption. The misperception that tends to be created by a few high-profile cases that all court action is collective and/or policy-driven has been dispelled by studies on domestic and transnational rights litigation.[49] Individual recourse to human rights courts is substantially different from rights litigation as a form of action with social reform goals.[50] This book is specifically interested in this latter kind of strategic human rights litigation that is driven by structural and policy reform goals, with emphasis on claims related to migrants and minorities. It explores the extent to which and ways in which this kind of litigation takes place in the Strasbourg Court and its institutional ramifications for the ECHR system. The next section discusses structural reform litigation as the first step and a recurrent phase of an experimentalist human rights regime based on international judicial enforcement.

3 International courts and human rights experimentalism

Human rights experimentalism can emerge in transnational settings where national governments have signed onto a treaty's broad framework norms but maintain wide discretion of how to put those to practice. These broad norms are domestically enforced through recurring cycles of interaction between states, non-governmental actors and other stakeholders, and treaty bodies.

In a judicially-enforced human rights treaty, this multi-level interaction unfolds in the following phases: 1) individual, legal and civil society actors engage in bottom-up rights claiming, involving problem-spotting, and the framing of local-national disputes and conflicts as human rights problems, often in connection to broader campaigns and social struggles (section 3.1); 2) the international court reviews rights claims and rules on whether human rights principles embedded in the treaty were violated; 3) national authorities of the violating state implement the international court's rulings; they incrementally enact specific and provisional measures over iterative cycles of domestic reform, review and assessment by the treaty's supervisory bodies (section 3.2); 4) non-governmental actors monitor state action, report to the supervisory treaty bodies and engage in follow-on action (repeat litigation, domestic follow-on litigation, campaigns, etc., section 2.3.3) (see Figure 2.1).

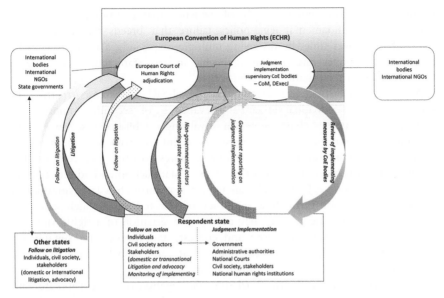

Figure 2.1 Transnational experimentalist dynamics in the ECHR regime

3.1 Transnational litigation and civil society mobilization

Transnational litigation of the strategic kind is the first phase in a judicially enforced human rights regime with experimentalist characteristics. It channels issues from the national-local level to an international court that applies and interprets broad normative principles in response to challenges of state action on human rights grounds. Human rights litigation, as already discussed, has increasingly been incorporated in the mobilization strategies of social groups and organizations that use the international legal system to advance goals of social and policy reform domestically. International treaties and court rules set the parameters for civil society involvement in rights litigation. In the ECHR system, NGOs a) represent individual petitioners, b) intervene as third parties (TPI) or amicus curiae, c) sponsor and support in a variety of other ways a case (i.e. by engaging in fact-finding, or providing new or expert information to the court).

Transnational structural reform litigation (SRL), as a specific variant of strategic legal action seeks to influence domestic law, policy and practice in accord with human rights norms. In the field of migration, for instance, it may be aimed at improving reception conditions for migrants and refugees, reforming asylum policy, or combatting ethnic discrimination in specific domains of state action. In the first place, SRL can take the form of *repeat litigation*, namely, legal action characterized by a large number of similar claims of human rights abuses in an issue area. These may variably involve disparate individual grievances, or deliberately strategic action. In either case, by lodging a large number of similar complaints, litigators build a body of evidence that exposes an entrenched situation or a fundamental legal-policy failure that breeds recurrent human rights abuses. Over time, by reviewing multiple cases, judges are able to make comprehensive policy intervention in specific areas of state action, elevating in this way, a court's reputation and authority.[51]

A second and distinctive kind of transnational SRL is *test case litigation*. In this variant, the individual litigant's grievance is of secondary importance. Instead, legal action is chiefly aimed at advancing established case law – challenging judicial interpretation, changing precedent, or extending the scope of treaty norms. It is also aimed at pressuring states to undertake reforms that promote rights protection in particular areas of state action and administration. Test case litigation seeks to make an impact not through a large number of repeat petitions, but through a small set of selected cases. Such cases are chosen for litigation because a) they exemplify a situation of a rights violation that the litigators seek to expose and contest, and b) they are suitable for making novel arguments and legal points that can compel judges to depart from precedent and to advance human rights law.

NGOs that engage in international strategic litigation closely collaborate with human rights lawyers. It is not rare for human rights lawyers to have a deeper commitment to a particular social cause that influences their professional legal practice.[52] Overall though, their motivation, degree of commitment to an underlying social cause, as well as their extent of connection to NGOs varies. Some may be affiliated with a NGO active on human rights issues. Others may pursue international rights litigation alone out of academic interest or as a matter of professional practice. Experienced lawyers follow closely the evolving human rights case law and can advance well-targeted and persuasive legal challenges. International rights litigation of the strategic kind may also be supported by international organizations and public institutions such as agencies working on human rights, non-discrimination and equality, especially those with a mandate to engage in litigation.[53]

Non-state actors who mobilize international human rights law on behalf of migrants and minorities comprise a diverse array of actors: multi-issue human rights organizations, international organization bodies, group-specific and issue specific advocacy organizations, legal or academic centres, community associations, public law organizations, and minority and migrant associations. Far from comprising, a unified social movement, these actors are situated in different states, they are knowledgeable of national or local issues, and they pursue various agendas. Some of those collaborate with NGOs in other countries around issues or cases of common interest to exchange information and to advance human rights.[54] Altogether, a wide variety of committed non-governmental actors, alongside international bodies and transnational networks make up an open, fragmented and multi-level European human rights field.[55]

In the frame of a treaty enforced by an international court, civil society organizations and transnational networks, alongside expert lawyers, play a critical role in generating the interactive and bottom-up dynamics that underpin human rights experimentalism. In the first place, NGOs, ranging from large transnational entities to small human rights groups with local knowledge, identify issues from the ground, and provide information about the local-national context. Through litigation, they bring the issues that are problematic from a human rights perspective to the attention of an international court. NGOs in collaboration with qualified lawyers construct national-local problems as human rights breaches by invoking broad and open-ended treaty norms. The initial stages of framing an issue or grievance in human rights terms and making it the subject of a complaint before an international court, may sometimes be less consciously strategic, and it may be inchoate or even fortuitous.[56]

Equally importantly, NGOs also generate and provide detailed factual information to expose the systemic nature of possible rights violations. The latter is particularly crucial in a system like the ECHR that adjudicates only individual cases, and does not recognize class actions, or group remedies. Documentation about structural human rights problems enables litigants to advance precedent-challenging and innovative claims, and the international court to make decisions that impact on policy areas domestically. The financial, organizational and other resources that large NGOs can generate are vital for the labor-intensive and resource-demanding tasks of fact-finding research to build a strategic litigation case. As part of transnational coalitions and networks, NGOs mobilize litigation and other strategies, and bring relevant and interested groups and actors into contact with one another. International court rulings are more likely to create pressure for states to tackle human rights abuses and to pursue social and policy reform, when they are deployed by actors with substantial material and organizational resources.[57]

Experimentalism is inherent in the uncertain and at times innovative ways in which litigants, lawyers, and civil society actors invoke treaty norms to construct local and national problems as human rights claims before an international court. Strategic litigators "work hard to develop arguments that stretch the meanings of rights and rules to wedge themselves into the litigation process".[58] They are willing to take high risk legal action with uncertain outcome, and seek an authoritative judicial ruling that they believe will have an impact on a salient social issue beyond the courtroom.[59] The expectation of a courtroom loss does not necessarily dissuade activists from litigating a case.[60] They look for "cracks" in established case law and press for a different approach.[61]

Experimentalism also underpins the incremental and longer-term approach that strategic litigators take, even if their arguments initially fail to convince judges. An experienced lawyer and seasoned litigator in international courts refers to this as the "value of persistence": "arguments that fall short [at convincing a court] at first, may gain traction over time, particularly when premised on a body of evidence that accumulates gradually".[62] When relevant and appropriate test cases arise, they follow through with successive litigation and press anew with legal argumentation on particular points of law. NGOs and other non-governmental actors engaging in litigation or acting as TPIs also bring to the attention of a human rights court normative shifts and legal developments in other states, as they try to convince the court to depart from precedent.[63] Over time, by reviewing test cases or multiple repetitive cases, international judges are able to make comprehensive policy intervention, and promote their court's reputation and authority.[64]

Systematic and proactive participation of non-governmental actors and stakeholders is central in a transnational regime of human rights experimentalism. A number of NGOs engaging in international rights litigation, including in the ECHR, tend to be "repeat players" (RP): they have built their reputation and accumulated expertise through a series of cases in an issue area. Galanter compellingly expounded how repeat players who regularly litigate in courts have an inherently advantageous position (vis-à-vis litigants who take to court once, "one-shotters") in formally neutral but routinely overloaded legal systems.[65] Besides being able to generate funding and access expert lawyers, RP have low start-up costs, advance knowledge and experience in how to frame an issue or conflict in legal and human rights terms, and established credibility in the field. They have established their vantage point over time through systematic interaction with the legal and justice system.

3.2 Judicial decision-making and implementation

Over the past two decades, international human rights courts have increasingly been confronted with cases involving structural problems not only in authoritarian states but also in established or backsliding democracies.[66] Structural problems exist when human rights breaches are linked to deficiencies in national legislation, and in administrative or judicial practice, that potentially disaffect large numbers of people.[67] Structural human rights problems, this book posits, form the basis for a shift in the functioning of human rights regimes in an experimentalist direction.

Human rights courts review individual claims and apply general treaty norms in issues from diverse national and local contexts. In their contentious judgments or advisory opinions, they tend to take a dynamic rather than static or "originalist" approach: they re-evaluate treaty norms in the light of changing social conditions, developments in international and national law, and shifting normative standards.[68] National authorities of respondent states must give effect to adverse rulings. Their obligation to adopt measures not only in the individual case concerned but also in order to prevent repetition of similar violations (called structural orders, general measures, or other) is inscribed in all regional human rights systems.[69] Thus, adverse rulings may call for legislative or administrative reforms, and judicial or other changes such as dissemination of court judgments, training or recruitment of new personnel, among others.[70]

In an experimentalist regime, adverse human rights rulings issued by an international court foremost function as "destabilizers" of the domestic status quo and as catalysts for domestic reform. They signal that established structures and practices in a particular domain of state action are untenable from a human rights perspective. They pronounce whether a state violated human rights embedded in a treaty but rarely prescribe top-down orders for structural reform to states. What specific measures are necessary to restructure domestic policy and practice in line with human rights is entirely the responsibility of national authorities.

Regional human rights regimes commonly embody this decentralized architecture: they recognize wide discretion to national authorities in determining the means to secure human rights in domestic policy and practice.[71] While their approach to remedies varies – from mostly declaratory as in the ECtHR and in the African Court of Human Rights to more prescriptive, as the Inter-American Court of Human Rights – overall, they refrain from ordering national authorities to make specific changes in national legislation, administrative or judicial practice.[72] The courts' remedial approach also varies even within each regional human rights regime, depending on the kind of cases they are dealing with (i.e. as in complex problems or in a small number of "pilot" judgments in the ECtHR).

Decentralization and a large margin of discretion to national authorities reflect the subsidiary and complementary nature of regional human rights regimes. They are meant to preempt unfettered international judicial interference with state sovereignty and democratic decision-making at the national level. Treaty bodies can maintain their own legitimacy by giving large space to the state to decide how to put human rights rulings into domestic policy and practice.[73] At the same time, this decentralized construction renders these regional treaties conducive to the growth of transnational human rights experimentalism.

Domestic enforcement of broad treaty norms does not end with a court ruling – indeed, this is only the beginning. Judicially enforced human rights regimes tend to assign the supervision of state implementation to the political organs of the respective regional organizations.[74] The ECHR is a case in point that assigns external supervision over judgment implementation to the Committee of Ministers (CoM), comprising of delegates of the signatory states. These external supervisory bodies monitor and periodically assess state implementation of human rights rulings until they are satisfied with the adequacy of measures and terminate their supervisory. How prescriptive human rights rulings are, is not only a feature of an international court's remedial approach. It is also shaped by the review process exercised by the treaty bodies that are responsible for overseeing state implementation of court rulings.[75]

From such a perspective that considers the twin role of both judicial and non-judicial treaty bodies, Newman has distinguished three models of remedial practice of human rights regimes. First, in the "direct remedy model", the tribunal and the supervisory treaty body specify in full detail the remedial actions that government officials must carry out. Secondly, in the "monitoring model", the international court articulates the range of parameters within which national officials must choose what implementing measures to adopt at the national level. Thirdly, in the "negotiation model", the human rights court and the supervisory treaty body create a broad framework and facilitate negotiation among different actors (governmental, various public and non-state stakeholders) to determine appropriate measures and reforms. The instruction to negotiate may be explicit or implicit.[76]

Human rights experimentalism is likely to emerge in a treaty-based regime, in which judgment implementation takes place along the lines of the "negotiation model". The latter is more likely to prevail in domains marked by systemic human rights problems that call for domestic reform. Structural problems are linked to the operation of large and complex administrative systems, or to entrenched structures and discriminatory attitudes. They also involve the interaction of, and conduct between a multiplicity of actors, at different levels of decision-making, who are affected by such a reform. Government-proposed measures to redress structural violations may not be sufficient or appropriate, or they may be strongly contested by those who must put them into practice. They may also leave gaps and ambiguities, and they cannot anticipate all future contingencies[77] due to a) incomplete knowledge, b) resistance among authorities and evasive compliance, c) uncertainty as to how human rights violations are redressed beyond the individual dispute at hand. For all these reasons, domestic implementation of judgments involving structural reform resembles a continuous process of negotiation among treaty bodies, states and non-governmental actors.

Last but not least, transnational experimentalism is marked by a move away from the state-centric nature of international human rights regimes in the earlier days of their establishment.[78] Domestic implementation of international court rulings is typically the responsibility of the executive. Its designated departments often coordinate remedial action with other state actors, pre-eminently the judiciary, human rights institutions, parliaments, and competent administrative authorities (i.e. police, schools, etc.). In an experimentalist setting, state implementation of treaty norms and judgments involves not only government and state authorities but also the systematic engagement of a variety of non-governmental actors and stakeholders. They regularly interact with supervisory treaty bodies in the implementation phase and seek to influence and pressure for the enactment of rights expansive reforms in areas, in which international court rulings pronounce violations.

A trend towards opening up enforcement mechanisms to the participation of non-governmental actors in the design and follow up of remedial measures is evidenced in many regional human rights regimes, including in the ECHR. Since the 2000s, non-state actors (NGOs, national human rights institutions, interest groups, some international bodies) can engage not only in ECHR litigation but also in the judgment implementation phase. They submit their own views and "shadow" action plans and reform proposals, monitor the governments' enacted measures, draft reports to state authorities and to international organizations, engage in follow-up litigation, and do advocacy work, among others. Likewise, in human rights systems where advisory proceedings are in place (international courts empowered to deliver advisory opinions), relatively open procedures allow for widespread participation of all parties to the treaty, including NGOs and individuals.[79] The Inter-American Court of Human Rights too has advanced innovative approaches to remedies that place "a special emphasis on the active participation of victims in the design and follow-up of remedies". It has also pursued procedures, such as convening (for the first time in 2008) compliance hearings "to provide the parties with the opportunity to present their evidence and arguments orally".[80]

In an experimentalist human rights regime, the engagement of non-governmental actors and stakeholders injects into judgment implementation an important participatory and deliberative dimension. It also brings openness and transparency in what is otherwise a bureaucratic and formalistic task. Increased participation can take place as a result of changes in treaty rules and practices. It is also driven by the vibrancy of civil society and the existence of national structures of democratic deliberation and human rights advocacy. Civil society organizations and other stakeholders may mobilize within and outside of the formal implementation process. They seize an international court's declared violation as an opportunity to mobilize further through advocacy or litigation before national courts and to pressure national authorities for reforms and policies grounded in human rights. Adverse international court rulings can focus the attention of authorities and of the general public on particular problems, and legitimize the arguments advanced by NGOs, stakeholders and human rights advocates vis-à-vis the state.

3.3 Assessment, domestic reform and follow-on action

A key feature of transnational experimentalist settings is the existence of feedback mechanisms. Institutionalized processes of iterative interaction between national-local actors and treaty bodies allow for the assessment and revision of initial remedies and for channelling new human rights claims from a country or region. The adoption of additional protocols to an international treaty years ater its original ratification (like the ECHR) is a manifestation of periodic and reflexive reconsideration of treaty norms. Through recurring cycles of litigation, judicial review and judgment implementation, state and non-state actors provide feedback to the international treaty bodies that interpret and apply these norms in different local-national contexts.

The feedback and iterative mechanisms are rooted in the expectation that critical lessons are learned through close contact and cooperation of national and international actors, as well as from expertise and experience from different countries. Learning from difference takes place as state and non-state actors share their knowledge from particular countries and regions and interact with treaty bodies that oversee the implementation of court rulings. Transnational networks of NGOs act as resources and information centers, "maintaining data bases of relevant information and drafting guidelines to help respond to particular kinds of complaints and identifying issues that arise repeatedly or in particular stages."[81] They draft guidelines of how to respond to particular kinds of complaints, they publish training materials, and organize training and learning workshops. Judicial and non-judicial treaty bodies also become repositories of information and knowledge about human rights problems and possible remedies.[82]

Feedback mechanisms are indispensable to a human rights regime that seeks to enforce general and uniform normative principles in countries with diverse political conditions and legal traditions. Their significance lies in the realization that embedding human rights protection in domestic structures and policies is rarely accomplished in a one-off action. Instead, human rights compliance has a strong provisional and open-ended quality that requires continuous engagement, reflection and oversight. In structural and complex human rights problems, initial remedies and policy responses are often incomplete. Their appropriateness and practical consequences cannot be fully foreseen when they are first enacted.

In judicially enforced, international human rights treaties, there are two main feedback mechanisms: a) monitoring and reporting by state and non-state actors in the context of judgment implementation, and b) follow-up and repeat litigation. Individuals, civil society and non-governmental stakeholders knowledgeable of local and national conditions, identify new gaps and lingering deficiencies in rights protection. They bring these to the attention of competent national authorities and international treaty bodies through their involvement in judgment implementation and follow-on litigation. Through repeat litigation, individuals and non-state actors challenge violations that arise due to earlier partial or ineffective remedies, or due to shifting conditions that create new human rights problems in the respondent state. They also invoke principles enunciated in earlier case law to bring similar complaints against other states that are parties to the treaty. Follow-up litigation may result in more expansive legal rulings, or conversely, it may lead adjudicators to narrow prior findings and remedies.[83]

Human rights experimentalism also involves follow-on action at the domestic level in the respondent state. Legal activists, civil society, advocacy groups and other stakeholders – at times in continuation of their involvement in international rights litigation – invoke human rights rulings in order to pressure governments to change laws, policies or practices that breed rights abuses.[84] They may form part of "compliance constituencies" alongside judges, government officials, administrative agencies, and others, with the power to influence and enforce implementation of contentious decisions.[85] They may use the media for publicity, and bring more complaints before national and international courts, including to pressure for state compliance with earlier rulings. Mobilization around human rights implementation may come up against counter-mobilization and backlash politics that "tries to overturn a precedent, abrogate or circumvent a ruling, or avert future losses in similar cases."[86]

The legal and social mobilization around an international court ruling is instrumental for human rights law and institutions to have any impact on domestic structural and policy change.[87] In fact, human rights judgments are arguably unlikely to trigger substantive reform on the ground unless they are connected to and incorporated in larger campaigns for social change.[88] Substantive human rights reform is rarely the result of a one-off action or a single judgment. Instead, it is an incremental and longer-term process, as scholars of international courts acknowledge. The domestic effects of human rights rulings in domestic policy and practice may take years to play out, "becoming fully evident only when publics inculcate a legal ruling, new actors enter the political arena, or legal entrepreneurs attempt to broaden the impact of a precedent."[89]

As long as human rights problems persist, the cycle continues from litigation to advocacy and pressure for implementation, to follow-up litigation in similar or related issues and implementation again. De Burca argues that for most part, iterative processes in the context of international human rights treaties have entailed "broadening the remit of those protected or the understanding of the right or issue in question, rather than narrowing or confining the original framework goals." This, however, does not exclude the possibility that in new conditions, governments might seek to rescind their earlier human rights commitments and to pressure for narrower interpretations of rights, or even to seek to withdraw from the original treaties.[90] Over time, judicial interpretations evolve in response to litigation, both relying on but also departing from precedent and leading to a sometimes expansive but other times restrictive evolution of case law.[91]

4 Concluding discussion

This chapter has analyzed the role of international institutions and rules – defining access and standing, judicial receptivity and precedent – in shaping the opportunities and constraints for international human rights litigation, based on a review of the relevant literature. Systematic and strategic human rights litigation though, that aims at domestic structural and policy reform, critically depends on the mobilization of a variety of legal and non-governmental actors. Through the resources that they can bring, expertise and organizational support, such actors constitute and sustain legal support structures for human rights litigation. In this book, the growth of national and transnational legal support structures and actors are viewed as indispensable in enabling vulnerable individuals and groups to seize opportunities for international rights litigation.

The rise and diversification of international rights litigation, specifically of the strategic kind, is central for the emergence of human rights experimentalism, as analyzed in section 3 of this chapter. It is a key mechanism through which individuals and non-governmental actors frame local and national issues into human rights claims before a regional and judicially based regime. Litigation and legal activism are key features of a court-based experimentalist human rights regime. Such a regime is nested in and develops out a decentralized and multi-level architecture. It involves the iterative interaction between treaty bodies, respondent states and a variety of non-governmental actors, in ongoing processes of human rights claiming, judgment implementation, and follow-on litigation and mobilization. Human rights experimentalism is shaped by bottom-up initiative, large discretion to state authorities, but also by multi-actor participation and deliberation in judgment implementation. State compliance and domestic human rights reform takes place over time, often through several cycles of litigation and judgment implementation.

This book posits that in certain areas of strategic and structural reform litigation, like those related to the rights of minorities and migrants, the ECHR evolves into one of transnational human rights experimentalism. The next chapter sets out the ECHR institutional context in which the rise in minority- and migrant-related litigation took place. It describes and analyzes the structural reforms of the ECHR regime from the 1990s onwards and how they transformed international legal opportunities and constraints for ECHR minority- and migrant-related litigation. Chapters 4 and 5 explore the role of legal support actors, particularly that of civil society, in the growth of human rights litigation related to minorities and migrants, respectively. Chapters 6 and 7 examine the domestic implementation of Court rulings related to Roma and migrants, and the extent to which the evolving system resembles one of human rights experimentalism.

Notes

1 Gráinne de Búrca, *Reframing Human Rights in a Turbulent Era* (Oxford: Oxford University Press, 2021), 46.
2 *M.S.S. v Belgium and Greece*, no. 30696/09, 21 January 2011, §399.
3 Robert Keohane, Andrew Moravscik and A.-M. Slaughter, "Legalized Dispute Resolution: Interstate and Transnational," *International Organization* 54, no. 3 (2000): 457–488.
4 Karen J. Alter, *The New Terrain of International Law – Courts, Politics, Rights* (Princeton: Princeton University Press, 2014), 5–6.
5 Rachel A. Cichowski, "Introduction: Courts, Democracy, and Governance," *Comparative Political Studies* 39, no. 1 (2006a): 7.
6 Lisa Vanhala, *Making Rights a Reality? Disability Rights Activists and Legal Mobilization* (Cambridge: Cambridge University Press, 2011).
7 Ellen Ann Andersen, *Out of the Closets and Into the Courts – Legal Opportunity Structure and Gay Rights Litigation* (Ann Arbor: The University of Michigan Press, 2006).
8 Gesine Fuchs, "Strategic Litigation for Gender Equality in the Workplace and Legal Opportunity Structures in Four European Countries," *Canadian Journal of Law and Society* 28, no. 2 (2013): 189–208.
9 Gianluca De Fazio, "Legal opportunity structure and social movement strategy in Northern Ireland and the United States," *International Journal of Comparative Sociology* 53, no. 3 (2012): 6–7. On the legal opportunity structure, see also Rhonda Evans Case and Terri E. Givens, "Re-engineering Legal Opportunity Structures in the European Union? The Starting Line Group and the Politics of the Racial Equality Directive," *Journal of Common Market Studies* 48, no. 2 (2010): 223–225; Andersen, *Out of the Closets and Into the Courts – Legal Opportunity Structure and Gay Rights Litigation*, 8–14.
10 Rachel Cichowski, *The European Court and Civil Society – Litigation, Mobilization and Governance* (Cambridge University Press, 2007); Boyle Heger, Elizabeth and Melissa Thompson, "National Politics and Resort to the European Commission on Human Rights," *Law & Society Review* 35, no. 2 (2001): 321–344; James Cavallaro and Stephanie Erin Brewer, "Re-evaluating Regional Human Rights Litigation in the Twenty-First Century: The Case of the Inter-American Court," *American Journal of International Law* 102, no. 4 (2008): 768–827; Lisa Conant, "Who Files Suit? Legal Mobilization and Torture Violations in Europe," *Law and Policy* 38, no. 4 (2016): 280–303.

11 On political opportunity structure, see Sydney Tarrow, "States and opportunities: The political structuring of social movements," in *Comparative perspectives on social movements*, eds. Doug McAdam, John D. McCarthy and Mayer N. Zald (Cambridge: Cambridge University Press, 1996), 54.

12 De Fazio, "Legal opportunity structure and social movement strategy in Northern Ireland and the United States," 6.

13 Article 34 ECHR. See Council of Europe, *Practical Guide on Admissibility Criteria* (Strasbourg: Council of Europe, 2014), 12–14.

14 Andersen, *Out of the Closets and Into the Courts,*13.

15 Lisa Conant, "Individuals, Courts and the Development of European Social Rights," *Comparative Political Studies* 39, no. 1 (2006): 76–100.

16 Evans Case and Givens, "Re-engineering Legal Opportunity Structures in the European Union?," 236.

17 See Council of Europe, *Environment and the ECHR*, European Court of Human Rights Fact Sheet, 21 July 2021, https://www.echr.coe.int/documents/fs_environment_eng.pdf.

18 Social movement scholars have drawn the distinction between structural and more volatile or contingent factors that shape political opportunities for collective action. See William A. Gamson and David S. Meyer, "Framing political opportunity," in *Comparative perspectives on social movements*, eds. Doug McAdam, John D. McCarthy and Mayer N. Zald (Cambridge: Cambridge University Press, 1996), 280–282; Ruud Koopmans, "Political. Opportunity. Structure. Some Splitting to Balance the Lumping," *Sociological Forum* 14, no. 1 (1999): 93–105. For applying the distinction between structural and contingent variables in relation to legal opportunities, see Chris Hilson, "New social movements: the role of legal opportunity," *Journal of European Public Policy* 9, no. 2 (2002): 241–243.

19 Different terms are used in the scholarly literature – judicial receptivity, judicial activism, judicial agendas – to denote essentially the same thing, namely, the preferences and views of judges concerning which issues and rights are important, and how they ought to be interpreted and decided.

20 Erik Voeten, "The Impartiality of International Judges: Evidence from the ECtHR," *American Political Science Review* 102, no. 4 (2008): 417–433.

21 Vanessa Baird and Tonja Jacobi, "Judicial Agenda Setting through Signaling and Strategic Litigant Responses," *Journal of Law and Policy* 29 (2009): 216–219; 222.

22 Baird and Jacobi, "Judicial Agenda Setting through Signaling and Strategic Litigant Responses," 216.

23 De Fazio, "Legal opportunity structure and social movement strategy in Northern Ireland and the United States," 3–22; Hilson, "New social movements: the role of legal opportunity," 243.

24 Hilson, "New social movements: the role of legal opportunity," 250.

25 Karen Alter, "The EU's Legal System and Domestic Policy: Spillover or Backlash?" *International Organization* 54, no. 3 (2000): 498; Karen Alter and Jeannette Vargas, "Explaining Variation in the Use of European Litigation Strategies," *Comparative Political Studies* 33, no. 4 (2000): 453–454.

26 Marc Galanter, "Why the 'Haves' Come out Ahead: Speculations on the Limits of Legal Change," *Law and Society Revie: Litigation and Dispute Processing: Part One* 9, no. 1, (1974): 135.

27 Shannon Portillo, "Social Equality and the Mobilization of the Law." *Sociology Compass* 5, no. 11 (2011): 949–956; Evans and Givens, "Re-engineering Legal Opportunity Structures in the European Union?" 224.

28 Vanhala, *Making Rights a Reality?*, 39.

29 Kristin Bumiller, "Victims in the Shadow of the Law: A Critique of the Model of Legal Protection," *Signs* 12, no. 3 (1987): 421–439.

30 Robert D. Benford and David A. Snow, "Framing Processes and Social Movements: An Overview and Assessment." *Annual Review of Sociology* 26 (2000): 631; William A. Gamson, and David S. Meyer, "Framing political opportunity," 276, 283.

31 Doug McAdam, John D. McCarthy and Mayer N. Zald, "Introduction: Opportunities, mobilizing structures, and framing processes – toward a synthetic, comparative perspective on social movements," in *Comparative perspectives on social movements*, eds. Doug McAdam, John D. McCarthy and Mayer N. Zald (Cambridge: Cambridge University Press, 1996), 6; Benford and Snow, "Framing Processes and Social Movements," 624.

32 Vanhala, *Making Rights a Reality?*, 105–107.

33 Holly J. McCammon and Allison R. McGrath, "Litigating Change? Social Movements and the Court System," *Sociology Compass* 92, no. 2 (2015): 133; Tanja A. Börzel, "Participation Through Law Enforcement The Case of the European Union," *Comparative Political Studies* 39, no. 1 (2006): 147–148; Andrew Boon, "Cause Lawyers in a Cold Climate," in *Cause Lawyering and the State in a Global Era*, eds. Austin Sarat and Stuart Scheingold (Oxford: Oxford University Press, 2001), 144, 148; Catherine R. Albiston and Laura Beth Nielsen, "Funding the Cause: How Public Interest Law Organizations Fund their Activities and Why it Matters for Social Change," *Law and Social Inquiry* 39, no. 1 (2014): 62–96.

34 Charles Epp, *The Rights Revolution* (Chicago: University of Chicago Press, 1998), 140–145. See also
    Carol Harlow and Richard Rawlings, *Pressure Through Law* (London: Routledge 1992), 293.

35 Epp, *The Rights Revolution*, 205.

36 Epp, *The Rights Revolution*, 201–202.

37 See Liora Israel, "Rights on the Left? Social Movements, Law and Lawyers after 1968 in France," in *Rights and Courts in Pursuit of Social Change*, ed. Dia Anagnostou (Oxford: Hart Publishing, 2014), 79–103.

38 Wibo van Rossum, "The roots of Dutch strategic human rights litigation: comparing 'Engel' to 'SGP'," in *Equality and human rights: nothing but trouble? Liber Amicorum SIM Special 38*, eds. Titia Loenen, Marjolein van den Brink, Susanne Burri, Jenny Goldschmidt (Utrecht: SIM/Universiteit Utrecht, 2015), 387–399.

39 Leila Kawar, *Contesting Immigration Policy in Court – Legal Activism and Its Radiating Effects in the United States and France* (Cambridge: Cambridge University Press, 2015); Israel, "Rights on the Left? Social Movements, Law and Lawyers after 1968 in France," 79–103.

40 Conant, "Who Files Suit? Legal Mobilization and Torture Violations in Europe," 295.

41 Lisa Vanhala, "Anti-discrimination policy actors and their use of litigation strategies: the influence of identity politics," *Journal of European Public Policy* 16, no. 5 (2009): 741.

42 European Council on Refugees and Exiles and European Legal Network on Asylum (ELENA), *Survey on Legal Aid for Asylum Seekers in Europe* (October 2010), 6.

43 R. Keohane et al., "Legalized Dispute Resolution: Interstate and Transnational," 465.

44 See Alter and Vargas, "Explaining Variation in the Use of European Litigation Strategies," 477; Rachel A. Cichowski, "The European Court of Human Rights, Amicus Curiae, and Violence against Women," *Law and Society Review* 50, no. 4 (2016): 893.

45 Theresa Squatrito, "Conditions of democracy-enhancing multilateralism: expansion of rights protections in Europe?" *Review of International Studies* 38, no. 4 (2012): 724.

46 See Alter and Vargas, "Explaining Variation in the Use of European Litigation Strategies," 478–479.

47 Loveday Hodson, *NGOs and the Struggle for Human Rights in Europe* (Oxford: Hart Publishing, 2011); Cichowski, "The European Court of Human Rights, Amicus Curiae, and Violence against Women," 890–919; Lloyd Hitoshi Mayer, "NGO Standing and Influence in Regional Human Rights Courts and Commissions," *Brookings Journal of International Law* 36, no. 3 (2011): 911–940.

48 Cichowski, *The European Court and Civil Society.*
49 Laura Beth Nielsen, Robert L. Nelson and Ryon Lancaster, "Individual Justice or Collective Legal Mobilization? Employment Discrimination Litigation in the Post-Civil Rights United States," *Journal of Empirical Legal Studies* 7, no.2 (2010): 175–201.
50 See Alter and Vargas, "Explaining Variation in the Use of European Litigation Strategies," 478.
51 Baird and Jacobi, "Judicial Agenda Setting Through Signaling and Strategic Litigant Responses," 216.
52 On cause lawyers, see Austin Sarat and Stuart Scheingold, eds., *Cause Lawyers and Social Movements* (Stanford: Stanford University Press, 2006).
53 Alter and Vargas, "Explaining Variation in the Use of European Litigation Strategies."
54 Margaret Keck and Kathryn Sikkink, *Activists Beyond Border – Advocacy Networks in International Politics* (Ithaca: Cornell University Press, 1998), 2.
55 In line with the perspective of Keck and Sikkink, the metaphor of a network underscores how relationships among NGOs, lawyers and activists are established and maintained. See Keck and Sikkink, *Activists Beyond Borders - Advocacy Networks in International Politics*, 6.
56 See McAdam, McCarthy and Zald, "Introduction: Opportunities, mobilizing structures, and framing processes," 16.
57 Lisa Conant, *Justice Contained* (Ithaca: Cornell University Press, 2002), 22–23.
58 De Fazio, "Legal opportunity structure and social movement strategy in Northern Ireland and the United States," 9.
59 See the view of a strategic litigation practitioner, Adam Weiss, "What is Strategic Litigation," *ERRC* (blog), 1 June 2015, http://www.errc.org/blog/what-is-strategic-litigation/62.
60 Douglas NeJaime, "Winning Through Losing," *Iowa Law Review* 96 (2011): 941–1003.
61 Vanhala, *Making Rights a Reality?*, 20.
62 James Goldston, "The Struggle for Roma Rights: Arguments that Have Worked," *Human Rights Quarterly* 32, no. 2 (2010): 317.
63 Alastair Mowbray, "An Examination of the European Court of Human Rights' Approach to Overruling its Previous Case Law," *Human Rights Law Review* 9, no. 2 (2009): 199.
64 Baird and Jacobi, "Judicial Agenda Setting Through Signaling and Strategic Litigant Responses," 216.
65 Galanter, "Why the 'Haves' Come out Ahead: Speculations on the Limits of Legal Change," 95–160.
66 Lawrence Helfer, "Redesigning the European Court of Human Rights: Embeddedness as a Deep Structural Principle of the European Human Rights Regime," *European Journal of International Law* 19, no. 1 (2008): 129; Alexandra Huneeus, "Reforming the State from Afar: Structural Reform Litigation at the Human Rights Courts," *Yale Journal of International Law* 40, no. 1 (2015): 1–40.
67 Mart Susi, "The Definition of a 'Structural Problem' in the Case-Law of the European Court of Human Rights Since 2010," *German Yearbook of International Law* 55 (2012): 385–418.
68 Mowbray, "An Examination of the European Court of Human Rights' Approach to Overruling its Previous Case Law," 191; Alastair Mowbray, "The Creativity of the European Court of Human Rights," *Human Rights Law Review* 5, no. 1 (2005): 63–64; Dinah Shelton, "Performance of Regional Human Rights Courts," in *The Performance of International Courts and Tribunals*, eds. Theresa Squatrito, Oran R. Young, Andreas Follesdal, Geir Ulfstein (Cambridge: Cambridge University Press, 2018), 137.
69 Başak Cali, "Explaining variation in the intrusiveness of regional human rights remedies in domestic orders," *International Journal of Constitutional Law* 16, no. 1 (2018): 216.

70 Charles F. Sabel and William H. Simon. "Destabilization Rights: How Public Law Litigation Succeeds," *Harvard Law Review* 117, no. 4 (2004): 1079.

71 Shelton, "Performance of Regional Human Rights Courts," 133.

72 Cali, "Explaining variation in the intrusiveness of regional human rights remedies," 214–234.

73 Rachel Murray and Clara Sandoval, "Balancing Specificity of Reparation Measures and States' Discretion to Enhance Implementation," *Journal of Human Rights Practice* 12, no. 1 (2020): 111.

74 Cali, "Explaining variation in the intrusiveness of regional human rights remedies," 228.

75 Gerald L. Newman, "Bi-Level Remedies for Human Rights Violations," *Harvard International Law Journal* 55, no. 2 (2014): 336.

76 Newman, "Bi-Level Remedies for Human Rights Violations," 329.

77 Sabel and Simon, "Destabilization Rights: How Public Law Litigation Succeeds," 1069.

78 De Búrca, *Reframing Human Rights in a Turbulent Era*, 41.

79 Dinah Shelton, "Performance of Regional Human Rights Courts," in *The Performance of International Courts and Tribunals*, eds. Theresa Squatrito, Oran R. Young, Andreas Follesdal, Geir Ulfstein (Cambridge: Cambridge University Press, 2018), 138.

80 Cali, "Explaining variation in the intrusiveness of regional human rights remedies," 220.

81 Gráinne De Búrca, "Human Rights Experimentalism," *American Journal of International Law* 111, no. 2 (2017): 296.

82 De Búrca, "Human Rights Experimentalism," 296–297.

83 Karen J. Alter, Laurence R. Helfer and Mikael Rask Madsen. "How Context Shapes the Authority of International Courts." *Law and Contemporary Problems* 79, no. 1 (2016): 22–23.

84 Alter, *The New Terrain of International Law*, 5–6.

85 Alter, *The New Terrain of International Law*, 50–53.

86 Alter, Helfer and Madsen, "How Context Shapes the Authority of International Courts," 22–23.

87 Epp, *The Rights Revolution*, 198.

88 Cavallaro and Brewer, "Re-evaluating Regional Human Rights Litigation in the Twenty-First Century: The Case of the Inter-American Court," 768, 788.

89 Alter, Helfer and Madsen, "How Context Shapes the Authority of International Courts," 23.

90 De Búrca, "Human Rights Experimentalism," 296.

91 Susanne K. Schmidt, "Who cares about nationality? The path-dependent case law of the ECJ from goods to citizens," *Journal of European Public Policy* 19, no. 1 (2012):12.

3 From politics to law

ECHR reform and legal opportunities

The rise of the individual as a holder of rights emanating from an international convention like the ECHR was a revolutionizing feature in the post-World War II evolution of international law. For the first time, individuals, and under certain conditions organizational entities, could bring claims before the ECHR bodies, alleging breach of human rights by a Contracting State. Governments though viewed the possibility of individuals to hold states accountable before an international court, as an unacceptable encroachment upon national sovereignty.[1] From the start, they resisted international judicial review of state actions and agreed to place structural limitations on individual access. The European Commission of Human Rights (hereby ECommHR, or the Commission) and the European Court of Human Rights (hereby ECtHR, or the Court) were even less intended to become settings where individuals from minorities and migrants, would regularly turn to challenge state practices on grounds of rights protection. International judicial oversight over executive action in areas close to the heart of a state's sovereign powers was particularly objectionable and strongly opposed.

In the following decades though, the ECHR underwent far-reaching changes in its structures and rules that expanded individual and non-governmental access to it. These occurred mostly incrementally, but major reforms were also introduced in the 1990s that drastically restructured the system. By the late 1990s, individual and other non-state actors could directly and regularly challenge state action before the Strasbourg Court on human rights grounds. This chapter provides an overview of the original institutional and juridical features defining access and standing in the ECtHR. It analyzes how these evolved and transformed over time, specifically in relation to claims related to migrants and minorities. Through process tracing, the analysis sheds light to a faintly visible upward trend in minority- and migrant-related litigation in the second half of the 1980s, a critical juncture, when the Court pronounced a number of milestone rulings.

In the 1970s, the Commission and the Court ushered in a bolder approach and began to exercise greater scrutiny over state restrictions of certain rights. They did so especially in cases involving social values and mores, in which a common European consensus appeared to exist.[2] The Convention as a "living instrument"[3] that must be interpreted in the light of societal changes, the principle of "autonomous interpretation" from the national legal and constitutional traditions[4], and

DOI: 10.4324/9781003256489-3

the "effective and practical protection" of European human rights[5], were all enunciated in the course of that decade. The new and dynamic approach that these conveyed, both reflected and in turn reinforced a profound shift in the Convention. It progressively transformed from a system founded upon inter-governmental diplomacy into a legalized rights review system.[6] The onset of the Helsinki process[7] and the rapprochement in East-West relations created an international milieu more receptive to human rights.[8]

The approach of the Commission and the Court though did not exhibit a similar openness to minority- and migrant-related claims. They were reluctant to hold national governments accountable for alleged breaches related to ethnic-cultural diversity or immigration. Strong deference to state governments stemmed from concerns not to alienate the Contracting States and undermine their fledgling support for the Strasbourg organs at the time. It helped establish the reputation of the ECHR adjudicatory bodies as unthreatening to national specificities, and to entrench the system's judicial authority in the longer run.[9]

From the 1960s onwards, several petitions from non-nationals to the ECHR challenged their deportation on non-refoulement grounds and sought political asylum in countries like Belgium, the UK, the Netherlands and elsewhere. They were either declared inadmissible or were struck out.[10] The few decisions and judgments that the Commission and the Court issued in the 1960s and the 1970s were mostly unfavorable to the claims raised by migrants and minority members. The first two sections of this chapter provide an overview of the original structural and institutional characteristics that restricted individual access and standing in the ECHR bodies. They also examine the responses of the Commission and the Court to minority- and migrant-related litigation in the 1960s and the 1970s.

Over the next decades, changes in rules and practices bolstered the judicial arm of the ECHR system (the Court) in relation to its political pillar (the Committee of Ministers (CoM)) and consolidated the legalization of the system. Changes improved the position of individual litigants vis-à-vis states and allowed third parties to intervene in legal proceedings. The reform momentum continued and culminated with a major institutional restructuring of the ECHR in the 1990s. In 1998, Protocol 11 (P-11) abolished the ECommHR, created a single Court, and rendered it mandatory for states to accept the right of individuals to petition it. In the 2000s, changes in the working methods of the Committee of Ministers (CoM) further opened up the system, allowing for the participation of non-governmental actors in the judgment implementation process. Sections 3–5 examine the changes in ECHR rules and practices defining the access of individuals and other non-state actors in the judicial and post-adjudication proceedings.

1 Structural and juridical constraints in the original ECHR system

Until the 1990s, Convention rules rendered optional the right of individuals to petition the ECtHR. This right was dependent on each Contracting State's acceptance of the Court's jurisdiction. Individual applications were initially lodged with the ECommHR. If the Commission considered a petition admissible, it could refer the case to the Court for a judgment on the merits, it could seek a friendly settlement, or it could refer the case to the Committee of Ministers (hereby CoM). In this latter instance, the applicant had absolutely no status before the CoM, an intergovernmental rather than judicial body made up of state representatives. While the CoM was assigned an important role, the Court was relegated to a secondary place in the Convention system.

Unsurprisingly, during the 1950s and 1960s, the ECommHR took a cautious and restrictive approach so as not to provoke reactions from states. It declared few petitions admissible with a view to gaining the confidence of those states that had not yet accepted the optional clauses.[11] It also referred most cases to the CoM rather than to the ECtHR, for a final decision on the merits.[12] By the early 1970s, the Court's case law on most of the substantive rights of the Convention was scant or non-existent.[13] It mostly consisted of non-admissibility decisions and Commission reports that lacked the status of court rulings and could not raise public awareness about the tribunal's existence.[14]

Convention rules also placed individuals in a thoroughly unequal position in legal proceedings vis-à-vis states. Individuals and other non-state actors had very limited access, standing and rights of audience in legal proceedings before the ECHR. Even if a state had accepted the Court's jurisdiction, a litigant was still not able to bring a claim directly to the Court and to communicate her views before it. Individual applicants could only deposit an application with the ECommHR.[15] While they were granted an equal status in the confidential proceedings before the Commission, they did not have an equal status (to that of State parties) in proceedings before the Court.[16] Legal standing before the ECtHR was limited to the agents representing State parties, who could be assisted by advocates or advisers.[17]

The limited standing and rights of audience of individual applicants, and national government resistance all transpired in the first case that was reviewed by the ECtHR. *Lawless v Ireland* concerned detention without trial of an applicant, who was suspected of being a member of the Irish Republican Army (IRA).[18] In the procedure before the Court, the applicant did not have rights of audience, unlike the respondent state, and he was not to be regarded as a party to the judicial proceedings.[19] The ECHR (Article 31) designated only the CoM and the respondent state as recipients of the Commission's report.[20] The Court issued "a reasonably government-friendly" judgment that did not find a human rights violation. It justified detention by accepting too readily and without much supporting evidence that the Irish government was facing an emergency threatening the life of the nation.[21]

At the same time, despite opposition from the Irish government, the ECommHR amended the rules as to allow the applicant's lawyer, the eminent Seán MacBride, to attend the hearing and represent the applicant's views before the Court.[22] MacBride was one of the founders of Amnesty International, and a prominent figure in the nascent at the time international human rights movement. In the following years, the applicant's representative would be allowed to participate in the oral hearings before the Court as an assistant of the ECommHR.[23]

1.1 Minority rights and state abuses under a state of emergency

In the 1960s and 1970s, a few petitions from minority individuals were deemed admissible by the Commission, but less than a handful were referred to the Court for a judgment.[24] They concerned minority culture and language, discrimination in the enjoyment of rights such as education, political representation,[25] and access to justice,[26] among others. A string of petitions was linked to the language conflict between the French-speaking and the Flemish-speaking communities in Belgium.[27] Aggrieved and politicized minority groups among the French-speakers, petitioned the ECtHR to contest national legislation that had divided Belgium into four linguistic regions – Dutch, French, German regions and the Brussels conurbation – with each given permanent boundaries. It also provided for the exclusive use of Dutch, French and German in the public sector in the respective regions.[28]

In the landmark *Belgian Linguistics* case, French speakers, who were a minority in the Flemish area[29], claimed that education legislation discriminated against them, as they could not receive instruction in their mother tongue.[30] Before the Court, they were represented by Paul Guggenheim, a prominent Swiss scholar of international law and formerly a judge of an international court. In a sharply divided 1968 judgment, the ECtHR opined that the right to education implied the right to be educated in the national language, but it did not require that the parents' linguistic preferences be respected. While it found that Belgium violated the right to education and the prohibition of discrimination, the judgment was "soft" on the government: it pronounced a breach in respect to only one of the four educational acts challenged by the applicants, and only for certain French-speaking children.[31]

The landmark *Belgian Linguistics* cases starkly revealed how much politics weighed upon the Commission and the Court, and how yielding they were to the respondent state in their review of the relevant national legislation. It also showed how apprehensive states were about an international court with jurisdiction to review alleged violations over such sensitive matters as minority rights. The Belgian government had not only opposed the referral of the case to the Court. It also protested the judgment issued against it by threatening to withdraw its acceptance of the right to individual petition.[32]

The deferential (to states) approach of the ECommHR and the ECtHR run through all the minority-related cases that they reviewed in the 1960s and the 1970s. In the *Inhabitants of Les Fourons*, brought by the Regional Association for the Defense of Liberties on behalf of 165 heads of German-speaking families, who wanted their children to receive their schooling in French, the Commission's decision did not dispute the territorial principle in language legislation. As in the *Belgian Linguistics* judgment, it declined to recognize a positive duty for the Belgian government "to establish or subsidize a particular system of education" or education in a minority language different from the language spoken by the majority.[33] In the 1970s, the Commission rejected claims to territorial autonomy by Jura autonomists in the Canton of Berne. It conceded a wide margin of appreciation to national authorities when they were confronted with a foreseeable danger affecting public safety and order.[34] The ECHR organs also viewed the differential treatment of linguistic, religious and other minority groups as legitimate.[35] They did so also in the context of consociational arrangements aimed at achieving inter-communal balance and political stability.[36]

In those early years, minority-related claims before the ECHR bodies were often expressions of political discontent, out of place with the intrinsic logic of an international convention. For instance, complaints were lodged by disgruntled Sudeten Germans, who saw their hopes for reclaiming their property in Czechoslovakia fade away with the 1973 treaty signed between Czechoslovakia and the Federal Republic of Germany.[37] They were also brought by individuals and ethnic groups resentful about the Suriname's independence from the Netherlands that had allegedly passed the island to settlers of the Dutch colonial era rather than to its original Indian inhabitants.[38] Such claims reflected a lack of understanding of the Convention, how the rights it guaranteed were applied to provide protection, as well as the nature and scope of those rights. In turn, the little developed and largely unknown case law at the time prevented the Strasbourg organs from communicating with clarity how litigants could frame their grievances as human rights claims.

Another string of minority-related petitions in the ECHR system in the 1960s-1970s were related to the inter-communal conflict between Protestant unionists and the Catholic nationalists (minority) in Northern Ireland. The British government had declared a national emergency in connection with the activities of the Irish Republican Army (IRA) in the region. This allowed it to temporarily withdraw from its human rights obligations under the Convention.[39] Direct rule was imposed from London in an attempt to deal with inter-communal violence.[40] Emergency measures bolstered executive powers and curtailed the rights of individuals accused or suspected of involvement in terrorist activities. Domestic courts in the UK tended to acquit security forces accused of killings.[41] This gave rise to strong perceptions about "miscarriages of justice" in the UK's common law system.[42]

Following the UK's acceptance of the right to individual petition in 1966, the situation in Northern Ireland set the stage for a large number of petitions to the ECHR. They sought protection of individuals from rights abuses related to the actions of security forces and paramilitary groups in the region.[43] Human rights petitions from Northern Ireland also raised issues related to electoral rights[44], freedom of expression and association[45], and discrimination in housing, employment and education, besides claims related to emergency legislation.[46] Notably, the Commission, rejected nearly all of those petitions, which originated mainly from Catholics, as inadmissible, or it found that rights' restrictions were justified on grounds of national security.[47]

The wave of litigation related to the inter-communal conflict in Northern Ireland was closely linked to the emergence of a civil rights movement in the region and in the UK. Old and new public interest and civil society organizations like the National Council for Civil Liberties (NCCL, the predecessor of Liberty), the

Campaign for Social Justice (CSJ) and the Northern Ireland Civil Rights Association (NICRA) had been active in denouncing the discrimination experienced by Catholics in Northern Ireland. They exhibited a distinctive legal orientation defined by the use of law and legal tactics as key tools for seeking rights and social change.[48] In the context of escalating tensions between Protestants and Catholics, they supported applicants in pursuing cases before domestic courts and in the ECHR system. They often solicited support from committed human rights lawyers, like Kevin Boyle and James Heaney (a US-based lawyer).[49] Legally-oriented civil society groups, along with the introduction of government sponsored legal aid programs, would form over the next decades the backbone of a well-developed legal support structure. The latter was arguably instrumental in the growth of rights claims before UK courts and the ECHR.[50]

Out the large number of petitions related to the conflict in Northern Ireland, only one was referred to the ECtHR for a judgment – the interstate case of *Ireland v the UK*.[51] In this case, the Court once again found internment without trial justified on grounds that the UK was still faced with an "emergency situation". It rejected the claim that the security forces operationalized emergency measures by favoring "loyalists" suspected of terrorism while discriminating against nationalists.[52] The judgment fueled into strong criticisms of the Strasbourg Court for what was perceived as lack of impartiality[53] and "near-total abdication to government discretion".[54] At the same time, the Court expressed concern about the failure of British authorities to carry out internal police investigations and to prosecute those found guilty. On this ground, its judgment did find a violation of Article 3 ECHR (prohibition of torture and inhuman treatment). The adequacy and effectiveness of internal police investigations into allegations of abuse arose as a major issue after 1975. From that point on, the UK's security policy in Northern Ireland abandoned internment without trial and shifted towards a criminal prosecution policy aimed at obtaining confessions and convictions.[55]

In sum, a substantial number of minority-related petitions were brought to the ECommHR and the ECtHR in the 1950s – 1970s. They originated from highly mobilized minorities, such as the French speakers in Belgium (applicants were at times themselves involved in local or national politics), as well as from the inter-communal conflict in Northern Ireland. A few pioneering lawyers with expertise in international law and human rights, and lawyers with activist and leftist leanings provided legal representation to applicants. Minority-related claims raised in the ECHR bodies were at times polemical; they did not resonate with the spirit of the Convention, and thus failed to pass the admissibility stage. As ECHR procedural rules and the relevant case law were underdeveloped, it is suggested that "...there was understandably a degree of uncertainty as to what would or would not pass muster in Strasbourg".[56] In response to minority-related petitions, the ECommHR and the ECtHR were highly reluctant to condemn state actions in situations involving ethnic-cultural diversity and conflict. Above all, they tended to justify executive action in cases involving threats to security and public order, as those related to inter-communal violence in Northern Ireland.[57]

1.2 Discrimination against immigrants (and why the United Kingdom)

In the 1960s and 1970s, a small number of petitions were lodged by foreigners and migrants, mostly challenging deportation orders by national authorities.[58] They mainly originated from the United Kingdom, the first state in Europe to seek to regulate immigration through restrictive rules. The UK had longstanding and extensive ties with citizens of Commonwealth countries, among which free mobility was maintained. In the 1960s, British authorities introduced rules to control immigration of persons not born in the UK or persons not holding a passport issued by the British government.

Complaints brought to the ECommHR concerned the refusal of immigration authorities to allow the entry of family members of British and Commonwealth citizens of Pakistani and Indian origin, into the UK.[59] The most important early immigration case in the ECHR, the *East-Africans Asians case*, was lodged by British citizens of Asian descent, who had been forced to flee the newly independent countries of Uganda and Kenya. They challenged provisions of the highly controversial 1968 Commonwealth Immigration Act that denied Commonwealth British citizens from Asia, who were residents of East Africa, entry to the UK.[60]

Until the 1980s, the ECommHR was generally reluctant to refer migrant-related cases to the Court for a judgment, being subject to strong pressure from state governments to refrain from it. In its lengthy admissibility decision in the *East Africans* case in 1970, the Commission found the differential treatment between citizens of the UK and the Commonwealth to be discriminatory on racial grounds.[61] The British government reacted strongly against it. It criticized the Commission for engaging in judicial review of legislation passed by an elected parliament and threatened to withdraw its acceptance of the right to individual petition.[62] Under such pressure, the Commission stopped short of referring the case to the Court for a judgment, but it instead referred it to the Committee of Minister (CoM) for a final decision. As the British government intensively lobbied state delegates to persuade them not to vote in favor of the Commission's verdict, the CoM was unable to reach a decision. "Non-decisions" of the sort were a focal point of criticism. They were a manifestation of the political underpinnings of the Convention system that hampered its legalization.[63]

The early migrant-related cases from the UK were brought to the ECHR as part of broader strategies for rights and policy change, with the support of pioneering lawyers and NGOs, like the Joint Council for the Welfare of Immigrants (JCWI). Established in 1967, the JCWI was part of an emergent movement for the civil rights of non-white immigrants in the UK, at a time when race relations became increasingly politicized. Alongside a variety of other organizations, it mobilized to oppose discriminatory and restrictive immigration policies.[64] A variety of NGOs – some with a general civil rights goals, and others with a specific migration focus, or with a public law orientation incorporated ECHR litigation among their mobilization strategies.[65] They often cooperated with pioneering civil rights lawyers, like Anthony Lester, counsel in the *East Africans* and the *Alam Khan* cases, and formerly a representative of Amnesty International, reporting on racism in America's deep-south. Having been involved in UK immigration policy on behalf of the progressive segments of the Labor Party government (the 1976 Race Relations Act), he pursued ECHR litigation to challenge the controversial 1968 immigration legislation.[66]

It is noteworthy that a large number of petitions in the ECHR originated from the UK, following its acceptance of the right to individual petition in 1966. The inter-communal conflict in Northern Ireland and the legal restrictions to immigration undoubtedly set the stage for recurrent breaches of Convention rights. Meanwhile, a strongly entrenched tradition of parliamentary supremacy, combined with the UK's lack of a written bill of rights (until the passage of the Human Rights Act in 1998), limited domestic judicial review of legislation and rendered the ECHR system as the only alternative venue. Most importantly though, the growth of ECHR litigation from the UK was directly linked to the mobilization of a variety of legal and non-governmental actors seeking social and policy change. More than any other European country, the UK saw in the 1960s and 1970s the rise of a vibrant civil rights movement that regularly made use of legal tactics to challenge state abuses in Northern Ireland and restrictions targeting non-white migrants.

In sum, up until the 1980s, the ECHR regime was not open or inviting to minorities and migrants seeking international rights protection. The limits to individual access and standing, and the deferential stance vis-à-vis state governments, described earlier, possibly discouraged individuals from systematically pursuing human rights litigation. The ECHR bodies were in turn deprived of the opportunity to develop a case law that would respond to the concerns and claims of minorities and migrants. The 1980s though were a turning point. In the first place, they marked the beginning of a series of changes in ECHR rules and structures that would fully legalize its international judicial review mechanism over the next decade. The next section describes and analyzes these structural changes.

2 From incremental changes to systemic overhaul

In the 1980s, a series of incremental changes that had been taking place, undermined the intergovernmental underpinnings of the ECHR, and transformed it into a legal system of international rights review. The ECommHR, but also states, started to refer more cases to the Court, gradually leading to the depoliticization of proceedings.[67] In the first place, it was no longer required for the CoM to give its approval to a decision or judgment issued by the ECHR bodies in order to render it final. The CoM began to regularly endorse the ECommHR's conclusions (unlike in earlier periods, when it often refused to ratify its decisions, as it had done in the *East African Asians* case). The CoM also revised its Rules of Procedure in order to reduce discrepancies between its decisions and those issued by the Court.[68] These shifts both reflected and reinforced the legalization of the ECHR system. The Court emerged as the main actor, shaping with its jurisprudence the substantive law of the Convention.

Changes also strengthened the procedural status and standing of the individual applicant vis-à-vis states in proceedings before the Court and introduced the possibility for third party intervention. In 1982, the revised Rules of the Court expressly recognized the individual's rights of audience, institutionalizing a practice that had already been taking place in the preceding years: they allowed the applicant to present (through her lawyer) her case before the Court, and thus to be directly involved as a party in international legal proceedings.[69] The applicant could now be consulted by the President of the Chamber hearing her case, receive copies of the documents filed and the judgments, request the adoption of interim measures or measures for obtaining evidence, file written pleadings, appear at oral hearings, and submit a claim for "just satisfaction".[70] By the 1980s, Court rules defining the status of individuals had evolved to such an extent that they came into direct conflict with the original Convention (Articles 44 and 48 stipulated that the individual applicants were unable to refer cases to the Court).[71]

Thirdly, the 1982 revision of the Rules of the Court (Article 37(2)) empowered the President of the Court to invite or grant leave to any Contracting State or to any person concerned other than the applicant, to submit written comments "on issues which [the President] shall specify".[72] The Court and the Commission already could, at their initiative or at the initiative of a state party, hear a witness or expert in a case. But the 1982 amendment enabled non-state entities to request to intervene and submit written (and not only oral) comments in a case under review by the Court.[73] In the second half of the 1970s, the Court had already received (but did not grant leave to) two requests from lawyers and a NGO, and one from the UK government, to intervene and make their views known to the Court.[74] The possibility for TPI was arguably introduced in response to persistent pressure by the UK, where the practice of amicus curiae had been well established in the domestic legal system[75], rather than in response to civil society pressure, as others have argued.[76] The UK government was arguably in favor of it in order to be able to convey its views in matters of interest in the ECommHR and the ECtHR. This procedure, however, would subsequently come to be mostly used by non-governmental actors who would increasingly seek to intervene as third parties in proceedings before the ECtHR.[77]

The above structural changes strengthened access and standing for individuals and opened new opportunities for non-governmental actors to participate in proceedings before the ECtHR. They did so at a time when more states accepted the right to individual petition. While until the mid-1970s, only four states had accepted it (the UK, Denmark, Belgium and the Netherlands), more states did so in the second half of the decade (Italy, Switzerland and Portugal). In the 1980s, five more countries for the first time accepted the right to individual petition: France in October 1981; two south European countries that had made a transition to democracy in the 1970s (Spain in July 1981 and Greece in November 1985); Turkey in January 1987 and Cyprus in January 1989. Even as more countries accepted the right to individual petition, governments were far from enthusiastic with the legalization of the ECHR system, yet they did not have control over its institutional development either.[78]

In the 1990s, a period of profound transformation in Europe, the ECHR adjudicatory system underwent far-reaching reform. Accumulated changes from the preceding decades and a rising number of petitions gave strong impetus to its restructuring.[79] Reforms in the early 1990s had sought to augment the capacity of the ECommHR and the ECtHR to handle their rising workload. The new protocol (Protocol 9) that entered into force in October 1994, allowed an applicant, whose petition had been the subject of a report by the Commission, to refer his/her own case to the Court, regardless of whether the Commission or the respondent State conceded to this referral. This both reflected and reinforced the individual's upgraded status as a party to the proceedings.[80] Protocol 9 though never entered into force, as some states, including France and the UK, refused to ratify it. Besides, the challenges of eastward expansion soon rendered the scope of this reform inadequate.

In the most far-reaching overhaul that the Convention system had ever experienced, Protocol 11 (hereby P-11) institutionalized many of the changes in Convention rules and practices that had been taking place since the 1980s. It abolished the Commission and established a single Court with mandatory jurisdiction that individuals and other non-state actors could directly access. While the CoM retained its main function in supervising the execution of judgments (Art. 54 ECHR), P-11 put an end in its decision-making role in rights review. The new, single and full-time Court would decide both on the admissibility and on the merits of alleged rights violations brought before it. P-11 also rendered the individual petitioner "a full party to the proceedings before the Court" on a par with states and enhanced the transparency of these proceedings.[81] It did not though extend standing to NGOs that can submit a petition to the ECtHR only on the condition that the rights of the organization itself (or of each one of its members) are violated.[82]

Most importantly, P-11 sealed the right to individual petition by making it obligatory for all Contracting States (old and new ones) to accept it. Unlike earlier protocols, it excluded the possibility for states to make any reservations. To be sure, already in the 1980s, more states, such as Greece, Turkey, France, had accepted the right to individual petition. While several states had by the 1990s accepted the right to individual petition, they continued to be sceptical about submitting their laws and practices to judicial rights review by an international court. For instance, as late as the mid-1990s, the UK government threatened to withhold renewal of the right to individual petition in reaction to the *McCann* judgment.[83] The obligatory nature of the Court's jurisdiction established with P-11 prevented states from raising anew barriers to individual access when they felt that ECtHR rulings were not in accord with their national preferences.

Following the disintegration of communist regimes, many states in Central-East and Southeast Europe (CESE) and the former Soviet Union, opted for accession to the Council of Europe (CoE) and the ECHR. The Convention's eastward expansion in the 1990s critically added to pressures for large-scale systemic reform. It accelerated the radical restructuring of the system that occurred with the entry into force of Protocol 11 ECHR (1 November 1998). The accession of twenty new states in the ECHR (from 27 to 47 states today) in the 1990s massively expanded the Court's jurisdiction to a geographical area with a population of 800 million – all potential litigants with the right to bring proceedings against states.

Eastward expansion also brought new challenges regarding the nature of rights violations, that were qualitatively different from those that the ECHR system had been accustomed to handle.[84] Most of the newly democratized, ex-communist states had problematic rule of law standards that diverged from the ECHR. Following their acceding to it, the Court began to be increasingly confronted with human rights breaches of a repetitive and structural nature.

The reforms ushered in with P-11 further consolidated the participation of non-governmental and civil society actors as Third Parties in legal proceedings before the Court. Third Party Intervention (hereby TPI), which was previously covered by the Rules of the Court, was incorporated as a permanent feature of the ECHR (as Article 36(2)).[85] Over the next years, opportunities for non-state actors to participate as third parties further expanded. The 2003 amended Rules of the Court reaffirmed and strengthened the ability of Third Parties to intervene in legal proceedings, not only by submitting written comments, but also (in exceptional circumstances) by taking part in a hearing. The right to intervene as a Third Party was also extended to the Council of Europe's Commissioner for Human Rights of Human Rights.[86]

The ECtHR invites or grants leave to a non-state actor to act as a Third Party on grounds that the party be "concerned" and its intervention is in the "interest of the proper administration of justice." NGOs with a general interest in or specific knowledge of an issue are generally allowed to submit an amicus brief and assist the Court in reaching a decision, as some claim.[87] Others though state that a substantial number of requests for TPI are refused.[88] The Court has recognized a broad range of non-state actors as legitimate to act as TPIs. These include a) persons other than the applicant, who have an interest in the domestic proceedings of a case brought before the ECtHR, b) entities, groups or individuals with relevant legal expertise or factual knowledge, and c) interest groups with views closely aligned to the applicant.[89] The Court for most part pays close attention to the content of these briefs, especially if they are submitted by large and well-established NGOs.[90] Several NGOs participate as TPIs before the ECtHR. They seek to challenge national laws and practices, to establish precedents, to inform the Court, and expand the judicial interpretation of Convention provisions.[91]

In sum, by the end of the 1990s, institutional reforms abolished all remaining structural barriers to directly access the Court and expanded the opportunities for individual and non-state actors to engage in legal proceedings before it. With its full-fledged legalization, the ECHR formed an unusually open transnational legal system. Any individual from the 47 Contracting States could bring a complaint in it without paying fees, without being represented by a lawyer, and even by writing a letter in his/her own language. Legal aid could be granted to petitioners to cover the application fees and even the fees for legal representation.[92] Individuals who were disgruntled with the failure of states to protect their rights, could turn to the ECHR with expectations to receive a fair hearing and get vindicated. As human rights litigation grew, the Convention's enforcement machinery increasingly came under pressure. In the next decade, the regime's restructuring extended to the Committee of Ministers (CoM) supervisory system of judgment execution, to which we turn in the next section.

3 Reform of the supervisory system of judgment execution

Up until 2000, little was known about the ECtHR judgment implementation process and the role of the CoM in it. The Committee's supervisory work, assisted by the Department for the Execution of Judgments, involved exchanges over remedial measures exclusively with government officials of the respondent state, that took place entirely behind closed doors.[93] The CoM oversight was admittedly lax and highly deferential to national authorities who typically responded with minimal and mainly individual measures to remedy the violations pronounced by the Court.[94] By the early 2000s, a mounting case load and increasing numbers of repetitive cases emanating from structural human rights deficiencies, raised profound concerns about the effectiveness of the system. They intensified pressures for reform of the judgment execution and CoM supervisory process.

In the course of the 2000s, the CoM supervisory mechanism over ECtHR judgment implementation underwent profound reconfiguration through a series of changes in the Committee's working rules (in 2004, 2006 and 2010). Changes aimed to enhance its efficacy in tackling structural human rights problems and overall to improve implementation. They transformed the CoM supervisory mechanism in three fundamental ways. In the first place, the communications between the respondent state and the CoM were no longer confidential but became public. They provide comprehensive information regarding the measures national authorities undertaken and generally about the state of progress in the execution of pending judgments.[95] The adoption of P-14 further entrenched the transparency and openness of the execution process.

Secondly, in supervising judgment implementation, the CoM began to concentrate its efforts and time on the most important and difficult cases involving structural and complex human rights problems. In the first place, leading cases are identified by the Court or the CoM and distinguished from repetitive ones; they reveal a new systemic problem and require the respondent state to undertake general measures to redress it. Furthermore, in 2010, a twin-track procedure was introduced that applies to adverse judgments either a) the standard procedure, in which the CoM exercises limited control and scrutiny, or b) the enhanced procedure.

The CoM reserves the standard procedure for those cases in which the implementation measures are clear and less contested. On the other hand, it places cases raising major structural and complex problems under enhanced supervision.[96] Judgments under enhanced supervision are examined as a matter of priority and the CoM assumes a more active role in assisting respondent states' authorities to adopt and implement remedial measures. In these ways, the supervisory system centered on the CoM has largely departed from a case-by-case approach. In practice, it applies its oversight and monitoring in particular areas of state administration and action marred by persistent or serious gaps in rights protection.

When the Court's final judgment is transmitted to the CoM, the Department for the Execution of Judgments initiates consultations with the respondent state on measures that need to be taken. Under the new working methods introduced as of January 2011 (following the entry into force of Protocol 14 ECHR), respondent states are required to submit action plans and report the implementing measures that they intend to take within six months from the time a judgment becomes final. This information is assessed by the CoM that may also conduct its own research, and it may require the respondent state to present statistics that show tangible improvement of the respective human rights situation.[97] When the CoM deems that implementing measures are sufficient to remedy the underlying violation, it terminates its supervision of a case by adopting a final resolution. Overall, the CoM became significantly more involved in reviewing the efficacy of the measures adopted by states to remedy violations found by the Court, in comparison to the period prior to 2000s (see CoM, 2013: 21–27).

Last but far from least, changes in the CoM working rules for the first time allowed non-governmental actors to intervene in the judgment execution process.[98] NGOs had actively lobbied for changing those rules as to allow them to also participate in implementation.[99] The introduction of Rule 9 in the working rules provided this opportunity. NGOs, national human rights institutions (NHRIs) and other stakeholders (including international organizations and other CoE organs such as the Parliamentary Assembly of the Council of Europe (PACE) and the CPT) can now make submissions on judgments under supervision by the CoM.[100] Non-governmental actors who are knowledgeable of the local-national context and have an interest in the issue raised by a ruling can monitor closely respondent states' actions. They can submit their own "shadow reports" providing to the Department of Execution important information about what is happening at the domestic level, clarify and assess critically the states' implementing measures, propose alternative and more effective forms of action, and highlight issues of concern – all essential input which the CoM is unable on its own to generate.[101]

4 ECHR opportunities for litigation and the limits to individual access

The overhaul of the ECHR in the 1990s that fully liberalized individual access and standing, as described in section 3, expanded international opportunities for litigation, in a vast geographic area of 800 inhabitants. The system's restructuring forms an important backdrop in the overall rise of human rights litigation. Yet, it was not the factor that originally sparked an interest and sporadic efforts of minority individuals and migrants to bring petitions in the ECHR. In these areas, an upward, even if faintly visible, trend in ECHR litigation was already noticeable in the 1980s, as Figures 3.1 and 3.2 show. In fact, the 1980s was a critical turning point for human rights litigation related to migrants and minorities. In these areas, a small number of lawyers and members of mobilized minorities were familiar with the incremental changes taking place in the ECHR and were able to discern its

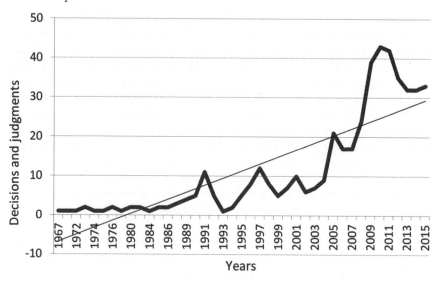

Figure 3.1 Migrant-related decisions and judgments over time, 1967–2015.

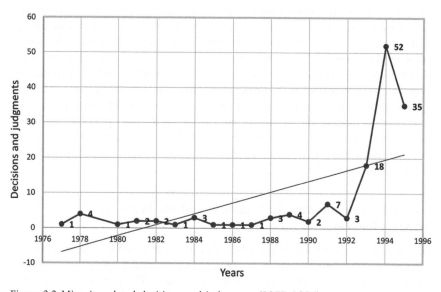

Figure 3.2 Minority-related decisions and judgments (1977–1996)

potential for rights advancement. In response to a small number petitions that they pursued, the ECHR bodies issued milestone rulings that resonated with and made the Convention relevant for the concerns of minorities and migrants, as we will see in the next section.

Despite the liberalization of access and standing in the 1990s, individuals continued to face marked constraints when seeking rights protection in the Strasbourg

Court. The liberalization of procedural access of individuals went hand in hand with profound restrictions regarding their substantive access to the Convention system.[102] Following the entry into force of P-11, the ECHR system continues to limit the number of complaints that are admitted for a judicial review on the merits – a hurdle that became particularly pronounced as the number of human rights complaints rose. While any individual can submit a petition to the Strasbourg Court, a petitioner's chances of reaching the stage of merits-based review are extremely small – at around 5%.[103] In view of this, the structural opportunities for individuals to obtain a substantive review of their grievances by the ECtHR, are not as open as it is commonly depicted.[104] The admissibility criteria include: exhaustion of domestic remedies, time limits, and rejection on grounds that an application is "manifestly ill-founded", incompatible with Convention provisions, or an abuse of the right to individual petition (Article 35 (3) ECHR). They allow the ECtHR a significant degree of control to select the cases that it reviews on the merits, and to shape its judicial agenda.[105]

The admissibility constraints in seeking a judicial rights review in the Strasbourg Court grew instead of narrowing in the 2000s.[106] Protocol 14 (P-14) introduced the "significant disadvantage" criterion that allows the Court to reject rights claims that do not "attain a minimum level of severity to warrant its consideration".[107] Rules that were introduced with Protocol 15 (P-15),[108] such as the reduction of the time limit to lodge an application from six to four months, are likely to further restrict individual access to the Court and curb the inflow of petitions, especially for the most vulnerable victims of human rights violations.[109] Altogether, the amended admissibility rules and the new filtering scheme introduced with P-14 and P-15 render the ECtHR even less accessible to individuals who are victims of rights breaches.[110] NGOs have sharply contested the increasingly stringent admissibility rules. Based on such rules, large numbers of petitions are rejected as inadmissible, and arguably without much justification.[111] NGOs view these as taking the Court away from its mission of delivering individual justice and putting it on the trail of becoming a constitutional court.[112]

The very small percentage of petitions that are in the end retained for a review on the merits demonstrates the fiction of the idea that any individual, affected by arbitrary state action, can alone, effectively access the ECtHR to claim her rights. In fact, accessing the ECtHR is a complex and fraught with hurdles reality for persons seeking international judicial review of alleged rights breaches in substance. Admissibility rules and practices are not commonly considered as part of the legal opportunity structure. Yet, low levels of admissibility to a merits-based review – the stage of the process that has most meaning and value – are an overpowering barrier to accessing international justice, particularly for persons who are vulnerable, and those who lack sufficient legal, financial and other resources and support. The formidable challenge for an individual to bring a compelling claim that is admitted for review on the merits comes on top of the demanding requirement to exhaust domestic remedies.

The vast majority of minority- and migrant-related petitions in the ECtHR are also rejected mostly as manifestly ill-founded. Even though systematic data on admissibility of migrant- and minority-related petitions is lacking, country-specific data shows that the overwhelming number of migrant-related petitions against the United Kingdom are rejected as inadmissible.[113] What is important here is that the chances for individual applicants to receive a merits-based, judicial rights review of their claim are practically moot without, at a minimum, support and guidance by a qualified, knowledgeable and experienced lawyer. Such a lawyer must be familiar with the technicalities of ECHR legal procedure, and with evolving jurisprudence in an issue area, in order to formulate an individual grievance into a sound human rights claim. For a complaint to be considered meritorious by the Court, it does not suffice to merely address an issue that national authorities did not consider or on which they erred. It also has to raise novel and persuasive claims that engage the Court with points of law it did not consider before.

For litigation to have any prospects to break through the admissibility hurdles and lead to a review on the merits, affordable and qualified legal guidance and representation are essential from the early stages of filing a complaint in the ECtHR. Availability of financial resources and organizational support may also be necessary depending on the complexity of a case. A large number of petitions are deposited by individuals without the help of a lawyer, and the vast majority of those are rejected as inadmissible.[114] In the case of Russia, – a country from which 16% of minority-related judgments in our sample originate – Dikov highlights as significant, but also unenviable, the fact that the vast majority of complaints, many of which are legally and factually complex, are at this early admissibility stage decided without a lawyer. He attributes this to the limited financial means on the part of applicants, or the lack of a culture of using a lawyer in Russia.[115] Financial resources, legal expertise and organizational support are particularly crucial in enabling vulnerable or disadvantaged individuals, such as non-nationals, to attain a merits-based review in the Convention system.[116]

Thus, in order to understand the rise in minority- and migrant-related litigation, it is necessary to pay attention to the capacities and resources that enable or constrain many Europeans, especially those among the most vulnerable and those in states with a dismal human rights record overall, to seek redress for rights violations before the ECtHR.[117] Availability of various kinds of legal, organizational and financial support to enable vulnerable persons, or individuals who are affected by systemic or incidental rights breaches in a country, is especially critical if we consider the powerful constraints facing them in gaining substantive access to the ECHR system. NGOs have time and again argued that states should allocate financial resources to lawyers and NGOs, and provide legal aid to potential applicants to help ensure that the claims brought to the ECHR are valid, and thus to reduce the large number of inadmissible applications.[118] As the next two chapters show, the milestone rulings that the Court issued in the 1980s in relation to migrants and minorities were outcomes of cases, in which litigants benefited from various levels and kinds of quality legal expertise and/or organizational support.

5 The rise of nascent legal activism

Up until the 1980s, ECHR structures and rules limited individual access to the Court and assigned petitioners a highly unequal status vis-à-vis states. In the few migrant- and minority-related cases that they reviewed, the Commission and the Court tended to concede wide discretion to the respondent states in claims related to cultural and linguistic rights, inter-communal conflict in Northern Ireland and immigration control – all considered to lie at the heart of state sovereignty. Incremental changes in the ECHR structures and rules from the 1980s onwards liberalized access and standing of individuals, culminating with the entry into force of P-11. The common depiction of the post-P11 adjudicatory system through, as open and accessible to all, overlooks the profound constraints that individuals face in accessing substantive justice. In practice, the road to attaining a merits-based rights review in the ECtHR is demanding and burdensome for ordinary and especially vulnerable individuals. Substantive access to the ECHR critically depends on the legal and other resources that are available to support litigants.

Legal opportunities for minority- and migrant-related litigation in the ECtHR had started to appear earlier than the 1990s restructuring. They emerged out of a few milestone decisions and judgments that expanded the content and scope of Convention provisions in directions that resonated with minorities and migrants' concerns. The Court's pronouncement of bold and innovative jurisprudential principles in the preceding decade, had greatly enhanced its authority and possibly emboldened it. Meanwhile, international organizations like the OSCE increasingly engaged in standard setting around minority protection. Safeguarding human rights and the protection of ethnic and national minorities was incorporated in their agenda, and it was viewed as an essential component of a democracy. European organizations and fora also expressed strong concerns about the failure of human rights to protect migrants and asylum-seekers.

In this shifting international and European context of the 1980s, an increased number of petitions from migrants and minority members were brought to the ECHR bodies. Petitions originated from indigenous cultural minorities in Scandinavian countries, from well-organized and assertive religious, linguistic and ethnic minorities from Greece, Belgium and Spain, as well as from aggrieved minorities in the United Kingdom and elsewhere. These legal actions were linked to the politicization of various autochthonous minorities in different European countries. Their recourse to the ECHR system was often aimed at obtaining a favorable Court ruling that would enhance their leverage and negotiating power vis-à-vis the state government. A growing number of petitions were also brought by immigrants who challenged their deportation on human rights grounds at a time that European governments began to tighten immigration policies. They mostly originated from the United Kingdom, the Netherlands and France, and less so from Germany, Sweden, Denmark and Austria – all host countries for large numbers of migrant populations.

This early wave of minority- and migrant-related litigation in the 1980s and early 1990s in the ECHR was also closely connected to the nascent activism of human rights lawyers and organizations. A number of lawyers and academics in

European countries were aware of developments in the ECHR and its case law. They were following international human rights law for various reasons – out of academic interest, a commitment to different social causes, as an extension of their expertise in constitutional law or of their ordinary legal practice. Being knowledgeable of the ECHR, they could discern the emerging opportunities for international litigation. In a few cases, they supported minority individuals and non-nationals to frame their issues and grievances as human rights claims. In less than a handful of cases, human rights organizations intervened as third parties to buttress the applicants' claims before the Court. Many of the lawyers and NGOs who engaged in ECHR litigation were pioneering actors in a diverse and increasingly legalized, transnational human rights field. They both seized and in turn helped advance legal opportunities, which changing rules and enhanced individual and organizational access in the ECHR system had opened.

In response to early litigation, a small number of decisions and judgments issued by the ECHR bodies expanded the normative scope of Convention provisions and made them relevant for minorities and migrants. In particular, they established the non-refoulement principle, applied the right to family life for migrants faced with expulsion, acknowledged the freedom of individuals to express pro-minority views, and affirmed that minority cultural practices could receive protection under the right to private and family life. The relevant ECHR decisions and judgments expanded the possibilities for framing minority and migrant issues as human rights claims. They fueled into a fledgling but proactive trend of rights litigation on behalf of minorities and migrants that would unfold over the next two decades. As the wall that had divided Europe between East and West was coming down, a proliferation of legal and civil society actors, attracted by the lure of international human rights law, discovered the opportunities emerging in the ECHR system.

These developments marked from the 1990s onwards the Court's systematic engagement with issues related to minorities and the entry, stay and integration of non-nationals in European societies. Migrant- and minority-related litigation in the ECHR rose sharply and spread to more European countries, at a level unprecedented in comparison to the previous decades. The content of claims also diversified, framing a wide variety of issues as human rights. By drawing on a large dataset of related decisions and judgments, the next two chapters provide an overview of these critical developments and the relevant case law of the ECtHR. In exploring the growth of minority- and migrant-related claims in the ECHR, they examine variable patterns of claims in different countries and issue areas, the resources and the actors involved, and the role of civil society in human rights litigation.

Notes

1   Henry G. Schermers, *The Merger of the Commission and Court of Human Rights (Protocol 11 to the European Convention on Human Rights)* (Saarbrucken: Europa-Institut Universitat des Saarlades, 1994), 3–4; Ed Bates, *The Evolution of the ECHR: From Its Inception to the Creation of a Permanent Court of Human Rights* (Oxford: Oxford University Press, 2010), 12.

2 See for instance the landmark judgment of *Sunday Times v the United Kingdom*, no. 6538/74, 26 April 1979.

3 *Tyrer v UK*, no. 5856/72, 25 April 1978.

4 *Engel and Others v the Netherlands*, no. 5100/71, 8 June 1976.

5 *Marckx v Belgium*, no. 6833/74, 13 June 1979.

6 A number of studies provide cogent and detailed accounts of the evolution of the Convention system in this direction. See Bates, *The Evolution of the ECHR: From Its Inception to the Creation of a Permanent Court of Human Rights*; Michael, O'Boyle, David Harris, Ed Bates and Carla Buckley, *Law of the European Convention of Human Rights* (Oxford: Oxford University Press, 2009); Clare Ovey and Robin White, *The European Convention of Human Rights* (Oxford: Oxford University Press, 2006); Steven Greer, *The European Convention on Human Rights – Achievements, Problems and Prospects* (Cambridge: Cambridge University Press, 2006); Mikael Rask Madsen "The Challenging Authority of the European Court of Human Rights: From Cold War Legal Diplomacy to the Brighton Declaration and Backlash," *Law and Social Inquiry* 32, no. 1 (2007), 137–159.

7 Starting in 1972, the Helsinki process initiated discussions of human rights and fundamental freedoms and fostered cooperation between East and West, culminating in 1975 with the signing of the Helsinki Accords.

8 For a thorough account of the developments in international human rights during that period, see Aryeh Neier, *International Human Rights Movement – A History* (Princeton University Press, 2012), especially chapters 6 and 7. See also Ann Marie Clark, *Diplomacy of Conscience – Amnesty International and Changing Human Rights Norms* (Princeton University Press, 2001).

9 Madsen, "From Cold War Instrument to Supreme European Court," 151.

10 See Marie-Benedicte Dembour, *When Humans Become Migrants: Study of the European Court of Human Rights with an Inter-American Counterpoint* (Oxford University Press, 2015), 200–202.

11 Of the first 195 complaints that were deposited with the ECommHR, 178 were immediately rejected. See Schermers, *The Merger of the Commission and Court of Human Rights*, 8.

12 The Court had only issued judgments on 7 cases until 1974, 4 of which were on Article 5 ECHR. See Bates, *The Evolution of the ECHR*, 257.

13 Bates, *The Evolution of the ECHR*, chapter 6.

14 Bates, *The Evolution of the ECHR*, 217–220.

15 Rudolf Bernhardt, "Reform of the Control Machinery under the European Convention on Human Rights: Protocol No. 11," *American Journal of International Law* 89, no. 1 (1995): 146.

16 Bates, *The Evolution of the ECHR*, 202.

17 Anna Dolidze, "Bridging Comparative and International Law: Amicus Curiae Participation as a Vertical Legal Transplant," *European Journal of International Law* 26, no. 4 (2015), 867.

18 *Lawless v Ireland* (No. 3), no. 332/57, 1 July 1961. It was a test case to challenge the emergency anti-terrorist legislation in the UK, which, however, had not yet accepted the right to individual petition. Therefore, it was lodged against Ireland that had already accepted it, and where the IRA carried out preparations for its guerrilla attacks in Northern Ireland.

19 Ireland even disputed the right of the Commission to disclose its report to Mr. Lawless, the applicant, or to transmit his remarks to the Court. Bernhardt, "Reform of the Control Machinery under the ECtHR: Protocol No. 11," 148.

20 Bates, *The Evolution of the ECHR*, 205.

21 See Brice Dickson, *The ECHR and the Conflict in Northern Ireland* (Oxford: Oxford University Press, 2010), 37.

22 Bates, *The Evolution of the ECHR*, 202.

23   Bernhardt, "Reform of the Control Machinery under the ECtHR: Protocol No. 11," 148.

24   For a general overview, see Ad Hoc Committee for the Protection of National Minorities, *European Court and Commission of Human Rights, Case-law on cultural rights*, CAHMIN (95) (Strasbourg: Council of Europe, 29 March 1995).

25   *Rassemblement jurassien and the Unité jurassienne v Switzerland* (dec.), no. 8191/78, 10 October 1979.

26   *Isop v Austria* (dec.), no. 808/60, 8 March 1962.

27   *Roger Vanden Berghe v Belgium* (dec.), no. 2924/66, 16 December 1968; *Un Groupe d' Habitants de Leeuw-St. Pierre v Belgium* (dec.), no. 2333/64, 16 December 1968. *See* Council of Europe, *Yearbook of the ECHR 1965* (The Hague: Martinus Nijhoff, 1967), 355.

28   Christopher McCrudden and Brendan O'Leary, *Courts and Consociations: Human Rights versus Power-Sharing* (Oxford: Oxford University Press, 2013), 49–50.

29   The applicants (6 applications in total), who petitioned on behalf of their children were inhabitants of Alsemberg, Beersel, Antwerp, Ghent, Louvain, and Vilvorde, in the Dutch-speaking region.

30   Case *Relating to Certain Aspects of the Laws on the Use of Languages in Education in Belgium v Belgium*, nos. 1474/62, 1677/62, 1691/62, 1769/63, 1994/63, 2126/64, 23 July 1968.

31   Bates, *The Evolution of the ECHR*, 237–238.

32   Bates, *The Evolution of the ECHR*, 185.

33   *Inhabitants of Les Fourons v Belgium* (dec.), no. 2209/64, 15 December 1964, which was terminated by the CoM issuing a resolution on 30 March 1971. The applicants were represented by Léon Defosset, a lawyer with leftist leanings, who was committed to the Francophone and the federalist cause.

34   *Rassemblement jurassien' and the Unité jurassienne v Switzerland* (dec.), no. 8191/78, 10 October 1979.

35   See *Albert Grandrath v Germany* (dec.), no. 2299/64, 23 April 1965, § 48. The case concerned differential treatment of Jehovah's Witnesses in comparison to Evangelicals and Roman Catholics.

36   McCrudden and O'Leary, *Courts and Consociations*, 63–64.

37   *X v Germany* (dec.), no. 6742/74, 10 July 1975.

38   *X v Netherlands* (dec.), no. 7230/75, 4 October 1976.

39   Article 15 ECHR allows a state to temporarily derogate from its obligations under the ECHR "in time of war or other public emergency threatening the life of the nation .... to the extent strictly required by the exigencies of the situation." However, no derogation is allowed from Articles 2, 3 4 (paragraph 1) or 7 EHCR.

40   Leslie John Macfarlane, *Human Rights: Realities and Possibilities* (London: Macmillan, 1990) 33–34.

41   Stephen Livingstone, "And Justice for All? The Judiciary and the Legal Profession in Transition," in *Human Rights Equality and Democratic Renewal in Northern Ireland*, ed. Colin Harvey (Oxford: Hart Publishing, 2001), 131–162; see also Dia Anagnostou, "From Belfast to Diyarbakir and Grozny via Strasbourg: Transnational Legal Mobilisation Against State Violations in Contexts of Armed Conflict," in *Rights in Pursuit of Social Change – Legal Mobilisation in the European Multi-level System*, ed. Dia Anagnostou (Oxford: Hart Publishers, 2014).

42   Brice Dickson, "Miscarriages of Justice in Northern Ireland," in *Miscarriages of Justice – A Review of Justice in Error*, eds. Clive Walker and Keir Starmer (Oxford: Oxford University Press, 1999), 287–303.

43   Carol Harlow and Richard Rawlings, *Pressure Through Law* (London: Routledge, 1992), 254.

44   *X v UK* (dec.), no. 5155/71, 12 July 1976.

45   *Arrowsmith v UK* (dec.), no. 7050/75, 16 May 1977.

46 *X and Y v UK* (dec.), nos. 5459/72, 5301/71, 5302/71, 12 July 1976; *X, Y and Z v UK* (dec.), nos. 5727/72, 5744/72 and 5857/72, 12 July 1978.

47 Brice Dickson, *The ECHR and the Conflict in Northern Ireland* (Oxford: Oxford University Press, 2010), 48–51.

48 For an overview of these trends in the UK, see Harlow and Rawlings, *Pressure Through Law*.

49 In 1969, the NCCL created a legal defense fund and became active in courts. See Epp, *The Rights Revolution*, 140–141.

50 Epp, *The Rights Revolution*, 142–3; see also Harlow and Rawlings, *Pressure Through Law*, 256.

51 *Ireland v the United Kingdom*, no. 5310/71, 13 December 1977. See also Dickson, *The ECHR and the Conflict in Northern Ireland*, 40–41.

52 Perhaps the greatest promise but also disillusionment for those seeking justice in the Strasbourg organs was the petition of *Donnelly and Others v UK* (dec.), no. 5577/72, 15 December 1975. It alleged ill-treatment of detainees by the police, and it sought to bring to light the existence of a systematic pattern of state abuse against individuals detained for suspected involvement in terrorist activities in Northern Ireland. The ECommHR found no violation, viewing the conducting of official investigations as enough proof that ill-treatment was not authorized at the higher level, despite the fact that few prosecutions or disciplinary actions resulted from such investigations. See Dickson, *The ECHR and the Conflict in Northern Ireland*, 38–40, 146.

53 Leslie C. Green, "Derogations of Human Rights in Emergency Situations," *Canadian Yearbook of International Law* 16 (1978): 92–115.

54 Joan F. Hartman, "Derogations from human rights treaties in public emergencies," *Harvard International Law Journal* 22, no. 1 (1981): 35.

55 Kevin Boyle, "Human Rights and Political Resolution in Northern Ireland," *Yale Journal of International Law* 9, no.1 (1982): 156, 163–64.

56 Dickson, *The ECHR and the Conflict in Northern Ireland*, 51.

57 *Stewart v UK*, no. 10044/82, 10 July 1984; *Farrell v UK* (dec.), no. 9013/80, 11 December 1982; *Kelly v UK* (dec.), no. 17579/90, 13 January 1993. For a thorough review, see Dickson, especially chapters 7 and 9.

58 See for example, *X v Federal Republic of Germany* (dec.), no. 6315/73, 30 September 1974; *X v Denmark* (dec.), no. 7465/76, 29 September 1976; *Philip Burnett Franklin Agee v United Kingdom* (dec.), no. 7729/76, 17 December 1976.

59 *Alam Khan v the UK* (dec.), no. 2991/66, 17 December 1968; *Singh v the UK* (dec.), no. 2992/66 (1967). These cases prompted the UK government to introduce legislation that conferred rights of appeal against decisions of immigration authorities to admit or remove persons from the country.

60 For a discussion of the background to the case, see Bates, *The Evolution of the ECHR*, 243–247.

61 *East African Asians v UK* (dec.), no. 4403/70 and 30 more applications, 14 December 1973.

62 For a discussion of the Commission's report and the attitude of the British government in regard to the *East Africans* case, see Bates, *The Evolution of the ECHR*, 244–247.

63 By 1977, the required two-thirds majority (Article 32 ECHR) of state delegates in the CoM could not be obtained to reach a decision in the *East African Asians v UK* case. In the end, under the pressure created by the case, the UK government allowed for the entry of all 31 applicants, while also raising the annual quota for entry. See Ed Bates, *The Evolution of the ECHR*, 244–246 and 413.

64 Epp, *The Rights Revolution*, 113–4.

65 Harlow and Rawlings, *Pressure Through Law*, 255; Laura Van den Eynde, "An Empirical Look at the Amicus Curiae Practice of Human Rights NGOs before the

European Court of Human Rights," *Netherlands Quarterly of Human Rights* 31, no. 3 (2013): 286.

66 Anthony Lester, "30 Years On," in *30 At the Turning of the Tide,* eds. Mayerlene Engineer, Julius Honnor, Louis Mackay, Olivia Skinner and Alice Trouncer (London: Commission for Racial Equality, 2006).

67 Bernhardt, "Reform of the Control Machinery under the European Convention on Human Rights: Protocol No. 11," 146.

68 Bates, *The Evolution of the ECHR,* 413–415.

69 Bernhardt, "Reform of the Control Machinery under the ECtHR," 148.

70 Bates, *The Evolution of the ECHR,* 402–403.

71 In 1994, the amending Protocol 9 was adopted in order to correct the discrepancies regarding the procedural status of the individual, which had developed between the original ECHR and the Court Rules, as they had subsequently been revised in the course of the 1980s.

72 Lance Bartholomeusz, "The Amicus Curiae before International Courts and Tribunals," *Non-State Actors and International Law* 5, no.3 (2005): 234.

73 Dolidze, "Bridging Comparative and International Law," 868.

74 The requests were made in the following cases: *Tyrer v UK,* no. 5856/72, 25 April 1978; *Winterwerp v the Netherlands,* no. 6301/73, 24 October 1979; and *Young, James and Webster v. United Kingdom,* no. 7601/76, 13 August 1981. In 1989, the Court's amended Rules of Procedure included a more permissive provision on non-party submissions. See Anna-Karin Lindblom, *Non-Governmental Organisations in International Law* (Cambridge University Press, 2005), 329.

75 Anna Dolidze, "Bridging Comparative and International Law," 878–9.

76 Rachel A. Cichowski, "Civil Society and the ECtHR," in *The ECtHR between Law and Politics,* eds. Jans Christoffersen and Mikael Rask Madsen (Oxford: Oxford University Press, 2011), 86–87.

77 Cichowski, "Civil Society and the ECtHR," 84–87.

78 In the 1980s, countries like Germany had reduced the period of their acceptance of the optional clauses, while the UK's renewal was anything but certain. Bates, *The Evolution of the ECHR,* 427–8.

79 Bates, *The Evolution of the ECHR,* 393.

80 This was Protocol 9 that opened for signature in 1990. Before it was expected to enter into force in 1994, P-9 was abandoned, as preparatory works for a new reform were launched.

81 Bernhardt, "Reform of the Control Machinery under the ECtHR," 150–151.

82 Lloyd Hitoshi Mayer, "NGO Standing and Influence in Regional Human Rights Courts and Commissions," *Brookings Journal of International Law* 36, no. 3 (2011): 917; Marco Frigessi Di Rattalma, "NGOs before the ECtHR: Beyond Amicus Curiae Participation?" in *Civil Society, International Courts and Compliance Bodies,* eds. Treves, Tullio, Marco Frigessi di Rattalma, Attila Tanzi, Alessandro Fodella, Cesare Pitea, and Chiara Ragni (The Hague: Asser Press, 2005), 59–60. In the ECHR system, non-governmental actors cannot bring a complaint about the compatibility of national legislation with the Convention *in abstracto,* or a claim of public interest in the form of *actio popularis.*

83 Vaughne Miller, *Protocol 11 and the New European Court of Human Rights* (House of Commons Library, Research Paper 98/109, 4 December 1998), 19.

84 Bates, *The Evolution of the ECHR,* 452–453.

85 Bartholomeusz, "The Amicus Curiae before International Courts and Tribunals," 234.

86 Van den Eynde, "An Empirical Look at the Amicus Curiae Practice of Human Rights NGOs," 291.

87 Lindblom, *Non-Governmental Organisations in International Law,* 344–345.

88 See Laura Van den Eynde, "Litigation Practices of Non-Governmental Organisations before the European Court of Human Rights" (European Master's Degree in Human

Rights and Democratisation: Awarded Theses of the Academic Year 2009/2011, Marsilio Editori, 2011), 281.

89 Bartholomeusz, "The Amicus Curiae before International Courts and Tribunals," 236–240.

90 Lindblom, *Non-Governmental Organisations in International Law*, 345.

91 Van den Eynde, "Litigation Practices of Non-Governmental Organisations before the European Court of Human Rights," 245, 297.

92 Rules 100–105 (formerly Rules 91–96). See European Court of Human Rights, *Rules of the Court*, (Strasbourg: Council of Europe), January 2016.

93 Lucja Miara and Victoria Prais, "The role of civil society in the execution of judgments of the ECtHR," *European Human Rights Law Review* 5 (2012): 529. See also S.K. Martens, "Commentary," in *Compliance with Judgments of International Courts*, eds. M.K. Bulterman and M. Kuijer (The Hague: Martinus Nijhoff Publishers, 1996), 77.

94 Martens, "Commentary," 77.

95 Ed Bates, "Supervising the Execution of Judgments Delivered by the ECtHR: The Challenges Facing the Committee of Ministers," in *European Court of Human Rights Remedies and Execution of Judgments*, eds. Theodora Christou and Juan Pablo Raymond (London: The British Institute of International and Comparative Law, 2005), 60.

96 Miara and Prais, "The role of civil society in the execution of judgments of the ECtHR," 532. See also Déborah Forst, "The Execution of Judgments of the European Court of Human Rights," *Vienna Journal of International Constitutional Law* 7, no. 3 (2013): 13.

97 Miara and Prais, "The role of civil society in the execution of judgments of the ECtHR," 531.

98 Rules of the Committee of Ministers for the supervision of the execution of judgments and of the terms of friendly settlements (adopted by the Committee of Ministers on 10 May 2006 at its 964th meeting and amended on 18 January 2017 at its 1275th meeting).

99 The AIRE Centre, Amnesty International and EHRAC, "Council of Europe: Recommendations to facilitate inclusion of civil society in ensuring the implementation of judgements of the ECtHR and debates on the future of the Court". Available at https://www.amnesty.org/en/wp-content/uploads/2021/08/ior610242005en.pdf

100 Nicholas Sitaropoulos, "Supervising Execution of ECtHR Judgments Concerning Minorities: The Committee of Ministers Potentials and Constraints," *Annuaire International des Droits de l' Homme* 3 (2008): 530–532.

101 Miara and Prais, "The role of civil society in the execution of judgments of the ECtHR," 534–535; Aysel Küçüksu, "In the Aftermath of a Judgment: Why Human Rights Organisations Should Harness the Potential of Rule 9," *Strasbourg Observers* (blog), 3 March 2021, https://strasbourgobservers.com/2021/03/03/in-the-aftermath-of-a-judgment-why-human-rights-organisations-should-harness-the-potential-of-rule-9/?subscribe=pending#504.

102 On this distinction, see Janneke Gerards and Lize R. Glas, "Access to justice in the European Convention on Human Rights system," *Netherlands Quarterly of Human Rights* 35, no. 1 (2017): 13–15.

103 The average rate for the period of 1959–2017 was 5.7% and reflects the number of judgments delivered against the total number of petitions submitted to the ECHR system (see ECHR Overview Statistics 1959–2017, available at https://echr.coe.int/Documents/Overview_19592017_ENG.pdf). The overwhelming majority of applications (around or more than 95%) are rejected for failure to satisfy one of the admissibility criteria laid down by the Convention. See *European Court of Human Rights – Practical Guide on Admissibility Criteria* (Strasbourg: Council of Europe, 2011), 7; Bates, *Law of the ECHR*, 758.

104 The opaqueness of the admissibility process (i.e. the Court did not publish any data on common grounds for rejection) has been criticized by activists and researchers. See

Ben Jones, "European Court of Human Rights: is the admissions system transparent enough?" UK Human Rights Blog (blog), 27 January 2012, http://ukhumanrights blog.com/2012/01/27/european-court-of-human-rights-is-the-admissions-system-transparent-enough-ben-jones/.

105 On admissibility, see Andrew Tickell, "Dismantling the Iron-Cage: the Discursive Persistence and Legal Failure of a 'Bureaucratic Rational' Construction of the Admissibility Decision-Making of the ECtHR," *German Law Journal* 12, no. 10 (2011): 1798. See also Paul Harvey, "Is Strasbourg obsessively interventionist? A view from the Court" *UK Human Rights Blog* (blog), 24 January 2012, http://ukhumanrightsblog.com/2012/01/24/is-strasbourg-obsessively-interventionist-a-view-from-the-court-paul-harvey/.

106 See Nikos Vogiatzis, "The Admissibility Criterion under Article 35(3)(b) ECHR: A 'Significant Disadvantage' to Human Rights Protection?" *International and Comparative Law Quarterly* 65, no. 1 (2016): 185–211.

107 Protocol No. 14 to the ECHR entered into force on 1 June 2010. It expedited the admissibility stage and introduced a new admissibility criterion that empowers the ECtHR to reject petitions in which "the applicant has not suffered a significant disadvantage". Council of Europe, *The new admissibility criterion under Article 35 § 3 (b) of the Convention: case-law principles two years on* (ECtHR Research Report, Strasbourg: Council of Europe, 2012), 10.

108 Adopted in 2013 but not ratified at the time of this writing in 2018.

109 Article 4 of Protocol 15, as it alters Article 35 (1) of the ECHR.

110 Marie-Aude Beernaert, "Protocol 14 and New Strasbourg Procedures: Towards Greater Efficiency? And at What Price?" *European Human Rights Law Review* 5 (2004): 556–557.

111 Michael O' Boyle, "On Reforming the Operation of the European Court of Human Rights," *European Human Rights Law Review* 1 (2008): 4. See also Christina G. Hioureas, "Behind the Scenes of Protocol No. 14: Politics in Reforming the European Court of Human Rights," *Berkeley Journal of International Law* 24, no. 2 (2006): 718–757; Open Society Justice Initiative, *The Application of the 'Significant Disadvantage' Criterion by the European Court of Human Rights* (New York: Open Society Justice Initiative, November 2015), 3.

112 Council of Europe, *Joint NGO Statement on Protocol 15 to the ECHR*, 24 June 2013. See also Andrew Tickell, "Radical but risky changes afoot at the European Court of Human Rights." *UK Human Rights Blog* (blog), 9 July 2013, https://ukhumanrights blog.com/2013/07/09/radical-but-risky-changes-afoot-at-the-european-court-of-human-rights-andrew-tickell/.

113 In about three-quarters of the inadmissible cases, the petitioner failed to pursue his/her application, normally after filing a request for interim measures (under Rule 39) to halt his/her removal, which was refused by the Court. See Harvey, "Is Strasbourg obsessively interventionist? A view from the Court."

114 Grigory Dikov, "The ones that lost: Russian cases rejected at the European Court," *Open Democracy*, 7 December 2009, https://www.opendemocracy.net/od-russia/grigory-dikov/ones-that-lost-russian-cases-rejected-at-european-court; Lubomir Majercik, "The Invisible Majority: The Unsuccessful Applications Against the Czech Republic Before the ECtHR," *CYIL* 1 (2010): 217–222.

115 Dikov, "The ones that lost: Russian cases rejected at the European Court".

116 See Dembour, *When Humans Become Migrants*, 232.

117 Guasti, Petra, David S. Siroky and Daniel Stockemer, "Judgment without justice: on the efficacy of the European human rights regime," *Democratization* 24, no. 2 (2016): 226–243.

118 Amnesty International, *Joint Response to the Proposals to Ensure the Future Effectiveness of the European Court of Human Rights* (1 December 2003), § 11.

Part I

Litigation and legal mobilization

4   Seeking protection of minorities and victims of armed conflict

From the 1990s onwards, minority-related litigation in the ECHR started to rapidly grow and diversify. Many claims and rulings targeted "new" states in Central-East and Southeast Europe (CESE) and the former Soviet states, such as Russia that joined the Convention in the 1990s. Many though also originated from "old" states, such as Greece and Turkey, that had already accepted the right to individual petition in the ECHR in the mid-1980s. From the 1990s onwards, individuals from minorities such as the Muslims and Turks in Greece and Bulgaria, Kurds in Turkey, Chechens in Russia, Gypsies and Travellers in the UK, the Roma in CESE, began to systematically bring cases in the Strasbourg Court. This chapter explores the factors and conditions that prompted an increasing number of individuals from various ethnic, cultural and religious minorities to take recourse to the ECHR system. It also examines the extent to which the respective human rights litigation is connected to broader mobilization strategies for social and political change.

The growth in minority-related human rights litigation cannot be understood outside of the normative, institutional and geopolitical developments in the second half of the 1980s and in the 1990s in Europe. During that time, the international community was concerned about the destabilizing effects of inter-communal and national conflicts that had erupted after the demise of communist regimes in East Europe. The disintegration of federated states, and the break-out of war in the former Soviet Union and in Yugoslavia, alerted to the dangers of assimilationist policies against ethnic-national minorities. Countries in West Europe also witnessed the assertion and politicization of various ethnic-linguistic groups and indigenous cultures in Belgium, Netherlands, Norway and elsewhere.

Growing international concern about inter-ethnic tensions galvanized efforts to advance normative standards related to minority protection. European and international institutions, such as the Council of Europe (CoE), the Organization of Security and Cooperation in Europe (OSCE), and the European Union, began to actively engage in standard setting related to the protection of minorities. In 1990, a milestone document released at the Copenhagen Meeting of the OSCE (it was Conference on Security and Cooperation at the time) dedicated a whole chapter on the protection of minorities that was viewed as central to the human dimension of security.[1] Significantly, it also included a specific reference to the "particular problems of Roma/Gypsies".[2] The normative advances in this area cemented a close interconnection

DOI: 10.4324/9781003256489-5

between human rights and the protection of minorities. Both were defined as funda-mental components of democracy and a rule of law system.

In this evolving normative milieu of the 1980s and early 1990s, the Council of Europe sought to render the ECHR more relevant to the protection of ethnic minorities. A proposal for an additional protocol to the ECHR on minority protec-tion was put forth in the 1993 Vienna Summit of the Council of Europe (CoE), however, it was withdrawn due to a lack of consensus among states.[3] In its place, the CoE adopted in 1994 the Framework Convention for the Protection of National Minorities. It was the first multilateral instrument that reflected the normative devel-opments that had taken place in the area of minority protection.[4] The Framework Convention maintained the individual human rights frame but it also acknowledged the need to safeguard the associative dimension of cultural-religious rights of mino-rities.[5] Despite its non-binding nature, it placed the protection of minorities firmly within the CoE bodies and influenced the ECHR interest in and approach to minority-related claims.

In this context, an increasing number of minority-related petitions in the 1980s and early 1990s were brought before the ECHR bodies that gradually became more attentive to the claims that they raised. Despite an initially timid approach, they issued decisions and judgments that extended Convention provisions to claims raised by minorities. The first part of this chapter examines those early cases and the responses of the ECHR bodies. The resulting case law established the legal ground for further litigation involving minorities that rapidly grew from the 1990s onwards. On the basis of extensive case law data, the first section of this chapter further explores the growth and diversification of minority-related human rights litigation, the issues that it raised, the targeted countries, and the engagement of civil society actors in it.

The growth of minority-related claims, this chapter argues, was not a plain con-sequence of enhanced institutional access to the ECtHR or a matter of course con-sequence of the Convention's eastward enlargement. Instead, it was made possible by the growth of legal support actors and structures, including civil society organiza-tions. Human rights litigation was deployed as a central or supplementary component of mobilization strategies by or on behalf of minorities in particular countries and regions. It sought to challenge restrictive state policies, rights abuses in regions of armed conflict, and discrimination of marginalized minorities. Sections 3–5 of this chapter identify and analyze distinctive patterns of ECHR litigation and mobili-zation strategies related to various ethnic and national minorities. They analyze how ECHR litigation grew as a) a tool for internationalizing minority politics and rights claims (Southeast Europe and Turkey), b) a strategy of transnational legal support networks against state abuses in regions of armed conflict, and c) a form of civil society activism to combat discrimination and promote domestic policy reform (Roma minorities).

1 The growth in minority-related litigation in the ECHR

A time-series depiction of ECHR minority-related decisions and judgments shows that minority-related litigation started to visibly increase in the first half of the

1990s (see Figure 4.1). Whereas in 1960–1990, the ECommHR and the ECtHR had issued 29 minority-related decisions and judgments, in 1991–2013 they issued 462 related rulings.[6] In an increasing and diversifying trend of minority-related litigation, claims principally targeted Turkey and Russia, where an armed conflict has been ongoing in Chechnya. It also targeted CESE countries, such as Bulgaria, Romania, Hungary and others. We can distinguish a) the period of the 1980s and early 1990s when the ECHR bodies established a few important principles in their case law that were relevant for minorities, and b) the period from the early 1990s onwards when the rise in related human rights complaints spiralled.

1.1 Early advances in ECHR minority-related case law

In a broader context of international standard-setting activities in the area of minority protection in the 1980s and early1990s, a number of petitions prompted timid but significant advances in the interpretation of ECHR principles by the Court and the Commission. Politicized minorities, such as the Slovenes in Austria, and Bretons in France, or indigenous people seeking recognition of their historical rights, pursued human rights litigation to advance their demands vis-à-vis the state. In countries like Sweden and Norway, prominent jurists, such as Thomas Cramer, former Swedish Ombudsman, had taken on to make aboriginal rights litigation (before Norwegian and Swedish courts, and the ECHR) a central political strategy of Sweden's Saami organizations.[7] In other cases, Norwegian Lapps voiced before the ECHR bodies a generalized grievance against the failure of Norway to recognize their language and culture, which involved historical rights

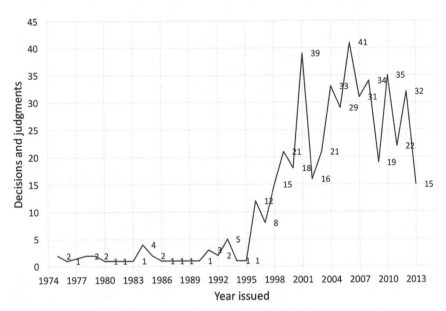

Figure 4.1 ECtHR minority-related decisions and judgments, 1974–2013

to land use, reindeer breeding, hunting and fishing.[8] In another string of petitions, French-speakers in Belgium, and Frisians aspiring for some form of local or regional autonomy in the province of Friesland (north of the Netherlands) claimed the right to use minority language in the electoral process.

In response to this early wave of minority-related litigation, the ECHR bodies rejected claims to recognize collective and cultural rights of minorities. They consistently interpreted the Convention as not guaranteeing rights such as the use of minority language in the election process, forms of territorial autonomy, or special electoral arrangements.[9] In other cases, UK Travelers' claims to lead a distinct way of life[10] and claims of others to use minority language in court as an expression of one's cultural identity[11] were rejected at the admissibility stage. Minority claims to preserve a culturally distinct way of life when it conflicted with other public priorities or government decisions, also did not find sympathy with the ECHR bodies. In its decision in *G. and E. v Norway* in 1983, the Commission argued that restrictions imposed upon hunting and reindeering in areas populated by Saami, did not infringe their customary rights that they could still enjoy in other areas. It affirmed that the Convention guarantees certain rights to everyone, but it does not recognize specific rights for minorities. While the construction of a hydroelectric dam admittedly interfered with the right to private and family life (Article 8 ECHR), the ECommHR saw it as necessary in a democratic society in the interests of the economic well-being of the country.[12]

At the same time, the Court and the Commission, amidst significant internal dissent, for the first time acknowledged that certain Convention provisions were applicable to and relevant for the concerns voiced by minorities. Even as it declined to extend protection to Saami customary rights when these conflicted with economic development, the ECommHR conceded that "a minority's lifestyle may, in principle, fall under the protection of private life, family life, or home".[13] By framing the protection of a distinct culture and way of life as a right to private and family life (Article 8 ECHR), the Commission's response to the *G. and E. v Norway* presaged a new and potentially more receptive approach. It opened possibilities for framing claims to protect minority views and cultures as human rights and provided a basis for substantial litigation in the coming years.

Individuals belonging to minorities started to invoke Articles 8–11 ECHR – right to private and family life, religious freedom, freedom of expression and association – at times in conjunction with the non-discrimination principle (Article 14 ECHR), to claim protection of their political views, religious beliefs or cultural identity. The Commission and the Court reviewed the respective claims by applying the well-known balancing and proportionality review. They examined whether state-imposed limits in the exercise of these rights were justified in a democratic society by the need to preserve national security and territorial integrity, to prevent disorder or crime and to protect the rights of others. Over the next decade, the Court established this approach and highlighted pluralism as a fundamental aspect of a democratic society that the Convention seeks to safeguard.[14] While pluralism was originally understood to protect the diversity of ideas and opinions, it was also extended to the diversity of religious beliefs, as well as of ethnic and cultural identities.[15]

The ECtHR milestone ruling of *Castells v Spain* in 1992 reflected this new approach to minority-related claims. In the 1980s, Spanish courts had convicted the applicant, Miguel Castells, a Member of Parliament (MP) and supporter of Basque nationalism, for publishing an article that accused the government of sheltering right-wing extremists allegedly responsible for killings.[16] The applicant was represented before the ECtHR by D. Korff, an international human rights lawyer based in London, and an academic, who had also litigated other high-profile cases in Strasbourg.[17] The ECtHR found the applicant's conviction to contravene his freedom of expression (Article 10 ECHR) and to be unnecessary in a democratic society. It stressed that it was especially important for political representatives to be able to express their views on matters of public interest, including critical opinions of the government. While the judgment did not in any way affirm minority rights or separatism, it showed that Articles 8–11 ECHR could provide significant protection to individuals expressing views or opinions favorable to minorities. In response to this judgment, the Spanish Constitutional Court changed its jurisprudence on issues of defamation and freedom of expression in order to conform to the ECtHR case law.[18]

In another milestone ruling, the ECtHR applied the proportionality review in a case involving minority religious freedom. It concerned the criminal prosecution of a Jehovah's Witness on charges of proselytism in Greece where the political and legal system granted privileges to the prevailing Christian Orthodox religion.[19] *Kokkinakis v Greece* was an instance of strategic litigation brought with the support of Jehovah's Witnesses Association in Greece, representing a highly active religious community. The Association was eager to pursue ECtHR litigation as part of its international mobilization strategy, and quickly seized the opportunity to do so soon after Greece accepted the right to individual petition in 1985. Kokkinakis was represented in the ECtHR by a constitutional law professor, and president of the Hellenic League of Human Rights (a human rights NGO). In its landmark judgment in 1993, the Court distinguished between propagation of one's faith and improper proselytism and found no evidence of the latter. It thus considered the applicant's conviction for proselytism a violation of his religious freedom (Article 9 ECHR).[20] The case marked the beginning of an international litigation strategy for Jehovah's Witnesses, but also for other religious minorities in Greece and elsewhere.[21]

The ECtHR also began to scrutinize more government arguments about the presumed exigency of rights restrictions for reasons of national security and intercommunal conflict. The legal activism of UK-based civil and human rights organizations in the ECHR was behind a few milestone judgments, such as *Brogan and Others v the UK* in 1988 that was brought by the Northern Ireland Council for Civil Liberties (NCCL).[22] The ECtHR found detention on mere suspicion of involvement in terrorist activities to contravene Article 5 ECHR. As Third-Party interveners, Amnesty International and Liberty contended that evolving international standards ruled out incommunicado detention and required that the detainee be allowed access to lawyers and family members.[23] The UK government declared a new derogation in order to avoid more adverse judgments.[24] In response to *Brannigan and McBride*, the Court, in a highly divided judgment in 1993, upheld this new derogation on grounds that formal habeas corpus safeguards were sufficient to protect detainees from abuses.[25] At the same time, it also noted that this "[state] power is not unlimited and cannot go beyond the 'extent strictly required by the exigencies' of the crisis"[26], thus leaving the door half open for further litigation.

In sum, in the early wave of minority-related litigation in the 1980s and early 1990s, individuals from highly politicized minorities raised various claims before the ECHR related to cultural identity, public participation, and state action in the context of inter-communal conflict. A few lawyers and academics, who were knowledgeable of the ECHR, as well as non-governmental organizations in the still nascent, at the time, field of human rights played a pivotal role: they enabled and supported petitioners to frame their grievances as human rights claims before the ECHR bodies. They both seized and also helped expand ECHR opportunities for international rights litigation. Legal and civil society activism – limited at the time to be sure – led to milestone decisions and judgments that interpreted Convention provisions in ways that resonated with issues of interest and concern for minorities. By extending the scope of the Convention, the relevant rulings paved the way for more minority individuals to pursue human rights litigation.

1.2 Diversification of claims, actors and targeted countries

Since the 1990s, minority-related petitions in the ECHR rapidly increased but also diversified. Many raised claims that followed the same line of case law that was developed in the early litigation wave described in the previous section. They challenged restrictions imposed upon the religious freedom of historical Muslim minorities and Jehovah's Witnesses, limits to the registration of ethnic minority associations, and the dissolution of minority associations and political parties holding views favorable to minorities.[27] Many also challenged the prosecution of individuals (journalists, human rights activists, editors-in-chief, book authors, and members of minority religions or associations) expressing pro-minority views. Most of those minority cases originated from Turkey, and secondarily from Greece and Bulgaria (ethnic Turks, Slav-Macedonians), but also in smaller numbers from Spain (Basques), Poland, Romania and other East European countries (section 2.1).

A second subset of human rights litigation, which is not conventionally understood as minority-related, has challenged before the ECtHR state abuses arising in areas of internal armed conflict linked to or caused by inter-ethnic strife. Complaints about abuses related to arrest and detention by security forces, property destruction and extra-judicial killings have arisen from Northern Ireland, and on much larger scale from the Kurdish minority in Turkey, and from individuals caught in the conflict between Russian security and Chechen separatist forces (section 2.2). In this latter and voluminous string of litigation, the Court applied and interpreted ECHR provisions in contexts of armed conflict, thus crossing over into a terrain that typically appertains to international humanitarian law.[28] A third subset of minority-related litigation that grew in the 1990s and 2000s challenged ethnic discrimination and racism in law enforcement, education, social service provision, and other sectors, largely in cases involving Travelers and Roma (section 2.3).

Applicants in minority-related cases were mostly individuals (50% male, 18% female, and 25.7% by women and men together) and only 6.3% of the petitions were brought by organizational entities (such as religious organizations, cultural associations and political parties). The limited number of organizations and minority groups acting as litigants can be attributed to the stringent, so-called "victim" requirement: the collective entity and all members belonging to it must show to be victims of the alleged abuse, in order to be able to bring a claim in the ECHR (Article 34 ECHR). It is extremely difficult for minority groups to show that each one of their individual members has been affected by the violation claimed and has authorized the lodging of an application to the Court. Unlike in legal persons, "the modes of membership of [minority] groups are not legally organized and are therefore neither identifiable nor verifiable for the purpose of ascertaining whether the mode of affiliation is destructive of freedom or discriminatory."[29]

Overall, the ECtHR has displayed a more receptive approach since the 1990s, taking into account evolving norms and standards of human rights and minority protection.[30] Once a minority-related claim is admitted for a review on the merits, the chances for the applicant to be vindicated by the ECtHR are high: in eighty-five percent of all minority-related cases that were admitted for a review on the merits, the ECtHR pronounced at least one violation of the Convention (see Figure 4.2). It did not find a violation in only 6% of the cases that it reviewed on the merits while 9% were resolved through friendly settlements. The Court is especially likely to find a violation in cases involving inhuman treatment, bodily harm, death or disappearance (Articles 2 and 3 ECHR), but much less likely in response to claims related to minority culture and language (see Figure 4.3).

At the same time though, the ECtHR has generally been unreceptive to discrimination claims raised by individuals belonging to minorities. Applying stringent evidentiary standards,[31] the Court found ethnic, racial or religious discrimination in a small percentage of judgments that raised claims of discriminatory treatment (in 34 out of 236 judgments in which violation of Article 14 ECHR was claimed, or in 14.4%). Notably, half of these judgments were brought by Roma, and they mostly involved procedural or substantive violations related to inhuman or degrading treatment (Article 3 ECHR), and the right to education (Article 1 of Protocol 2).[32]

Minority-related complaints are brought to the ECtHR by individual litigants with support either of lawyers alone, or by civil society organizations. Most of the cases raising issues of minority political participation and public expression under Articles 10–11 ECHR are brought by individuals with the support of lawyers, at times with behind-the-scenes approval or backing of minority associations. Such cases rarely require large amounts of documentation and fact-finding, but they usually depend upon appropriate and skilful crafting of legal argumentation before the ECtHR.

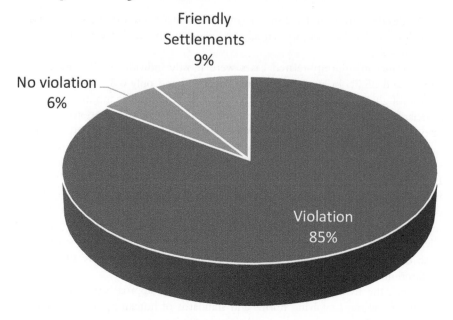

Figure 4.2 Judicial outcomes in minority-related cases, 1960–2013

At the same time, slightly over half of minority-related cases are supported by various civil society and/or minority organizations. Their involvement takes different forms, besides acting as litigants in a small number of cases: they intervene as Third Parties (TPIs), they provide legal support and representation to applicants, collect necessary documentation and generally assist in preparing the case file with in-house or external lawyers. In all its different forms, NGO involvement in minority-related ECHR litigation is substantial – in 51% of all related decisions and judgments of our dataset for the period 1960–2013 (see Figure 4.3). The extent of their involvement varies across issue areas. It is far more frequent in cases of severe rights abuses in conditions of armed conflict (involving death or disappearance, ill-treatment or torture) in Russia and Turkey. Eighty percent of the decisions and judgments against Russia in our data set (or 60/75) were brought before the ECtHR with the support by NGOs – comprising a relatively small number of "repeat players." These are cases that are often very demanding in terms of evidence gathering.

Civil society engagement is also high in ECHR minority complaints related to religious freedom and ethnic-racial discrimination. Religious organizations often act as litigants, or litigants are often connected with and/or supported by religious associations. The high incidence of civil society involvement in minority religious freedom cases in part reflects the high levels of Jehovah's Witnesses (JWs) mobilization in the ECHR system. JWs are a well-organized, transnational religious community that has for decades pursued an international strategy of rights litigation and advocacy. A high level of civil society engagement is also evidenced in

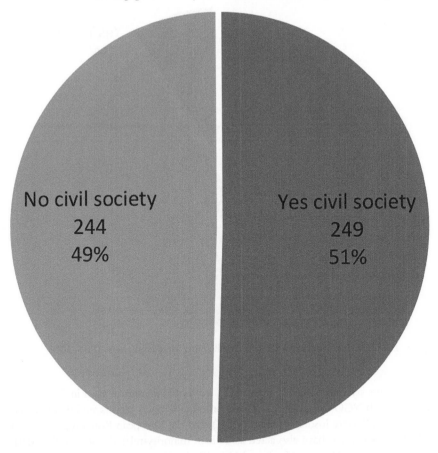

Figure 4.3 Civil society involvement in ECtHR minority-related cases (TPIs and other forms), 1960–2013

Roma-related cases, many of which have systematically raised discrimination claims. Domestic and transnational Roma rights NGOs mainly in Central-East and Southeast Europe (CESE) have actively pursued a litigation strategy before national courts and the ECtHR over the past two decades.

Significantly more limited is the engagement of civil society organizations as third-party interveners (TPIs) in minority-related cases before the ECtHR. Generally, third party intervention (TPI) occurs in a small percentage of all minority-related judgments – in 38 out of the 402 related judgments issued until 2013 (or 9%, see Figure 4.4). NGOs submitted amicus briefs in only 22/38 (or 7%) minority-related cases involving TPI[33], most frequently in cases involving gross violations and bodily harm (Articles 2 and 3 ECHR).

NGOs select strategically the cases in which they request leave to intervene as third parties and provide specialized and expert knowledge to the Court. They are relatively few in number, predominantly UK-based, and a handful or so of them are repeat

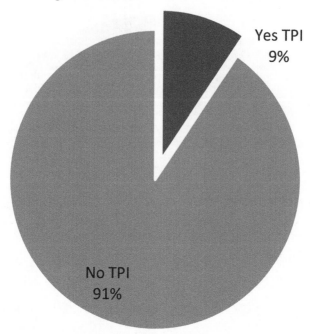

Figure 4.4 Third Party Intervention in ECtHR minority-related cases, 1988–2013

players. Amnesty International in particular, submitted an amicus brief in 7 out of 28 cases in which NGOs acted as TPIs. Other prominent repeat players are Liberty, Interrights, Open Society Justice Initiative (OSJI), and the European Roma Rights Center (ERRC). NGOs that have also acted as TPIs in minority-related cases are the AIRE Center, the Greek Helsinki Monitor, Article 19, the Norwegian Helsinki Committee, and a couple of others that are specialized and single-issue groups.[34] Some NGOs manifest a preference to engage as TPIs (such as Liberty, Justice and Amnesty International), while others tend to support applicants to bring cases before the ECtHR (such as the Kurdish Human Rights Project, the EHRAC). Some NGOs, such as the ERRC and the AIRE Center, do both.

As third parties, NGOs' interventions tend to be concentrated in high importance and Grand Chamber cases. These cases raise new and innovative points of law that a party in proceedings may not wish to raise.[35] NGOs intervened in 24% of high importance rulings (Case Reports and Level 1), but only in 3% of low importance judgments (Level 2 and Level 3 cases, see Figure 4.5). High importance and Grand Chamber judgments set precedents and shape the normative scope and meaning of Convention principles that are applied to a larger number of cases.[36] Thus, the potential influence of TPIs over the development of the case law, is significantly higher than the overall small number of their amicus submissions might suggest.

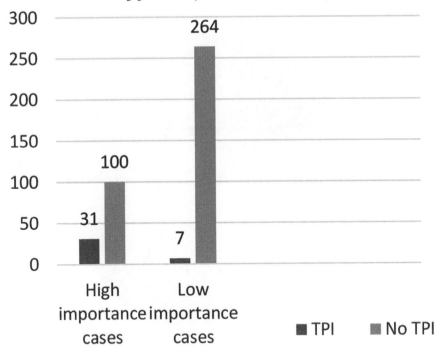

Figure 4.5 Third Party Intervention in ECtHR minority-related judgments by level of importance, 1988–2013

2 Strategic human rights litigation

The overall rise in minority-related ECtHR claims since the 1990s was directly linked to the development of proactive, systematic and strategic international legal action in particular issues, minorities, and countries or regions. In 1990–2013, the bulk of minority-related decisions and judgments originated from five states: Turkey, Russia, the United Kingdom, Greece, and Bulgaria account for 81% of all minority-related decisions and judgments (Figure 4.6). Turkey alone accounts for 46% of all minority-related judgments and decisions that are included in the data set compiled for this study. A variety of civil society actors and NGOs were instrumental in enabling, supporting, and even initiating, human rights litigation in this area. They did so as part of broader mobilization and advocacy strategies on behalf of minority groups or broader causes of rights advancement. This section explores how human rights litigation grew a) as a tool for internationalizing minority rights and politics (Southeast Europe and Turkey), b) a strategy of transnational legal support networks against state abuses in armed conflict, and c) a form of civil society activism to combat discrimination and promote domestic policy reform (Roma minorities).

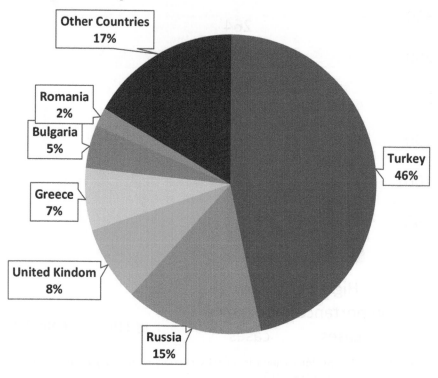

Figure 4.6 Respondent states in minority-related decisions and judgments, 1960–2013

2.1 State restrictions to the public participation of minorities

Why did individuals from a few religious and ethnic minorities, mostly from Turkey, Greece and Bulgaria, bring large numbers of claims against their state to the Strasbourg Court? International human rights litigation emerged as an opportunity after these countries accepted the right to individual petition in the 1980s and early 1990s, in the context of domestic constraints facing minorities. National laws and practices in Greece, Bulgaria and Turkey imposed restrictions on the expression and associational life of minorities and came into conflict with minority aspirations. Greece and Bulgaria denied the existence of, or refused to recognize, minority groups that defined themselves as Turkish (in Greece) and Macedonian (both Greece and Bulgaria). National authorities withheld registration of associations that bore the name of non-recognized minorities, or they restricted in other ways their right to organize in the public sphere. They typically justified these restrictions on grounds of preserving national security and territorial integrity, to prevent disorder or crime, and to protect the rights of others. National courts in turn were unwilling to uphold rights against restrictions on religious freedom and the establishment of minority associations and political parties.[37]

Domestic constraints combined with international opportunities to resort to the ECHR system set the context for rising litigation. Constrained in pursuing their demands through domestic legal and political institutions, individuals belonging to religious and ethnic minorities and their organizations[38] sought to mobilize international law and litigate in the ECtHR. For Jehovah's Witnesses (JWs), for instance, repeat ECtHR litigation from the 1990s onwards became the corner-stone of their mobilization strategy in several countries. They brought over fifteen complaints against Greece, and more against Turkey and other countries, related to the establishment and operation of places of worship,[39] conscientious objectors, and proselytism, among others.[40] The mobilization strategies and resources of the different minority groups shaped the timing and extent to which they deployed ECHR litigation to advance their grievances and exert pressure upon governments to reform restrictive laws and practices. Sizeable ethnic minorities on the other hand, like the Turks in Bulgaria and the Hungarians in Romania, who gained representation and were able to influence governments through established min-ority political parties in national parliaments, did not opt for a ECtHR litigation strategy.

From the 1990s onwards, individuals from the Turkish Muslim minority in Greek region of Thrace systematically engaged in ECtHR litigation to advance the minority's claims to self-determination.[41] Complaints challenged the refusal of Greek authorities to recognize the religious leaders (muftis) elected by the com-munity, as a violation of religious freedom.[42] They also challenged the refusal of Greek courts to register minority associations bearing the adjective 'Turkish' (as in the Turkish Association of Ksanthi), on grounds that they propagated the exis-tence of a Turkish minority in Greece and threatened public order. While con-cerning a symbolic issue of ethnic-cultural identity recognition, the claim was directly at odds with Greek state policy that recognizes a Muslim minority in Thrace (based on the 1923 Lausanne Treaty) and denies the existence of a Turk-ish minority.[43] In all the relevant minority petitions, the ECtHR, in line with its well-established case law, was not convinced that the Turkish-named minority associations constituted a threat to public order or to democratic society. It found the above restrictions to be disproportionate and to infringe freedom of associa-tion (Article 11 ECHR).[44]

Human rights litigation by Thrace's minority was pursued on the sidelines of a political mobilization strategy that relied on the support of their kin-state (Turkey). From the 1990s onwards, systematic recourse to the ECHR was a deliberate and interest-driven reorientation of its mobilization strategy that was endorsed by the minority's key political actors in Greece and abroad: the minor-ity's leaders in Thrace; the kin-state officials (in the foreign ministry in Turkey and in its consulate in Thrace); and the network of the minority's organizations in diaspora, mostly in Turkey and in Germany.[45] In the 5th International Assembly of Western Thrace Turks in Istanbul in 2006, ECtHR litigation was highlighted as a central component of the minority's international and domestic political strat-egy.[46] Turkey as the "kin-state" eventually embraced the shift to a Europeanized and human rights strategy, arguably in order to legitimate its role as "guardian" of the minority of Western Thrace and provided resources for the minority to engage in it.[47]

Individuals from Slav Macedonian minorities also brought complaints to the ECtHR against Greece and Bulgaria, albeit far more limitedly than Turkish Muslims in the Greek region of Thrace. They did so primarily to challenge the official denial of the existence of such minorities, which was manifested in restrictions that the authorities imposed upon associations bearing the name 'Macedonian' (i.e. dissolution or refusal to register Macedonian minority associations).[48] Unlike Turkish Muslims in Thrace, Slav Macedonians did not possess the level of organization and legal support from within the community to systematically engage in ECtHR litigation. Notably, Greek and Bulgarian lawyers were overwhelmingly unwilling to legally represent Slav Macedonians in Greek courts or in the ECtHR, out of concern not to be perceived as unpatriotic. Legal representation in the few cases that they took in Strasbourg was provided by a few committed lawyers outside of the minority community. In Bulgaria, less than a handful of activist lawyers linked to human rights organizations, assisted Slav Macedonians to frame restrictions in their political participation as human rights violations.[49]

The largest – by far – string of minority-related ECHR litigation since the 1990s involved complaints by or on behalf of Kurds to challenge restrictive laws and policies in Turkey. A primary cause and target of related complaints was the Turkish Criminal Code (Article 301 that replaced Article 159 in May 2008) that rendered punishable views that were considered to "denigrate" Turkishness, the Parliament and other public institutions, such as the judiciary or the military. It also incriminated acts or views seen to incite "hatred or hostility on the basis of distinction between social classes, races, religions, denominations or regions"[50], and the dissemination of propaganda "aimed at undermining the territorial integrity of the Republic of Turkey or the indivisible unity of the nation".[51] On the basis of these provisions, authorities prosecuted individuals who publicly expressed dissenting or critical views of Turkey's policies towards the Kurds and other minorities.[52] National legislation also provided for the banning and dissolution of political parties that accepted the existence of minorities in Turkey, and promoted the use of non-Turkish language and culture.[53] On the basis of such provisions, pro-Kurdish parties were dissolved for expressing pro-minority views, often solely in the content of their party programs.

The Turkish government accepted the right to individual petition in 1987 – a strategic move to enhance the country's prospects for EU membership. At the time, knowledge about the Convention and the necessary legal expertise to bring complaints before the ECtHR were lacking, but they developed quickly in the following years. In the early 1990s, less than a handful of Kurdish lawyers with strong interest in human rights, some of them involved in Kurdish politics, began to take cases to the ECHR on their own, despite the threats and intimidation targeting those defending Kurds. Some of them, like Tahir Elci, subsequently helped found organizations like the Human Rights Foundation of Turkey. Others, like Sezgin Tanrikulu and Hasip Kaplan, would become Members of the Turkish Parliament with pro-Kurdish parties.[54]

Kurdish lawyers, activists and political leaders sought to build the legal expertise and organizational capacity to engage in international rights litigation in order to challenge domestic restrictions and advance their demands. In 1994, a group of Kurdish lawyers in Istanbul established the Foundation for Society and Legal Studies (TOHAV) that would collaborate with the London-based Kurdish Human Rights Project (KHRP), which is discussed in the next section.[55] By the mid-1990s, the Diyarbakir Bar Association was providing ECHR training to hundreds of lawyers, helping diffuse knowledge and build capacity for using the ECHR individual petition mechanism.[56] The issuing by the ECtHR of landmark judgments like *Aksoy v Turkey* that for the first time acknowledged the incidence of torture by security forces in South East Turkey[57], further galvanized such legal capacity building.

In the course of the 1990s, Kurdish lawyers, at times in cooperation with national human rights organizations, brought numerous complaints to the ECtHR to challenge the persecution of individuals expressing pro-minority views and the dissolution of associations and political parties expressing pro-Kurdish views.[58] In the first case in this string of claims, Medhi Zana, former mayor of Diyarbakir and a legendary figure, claimed that his imprisonment for making statements in support of "the PKK national liberation movement" violated his freedom of expression (Article 10 ECHR). The ECtHR did not find a violation of Article 10 in *Zana v Turkey*. Yet, this judgment alongside the one in *Castells v Spain* discussed earlier, set landmark precedents. By highlighting that state authorities must provide compelling justification for restricting pro-minority views, they paved the way for many more related claims.[59] In most cases raising claims under Articles 10 and 11 ECHR, the ECtHR found that Turkish authorities did not provide adequate justification for banning or closing down newspapers, political parties or associations of minorities on grounds of national security. In those complaints alleging violations of civil liberties, unlike those raising claims about special rights of minorities, the Court recognized a narrow margin of appreciation for states.[60]

Other religious, ethnic and cultural minorities in Turkey and other countries began to pursue, more or less systematically, ECtHR litigation to challenge restrictive domestic laws and practices, and to advance their claims. In the 2000s, Alevis (non-Sunni Muslims) and their organizations (such as the Alevi-Bektashi Federation (ABF) and the Pir Sultan Abdal Association) overcame their initial reluctance and concern not to be associated with Kurdish groups. They began to bring cases before the ECtHR to contest restrictions on practicing their religious freedom, including in regard to the teaching of religion based on the dominant Sunni Islam, in Turkish schools.[61]

Beyond Turkey, several complaints to contest state restrictions on their religious freedom and cultural identity[62], associational life, or political and electoral participation[63] were brought against Scandinavian countries, Spain, Poland and other countries. In formulating its approach in such kinds of cases under Articles 10 and 11 ECHR, the ECtHR referred to evolving international norms of minority protection embodied in the CSCE Copenhagen Document on the Human

Dimension and the Framework Convention for the Protection of National Minorities (FCPNM).

In sum, minorities increasingly pursued ECtHR litigation from the 1990s onwards, primarily in countries where laws, policies or judicial approach allowed restrictions in their political participation and in their religious, cultural and associational life. Individual human rights complaints were often endorsed, supported or orchestrated by minority organizations in the frame of political campaigns to advance their demands vis-à-vis states. ECtHR litigation became more systematic when a) it was explicitly incorporated in collective strategies to internationalize minority grievances, and b) the necessary legal expertise and organizational support was available. These conditions were especially critical for the growth international rights litigation in cases involving gross state violations in the context of armed conflict. Litigation in this area was characterized by the formation of national and transnational networks of lawyers and human rights organizations that motivated and enabled large numbers of individuals to bring complaints before the ECtHR. The next section explores ECHR litigation in Northern Ireland, in southeast Turkey and in Chechnya in Russia.

2.2 National and transnational legal support structures and networks

From the 1990s onwards, complaints in the ECHR system condemning state abuses in contexts of armed conflict sharply increased. The Convention explicitly allows contracting states to derogate from their obligations when faced with an emergency that is seen to threaten national security and public order (Article 15 ECHR). Under a state of emergency, as in the UK in the 1960s and 1970s (linked to the inter-communal violence in Northern Ireland), exceptional powers may be transferred to the executive. From the 1970s onwards, numerous petitions to the ECtHR challenged the scope and limits of such executive prerogative and raised claims that had been denied by domestic courts. Complaints alleged unlawful arrest and detention, ill-treatment of prisoners convicted on terrorist-related charges, and of individuals in custody by the British army or the police, as discussed in chapter 3.

In no other minority-related issue area has the ECHR system seen a rise in litigation as voluminous as the one involving egregious violations occurring in a state of emergency and armed conflict. For the 1960–2013 period, nearly two-thirds of all minority-related ECHR decisions and judgments against the UK involved allegations of such abuses. In Turkey, petitions by Kurds made up more than 90% of all minority-related cases in the ECtHR. The bulk of those were directly linked to the state of emergency and armed conflict in the southeast of the country (105 out of the 220 decisions and judgments against Turkey in my dataset). Nearly 40% of the minority-related judgments that the ECHR organs issued in 1960–2013 involved such claims (see Figure 4.7). In exploring the factors that led to the spiralling of those claims, we must trace why they originally emerged in the UK, and subsequently in Turkey and Russia.

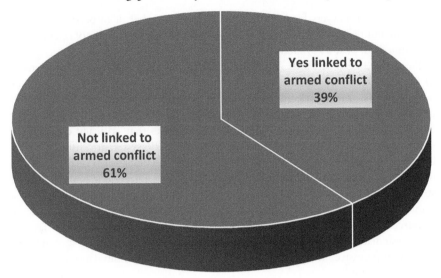

Figure 4.7 Minority-related decisions and judgments related to state of emergency and armed conflict, 1960–2013

In the 1990s and 2000s, a new wave of ECtHR litigation related to state abuses in contexts of inter-communal violence and armed conflict. In the first place, several complaints were related to the inter-communal conflict in Northern Ireland. They were brought against the UK at a time that a vibrant domestic human rights movement was marshalling support for the passage of the Human Rights Act. Lawyers were more at ease in taking such complaints to the ECtHR, in comparison to the earlier period, in the light of declining inter-communal tensions and the peace process marked by the 1998 Good Friday Agreement. In some cases, they joined forces with international NGOs like Amnesty International, the International Federation of Human Rights, British-Irish Rights Watch, and the International Commission of Jurists, to call for a public inquiry into the death of lawyer of Pat Finucane, a high-profile case also decided by the ECtHR.[64] In other cases, human rights organizations acted as third-party interveners to support related claims advanced by petitioners before the Strasbourg Court.[65]

Meanwhile, another region that was the site of armed conflict came under the jurisdiction of the ECHR when Turkey accepted the right to individual petition in 1987. That year, the Turkish government had also declared a state of emergency in the southeast of the country, where operations by security forces were underway to quash a Kurdish militant movement led by the Kurdistan Workers' Party (PKK). Large-scale human rights violations were committed against civilians. They were fended off from judicial review by the country's Constitutional Court and domestic courts, based as they were on statutory orders issued under the state of emergency.[66] Thus, resort to international rights litigation emerged as the only alternative course of action for those who suffered abuses. Initially, a small number of lone Kurdish lawyers filed the first few petitions on behalf of persons claiming inhuman and degrading treatment by security forces during a military operation in the immediate post-1987 period.[67]

From the 1990s onwards, Kurdish ECtHR litigation condemning the actions of security forces in southeast Turkey rapidly grew as a result of two key developments: a) the decision by domestic human rights organizations to pursue an international litigation strategy to advance rights and justice for Kurds, and b) the forging of transnational networks that critically contributed to building the legal and organizational capacity for systematic human rights litigation. In the early 1990s, the Human Rights Association (IHD, Turkey's first human rights NGO established in 1987) and its Diyarbakir branch made a strategic and internally divisive decision to take on the Kurdish issue as a priority and to pursue an international legal strategy around it.[68] Lack of resources and familiarity with the ECHR though, prevented young IHD lawyers from systematically bringing complaints. Operating in a region where state violence was pervasive, they were also faced with constant intimidation, imprisonment, and death.[69]

In the early 1990s, the establishment of a transnational partnership between the IHD and the London-based Kurdish Human Rights Project (KHRP) helped domestic organizations and lawyers surmount the above constraints. Established in 1992 by a Kurd in self-exile and human rights lawyer in the UK, it sought to use human rights law to defend Kurdish victims against rights abuses in southeast Turkey.[70] Notably, the KHRP worked together with British lawyers with experience in ECHR litigation in Northern Ireland, into which they tapped to frame abuses in southeast Turkey into human rights claims.[71]

The KHRP international human rights expertise was joined with the IHD's profound knowledge of local and national conditions in Turkey.[72] Domestically, the IHD and its lawyers carried out the indispensable groundwork for the legal cases. They identified cases and victims, engaged in fact-finding, gathered essential evidence, corresponded with Turkish authorities, filled cases in domestic courts, and prepared draft case files. The KHRP provided legal representation to petitioners and supported the preparation of case files: it translated Turkish documents in English, identified missing information, provided critical analyses of the government's position, and it connected with forensic experts who assessed the evidence submitted by the Turkish government.[73] The KHRP-IHD strategy relied not on the selection of test cases but in the lodging of a large number of similar petitions to demonstrate the existence of administrative practices of systematic rights abuses. Over the course of the 1990s and in the 2000s, they brought to the ECtHR a large number of complaints concerning extra-judicial killings,[74] disappearances, property destruction[75] and other issues that led to advances in the Court's case law.[76]

This string of Kurdish human rights litigation both relied on and contributed to expanding the ECtHR case law from Northern Ireland. *Aksoy v Turkey* affirmed that it is up to the Court to rule whether state actions under a state of emergency have gone beyond the "extent strictly required by the exigencies of the crisis"[77], expanding the approach charted in *Brannigan and McBride v the UK*.[78] In the seminal judgment of *McCann and Others v UK*, a sharply divided ECtHR for the first time established the requirement for an effective State investigation into deaths caused by security forces.[79] In subsequent judgments from Northern Ireland and Turkey, the Court further elaborated that an "effective" investigation must be thorough, impartial and timely. It must probe the circumstances surrounding the use of force and the resulting loss of life and prosecute those State actors found responsible.[80]

Gül v Turkey and other judgments drew on *McCann v UK*, to underscore the obligation of the state to promptly and thoroughly investigate killings by security forces by taking into account all surrounding circumstances.[81] In *Akdeniz and Others* and in scores of other cases, the ECtHR affirmed the state's obligation to prevent, investigate and account for all deaths and disappearances under Article 2 ECHR, even if the evidence to prove direct state responsibility was lacking; and to take preventative measures to protect Kurds who were at risk of being victims of unlawful attacks and attacks by unknown perpetrators in Southeast Turkey.[82] In *Kurt*, the ECtHR did not accept circumstantial evidence and data showing an officially tolerated practice of disappearances in the region. Subsequently, though, it conceded that when authorities were unable to explain what happened to a person who vanished after his/her apprehension or detention, that person must be presumed dead.[83] It shifted the burden of proof to the state to provide a plausible explanation about the disappeared person's fate.[84]

In the 2000s, international litigation against state abuses in southeast Turkey continued even as Kurds' faith in the ECHR system declined. The role of the transnational KHRP-IHD partnership receded and that of domestic organizations, such as the Diyarbakir Bar Association, and the Istanbul-based Foundation for Society and Legal Studies grew. Along with expert lawyers, they provided a robust legal support structure for ongoing ECtHR litigation. Several trainings conducted in the previous decade, including by the KHRP and the IHD, and accumulated experience with litigation in Strasbourg had diffused ECHR knowledge and expertise domestically.[85] The ECtHR though became less willing to scrutinize alleged violations, in the light of human rights reforms linked to Turkey's official candidacy for EU accession in 1999. For instance, the Court struck out cases in response to the Turkish government's unilateral declaration of regret of an individual's death by security forces and monetary compensation.[86] In *İçyer v Turkey,* it also rejected, prematurely, as inadmissible complaints related to forced displacement and village/property destruction[87] invoking the passage of a domestic law that provided compensation to those displaced.[88]

The Kurdish cases from Turkey established a firm legal basis in the ECHR for violations in contexts of armed conflict by 1998 when Russia ratified the Convention. In the 1990s, the Russian government dispatched federal troops to quash a secessionist movement in the southern region of Chechnya. The region became the theatre of egregious state abuses, perpetrated by security forces with impunity in the absence of domestic legal remedies.[89] Soon following Russia's accession to the ECHR, several complaints were lodged by individuals with the support of a few domestic human rights organizations and lawyers, willing and capable to seize opportunities for ECHR litigation. Set up by the Russian NGO Memorial, which had grown out of dissidents' movement in the Soviet period, the Memorial Human Rights Center filed the first few petitions, after sending a young lawyer to gather evidence and interview victims in the region.[90] Large numbers of cases from Chechnya were also brought to the ECtHR with the support of the Committee for the Prevention of Torture (CPT), an NGO in the city of Nizhny Novgorod. The CPT specifically investigated allegations of torture by state agents, and represented victims at the national level and before the ECtHR.[91]

In bringing complaints against gross violations in the ECtHR, human rights organizations and lawyers in Russia and Chechnya established transnational partnerships, as their counterparts in Turkey had done. In the late 1990s, the Moscow branch of Human Rights Watch (HRW) set up the Stichting Chechnya Justice Initiative (subsequently, Stichting Russian Justice Initiative (SRJI)) with funding from the Dutch government. The SRJI provided legal assistance and support to individuals bringing complaints to the Strasbourg Court.[92] Both the HRW and the SRJI had been following closely the proliferation of the Kurdish cases in the ECtHR. They anticipated that the situation in Chechnya would become a new context for large numbers of ECtHR complaints following Russia's ratification of the Convention.[93] Over the next decade, the SRJI became a very important actor in cases from Chechnya and the North Caucasus.[94] Meanwhile, British lawyers with contacts in Russia and experience in Northern Irish and Kurdish litigation in the ECtHR, set up in London the European Human Rights Advocacy Center (EHRAC) with a large grant by the European Commission in 2003. They forged a partnership with Russian NGO Memorial and provided assistance and capacity building to Russian NGOs and human rights monitors in Chechnya and elsewhere for litigation in the ECtHR.[95]

The vast majority of the Chechen cases were lodged in the ECtHR with the support of domestic and international NGOs (nearly 80% of the relevant cases in our dataset). Transnational partnerships between Russian and Chechen NGOs and human rights organizations abroad provided critical legal and financial resources for repeat and systematic ECtHR litigation. By bringing together human rights lawyers and organizations who were repeat players in the ECtHR, with lawyers and domestic organizations with knowledge of and access in the region, these transnational networks were able to generate large numbers of cases. They collected documentation to frame state abuses in Chechnya into human rights claims, and supported many civilian victims to access the ECtHR.[96] The SRJI and EHRAC networks supported the bulk of Chechen litigation in cooperation with the NGO Memorial and its lawyers in the region, who collected the evidence and did the groundwork for the legal cases.[97] They also conducted large numbers of training activities and workshops for Russian lawyers and other organizations on human rights litigation.[98] The SRJI and Memorial-EHRAC further placed emphasis on advocacy and pressure for implementing ECtHR judgments against Russia.[99]

The Chechen cases drew from and further advanced the ECtHR case law involving abuses in contexts of armed conflict. They concerned enforced disappearances,[100] extra-judicial killings[101] and injuries of civilians,[102] destruction of homes and property,[103] torture and inhuman treatment, illegal detention and inhuman conditions of detention, indiscriminate use of force, and lack of effective investigation into the death of civilians during security operations by Russian forces,[104] among others. In response, the ECtHR further elaborated on the positive obligation of the state to conduct an effective investigation into deaths caused in army operations. In particular, it attributed responsibility not only to the actual perpetrators of killings, but also to those involved in planning an operation (i.e. whether they ensured a safe exit for civilians).[105] The obligation to carry out an effective investigation emphasized the rights of the victim more explicitly in the judgments coming out of Chechnya than in earlier cases from regions with armed conflict. Overall, the Court extended its depth of scrutiny and state reprimand in the Chechen cases in comparison to the Kurdish and Northern Irish cases, in a country where existing standards fell well below the minimum.[106]

As in southeast Turkey, the large number of applications enabled the Court to acquire a thorough understanding of the specific context of violence and impunity in Chechnya. This was crucial for deciding cases on incomplete evidence, such as those involving the widespread phenomenon of disappearance of individuals after being taken to state custody.[107] Building on earlier precedents on the right to life and the prohibition of torture from southeast Turkey and Northern Ireland, the ECtHR began to rely more on inferences and presumptions of fact in the Chechen cases. It thus loosened the high evidentiary standards that it had maintained in the earlier Kurdish cases. It had earlier required applicants to prove beyond reasonable doubt that the disappeared was dead, and that the government was complicit in the killing.[108] The Court emphasised more than before the failure of the Russian government to disclose information to rebut the applicants' claims, and to provide alternative explanations.[109]

The unprecedented increase of complaints related to state abuses in contexts of armed conflict was not a plain consequence of enhanced structural access of individuals to the ECtHR. Instead, it was critically driven by legal and organizational actors with the knowledge, strategic motivation and capacity to seize such opportunities. The emergence and operation of legal support structures in this area was distinctly and profoundly transnational, and they made it possible to systematically engage in ECtHR litigation. Transnational partnerships of legal actors and human rights organizations emerged as central in another area of rising ECtHR litigation concerning a highly vulnerable and marginalized ethnic-cultural minority – the Roma. They were instrumental not only in bringing large numbers of complaints in the ECtHR but also, as the next section shows, in developing a novel kind of structural reform litigation.

2.3 *Discrimination and structural reform litigation*

From the 1990s onwards, a rising trend of minority-related ECtHR litigation on Gypsies and Roma took place in the context of growing international concern about their plight. Their socioeconomic marginalization became particularly acute following the disintegration of state socialist regimes in Central East and Southeast Europe (CESE).[110] In 1993, the OSCE High Commissioner on National Minorities called for targeted government policies to deal with the distressing situation of Roma in education, employment, health care and general welfare.[111] In the second half of the 1990s, the European Commission included discrimination against the Roma in its periodic reviews of CESE candidate states for EU membership, who had to report on how they sought to tackle it.[112] The 1990s also saw the rapid development of anti-discrimination norms. A series of newly adopted EU directives prohibited discrimination, including on grounds of race/ethnicity – the Race Equality Directive (RED).[113] Significantly, these directives targeted not only direct but also indirect forms of discriminatory treatment. All EU member and candidate states had to transpose the anti-discrimination directives that could be invoked before courts and equality bodies.

In this favorable international and normative context, a number of NGOs mobilized to challenge ethnic discrimination and began to use law and courts, including the ECtHR, to advance Roma rights. The 1990s saw an unprecedented growth of legal support actors and structures in this area, both in West European countries like the UK, and in several CESE countries. Besides a proliferation of committed lawyers, these comprised Roma rights and human rights NGOs, equality bodies (established also in CESE in the frame of the EU accession process), and access to funding from the EU, national governments, and private sources, notably the Open Society Foundation (OSF). International NGOs, such as Human Rights Watch (HRW) Amnesty International (AI), the Minority Rights Group International, the Open Society Institute (OSI), and the International Helsinki Federation for Human Rights, criticized CESE governments for their treatment of the Roma and did research to document their human rights situation. Transnational networks of domestic and international NGOs, lawyers and activists were created and mobilized to advance Roma rights.[114]

Lawyers, Roma rights activists and NGOs, at times with the support of equality bodies, mobilized the resources to systematically engage in domestic and ECHR litigation as part of their broader strategies of advocacy and pressure. By bringing a large number of Roma-related claims before the ECtHR, they drew on and in turn helped expand anti-discrimination case law and the interpretation of other Convention rights. In the late 1980s and early 1990s, a handful of lawyers in the UK – a country with a strong tradition in public interest litigation and in anti-discrimination law – saw the international organizations' interest in Roma issues as an opportunity to pursue test case litigation.[115] With funding from private foundations (Nuffield, Rowntree), those lawyers[116] provided legal expertise and services to Travelers out of Cardiff Law School's Traveller Law Research Unit, and pursued litigation before domestic courts and the ECtHR.[117] They saw litigation as the only alternative to seek rights for Travelers and Roma who do not "constitute an effective pressure group or a popular cause for political vote seekers".[118]

In the 1990s, the UK lawyers brought a string of petitions to the ECHR bodies to condemn discrimination against Gypsy Travelers and to advance their right to a culturally distinct way of life. They specifically challenged city planning rules in the UK that prevented Travelers from stationing their caravans on land that they owned (due to environmental and planning regulations), or in especially designated sites (due to the lack of sufficient space).[119] The applicants claimed that restrictions imposed by local authorities prevented them from leading a culturally distinct way of life and breached their right to private and family life (Article 8 ECHR). Notably, they also argued that discrimination against Gypsy Travelers was structurally embedded in the UK's laws and administrative practices.[120] Most of the circa two dozen Travelers' applications against the UK in the 1990s were found inadmissible by the Strasbourg Court.

The ECtHR eventually recognized that a culturally distinct way of life can be seen as part of the right to private and family life. In the 1996 judgment in *Buckley*, the UK environmental planning and local administrative rules admittedly interfered with the Travelers' right to a family life (Article 8 ECHR). Yet, such interference was found to be necessary in a democratic society.[121] In 2001 in *Chapman v UK*, the Court invoked "an emerging international consensus recognizing the special needs of minorities and an obligation to protect their security, identity and lifestyle" to affirm the protection of a minority group's way of life under Article 8 ECHR.[122] In 2004, the Court at last accepted that the legislative restrictions that the UK placed on stationing caravans affected the Travelers' ability to have a home and maintain a distinct identity, violating their right to family life.[123] Yet, it did not see the failure of authorities to give special consideration to this distinct identity as discriminatory in breach of the Convention.[124] The Court continued to be aloof to claims of ethnic discrimination, particularly of a structural kind, as it is discussed in chapter 6.

Legal support actors and structures for Roma-related human rights litigation also flourished in post-communist CESE, in Bulgaria, Hungary, the Czech Republic, Romania and elsewhere. A new generation of lawyers, activists and NGOs sprang out of former dissident groups. Many were members and founders of national Helsinki committees that had been established during the communist period.[125] Their interest in and familiarity with the ECHR system rapidly grew in the 1990s through trainings provided with support from large organizations, such as Amnesty International, the International Helsinki Foundation and others, and funding from different European and US governments, and private foundations.[126] Many of those newly trained lawyers staffed the legal programs of, or cooperated with NGOs like the Bulgarian Lawyers for Human Rights, the European Integration and Human Rights Association, and NGOs specifically focusing on Roma rights.[127]

Several Roma and human rights NGOs across CESE turned to legal strategies that they saw as an instrument of social and democratic change in the rapidly transformational, post-communist period.[128] The Sofia-based Human Rights Project and Romani Baht, the Roma Center for Social Intervention and Studies in Romania (Romani Criss), the Legal Defense Bureau for National and Ethnic Minorities (NEKI) and the Chance for Children Foundation (CFCF) in Hungary and Poradna in Slovakia, all pursued Roma-related cases before domestic courts, equality bodies and the ECtHR, alongside their advocacy activities.[129] They engaged in repeat and strategic litigation concerning Roma segregation in schools, discrimination in the criminal justice system and housing, racially motivated crimes, and other issues. They framed their claims in reference to EU and international anti-discrimination law.[130]

The Budapest-based European Roma Rights Center (ERRC) emerged as a key actor in Roma rights litigation in CESE. It was established in 1996 jointly by US lawyers and Roma experts from Bulgaria (one of them had been a founder of the Bulgarian Helsinki Committee) and elsewhere, who had been active in Roma-related litigation before domestic courts. With funding from the Open Society Foundation (OSF), and with start-up logistical support from the Open Society Institute in Budapest, the ERRC made international human rights litigation a centerpiece of its strategy on Roma rights.[131] UK and US lawyers with experience in civil rights litigation (some of whom had worked in organizations like Human Rights Watch) and a belief in law as a tool for social change, were hired to develop the ERRC's litigation program. UK lawyers like Luke Clements, solicitor in many of the Gypsy Travelers cases, joined the legal advisory committee of the ERRC, and Anthony Lester became a member of the ERRC board. Prominent civil rights lawyers like Theodore Shaw, formerly President of the NCAAP Legal Defense Fund also sat on the ERRC Legal Advisory Panel.

The ERRC helped spring and sustain an extended network of transnational partnerships across many CESE countries that made possible systematic human rights litigation on Roma discrimination. With its superior organizational and financial resources, the ERRC maintained a leading role in ECHR litigation in the region. It drew from but also contributed to the growth of domestic legal support actors and structures by providing funding, expertise and support to lawyers and domestic NGOs for Roma-related ECHR litigation in countries like Croatia, Bulgaria and Greece, among others. The extended transnational network of Roma rights NGOs and activists, many of them collaborating in different cases with the ERRC, supported and made third party interventions in scores of Roma-related cases before the ECtHR.[132] They concerned ill-treatment of Roma by the police[133], incidents of racist insults and attacks against houses inhabited by Roma and the authorities' failure to carry out an adequate criminal investigation[134]; segregation in education[135]; housing and forced eviction from Roma settlements;[136] and sterilization without informed consent[137], and other issues.

3 Concluding discussion

The liberalization of individuals' direct access to the Court and the ECHR expansion to Central East Europe and the former Soviet Union form an essential backdrop for understanding the rise of ECHR litigation overall. Yet, the growth in human rights claims – regarding minority public participation, state abuses in contexts of inter-communal and armed conflict, and ethnic discrimination – as the foregoing analyses showed, was primarily driven by a variety of social and legal mobilization strategies. In particular, rising ECtHR litigation in these areas was made possible first by the expansion of legal support structures and actors in West Europe and in CESE countries. A proliferation of human rights lawyers, alone or in collaboration of national and transnational NGOs, provided indispensable support for minority individuals to engage in international rights litigation. They were able to discern expanding international legal opportunities, framed individual grievances and state abuses as human rights claims and mobilized the necessary resources and expertise for repeat and sustained litigation in the ECtHR.

Individuals from minorities and their associations, as well as civil society organizations used and supported international legal strategies to advance cultural identity claims, to challenge restrictive state policies and practices affecting the public participation of minorities, to condemn ethnic discrimination and to defend victims of gross violations in regions of conflict, among other goals. From the 1990s onwards, they did so in increasing numbers, often as part of broader mobilization campaigns to draw attention to minority grievances abroad and to pressure state governments at home. Politicized and well-organized minorities, like Muslims, Turks and Jehovah's Witnesses in Southeast European countries, cultural groups and indigenous peoples in Scandinavia and western Europe, brought several complaints to the ECtHR.

In response to several cases, the Court expanded its interpretation of the Convention in a direction that made it increasingly relevant for minority issues and grievances. In contexts of armed conflict, many cases would not have been brought before the ECtHR without support from local and organizational actors familiar with conditions in the region, and capable to access and collect the necessary factual information. Litigating such cases must meet high evidentiary standards, for instance, in order to prove that state authorities are implicated in killings and disappearance cases. Systematic gathering of data and rich contextual information were indispensable for building compelling human rights claims that influenced and at times expanded ECHR interpretations of rights violations in armed conflict.

In some issue areas, like ethnic discrimination against the Roma in CESE Europe, engaged lawyers and NGOs pioneered and developed structural reform litigation (SRL), a particular and highly contested form of strategic litigation. In SRL, the ECtHR reviews and issues judgments that necessitate state reform of entire policy sectors where policies, rules and systemic patterns of behavior (re) produce racism and ethnic discrimination. Roma-related ECtHR litigation is a case in point: it raises numerous complaints about institutional racism and structural discrimination in areas like housing, education, and the police, among others. More so than in any other kind of strategic legal action, SRL is incorporated in broader and ongoing advocacy and mobilization campaigns, as it is further explored in chapter 6.

The engagement of NGOs and minority actors in ECtHR litigation does not end with the issuing of a Court judgment. Indeed, in strategic litigation, the release of a judgment that pronounces a human rights violation creates the opportunity and a framework for ongoing advocacy and mobilization. Respondent states' authorities, as it is well known, are obliged to implement adverse judgments and remedy the pronounced violations. Since 2006, as already discussed in chapter 3, non-governmental and civil society actors can also participate in and provide input at the judgment implementation phase that is overseen by the Council of Europe Committee of Ministers. Chapter 6 shifts attention to state implementation of ECtHR judgments that condemn Roma segregation in schools in the Czech Republic, Croatia, Greece and Hungary as a form of indirect discrimination. It explores how the systematic involvement of non-governmental actors in litigation and implementation prompts the emergence of human rights experimentalism in the Convention system.

Notes

1   Patrick Thornberry and Maria Amor Martin Estebanez, *Minority rights in Europe – A review of the work and standards of the Council of Europe* (Strasbourg: Council of Europe Publishing, 2004), 17.

2   See Neukirch, Claus, Katrin Simhandl, Wolfgang Zellner, "Implementing Minority Rights in the Framework of the CSCE/OSCE," in *Mechanisms for the Implementation of Minority Rights Standards, Minority Issues Handbook Vol. 2* (Strasbourg: Council of Europe Publishing, 2005), 160.

3   The idea of an additional protocol to the ECHR on minority protection was originally proposed in the 1960s, but it was rejected by the Parliamentary Assembly (PACE) and the Committee of Ministers (CoM) of the Council of Europe (CoE). See Thornberry and Estebanez, *Minority rights in Europe – A review of the work and standards of the Council of Europe*, 40–42.

4   Council of Europe, *Framework Convention for the Protection of National Minorities*, 1 February 1995, ETS 157. See also Council of Europe, *Report on an additional protocol on the rights of minorities to the ECHR* (Parliamentary Assembly, Doc. No. 6742, 19 January 1993), https://assembly.coe.int/nw/xml/XRef/X2H-Xref-ViewHTML.asp?FileID=6772&lang=EN.

5   The FCPNM affirmed that the "protection of a national minority can be achieved through protection of the rights of *individuals belonging to* such a minority" who "may exercise their rights individually and in community with others" (paragraphs 31 and 37; emphasis added). See Florence Benoit-Rohmer, *The Minority Question in Europe – texts and commentary* (Strasbourg: Council of Europe publishing, 1996).

6   The ECtHR issued 450 decisions and judgments, and the ECommHR issued 32 decisions.

7   See Frank Cassidy, ed., *Aboriginal Title in British Columbia: Delgamuukw v The Queen – Proceedings of a conference held September 1991* (Lantzville, BC: Oolichan Books, 1992), 273–274.

8   *G. and E. v Norway* (dec.), no. 9278/81 and 9415/81, 3 October 1983; see also *Östergren and Others v Sweden* (dec.), no. 13572/88, 1 January 1991.

9   *Clerfayt and Mathieu-Mohin v Belgium*, no. 9267/81, 2 March 1987; *Clerfayt, Pierre Legros et al. v Belgium* (dec.), no. 10650/83, 17 May 1985; *Fryske Nasjonale Partij v Netherlands* (dec.), no. 11100/84, 12 December 1985. See *Informationsverein Lentia v Austria and others*, nos. 13914/88, 15041/89, 15717/89, 15779/89, 17207/90, 24 November 1993.

10 *P v UK* (dec.), no. 14751/89, 12 December 1990.

11 *Bideault v France* (dec.), no. 11261/84, 1 October 1986.

12 Timo Koivurova, "Jurisprudence of the European Court of Human Rights Regarding Indigenous Peoples: Retrospect and Prospects," *International Journal on Minority and Group Rights* 18, no. 1 (2011):10.

13 *G. and E. v Norway* (dec.), nos. 9278/81 and 9415/81, 3 October 1983.

14 Lourdes Peroni, "Minorities before the European Court of Human Rights," in *International Approaches to Governing Ethnic Diversity*, eds. Jane Boulden and Will Kymlicka (Oxford: Oxford University Press, 2015), 26–27.

15 Julie Ringelheim, *Diversite culturelle et droits de l' homme: La protection des minorites par la Convention Europeenne* (Brussels: Bruylant, 2006), 353–355.

16 *Castells v Spain*, no. 11798/85, 23 April 1992. Miguel Castells was MP in the Herri Batasuna (leftist Basque nationalist party), and leader of a political organization linked to the separatist ETA (*Euskadi Ta Askatasuna*). He was one of the lawyers who had defended the ETA in the famous "Burgos trial" staged by Franco in the late 1960s, to judge and execute 16 ETA members who had been arrested. See John L. Sullivan, *ETA and Basque Nationalism – The Fight for Euskadi 1890–1986* (London: Routledge, 2015), 95.

17 D. Korff was also counsel in the milestone case of *McCann and Others v UK*, no. 18984/91, 27 September 1995.

18 Committee of Ministers, Resolution DH (95) 93, 7 July 1995.

19 See Dia Anagnostou and Evangelia Psychogiopoulou, "Under what conditions can ECtHR rulings promote rights-expansive policy change? Religious and ethnic minorities in Greece," in *The European Court of Human Rights: Implementing the Strasbourg's Judgments into Domestic Policy*, ed. Dia Anagnostou (Edinburgh: Edinburgh University Press, 2013), 145–146.

20 *Kokkinakis v Greece*, no. 14307/88, 25 May 1993.

21 *Manousakis and Others v Greece*, no. 18748/91, 26 September 1996; *Tsirlis and Kouloumpas v Greece*, nos. 19233/91 and 19234/91, 29 May 1997; *Valsamis v Greece*, no. 21787/93, 18 December 1996; *Efstratiou and Others v Greece*, no. 24095/94, 18 December 1996; *Georgiadis v Greece* no. 21522/93, 29 May 1997; *Pentidis and Others v Greece*, no. 23238/94, 9 June 1997; *Tsavachidis v Greece*, no. 28802/95, 21 January 1999; *Thlimmenos v Greece*, no. 34369/97, 6 April 2000;

22 *Brogan and Others v UK*, nos. 11209/84, 11234/84, 11266/84 and 11386/85, 29 November 1988.

23 Anna-Karin Lindblom, *Non-Governmental Organisations in International Law* (Cambridge University Press, 2005), 333–334.

24 Brice Dickson, *The European Convention on Human Rights and the Conflict in Northern Ireland* (Oxford: Oxford University Press, 2010), 123.

25 For a detailed overview and analysis of the claims raised, see Susan Marks, "Civil Liberties at the Margin: the UK Derogation and the European Court of Human Rights," *Oxford Journal of Legal Studies* 15, no. 1 (1995): 80–81.

26 *Brannigan and McBride v UK*, nos. 14553/89 and 14554/89, 25 May 1993, § 43.

27 *Sidiropoulos v Greece*, no. 26695/95, 10 July 1998; *United Macedonian Organization Ilinden and Ivanov v Bulgaria*, no. 44079/98, 20 October 2005; *Emin and Others v Greece*, no. 34144/05, 27 March 2008; *Bekir Ousta v Greece*, no. 35151/05, 11 October 2007.

28 On the relationship and differences between human rights and international humanitarian law, see Juliet Chevalier-Watts, "Has human rights law become *lex specialis* for the European Court of Human Rights in right to life cases arising from internal armed conflicts?" *International Journal of Human Rights* 14, no. 4 (2010): 585–586.

29 On this issue in regard to legal persons, see *Chassagnou and others v France*, nos. 25088/94, 28331/95 and 28443/95, 29 April 1999. See Frederic Edel, *The prohibition of discrimination under the ECHR* (Human Rights files no. 22, Strasbourg: Council of Europe Publishing, 2010), 14–15.

30   Gaetano Pentassuglia, "The Strasbourg Court and Minority Groups: Shooting in the Dark or a New Interpretive Ethos?" *International Journal of Minority and Group Rights* 19, no. 1 (2012): 2.

31   Patrick Thornberry and Maria Amor Martin Estebanez, "Introduction," in *Minority Rights in Europe – A review of the work and standards of the Council of Europe* (Strasbourg: Council of Europe Publishing, 2004), 49.

32   See *DH and Others v Czech Republic*, no. 57325/2000, 13 November 2007.

33   The other TPIs are the governments of Azerbaijan, Russia, Romania and Cyprus, and a national human rights institution (the Northern Ireland Human Rights Commission).

34   These are the International Federation of Gynaecology and Obstetrics, Centre of Housing Rights and Eviction, and the Roman Education Fund, among others.

35   Loveday Hodson, *NGOs and the Struggle for Human Rights in Europe* (Oxford: Hart Publishing, 2011), 51–52.

36   Fifty-nine (or 14.4%) of the 410 minority-related judgments in our data set were issued by the Grand Chamber and the rest by the ECommHR or a Section of the Court.

37   Dia Anagnostou and Yonko Grozev, "Human rights litigation and restrictive state implementation of Strasbourg Court judgments: The case of ethnic minorities from Southeast Europe," *European Public Law* 16, no. 3 (2010): 401–418.

38   These minority groups were Alevis (non-Sunni Muslims), Kurds and Armenians in Turkey, Turkish, Muslim, or Slavic-speaking and Macedonian minorities in Greece and Bulgaria, Jehovah's Witnesses in all three countries.

39   *Manousakis and Others v Greece*, no. 18748/91, 26 September 1996; *Christian Association Jehovah's Witnesses v Bulgaria* (dec.), no. 28626/95, 3 July 1997.

40   Interview with a JWs activist in ECHR litigation, Dia Anagnostou, Athens, 3 March 2008.

41   *Sadik Ahmet v Greece*, no. 18877/91, 15 November 1996; *Sadik Ahmet v Greece* (dec.), no. 25759/94, 6 March 1997.

42   See for instance *Agga v Greece (no 2)*, nos. 50776/99 and 52912/99, 17 October 2002; *Agko v Greece* (dec), no. 31117/96, 20 October 1997; *Imam and Others v Greece* (dec.), no. 29764/96, 20 October 1997.

43   Konstantinos Tsitselikis, "Minority Mobilisation in Greece and Litigation in Strasbourg," *International Journal on Minority and Group Rights* 16, no.1 (2008): 45.

44   *Bekir-Ousta and others v Greece*, no. 35151/05, 11 October 2007; *Emin and others v Greece*, no. 34144/05, 27 March 2008; *Tourkiki Enosi Xanthis and others v Greece*, no. 26698/05, 27 March 2008, among others.

45   Jeanne Hersant, "Mobilizations for Western Thrace and Cyprus in Contemporary Turkey," in *Social Movements, Mobilization and Contestation in the Middle East and North Africa*, eds. Joel Beinin and Frédéric Vairel (Stanford: Stanford University Press, 2013), 167–182.

46   Final Declaration (5th International Assembly of Western Thrace Turks, Istanbul, 15–17 September 2006) (on file with author).

47   Minority political leader, interview, Athens, 23 May 2008.

48   *Stankov and the United Macedonian Organisation Ilinden v Bulgaria*, nos. 29221/95; 29225/95, 2 October 2001; *United Macedonian Organisation Ilinden and Ivanov v Bulgaria*, no. 44079/98, 20 October 2005; *Sidiropoulos and Others v Greece*, no. 26695/95, 10 July 1998; *Ouranio Toxo and Others v Greece*, no. 74989/01, 20 October 2005.

49   Dia Anagnostou, Interview with human rights lawyer in Sofia, Bulgaria (over Skype), 16 March 2012.

50   Article 312 of the Turkish Criminal Code in force at the material time.

51   Section 8 of the Prevention of Terrorism Act (Law No. 3713 of 12 April 1991) in force at the material time.

52 *Sürek v Turkey*, no. 24122/94, 8 July 1999; *Erdoğdu and Ince v Turkey*, no. 25067/94, 8 July 1999; *Erdoğdu v Turkey*, no. 25723/94, 15 June 2000; *Sener v Turkey*, no. 26680/95, 18 July 2000; *Polat v Turkey*, no. 23500/94, 8 June 1999; *Karataş v Turkey*, no. 23168/94, 8 July 1999, among many others. Writers (most infamously the novelist Orhan Pamuk), academics (like professors Baskin Oran and Ibrahim Kaboglu), journalists, publishers and human rights defenders, who expressed dissenting views on Kurds, Armenians and minorities more broadly, were convicted.

53 Law on Political Parties, no. 2820, 22 April 1983, Article 78(a) and Article 81. The same law also prohibited the formation of political parties with the name 'communist' 'national socialist', 'theocratic', etc.

54 Dilek Kurban, *Limits of Supranational Justice – The European Court of Human Rights and Turkey's Kurdish Conflict*, (Cambridge University Press, 2020), 207–208.

55 Dilek Kurban, "The Limits of Transnational Justice: The European Court of Human Rights, Turkey and the Kurdish Conflict" (Ph.D Dissertation, University of Maastricht, 2018), 127, 176.
   See also Sinem Yargiç, "The Need to Amend Turkish Legislation to Ensure Political Participation in Turkey," *Yönetim Bilimleri Dergisi* 21, no. 11 (2013): 208.

56 Kurban, "The Limits of Transnational Justice," 155.

57 *Aksoy v Turkey*, no. 21987/93, 18 December 1996.

58 *United Communist Party of Turkey and Others v Turkey*, no. 133/1996/752/951, 30 January 1998; *Socialist Party and Others v Turkey*, no. 20/1997/804/1007, 25 May 1998; *Freedom and Democracy Party (ÖZDEP) v Turkey*, no. 23885/94, 8 December 1999; *Yazar and Others and the People's Labour Party (HEP) v Turkey*, nos. 22723/93, 22724/93 and 22725/93, 9 April 2002; *Dicle for the Democratic Party (DEP) v Turkey*, no. 25141/94,10 December 2002, among many others.

59 *Zana v Turkey*, no. 18954/91, 25 November 1997. The ECtHR underscored the special circumstances of the case, with the applicant being an influential politician, who expressed support for the PKK at a time when the latter had carried out murderous attacks against civilians in southeast Turkey.

60 Mustafa Kocak and Esin Orucu, "Dissolution of Political Parties in the Name of Democracy: Cases from Turkey and the ECtHR," *European Public Law* 9, no. 3 (2003): 399–420.

61 *Hasan and Eylem Zengin v Turkey*, no. 1448/04, 9 October 2007; *Mancur Yalcin and Others v Turkey*, no. 21163/11, 16 September 2014. On Alevi mobilization and litigation before domestic courts and the ECtHR, see Elise Massicard, "Variations in the Judicialisation of the Alevi Issue – From Turkey to Europe," *Revue française de science politique* 64, no.4 (2014): 711–733.

62 *Konkama and 38 Other Saami villages v Sweden* (dec.), no. 27033/95, 25 November 1996; *Muonio Saami Village v Sweden*, no. 28222/95, 9 January 2001; *Johtii Sapmelaccatry and other v Finland*, no. 42969/98, 18 January 2005.

63 *Gorzelik and Others v Poland*, no. 44158/98, 17 February 2004. See also *Herri Batasuna and Batasuna v Spain*, nos. 25803/04 and 25817/04, 30 June 2009; *Etxeberria and Others v Spain*, no. 35579/03, 30 June 2009; *Herritarren Zerrenda v Spain*, no. 43518/04, 30 June 2009.

64 Dia Anagnostou, "From Belfast to Diyarbakir and Grozny via Strasbourg: Transnational Legal Mobilisation Against State Violations in Contexts of Armed Conflict." In *Rights in Pursuit of Social Change – Legal Mobilisation in the European Multi-level System*, edited by Dia Anagnostou (Oxford: Hart Publishing, 2014), 173–4.

65 See for example, *McCaughey and Others v the United Kingdom*, no. 43098/09, 16 July 2013.

66 Carla Buckley, *Turkey and the ECHR – A Report on the Litigation Programme of the Kurdish Human Rights Project* (London: KHRP, 2000), 4.

67 One of them was Hasip Kaplan, from a small Kurdish town, who took the case *Gürdogan, K. Müstak, B. Müstak, A. Müstak v Turkey (dec.)*, nos. 15202/89, 15203/89,

15204/89, 15205/89, 12 January 1993. Other lawyers were Sezgin Tanrikulu and Tahir Elçi. See Kurban, *The Limits of Transnational Justice*, 164 and 175.

68 Kurban, *The Limits of Transnational Justice*, 149–150.

69 Kurban, *The Limits of Transnational Justice*, 155–162.

70 Interview, Kerim Yildiz, London, 26 June 2012.

71 The KHRP worked with a large number of lawyers, initially with Kevin Boyle and Françoise Hampson from Essex University, who were renowned for their work in litigating cases from Northern Ireland, but also with many other lawyers from the UK and Turkey. See Buckley, *Turkey and the ECHR – A Report on the Litigation Programme of the Kurdish Human Rights Project*, 2.

72 For a detailed account of the origins of the KHRP, see Kurban, *The Limits of Transnational Justice*, 164–166.

73 Buckley, *Turkey and the ECHR – A Report on the Litigation Programme of the Kurdish Human Rights Project*, 75; Kurban, *The Limits of Transnational Justice*, 168.

74 Extra-judicial killing refers to "the taking of an individual life by government authorities or in the course of operations involving the use of lethal force by State agents without the minimal guarantees provided by the due process of law". See Carla Buckley, "The European Convention on Human Rights and the Right to Life in Turkey," *Human Rights Law Review* 1, no. 1 (2001): 36.

75 *Akdıvar and Others v Turkey*, no. 99/1995/605/693, 30 August 1996. This was a precedent-setting ruling concerning forced evictions and the burning of villages by security forces.

76 *Ağgül and Others v Turkey*, no. 33324/96, 22 May 2001; *Aygördü and Others v Turkey*, no. 33323/96, 22 May 2001; *Cemal and Nurhayat Güven v Turkey*, no. 31848/96, 22 May 2001; *Dilek v Turkey*, no. 31845/96, 17 June 2003; *İnce and Others v Turkey*, no. 33325/96, 22 May 2001.

77 See *Aksoy v Turkey*, no. 21987/93, 18 December 1996.

78 *Brannigan and McBride v UK*, nos. 14553/89 and 14554/89, 25 May 1993.

79 *McCann and Others v UK*, no. 18984/91, 27 September 1995.

80 Indicatively, see *McKerr and Others v UK*, no. 28883/94, 4 April 2000; *Shanaghan and Kelly v UK*, nos. 37715/97 and 30054/96, 4 August 2001; *Magee v UK*, no. 28135/95, 6 September 2000; *McShane v UK*, no. 43290/98, 28 May 2002; *Finucane v UK*, no. 29178/95, 1 July 2003. For a critical discussion of the UK investigative and prosecutorial processes, see Anthony Gordon and Paul Mageean, "Habits of Mind and "Truth Telling": Article 2 ECHR in Post-Conflict Northern Ireland," in *Judges, Transition, and Human Rights*, eds. John Morison, Kieran McEvoy, and Anthony Gordon (Oxford: Oxford University Press, 2007), 185–86.

81 *Gül v Turkey*, no. 22676/93, 14 December 2000; *Ergi v Turkey*, no. 23818/94, 28 July 1998. See also Carla Buckley, "The European Convention on Human Rights and the Right to Life in Turkey," 45–46.

82 *Akdeniz and Others v Turkey*, no. 23954/94, 31 May 2001; *Yaşa v Turkey*, no. 22495/93, 2 September 1998; *Tanrikulu v Turkey*, no. 23763/94, 8 July 1999; *Mahmut Kaya v Turkey*, no. 22535/93, 28 March 2000; *Kemal Kılıç, v Turkey*, no. 22492/93, 28 March 2000.

83 *Çakıcı v Turkey*, no. 23657/94, 8 July 1999; *Ertak v Turkey*, no. 20764/92, 9 May 2000; *Timurtaş v Turkey*, no. 23531/94, 13 June 2000.

84 *Timurtas v Turkey*, no. 23531/94, 13 June 2000; *Orhan v Turkey*, no. 25656/94, 18 June 2002; *Ipek v Turkey*, no. 25760/94, 14 May 2002.

85 Kurban, *The Limits of Transnational Justice*, 174.

86 *Akman v Turkey*, no. 37453/97, 26 June 2001.

87 *İçyer v Turkey* (dec.), no. 1888/02, 12 February 2006.

88 For a discussion on this, see Kurban, *The Limits of Transnational Justice*, 184–189.

89 Emma Gilligan, *Terror in Chechnya: Russia and the Tragedy of Civilians in War* (Princeton University Press, 2010), 9–12.

90 Gilligan, *Terror in Chechnya*, 186.
91 The lawyers working together with the Committee prepared and filed 84 complaints to ECtHR. See Committee Against Torture, accessed 20 December 2021, http://hragents.org/en-time/tl-kpp-en/#.
92 Gilligan, *Terror in Chechnya*, 186.
93 See Lisa McIntosh Sundstrom, "Russian NGOs and the European Court of Human Rights: A Spectrum of Approaches to Litigation," *Human Rights Quarterly* 36, no. 4 (2014): 857–858.
94 Out of a total of over 500 cases regarding grave human rights abuse in Chechnya and other North Caucasus republics that had been submitted to the Court by December 2015, the SRJI had represented clients from North Caucasus in almost 355 of those cases. It had won 179 cases at the European Court of Human Rights finding Russia responsible for grave violations of human rights in Chechnya, Kabardino-Balkaria and Ingushetia. See the SRJI website at https://www.srji.org/en/legal/.
95 Interview with representative from EHRAC, London 26 June, 2012.
96 By June 2014, the Memorial-EHRAC Program had submitted 242 Russian cases to the ECtHR and obtained judgments on 93 of them. See McIntosh Sundstrom, "Russian NGOs and the European Court of Human Rights: A Spectrum of Approaches to Litigation," 861.
97 By 2012, Memorial had four legal aid offices in Chechnya, in addition to judicial aid points in Ingushetia, Dagestan, and Kabardino-Balkaria. See Freek Van der Vet, "Seeking Life, Finding Justice: Russian NGO litigation and Chechen Disappearances before the ECtHR," *Human Rights Review* 13, no. 3 (2012): 308.
98 Van der Vet, "Seeking Life, Finding Justice," 308.
99 Sundstrom, "Russian NGOs and the ECtHR," 864.
100 *Tashukhadzhiyev v Russia*, no. 33251/04, 25 October 2011; *Umarova and Others v Russia*, no. 25654/08, 31 July 2012.
101 *Khashiyev and Akayeva v Russia*, nos. 57942/00 and 57945/00, 24 February 2005; *Musayev and Others v Russia*, nos. 57941/00, 58699/00 and 60403/00, 26 July 2007; *Estamirov and Others v Russia*, no. 60272/00, 12 October 2006; *Amuyeva and Others v Russia*, no. 17321/06, 25 November 2010.
102 *Isayeva, Yusupova and Bazayeva v Russia*, nos. 57947/00, 57948/00, 57949/00, 24 February 2005.
103 *Esmukhambetov and Others v Russia*, no. 23445/03, 29 March 2011.
104 *Inderbiyeva v Russia*, no. 56765/08, 24 September 2012; *Kadirova and Others v Russia*, no. 5432/07, 27 March 2012.
105 *Isayeva v Russia*, no. 57950/00, 24 February 2005; *Isayeva, Yusupova and Bazayeva v Russia*, nos. 57947/00, 57948 and 57949/00, 24 February 2005.
106 Chevalier-Watts, "Has human rights law become *lex specialis* for the European Court of Human Rights in right to life cases arising from internal armed conflicts?" 715–717.
107 See *Bazorkina v Russia*, no. 69481/01, 27 July 2006; *Bitiyeva and X v Russia*, nos. 57953/00 and 37392/03, 21 June 2007; *Medov v Russia*, no 1573/02, 8 November 2007, among many others.
108 Irum Taqi, "Adjudicating Disappearance Cases in Turkey: An Argument for Adopting the Inter-American Court of Human Rights' Approach," *Fordham International Law Journal* 24, no.3 (2000): 982.
109 Philip Leach, "The Chechen Conflict: Analysing the Oversight of the ECtHR," *European Human Rights Law Review* 6 (2008): 732, 748.
110 On the widespread attention given to Roma by European and international organizations in the 1990s, see Peter Vermeersch, *The Romani Movement* (Oxford: Berghahn Books, 2006), chapter 5.
111 Luke Clements, Philip A. Thomas and Robert Thomas, "The Rights of Minorities – A Romany Perspective," *OSCE Office for Democratic Institutions and Human Rights Bulletin* 4, no. 4 (1996), 6–7.

112 Vermeersch, *The Romani Movement*, 197.

113 See Council Directive 2000/43/EC of 29 June 2000 implementing the principle of equal treatment between persons irrespective of racial or ethnic origin (2002) OJ L180/22.

114 Vermeersch, *The Romani Movement*, 201–203.

115 Clements, Thomas and Thomas, "The Rights of Minorities – A Romany Perspective," 16.

116 They were specialists in public law (Keith Lomax), social care and disability law (Clements), environmental planning (Richard Drabble), and anti-discrimination law (Michael Beloff QC). Some were university professors, like Philip A. Thomas and Luke Clemens, others worked in private law firms, and others were acclaimed human rights lawyers (like Peter Duffy QC).

117 Lilla Farkas, "Mobilising for racial equality in Europe – Roma rights and transnational justice" (Ph.D Thesis, European University Institute, Department of Law, 2020), 169–171.

118 Clements, Thomas and Thomas, "The Rights of Minorities – A Romany Perspective," 5.

119 *Smith v UK* (dec.), no. 14455/88, 4 September 1991.

120 See for example, *Chapman v United Kingdom*, no. 27238/95, 18 January 2001, § 83, 93.

121 See *Buckley v UK*, no. 20348/92, 25 September 1996.

122 See *Chapman v the United Kingdom*, no. 27238/95, 18 January 2001.

123 *Connors v United Kingdom*, no. 66746/01, 27 May 2004.

124 *Chapman v UK*, no. 27238/95, 18 January 2001; *Beard v UK*, no. 24882/94, 18 January 2001; *Coster v UK*, no. 24876/94, 18 January 2001; *Jane Smith v UK*, no. 25154/94, 18 January 2001; *Lee v UK*, no. 25289/94, 18 January 2001. See also Ralph Sandland, "Developing a Jurisprudence of Difference," *Human Rights Law Review* 8, no.3 (2008): 489.

125 See Aryeh Neier, *The International Human Rights Movement – A History* (2012), 156.

126 Interview with human rights lawyer in Sofia, Bulgaria, 12 March 2012, conducted over skype. See also James Goldston, "Public Interest Litigation in Central and Eastern Europe: Roots, Prospects, and Challenges," *Human Rights Quarterly* 28, no. 2 (2006): 494.

127 Interview with human rights lawyer in Sofia, Bulgaria, 12 March 2012, conducted over skype.

128 Interview with co-founder of ERRC, London, 27 March 2012.

129 For a detailed description, see Farkas, *Mobilising for racial equality in Europe*, chapter 3.

130 Goldston, "Public Interest Litigation in Central and Eastern Europe," 507–511.

131 Interview with co-founder of ERRC, London, 27 March 2012.

132 Cases involving Roma have been brought against Bulgaria and Romania, but also from Croatia, Hungary, Slovenia, Slovakia, the Czech Republic and Greece, as well as from France, Italy and other countries.

133 See for instance, *Soare and Others v Romania*, no. 24329/02, 22 February 2011; *Cobzaru v Romania*, no. 48254/99, 26 July 2007; *Balogh v Hungary*, no. 47940/99, 20 July 2004; *Assenov and Others v Bulgaria*, no. 24760/94, 28 October 1998.

134 See *Koky et al v Slovakia*, no. 13624/03, 12 June 2012; *Tanase and Others v Romania*, no. 62954/00, 26 May 2005; *Gergely v Romania*, no. 57885/00, 26 April 2007; *Kalanyos and Others v Romania*, no. 57884/00, 26 April 2007.

135 *Orsus and Others v Croatia*, no. 15766/03, 16 March 2010; *Lavida and Others v Greece*, no. 7973/10, 30 May 2013.

136 *Yordanova and Others v Bulgaria*, no. 25446/06, 24 April 2012.

137 See for example, *R.K. v Czech Republic* (dec.), no. 7883/08, 27 November 2012.

5 Legal strategies for migrants' rights and policy change

Since the 1990s, migrants and asylum seekers brought a fast-rising number of claims in the European Court of Human Rights (ECtHR). Originating from many European countries, they raised diverse claims for rights protection in reference to various Convention provisions. Third-Country Nationals (TCNs) invoked their right to a family life and the principle of non-refoulement to prevent their deportation or to ask the ECtHR to temporarily suspend their removal until their case is fully examined. Others challenged the lawfulness and conditions of their detention, reception conditions and asylum procedures, and their access to social rights and the justice system, all on human rights grounds. The sharp rise of human rights litigation in this area is remarkable, considering that the Convention was never intended to be a legal regime that would adjudicate on claims linked to asylum and immigration. Why did migrants and asylum seekers take recourse to the ECtHR in increasing numbers? Who are the actors involved in the relevant complaints, which countries do these most frequently target, and what issues do they raise?

The rise in ECtHR migrant-related litigation cannot be understood outside the shifting political and social context of the late 1980s and the 1990s in Europe. During that time, the rights of migrants, refugees and displaced persons received increasing attention by international organizations like the United Nations (UN), the Organization of American States, the UN High Commission for Refugees (UNHCR), and others.[1] Simmering tensions around the presence of migrants in European societies sparked awareness and created pressure for the ECHR to step up its efforts in the protection of non-nationals. It had become clear that existing specialized instruments, such as the 1951 Geneva Convention on the Protection of Refugees, which were a product of the particular post-World War II context[2], could not address the changing nature of international migration in Europe. Many refugees came from Africa, Asia and the Middle East. They sought asylum in Europe, fleeing from countries that were devastated by civil war, natural disasters and grinding poverty, such as Somalia, the Democratic Republic of Congo, Rwanda, Afghanistan or Iraq. Yet, they could not establish persecution under one of the five grounds of the Geneva Convention (race, religion, nationality, membership of a particular social group or political opinion).

DOI: 10.4324/9781003256489-6

The growth of migrant-related ECtHR litigation was unrelated to the Convention's eastward expansion since the 1990s.[3] Litigation in this area started to grow in the second half of the 1980s and in the 1990s, primarily targeting the 'old' states of the CoE from West Europe, such as the United Kingdom (hereby UK), the Netherlands, France, and Belgium. Governments in these countries adopted new and expanded existing legal provisions and practices aimed at tightening immigration control.[4] They sought to curb migration of newcomers and asylum-seekers, but also to impose restrictions on the stay of second-generation migrants, often by adopting policies that were controversial from a human rights point of view. Migration into Europe increased and diversified not only in long-standing immigration countries, but also in south European states that had formerly been emigration countries. In the course of the 1990s and especially after 2000, Greece and Italy saw rapidly rising numbers of TCNs entering their territory, many without admission documents. These countries had weakly developed and deficient reception and asylum systems and encountered strong difficulties in managing increased immigrant inflows.

The structural reform of the ECHR in the 1990s expanded legal opportunities for individuals to access the Court, as we saw in chapter 3. It is doubtful though whether many migrants and asylum-seekers, mostly vulnerable individuals and thoroughly unfamiliar with the host society, would have been able and motivated to entreat an international court like the ECtHR; the latter had not even begun to develop a case law in this area until the 1990s. Probing into the rise of migrant-related litigation in the ECtHR, this chapter explores the growing interest and mobilization of various legal actors and non-governmental organizations (NGOs) in the field of migration and human rights law. It applies a process tracing approach and a time-series analysis to explore patterns of ECtHR migrant-related litigation and the civil society involvement in it.[5]

The 1980s were a turning point for human rights litigation related to migrants, when a number of milestone rulings broke new legal ground and paved the way for more related complaints. The first and second parts of this chapter examine the socio-legal developments in the area of migrants' rights in the 1980s and the Court's landmark rulings that rendered the ECHR relevant for migrants. The third part of the chapter traces the evolution of migrant-related litigation in the ECHR before and after the 1980s-90s. It draws on aggregate case law data of over 605 relevant judgments, to explore and analyze the countries that the relevant petitions most frequently targeted, the issues they raised, and the judicial outcomes. The fourth part explores the extent and nature of civil society involvement in cases brought to the ECtHR by migrants and asylum seekers, drawing on case law data and on ten interviews with lawyers and civil society activists. The fifth section examines structural reform litigation (SRL), a specific kind of strategic litigation developed with support from NGOs and other non-governmental actors to pressure for structural and policy reform within states.

This chapter argues that the rise in migrant-related ECtHR litigation was largely driven by the proliferation of legal support actors and structures in several European countries. A variety of non-governmental organizations (NGOs) seized international legal opportunities to support applicants and pursue broader strategic goals. Through synergies with lawyers, they challenged state action related to detention, reception and deportation of TCNs on human rights grounds. Large numbers of claims gradually pushed the Strasbourg Court to become extensively involved in issues related to immigration and asylum. In reviewing cases that had implications for state policies on immigration and asylum, the Court began to engage in a highly controversial form of international judicial rights review.

1 Legal activism and advances in ECHR case law

In the 1980s, the Council of Europe became increasingly concerned about the failure of governments to uphold migrants' rights in the midst of rising anti-immigrant attitudes in European societies. Such concerns were publicly voiced in a colloquy organized by the Council of Europe in Funchal, Madeira (Portugal) in October 1983 (the Funchal Colloquy), which was widely attended by politicians, civil servants, judges, lawyers and NGO representatives. In the course of that colloquy, the Convention system came under strong criticisms for failing to provide sufficient protection to migrants and asylum-seekers facing deportation. The latter was a strongly controversial issue, on which some Council of Europe officials took a notably self-critical stance. They strongly expressed the view that the human rights framework should be deployed proactively to protect the rights of migrants and promote their integration in Europe. The Colloquy's recommendations urged the ECHR adjudicatory bodies to take a more decisive stance on expulsion and deportation, as well as on procedural guarantees for those seeking asylum.[6]

As European governments tightened immigration policies, an increasing number of migrants and asylum seekers brought complaints in the ECHR organs.[7] They did so despite the fact that the ECHR does not guarantee a right to non-citizens to enter or stay in the territory of a given state, or a right to political asylum. Complaints mostly originated from the United Kingdom, the Netherlands and France, but also from Germany, Sweden, Denmark and Austria.[8] These were countries with migrants from former colonies, or countries with a significant migrant population that had arrived in the post-War years of the economic boom. In those early petitions, non-nationals sought to stop their deportation by raising claims under Article 3 ECHR (prohibition of inhuman and degrading treatment). While the ECommHR had recognized the relevance of Article 3 for expulsion cases, it had rejected the respective claims as inadmissible.[9] A few related complaints had led to decisions by the ECommHR or to friendly settlements, but only one was referred to the ECtHR for a judgment, and it was a seminal one – the case of *Abdulaziz, Cabales and Balkandali v UK* (1985).[10]

Abdulaziz, Cabales and Balkandali v UK was a test case supported by the Joint Council for the Welfare of Immigrants (JCWI), with the aim of challenging the UK's restrictive immigration law. The 1980 Immigration Rules allowed female spouses or partners to join their lawfully residing husbands in the UK. They did not though similarly allow for the entry of male spouses on grounds of protecting the domestic labor market.[11] The applicants were represented by a "dream team" of internationally reputed, human rights lawyers from the UK that included Rosalyn Higgins, M. Beloff, and S. Grosz, who argued that immigration rules were discriminatory. The ECtHR agreed that the differential protection enjoyed by female migrants in joining their husbands was not objectively justified and was a form of sex-based discrimination (Article 14 ECHR). While it rejected the claim that refusing entry to the husbands of the female applicants violated their right to family life (Article 8 ECHR), the Court for the first time noted that this right could be relevant for non-citizens seeking to enter or stay in a country. Significantly, it also stated that if extradition has consequences likely to breach a Convention right, this could engage the obligations of the Contracting state.[12]

By raising the possibility of extra-territorial responsibility in extradition, the *Abdulaziz Cabales and Balkandali* judgment paved the way for a major breakthrough in the ECHR case law over the next few years, in the case of *Soering*. This case did not involve a migrant or a refugee, but a German national, whose extradition from the UK was requested by the USA and the state of Virginia, where he was faced with charges of multiple homicide and the possibility of death penalty. Before the ECHR bodies, the applicant was represented by prominent UK lawyers specializing in migration and human rights. Building their case on the Court's earlier interpretation in *Abdulaziz, Cabales and Balkandali,* they pressed the claim that extradition to a country where one is likely to face inhuman and degrading treatment would breach Article 3 ECHR.[13] The Court's judgment in *Soering* for the first time unambiguously pronounced the prohibition of *refoulement* on the basis of Article 3 ECHR. It conceded that the applicant's extradition to the USA, where he was likely to be put on a death row, would engage the responsibility of the UK authorities and amount to inhuman and degrading treatment.[14]

The judgments in *Abdulaziz Cabales and Balkandali* and in *Soering* were products of the flourishing legal and civil society activism in the UK of the 1980s. Human rights organizations like Amnesty International (AI) seized the opportunities opened with the 1982 change in Court Rules to make a third-party intervention in the case of Soering.[15] In search for neutrality and a less politicized approach to human rights during the Cold War, AI pursued a legal strategy for some of the causes that it advocated.[16] While AI was unwilling to represent litigants before courts, it was keen to get involved in international legal proceedings as part of its campaign to pressure states and the United Nations to condemn judicially imposed capital punishment.[17] In its third-party submission in *Soering*, Amnesty argued that in the light of the evolving standards in Western Europe, the death penalty and exposure to the "death row phenomenon" should be considered inhuman and degrading treatment within the meaning of Article 3 ECHR. It should be considered inhuman even if at that time the ECHR (Article 2) allowed for the death penalty for someone convicted of a crime, for which such a penalty was provided for by law.[18] Significantly, the Court's judgment accepted both of these points in its final ruling.

The *Soering* judgment attracted a voluminous amount of commentary and it was undoubtedly of historical significance for the development of immigration law in Europe.[19] The ECtHR for the first time held Contracting Parties responsible "for all and any foreseeable consequences of extradition suffered outside of their jurisdiction".[20] *Soering* thus expanded the scope of the Convention and established a strong legal ground for individuals seeking political asylum in Europe. While it did not question the states' prerogative to expel non-citizens from its territory, it signaled that governments could no longer do so without appreciation of the conditions that the deported individual would likely face in the receiving state, even if that state lied outside of the ECHR jurisdiction.[21] The responsibility of the sending state could be triggered specifically in regard to the protection of Convention rights that had an absolute character, such as the prohibition of torture, and inhuman and degrading treatment.

Besides Amnesty International, a variety of other NGOs in the UK began to proactively deploy international legal strategies to challenge restrictive immigration policies. Old organizations like the Joint Council for the Welfare of Immigrants, and new ones like the Immigration Law Practitioners Association (ILPA, established in 1984) and Interrights (established in 1982), supported litigation. They pursued test cases on due process in deportation proceedings and on rules governing immigration more broadly.[22] Quasi-governmental Community Law Centers also provided legal assistance and advice in disadvantaged areas. As one of the few studies of that period states, "there [was] a spurt of enthusiasm for international pressure through law and networks [were] springing up in response".[23] Thatcher's anti-union policies, the perceived attack to basic civil liberties and the rise of racial tensions further fueled such legal activism.[24]

Progressive human rights lawyers in the UK, like Anthony Lester, Ben Birnberg, and others who were knowledgeable of the Convention, also defended applicants in cases that made further advances in ECHR case law. In many cases, they collaborated with migrants' rights advocates and organizations. David Burgess, a committed human rights lawyer who fought legal battles on behalf of individuals from marginalized groups, and Nicholas Blake, one of the UK's top immigration lawyers, represented applicants in the landmark case of *Vilvarajah and Others v UK*. The applicants were young Tamils, who belonged to a minority at the height of the inter-ethnic strife in Sri Lanka in the second half of the 1980s. They sought political asylum on grounds that they faced persecution if returned back to their country.[25] The ECtHR argued that the conditions of generalized violence in Sri Lanka were not substantial grounds for believing that the applicants would be exposed to inhuman and degrading treatment in breach of Article 3 ECHR. With a highly divided decision of the Commission though (7/7), the scope of non-refoulement protection for migrants was far from settled and would be pressed further in many more cases.

In the mid-1990s, another key milestone in the ECtHR immigration-related case law was *Chahal v United Kingdom* (1996) that considered non-refoulement in cases of TCNs suspected of involvement in terrorist activities. The applicants, who were Sikh, claimed that their deportation to the region of Punjab in India would expose them to the risk of persecution contrary to Article 3 ECHR, and that they did not have access to an effective domestic remedy (Article 13 ECHR).

The contested issue was whether such a remedy was possible at all, in view of the fact that state authorities could not divulge, as they claimed, sensitive for national security information. London-based NGOs, such as Amnesty International, Liberty, the AIRE Center and the Joint Council for the Welfare of Immigrants (JCWI) intervened as third parties to support the applicants' claims. The ECtHR attached weight to an Amnesty report to assess the situation in Punjab and to determine that deportation would put applicants at risk contrary to Article 3 ECHR. The Court also conceded that an effective remedy required independent scrutiny of the deportation order, and that a remedy "as effective as can be" did not meet basic human rights guarantees.[26]

Human rights lawyering and activism in the 1980s began to emerge in other European countries with substantial migrant population, such as the Netherlands. The country lacked a well-developed legal support structure and a legally oriented civil society sector. Yet, human rights had been flourishing as a legal specialization in the Dutch academia for some time. Academics were eager to bring petitions in the ECHR system, especially after successful attempts to do so in other domains of state action.[27] The ECtHR *Berrehab v Netherlands* judgment was a product of such academic interest in human rights litigation.[28]

Berrehab brought to light the situation of legally resident migrants who faced expulsion, due to loss of their residence permit, or a criminal conviction, even of a minor kind. National authorities refused to renew the applicant's residence permit (a national of Morocco) after he divorced from his Dutch wife. An ordinary attorney, who had handled the applicant's divorce in domestic courts, also represented him before the ECtHR. He framed the claims raised in *Berrehab* by collaborating with academics who were keen to advance human rights jurisprudence in this emerging field of law.[29] The judicial proceedings before the ECHR were fast-tracked (similarly to *Soering*), showing that the Commission was "by then determined to test the Convention's requirements regarding the expulsion of aliens before the Court".[30] The ECtHR found the applicant's expulsion to be a disproportionate interference with, and to contravene his right to family life (Article 8 ECHR). The *Berrehab* judgment further spurred interest in the ECHR and prompted Dutch lawyers to seek to frame other cases in human rights terms too.[31]

An increasing number of professional lawyers specialized in human rights in countries like France, the Netherlands and Sweden, and ordinary practicing attorneys worked together with academics in the still little developed at the time but fast emerging field of human rights law.[32] Cause lawyers, specialized human rights lawyers, ordinary attorneys, and law professors were all key actors in increasingly framing migrant issues as human rights claims and bringing them before the ECHR organs. In France, a distinctly French tradition of "cause lawyering" evolved and became diffused from the 1980s onwards. It could be traced back to the Algerian war of independence and the anti-colonial politics in France, as well as to the social movements of the 1960s.[33] Lawyers litigating in the ECtHR had received training in the famous "Ornano Office", the first radical law office in France, under the apprenticeship of leading human rights lawyers like Francis Teitgen.[34] Old human rights organizations like the LDH (*Ligue des Droits de l' Homme et du Citoyen*) and new rights-oriented organizations and networks became active in the field of migrants' rights. Organizations like GISTI (The Group for Information and Support to Immigrants) sought to mobilize the law against the rising appeal of anti-immigrant policies and right-wing politics of Le Pen's *Front National*.[35]

In sum, by the mid-1990s, legal and civil society activism around migrants' rights led to Strasbourg Court judgments that established the principle of non-refoulement and the right to family life, as basic pillars in the juridical protection of migrants against expulsion. These judgments sparked further interest in the ECtHR and expanded opportunities for more petitions by migrants and asylum seekers.[36] To be sure, while *Soering*, *Berrehab* and *Chahal* established the jurisprudential grounds for limiting state prerogative in deporting migrants, they did not provide a guarantee against expulsion. In fact, the Court placed a high threshold for determining the risk of an applicant facing deportation and a strong burden on the applicant to prove his/her allegations. This was made apparent in the case of *Cruz Varas and Others v Sweden* brought to the ECtHR by Percy Pratt, a prominent civil rights lawyer and advocate in Sweden. In this case, Swedish authorities had ordered the deportation of a couple with their son back to Chile under Pinochet.[37] The ECtHR did not find a violation of the non-refoulement principle, despite factual evidence (which had already been accepted by the Commission) that the applicant had been subjected to political prosecution and torture.

2 Patterns of migrant-related litigation

The advent of human rights lawyering, as well as legal and civil society activism in a few European countries were instrumental in bringing the early string of migrant-related cases in the ECtHR in the 1980s. The Court's milestone judgments discussed in the previous section further expanded opportunities for human rights litigation by non-nationals in more European countries. From the 1990s onwards, many more cases were brought to the ECtHR by migrants and asylum-seekers, raising claims that aimed to set limits to states' immigration control policies and practices. Figure 5.1 depicts this upward trend in the number of the relevant judgments that were issued by the Court between 1980 and 2020.

Migrant-related judgments target a large number of states, many from West and South European states, unlike minority-related litigation, which mostly originates from Central East and Southeast Europe and the former Soviet Union. Fifty-five percent of migrant-related judgments target the following eight states: the United Kingdom, France, Greece, the Netherlands, Sweden, Switzerland, Belgium and Italy (see Figure 5.2). Unlike minority-related litigation, ECHR migrant-related claims do not have a distinctive group-specific pattern. Petitioners are from more than forty different nationalities.[38] In sixty-eight percent of judgments the applicants are male, in twenty percent they are female, while twenty-percent of judgments involve both male and female applicants. A number of migrants have the nationality of the host state, most of them in the UK, France and the Netherlands.

Migrants and asylum-seekers raised a wide variety of claims before the ECtHR. They concern expulsion or non-entry of legally-resident Third Country Nationals

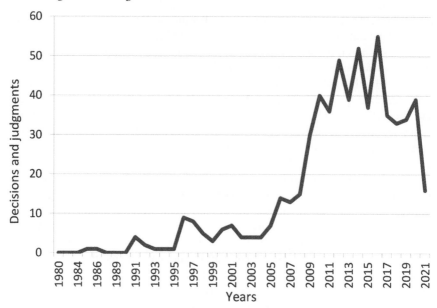

Figure 5.1 ECtHR migrant-related judgments, 1980–2020

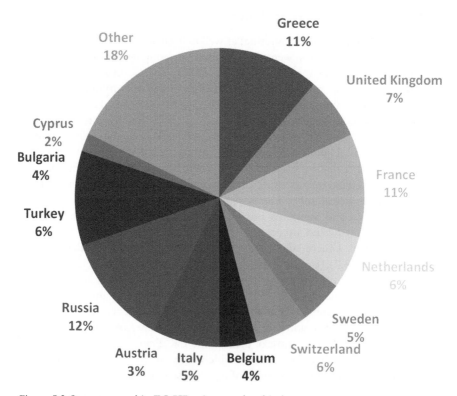

Figure 5.2 States targeted in ECtHR migrant-related judgments

(TCNs),[39] conditions and lawfulness of detention,[40] access to social provisions and jobs,[41] access to remedies and justice,[42] asylum procedure, attempt to prevent removal on grounds of non-refoulement,[43] inhuman treatment by police authorities,[44] the EU asylum law (the Dublin regulation),[45] and a variety of other issues.[46] By far, the largest number of decisions and judgments are related to asylum, removal and non-refoulement, and to the detention and expulsion of legally residing TCNs. Few are the judgments related to access to remedies and justice, social provisions and jobs. Figure 5.3 shows the distribution of migrant-related judgments across issue areas. Migrant-related petitions to the ECtHR are often accompanied by requests to the Court to apply Rule 39 interim measures, mostly in cases pending deportation or expulsion of the applicant(s). If granted, these require a respondent state to refrain from removing an applicant to a country where s/he may be at risk of inhuman and degrading treatment, while the examination of his or her case before the ECtHR is still pending.[47] The ECtHR finds at least one violation in the vast majority of the cases that it reviews on the merits and issues a judgment (75% of all judgments include a least one violation of the Convention), as Figure 5.4 shows.

The large increase in incoming migrants, the diversification of asylum-seekers' outlook, the expansion of restrictive immigration policies across Europe, and the

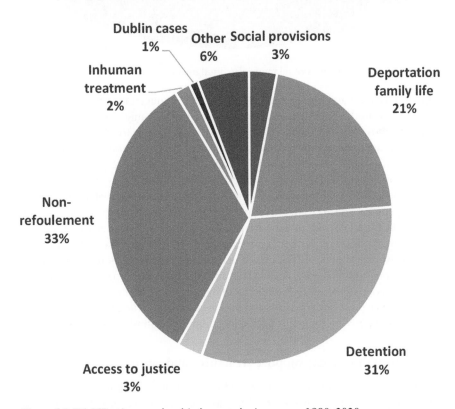

Figure 5.3 ECtHR migrant-related judgments by issue area, 1980–2020

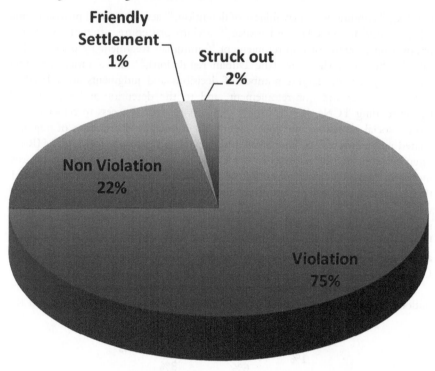

Figure 5.4 Judicial outcomes of migrant-related judgments, 1980–2020

deficient reception and asylum systems of the 'new' immigration countries in south Europe, all form the broader context for the rise of ECHR migrant-related litigation since the 1990s. What enabled increasing numbers of migrants to take recourse to the ECtHR though was an unprecedented expansion of legal support actors and structures from the 1990s onwards in many European countries. These comprised of: a) a proliferation of specialized lawyers with expertise in human rights and immigration law, b) the existence of legal aid schemes, c) a wide variety of civil society actors, including but not limited to migrants' rights organizations, that increasingly engaged in litigation as part of their mobilization strategies, and d) the formation of transnational networks of lawyers and non-governmental organizations that diffused knowledge and awareness of the ECHR. Such networks facilitated the flow of information among lawyers and NGOs across countries and enabled them to coordinate action to support litigation in the ECtHR on behalf of migrants. The next three sections of this chapter analyze these developments and how legal support structures and actors were critical for the growth of migrant-related litigation in the Strasbourg Court.

3 The growth of legal support structures and actors

The growth of legal support structures and actors in the area of migrants' rights in many European countries, was instrumental for their ability to engage in proceedings before domestic courts and increasingly in the ECtHR. In the first place, legal actors comprised an expanding cohort of practicing lawyers in different European countries, with knowledge of the ECHR and its potential relevance for migrants' issues. The availability of affordable and qualified legal expertise and representation provided applicants who were non-nationals with support and guidance to take legal proceedings before domestic courts and subsequently to file a complaint in the ECtHR. They were crucial from the early stages in enabling vulnerable or disadvantaged individuals, such as non-nationals, to attain a merits-based review in the Convention system.[48] Data shows that a very high percentage of migrant-related petitions (as of ECHR petitions overall) are rejected as inadmissible (as ECtHR complaints more broadly).[49] Petitions that were deposited without support from a lawyer familiar with the procedure before the Strasbourg Court and the relevant case law, were far more likely to fail to pass the admissibility stage.[50]

In the bulk of ECtHR migrant-related judgments in our dataset (in three out of four cases), applicants were represented by lawyers alone without apparent involvement of any organization or institution, as data presented in the next section shows. Lawyers took up cases and framed human rights claims to challenge deportation on non-refoulement grounds,[51] including in landmark cases (*Chahal*), or on grounds of the right to family life,[52] or conditions and lawfulness of detention,[53] and collective expulsion,[54] among others. They compellingly depicted the physical abuse suffered by a non-national while in police custody as tantamount to torture;[55] they framed the deportation of non-nationals as detrimental to the best interest of their children,[56] or unacceptable in view of the applicant's long period of residence, schooling and family life in France.[57] Lawyers also framed a situation of non-paid domestic labor as an instance of trafficking in humans contrary to the prohibition of slavery and forced labor (Article 4 ECHR)[58] and the deportation of a seriously ill non-national with a criminal conviction as a violation of the non-refoulement principle.[59]

Lawyers who represented non-nationals before the ECtHR had different specializations and varying motivations. They identified or came across relevant cases through a variety of channels, prepared the case files and represented the applicants before the ECtHR. They comprised specialists in human rights, international and constitutional law, academics, and professional practitioners in different areas of law (i.e. health, criminal law) who also developed an interest and expertise in immigration law. Many of them were academics, professors of constitutional, human rights or EU law, who maintained a legal practice (as in Greece), and who occasionally or systematically engaged in litigation before the ECtHR (as in the Netherlands or Belgium[60]), including on behalf of migrants. Others were professionals who had their own legal practice, or worked in smaller or larger, and at times prestigious law firms. Some were eager to advance human rights case law and/or to promote their reputation in case of a judicial victory before an international court, with varying commitment to migrants' rights per se.[61] In countries like the UK and the Netherlands, home to an active immigration bar and a strong pro bono tradition, an increasing number of professional lawyers also engaged in international litigation related to migrants and human rights.[62]

An important subsection of lawyers who represented migrants before the ECtHR were motivated by a commitment to advance progressive issues by using law to promote social change. Many of those legal practitioners engaged in rights litigation in the tradition of left-wing cause-lawyering that had its origins in the 1960s and 1970s.[63] In the case of *Amuur v France*, for example, two activist lawyers with expertise in labor law represented the Somali applicants (who obtained legal aid) before the ECtHR. The case was one among a series of similar legal challenges that those two lawyers pursued before the ECtHR, even after they had lost contact with the applicants.[64] Before the Court, *Amuur* challenged the practice of French authorities to detain non-nationals travelling into France in an international zone inside the airport, which the authorities considered extra-territorial (thus, beyond the reach of domestic legal rights guarantees), for long periods of time.[65] In the second half of the 1980s and early 1990s, trade union and migrant rights' associations (such as the newly established ANAFE[66]) had mobilized to challenge this practice. In the Netherlands too, left-wing lawyers established in the 1970s the Legal Aid Working Group on Immigration that trained legal practitioners in migration law and provided legal assistance.[67]

Secondly, legal support structures comprise a proliferation of legal aid schemes catering to migrants in most European countries. Legal aid encompasses legal information and advice, as well as legal assistance and representation.[68] Its availability is indispensable for migrants to take their case through the asylum system, the appeal procedure and the domestic court system. Without it, migrants would be unable to navigate complex procedures related to asylum, appealing against return or detention decisions, and pursuing international rights litigation.[69] Public duty lawyers or lawyers working for NGOs are providers of legal aid to migrants. Legal aid in part comes through state-funded programs that are variably available to migrants and asylum-seekers at first, second or appeal stage in different countries.[70] While they are chronically underfunded or they were cut down (i.e. in the UK after 2012), non-state resources for legal assistance apparently increased since the 1990s. Most European countries have hybrid schemes that combine publicly funded aid schemes with privately funded NGO support.[71]

It is not the levels of public legal aid alone that matter for the growth of ECtHR migrant-related litigation. A large number of human rights complaints and judgments, for instance, originates from Greece that has very limited state-funded legal assistance.[72] Legal aid is mostly available as ad hoc support from NGOs such as the Greek Council of Refugees, Metadrasi and the UNHCR that have sizeable litigation programs. Significantly, legal aid schemes bring many migrants, from early on upon their arrival into a country, into contact with lawyers and NGOs active on migrants' rights. NGOs legal assistance to migrants comes through programs funded by international (such as the UNHCR) and institutional donors (such as the EU's Asylum and Migration Integration Fund, AMIF), and by private foundations like the Open Society Justice Initiative (OSJI), the Open Society Foundations (OSF) and others.[73]

Since the 1990s, an increasing number and a wide variety of non-governmental organizations turned to law and legal tactics to challenge restrictive state policies on asylum and immigration. They pursued litigation before domestic and European courts with the goal of promoting advocacy for migrants' rights – an issue unpopular among electorates at the national level.[74] They were NGOs with a broad human rights agenda or with a specific focus on immigration. National and international human rights organizations[75], migrants' rights organizations[76], including European umbrella organizations assisting refugee NGOs (such as the European Council on Refugees and Exiles, ECRE), and academic, research and public law organizations have all engaged in ECtHR litigation.[77] They also comprise professional associations, like the Immigration Law Practitioners' Association (ILPA) in the UK; membership-based associations of lawyers, academics and consultants focusing on the legal aspects of immigration and migrants' rights like the Association of Juridical on Immigration (ASGI) and the *Unione Forense per la Tutela dei Diritti dell' Uomo* (UFTDU) in Italy; and NGOs that are active service providers to immigrants on the ground, like the Greek Council for Refugees (GRC) and Metadrasi, among many others, in Greece.

In the immigration field, NGOs take a variety of different roles from the early stages of the asylum procedure at the national level, depending on funding and capacity. They provide information on the procedure, assist asylum seekers with questionnaires, conduct country of origin research, attend asylum interviews, and facilitate contacts between asylum seekers and lawyers.[78] A significant contribution of a number of NGOs that is often invisible in human rights litigation, is that they provide pan-European research, they source expert opinions, and engage in training and capacity building.[79] In this way, they indirectly support and facilitate lawyers' work in preparing case files and representing TCNs before the ECtHR. Last but not least, legal support structures include National Human Rights Institutions (ombudsmen, national commissions, etc.) that in some countries were either directly involved in or indirectly supported human rights litigation on behalf of migrants.[80] In Greece, for example, reports by the Greek Ombudsperson based on its handling of large numbers of individual cases often provided rich documentation and legal arguments for lawyers bringing migrant-related cases in the ECtHR.

From the 2000s onwards, legal support structures and migrants' rights lawyering also grew in south European countries like Greece and Italy that had lacked a public law tradition. Repeat migrant-related litigation targeting these countries in the ECtHR did not arise until a relatively small but committed number of professional and activist lawyers began to engage in it. In Greece, from 2008–2009 onwards, a group of lawyers with a progressive and/or leftist orientation began to systematically bring migrant-related complaints before domestic courts and in the Strasbourg Court to challenge restrictive immigration detention practices and highly deficient asylum procedures.[81] A small number of NGOs also assisted migrants to engage in legal proceedings. In the case of *Horshill v Greece* (2013), for example, the NGO "Aitima" (meaning "claim") supported the applicant before domestic courts. It did so with resources from a legal aid program that was part of a larger action funded by the European Refugee Fund with the aim of informing refugees about their rights and of providing them with legal assistance.[82] An activist immigration lawyer subsequently represented the applicant before the ECtHR. NGOs like the Greek Council for Refugees (GCR) regularly brought into contact lawyers with non-nationals who were in reception centers or in detention.

The legal support structures that enabled and drove the rise in ECtHR migrant-related litigation flourished not only at the national but also at the transnational level. Many of the engaged NGOs, lawyers and lawyers' groups in different European countries participate in transnational European networks. The oldest and most important one in this area is the European Legal Network on Asylum (ELENA) that is run by the European Council on Refugees and Exiles (ECRE) in Brussels. As early as 1989, the Swedish lawyers, members of ELENA, brought to the ECHR system the landmark case of *Cruz Varas and others v Sweden* that concerned the interpretation of the non-refoulement principle under Article 3 ECHR. The ELENA network and its members across countries became increasingly involved in strategic litigation, alongside advocacy. Their broader strategic objective is to push for reforming national and European legislation and practices that are in breach of international human rights standards.

The ELENA network spans across thirty-three European countries. It comprises experienced legal practitioners, NGOs, academics and legal officers in ECRE member organizations, both formal legal entities and informal networks of legal practitioners. ELENA supports migrant- and asylum-related litigation at the national and European level by providing a nodal point for the exchange of information (including case specific information), for advice, and mobilization. Its legal updates inform lawyers and organizations supporting refugees, of recent developments in the field of asylum law. ELENA also facilitates cross-national learning (i.e. on national schemes and practices regarding the provision of legal aid) and collaboration among NGOs and practitioners.

From the 2000s onwards, the ELENA network supported Greek and Italian NGOs and lawyers to engage in litigation and advocacy to push for the reform of highly deficient asylum systems in the two countries.[83] Through the cross-national exchange of information and cooperation promoted by ELENA, NGOs and lawyers from different countries were also able to build a factual basis for coordinated legal challenges of Dublin transfers to Greece, Hungary and Italy, and to support domestic litigation on detention pending removal in Poland and Greece. Over the past twenty-five years, ELENA also conducted numerous trainings of lawyers on European and international asylum law.[84]

Transnational legal support structures also include a number of international human rights organizations like Amnesty International and Human Rights Watch. While they rarely provide legal representation to applicants, they nonetheless contribute in a diffused, indirect, and profoundly significant way to ECtHR migrant-related litigation through their broader human rights work. They do so by furnishing vital documentation, factual and country-specific information and expertise, often in the form of reports, from which the Court draws in examining the applicants' claims. This is all the more important considering the limited means that the ECtHR has to establish the facts of cases on its own.[85] Notably, one-third of all ECtHR migrant-related judgments made reference to and relayed findings of such human rights reports. In preparing their case and argumentation, lawyers also rely on such reports to substantiate applicants' claims.[86] In some cases, international human rights organizations wrote letters to the Court to back up applicants' claims against their deportation on non-refoulement grounds, or to document appalling detention conditions.[87] The next section examines the involvement of NGOs and lawyers in ECtHR strategic litigation related to immigrants.

4 Civil society strategies in the Strasbourg Court

NGOs and other non-governmental actors mostly engage in human rights litigation related to migrants from a strategic perspective. By taking a case to the Strasbourg Court, NGOs may seek to expose deficiencies in national laws and state practices from a human rights point of view, to support migrants' rights advocacy and to pressure governments to undertake rights-expansive reforms. Migrant-related cases come about in a variety of different ways to strategic litigators. Frequently, their strategic litigation efforts are embedded in a broader long-term strategy, stretching over a period of years. But the strategic value of a case is not always possible to determine at the outset on the basis of certain set criteria.[88] Interested NGOs may look for a case to take to the ECtHR with specific characteristics that allows them to challenge a national law or practice, and they contact a lawyer when such a case emerges.[89] Alternatively, they may get involved in cases at different stages of the process before the ECtHR.

Complaints may start off as individual rather than as test cases and their significance for broader legal and policy issues may become apparent later or retroactively. An experienced litigator acknowledges that "the vast majority of strategic cases come about because the lawyer has the ability to spot the strategic issue in a case and take it forward in a way that obtains the desired result".[90] Immigration lawyers and specialists are often well-aware how intensely political is immigration law. They can readily discern the strategic value of a case. For example, cases like *Saadi v Italy* that challenged the deportation of an individual suspected of involvement in terrorism, and *Hirsi Jamaa v Italy* concerning pushbacks at high sea, raised issues around which there was strong political contestation and NGO mobilization. Those cases were identified and initially handled by individual lawyers, who were well aware of the wider contested issues at stake.[91] NGOs, academics and the UNHCR became involved at a later stage when those cases were referred to the Court for a review on the merits.

The involvement of civil society actors in proceedings before the ECtHR is multifaceted and takes various forms. In the first place, NGOs act as applicants, which, however, is rare given the difficulty of meeting the ECHR "victim" requirement.[92] Secondly, NGOs provide direct support to applicants to bring a complaint before the ECtHR. They help formulate the specific issues and grievances into human rights claims, prepare their case file, and provide them with legal representation before the Court through in-house lawyers or in cooperation with lawyers from outside of the organization.

NGOs that provide such full-scale support, a kind of involvement that is often resource intensive, are relatively few, experienced and knowledgeable of the ECHR system. They do so in selected cases, in which they have an interest in the issues that are at stake, and which they believe have strong merit to be admissible.[93] NGOs find out about such cases mostly through contacts with lawyers, migrants' groups and other organizations. The AIRE Center is a well-known example of a highly active NGO that has systematically engaged in European rights litigation in such a holistic manner in cases involving vulnerable individuals and groups, including migrants, asylum seekers and refugees. Over the past twenty five years, it has taken a large number of cases to the ECtHR challenging the deportation of migrants on grounds of family life or the non-refoulement principle, in the UK and in other countries.[94] Other legally oriented, migrants' rights, human rights or issue specific NGOs, like Liberty, Redress (Seeking Reparation for Torture Survivors) the Greek Helsinki Monitor, and Service d' Aide Juridique aux Exiles (SAJE) have litigated cases in the ECtHR less systematically or only occasionally.[95]

A third and preeminently strategic kind of NGO involvement in migrant-related ECHR litigation is to make a Third-Party Intervention (TPI). TPI takes place in 15% of migrant-related judgments delivered by the Court. Twelve percent of the relevant amicus briefs are submitted by civil society actors, mostly by NGOs (see Figure 5.5). NGOs act as TPIs in a relatively small number of ECtHR migrant-related judgments. This might seem surprising, considering that the Court is generally permissive in allowing for third parties to make submissions to cases that it reviews on the merits.[96] The level of NGO engagement as third parties in migrant-related judgments though is still much higher than it is in the ECtHR litigation overall (which is reported in less than 1% of all cases).[97] In several cases NGOs coordinate their submissions or prepare a joint submission.[98]

TPIs are more frequent in migrant-related cases from the UK and the Netherlands (36.3% of all TPIs are in cases targeting these two countries). A number of UK-based NGOs are repeat players in TPI before the ECtHR in cases targeting not only the UK but also other countries: Amnesty International, Liberty, Justice, AIRE Center and Interrights. A much smaller number of amicus briefs is submitted by state governments (the UK, Netherlands, but also Belgium, Germany, Lithuania, Slovenia), international organizations (i.e. UN Committee against Torture, UN High Commissioners for Refugees, Council of Europe Commissioner for Human Rights) and occasionally by national human rights and equality bodies (i.e. the UK's Equality and Human Rights Commission).

One reason that TPIs takes place in a relatively small number of judgments is that third party submissions require expertise and investment of time. They are

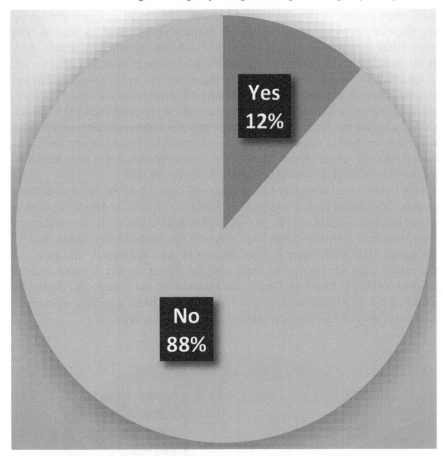

Figure 5.5 NGOs as TPIs in ECtHR migrant-related judgments, 1980–2020

attractive because they allow a human rights organization or other civil society actors to address legal points, advance principles, and make the Court aware of the importance of an issue, without engaging in full-scale litigation, which is often far more resource demanding. Besides providing specialized and technical knowledge to the Court, TPIs can present innovative and 'risky' arguments that a party in proceedings may not wish to raise.[99] When a case that is referred to the Court for a review on the merits attracts multiple TPIs (NGOs and others), its legal and political weight usually increases.

As TPIs, NGOs have argued against the detention, even brief, of asylum seekers whilst their claims are being processed[100], and that under EU law asylum seekers have the right to judicial review of their detention[101]; they have highlighted the inadequacy and uncertainty surrounding the extent of Council of Europe states' obligations to protect victims of human trafficking[102]; they have documented the deficient and superficial review process of asylum claims by national authorities at the French border[103]; they have advanced non-refoulement as a principle having the status of a peremptory, non-derogable norm of international law binding even upon states that are not a party to any international agreement; and they have challenged diplomatic assurances as insufficient to offset an existing risk of torture in the country where an individual is to be deported, even in cases entailing national security concerns and suspicion for applicants' involvement in terrorism.[104] NGOs also argued that the lack of a suspensive appeal against expulsion measures in French Guiana allowed the authorities to routinely expel non-nationals without any legal safeguards and judicial oversight, which caused serious infringements on their fundamental rights.[105] These are only some of the arguments advanced in third party submissions by NGOs in migrant-related cases before the ECtHR.

NGO mobilization in migrant-related judgments issued by the ECtHR is higher if we consider other forms of their engagement. NGOs are involved in 23% of all migrant-related judgments, acting as TPIs, providing organizational support to the applicant, or being associated with the lawyer who represents the applicant (see Figure 5.6).[106] Altogether, their involvement is most frequent in non-refoulement, detention and deportation cases (see Figure 5.6). States with the highest number of migrant-related judgments (United Kingdom, Greece, the Netherlands, and France) also display the most frequent NGO involvement in the respective legal claims, suggesting a close connection between civil society participation and human rights litigation.

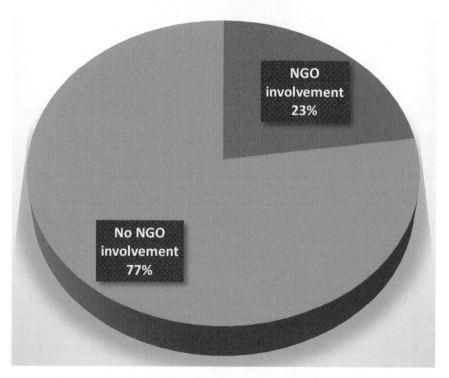

Figure 5.6 NGO involvement in ECtHR migrant-related judgments, 1980–2020

Civil society involvement was a critical factor behind the rise of ECtHR migrant-related cases since the 1990s. The case law data compiled for this study shows that the upward evolution of migrant-related judgments issued by the Court since the 1990s follows a trend parallel to the growth of civil society involvement (see Figure 5.7). At the same time, NGOs clearly do not dominate migrant-related litigation; most related cases are brought to the ECtHR without any organizational support of any kind, as we saw above. In the light of this, how do we understand the parallel and upward trend in migrant-related Court judgments and civil society involvement since the 1990s?

Even though civil society actors are involved in a relatively small number of ECtHR migrant-related judgments, their weight and potential impact is much greater. Their involvement tends to be concentrated in those cases that are classified as high importance, namely cases that are innovative and raise new legal issues. NGOs are involved in 65% of high importance cases (those published in case reports and Level 1 judgments), but only in 35% of low importance cases (Levels 2 and 3, that is the repetitive cases, see Figure 5.8). NGOs' interventions as third parties also tend to be concentrated in migrant-related cases that are referred to the Grand Chamber for a final judgment. More than half of Grand Chamber judgments (57%) have at least one amicus curiae, while less than 10% of judgments issued by a section of the Court have NGO third party submissions.

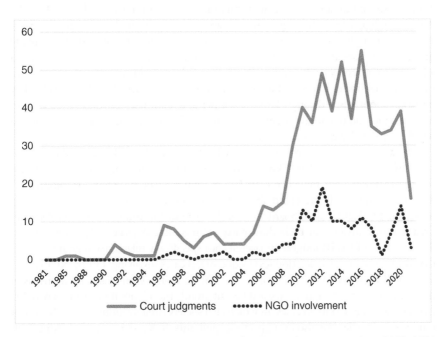

Figure 5.7 ECtHR migrant-related judgments and NGO involvement over time, 1980–2020

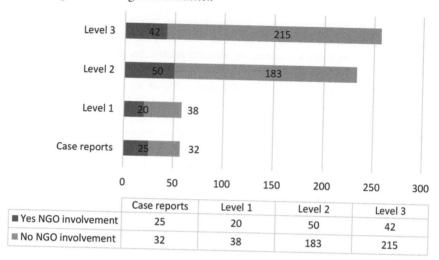

Figure 5.8 NGO involvement in ECtHR migrant-related judgments by level of importance, 1980–2020

NGOs specifically look for and are eager to intervene in high impact cases that
push forward the jurisprudence of the ECtHR. The decision by a civil society
entity to submit an amicus brief in a migrant-related case reviewed by the ECtHR
is commonly made at the stage when a case is communicated to the government,
and it is a highly strategic one. NGOs active in the ECHR system regularly
monitor the cases that are communicated to governments and have already been
admitted for a review on the merits. They request leave to intervene as third parties in
cases that raise issues that are of interest and a priority for them.[107] Alternatively, they
find out about cases through lawyers, formal and informal networks, who contact
human rights and public law organizations and notify them about an upcoming case, in
which they may have an interest in intervening.[108]

Scholars have debated the influence of NGOs in the ECHR and on the Court's
case law. Some argue that NGOs have a potentially significant impact,[109] others
though consider their influence over Court rulings to be moderate or minimal.[110]
The data of this study presented above does not show anything about the extent to
which the ECtHR takes on board and is influenced by the arguments that civil society
organizations advance in their third-party submissions. A large-scale study by Van
den Eynde on ECtHR judgments overall (not specifically related to migrants) argues
that the Court found a violation less frequently in cases involving TPI by NGOs than
in cases without NGOs as third parties.[111] The data of migrant-related judgments in
the present study though shows a different trend: the Court finds a human rights
violation at a higher rate in cases, in which civil society organizations are involved (not
only as third parties but also in supporting applicants; 87%), than in cases lacking such
involvement (75%).

Civil society activism, this study argues, has a central role in the legal support
structures and actors that drive migrant-related human rights litigation. While

non-governmental actors do not drive the bulk of migrant-related judgments in the ECtHR, they are strategically engaged in the most important cases, as the data presented above suggests. Grand Chamber judgments and high importance cases raise new issues of human rights law and establish the normative principles that the Court applies in a larger number of repeat or related claims.[112] In this sense, the case law that develops in the high importance cases also influences the legal opportunities and constraints for the kinds of rights claims that are subsequently raised before the ECtHR. By predominantly targeting its interventions in such kinds of cases, civil society activism in human rights litigation has a trailblazing quality: it helps shape the legal trends, normative standards, and framing of claims before the ECtHR.

5 Mobilizing human rights law for domestic structural reform

Structural reform litigation (SRL) is a distinctive kind of strategic legal action that principally attracts civil society engagement. It seeks to condemn national laws and practices that are closely linked to system-wide deficiencies in entire areas of state administration and generate breaches of human rights. A case may be strategically selected to expose system-wide problems in a particular area (i.e. immigration detention). Alternatively, a smaller or larger number of repeat individual complaints lead the Court to find human rights violations, that altogether bring to light a structural problem at the domestic level. Redressing such violations often necessitates far-reaching reforms to change structures and practices in administratively complex areas of state activity, such as immigration and asylum management. NGOs are the main actors who initiate or engage in ECtHR litigation as a tool of pressure for domestic structural reform.[113]

Over the past fifteen years, countries like Greece, Italy, Hungary and others, have been a target of judgments finding violations that stem from systemic deficiencies in migrant reception and asylum systems. Greece and Italy are the main countries of entry for the vast majority of irregular migrants and asylum seekers from Asia and Africa into the EU. In these countries, national judiciaries largely failed to engage in effective and thorough rights review of immigration related rules and practices.[114]

SRL against Greece and Italy in the ECtHR targeted national policies and practices related to immigration and asylum, including those that transposed and applied EU law, primarily the Dublin Regulation rules. In Italy, complaints brought before the ECtHR challenged arbitrary detention practices in the new "hotspots" located at the European borders (i.e. in the island of Lampedusa). In those "hotspots", arriving migrants undergo identification, registration and an initial determination of whether they have a potentially valid claim to international protection. In *Khlaifia and others v Italy*, the ECtHR found that migrants' detention in Early Reception and Aid Centers (*Centri di Soccorso e Prima Accoglienza*) did not meet basic habeas corpus rights, and that it was not subject to judicial review (violation of Article 5 ECHR).[115]

ECtHR litigation also raised human rights issues in the context of bilateral readmission agreements of the Italian government with third countries or transit countries, such as Libya, Tunisia, but also Greece.[116] In those cases, litigators argued that the presumption that these countries are safe for purposes of return, was at odds with the principle of non-refoulement. The informal nature of bilateral agreements, and the expedited returns of arriving migrants (push-backs, often performed on the high seas) that lacked basic procedural guarantees, all raised serious problems from a human rights perspective.[117] In *Sharifi and Others v Italy and Greece*, the ECtHR found that the applicants' automatic and indiscriminate expulsion by Italian border authorities to Greece, without providing them access to legal information and assistance regarding the asylum procedure, contravened the prohibition of collective expulsion (Article 4, Protocol 4 ECHR) and the principle of non-refoulement (Article 3 and 13 ECHR). It also condemned Greece on account of systemic deficiencies that obstructed the applicants' access to an effective asylum procedure (violation of Article 3 and 13 ECHR).

The cases described above raised wider and strongly contested issues in Italy's immigration and asylum management and attracted a high level of civil society engagement. A few experienced human rights' lawyers initially identified the cases through their contacts in Italy and abroad. Being were well-aware of the wider political and policy issues involved, they made contact with NGOs working on these issues. A number of NGOs (with national and transnational activity) and international bodies (mainly the UNHCR) provided documentation and information, and they also intervened as third parties before the Court. In *Sharifi*, the Special Rapporteur of the UN Human Rights Council and the Council of Europe Commissioner for Human Rights had already expressed concern about the automatic returns from Italy to Greece without any safeguards for the persons concerned. The ECtHR judgment referred to their reports. In their TPIs, NGOs like the AIRE Center and Amnesty International, and the UNHCR, strongly argued that such returns in the frame of the Italy-Greece 1999 readmission agreement lacked basic safeguards and violated non-refoulement. Their mobilization, along with the involvement of other civil society actors, such as the Association for Juridical Studies on Immigration (ASGI), would continue in the judgment implementation phase.

In the 2000s, concern was mounting among human rights and migrants' rights organizations about the asylum conditions in member states at the EU border, and the extent to which they guaranteed basic human rights standards. By virtue of their geographical position and EU law, Greece and Italy bore the brunt of most asylum claims by incomers. The EU's Dublin Regulation, assigns primary responsibility to state of first entry for processing asylum applications.[118] Lawyers and NGOs active on migrants' rights began to use litigation before national and European courts to challenge deficient asylum procedures in Greece by invoking non-refoulement and other human rights principles. By extension, they also challenged the presumption embedded in the Dublin Regulation that all EU Member States were "safe" for Dublin returns, namely, returns to the country where an asylum seeker first made his/her entry into the EU – largely Greece, and secondarily Italy. By doing so, the relevant court cases became directly entangled in highly contested issues and inter-state disagreements over the EU's asylum policy.

Extensive transnational contacts among human rights and migrants' rights organizations across Europe enabled them to identify cases and to build a factual basis for advancing related legal challenges. In 2006–2007, international organizations like the UNHCR and NGOs – Amnesty International, the Norwegian Helsinki Committee, Pro Asyl, and others – already provided documentation that attested to the poor living and detention conditions of those seeking international protection in Greece. In view of the extremely small chances that asylum applicants had in being granted international protection, they urged EU member states to suspend Dublin transfers to Greece.[119] Meanwhile, thousands of asylum seekers from different European countries were filing petitions to the ECtHR for interim measures in order to suspend their imminent return to Greece.[120] Several cases were also brought to the ECtHR to challenge deficiencies in domestic asylum systems related to reception conditions, the application procedure, and detention practices, among others. They mostly targeted Greece and Italy.

By challenging national reception and asylum systems, the "Dublin" string of human rights litigation sought to intensify pressure for domestic structural reform in countries like Greece, and indirectly, for change in EU asylum law. In one of the first related petitions to the ECtHR in 2008, *K.R.S. v UK*[121], the Court decided that procedural safeguards and evidence of non-removal to third countries were sufficient to render Greece "safe", despite strong evidence submitted by the UNHCR and human rights organizations to the contrary.[122] As the ECtHR issued an inadmissibility decision (instead of judgment of no violation), human rights organizations and NGOs active on the Dublin issue, such as the UNHCR, ECRE, ICJ and Amnesty International did not have the opportunity to express their views before the Court.[123] While the ECtHR was apparently reluctant to give due weight to the wealth of documentation on the poor asylum conditions in Greece, some governments, such as in Denmark, Iceland and Luxembourg, proceeded to suspend Dublin transfers to Greece.[124]

At the same time, the disappointment that the *K.R.S.* decision created, fueled into the determination of engaged lawyers, NGOs and advocacy groups in the UK and elsewhere to bring another case before European courts.[125] It was in this context of widespread NGO mobilization at the national and European level that the landmark *M.S.S. v Belgium and Greece* case emerged and prompted the ECtHR to revisit its position in the *K.R.S.* In its 2011 judgment in *M.S.S v Greece and Belgium*, the ECtHR found Greece in violation of the Convention on account of its seriously dysfunctional asylum system, but also Belgium for returning back the applicant to Greece. The substantial effects of this judgment at the national and EU level are discussed in detail in chapter 7.

6 Concluding discussion

The rise of ECtHR migrant-related litigation since the 1990s was directly linked to and made possible by the emergence of legal support actors and structures in an increasing number of European countries and transnationally. In the first place, legal support actors and structures comprised a proliferation of qualified human rights and immigration lawyers of diverse profiles and motivations (professionals in different areas, academics, cause lawyers). The turning point was in the 1980s when a relatively small number of human rights lawyers and mostly UK-based NGOs seized international legal opportunities, such as direct access to the ECtHR and the possibility for TPI, to bring cases and advance innovative human rights claims. The milestone judgments issued by the Court made the Convention relevant for migrants and asylum seekers, and further expanded legal opportunities for human rights litigation in this area. In the 1990s and the 2000s, legal support actors and structures in the area of migrants' rights rapidly grew across Europe.

While the vast majority of migrant-related complaints in the ECtHR were brought by individual lawyers, a wide variety of non-governmental organizations were critical actors behind a smaller number of strategic and high importance judgments. They included local community organizations, human rights, issue-specific organizations and migrants' rights associations, variably connected or not necessarily connected with each other. What they had in common is that they increasingly incorporated legal and human rights strategies in their repertoire of action. Funding from public legal aid programs and from private foundations enabled lawyers and NGOs to engage systematically in international rights litigation on behalf of migrants. Last but not least, a variety of national human rights institutions, international bodies, and non-governmental human rights organizations critically contributed to migrant-related human rights litigation by supplying indispensable factual information and country-specific documentation.

Legal support actors and structures played an indispensable role in rendering the ECHR system accessible to large numbers of migrants and asylum seekers. They identified and framed a diverse array of issues related to deportation, detention, asylum procedure into human rights claims that resonated and at times sought to advance existing case law; they transferred expertise in and knowledge of the ECHR system to lawyers and organizations in more European countries; they provided legal expertise, resources and organizational capacity to TCNs claiming state violation of their rights; and they exchanged information and coordinated legal action across countries and between the national and European level. NGOs also variably mobilized advocacy and pressure for reforms in immigration and asylum laws and policies. Since the 2000s, legal support actors and structures saw an unprecedented expansion through the establishment of transnational networks of lawyers, experts and NGOs.

A key offshoot of systematic non-governmental engagement in the ECtHR has been the growth of structural reform litigation (SRL), in the areas of immigration and asylum. It specifically targets human rights violations of a structural nature that emanate from defective rules and practices that are at odds with basic rights guarantees. The ECHR's encounter with structural human rights problems has posed far-reaching challenges to the Court's judicial review, and to the supervisory mechanism that oversees state implementation of adverse judgments. In order to redress systemic human rights violations, national authorities must implement domestic changes in state policies, administrative structures, and practices.

In this context, over the past twenty years, the ECHR supervisory system has undergone far-reaching changes with a view to exercising more effectively its oversight over domestic human rights reform. Following the 2006 rules of the CoM, many of the NGOs and international bodies that engaged in ECtHR litigation have extended their mobilization efforts in the judgment implementation phase too. Chapter 7 examines the domestic implementation of migrant-related judgments involving structural human rights problems and the increasing engagement of civil society actors in it. It argues that their expanded and systematic participation transforms the ECHR into a regime of experimentalist governance.

Notes

1   Antônio Augusto Cançado Trindade, *The Access of Individuals to International Justice* (Oxford: Oxford University Press, 2015), 133.
2   The Geneva Convention was designed to provide a legal status for those persons who found themselves outside their country of nationality or habitual residence and who feared prosecution as a consequence of "events occurring in Europe before 1 January 1951." Nuala Mole and Catherine Meredith, *Asylum and the ECHR*, Human Rights files No. 9 (Strasbourg: Council of Europe Publishing, 2010), 10.
3   Throughout the text, I use the term "migrants" generically to refer to all categories of third country nationals, including asylum seekers.
4   See Pauline GJ Maillet, "Exclusion From Rights Through Extra-Territoriality at Home: The Case of Paris Roissy-Charles De Gaulle Airport's Waiting Zone" (PhD Thesis, Wilfrid Laurier University, 2017), http://scholars.wlu.ca/etd/1908; Virginia Passalacqua, "Legal Mobilization and the Judicial Construction of EU Migration Law" (PhD thesis, EUI Florence, 2020).
5   Rachel A. Cichowski, "The European Court of Human Rights, Amicus Curiae, and Violence against Women," *Law and Society Review* 50, no. 4 (2016): 890–919; Lisa Conant, "Who Files Suit? Legal Mobilization and Torture Violations in Europe," *Law and Policy* 38, no. 4 (2016): 280–303.
6   For an overview of the discussions that took place during the Funchal Colloquy, see Marie-Benedicte Dembour, *When Humans Become Migrants: Study of the European Court of Human Rights with an Inter-American Counterpoint* (Oxford University Press, 2015), 156–158.
7   In the Funchal Colloquy, it was reported that in 1982 alone, 156 applications had been filed by foreigners (out of a total of 590 applications lodged with the Commission). See Dembour, *When Humans Become Migrants*, 158.
8   See Wolfgang Strasser, "Intervention by Mr. Wolfgang Strasser," in *Proceedings of the 2nd Colloquy on the European Court of Human Rights and the protection of refugees, asylum-seekers and displaced persons* (Strasbourg: Council of Europe Publishing, 19–20 May 2000), 47–49.
9   See for example, the following cases reviewed by the ECommHR: *Harabi v Netherlands* (dec.), no. 10798/84, 5 March 1986; *Lamraoui v the Netherlands* (dec.), no. 12180/86, 3 September 1991; *Hoodehe v UK* (dec.), no. 12492/86, 11 October 1988; *Zarrabi v UK* (dec.), no. 14458/88, 7 September 1989; *Rasu v the Netherlands* (dec.), no. 15902/89, 9 October 1990, among others.
10   *Abdulaziz, Cabales and Balkandali v UK*, nos. 9214/80, 9473/81, 9474/81, 28 May 1985.
11   See Donald Wilson Jackson, *The United Kingdom Confronts the ECHR* (Gainesville: University Press of Florida, 1997), 92–93.

12 See *Abdulaziz, Cabales and Balkandali v UK*, nos. 9214/80, 9473/81, 9474/81, 28 May 1985, § 59–60.

13 As early as the 1960s, the ECommHR had recognized the relevance of Article 3 for cases of extradition and expulsion. See the Commission's decision in *X. v Belgium* (dec.), no. 984/61, 29 May 1961; see also *X v Federal Republic of Germany*, no. 1802/62, 26 March 1963. Interestingly, in *Soering v the UK*, no. 14038/88, 7 July 1989, the ECommHR was highly divided, and rejected that in the particular circumstances of the case extradition in the USA would constitute violation of Article 3. Despite this favorable decision, the UK government still referred the case to the Court, in the hope of seeing a clear rejection of the broader legal principle of non-refoulement. See Dembour, *When Humans Become Migrants*, 203.

14 *Soering v the UK*, no.14038/88, 7 July 1989, § 101–102.

15 In the small number of third-party submissions before the ECtHR from 1983 until 1998, AI was one of the five most active NGOs engaging as amicus curiae, in cases mostly related to Article 3 ECHR. See Anna-Karin Lindblom, *Non-Governmental Organisations in International Law* (Cambridge: Cambridge University Press, 2005), 330–331.

16 The availability of funding from large philanthropic foundations, such as the Ford Foundation, for legally-oriented strategies reinforced increased professionalization among human rights organizations from the late 1970s onwards. See Yves Dezalay and Bryant Garth, "From the Cold War to Kosovo: The Rise and Renewal of the Field of International Human Rights," *Annual Review of Law and Social Science* 2 (2006): 243, 236–7.

17 Deen Zagorac, "International and Courts and Compliance Bodies: The Experience of Amnesty International," in *Civil Society, International Courts and Compliance Bodies*, eds. Tullio Treves, Marco Frigessi di Rattalma and others (The Hague: Asser Press, 2005), 38; Ann Marie Clark, *Diplomacy of Conscience – Amnesty International and Changing Human Rights Norms* (Princeton: Princeton University Press, 2001), 108–109.

18 Lindblom, *Non-Governmental Organisations in International Law*, 340–341.

19 Indicatively, see Susanne Zühlke and Jens-Christian Pastille, "Extradition and the European Convention - Soering Revisited," *Heidelberg Journal of International Law* 59, no.3 (1999): 750–784; Hemme Battjes, "Landmarks: Soering's Legacy," *Amsterdam Law Forum* 1, no. 1 (2008): 139–149.

20 *Soering v the UK*, no.14038/88, 7 July 1989, cited in Battjes, "Landmarks: Soering's legacy," 142.

21 Zühlke and Pastille, "Extradition and the European Convention - *Soering* Revisited," 750–751.

22 Charles Epp, *The Rights Revolution* (Chicago: The University of Chicago Press, 1998), 113 and 141.

23 Carol Harlow and Richard Rawlings, *Pressure Through Law* (London: Routledge, 1992), 248–250.

24 Mikael Rask Madsen, "France, the UK, and the 'Boomerang' of the Internationalisation of Human Rights (1945–2000)," in *Human Rights Brought Home: Socio-Legal Perspectives on Human Rights in the National Context*, eds. Simon Halliday and Patrick Schmidt (Oxford: Hart Publishing, 2004), 79.

25 *Vilvarajah and Others v UK*, nos. 13163/87, 13164/87, 13165/87, 13447/87, 13448/87, 30 October 1991. See also *Vijayanathan &. Pusparajah v France*, nos. 17550/90 and 17825/91, 27 August 1992.

26 Lindblom, *Non-Governmental Organisations in International Law*, 334–336.

27 Erik Larson, Wibo van Rossum and Patrick Schmidt, "The Dutch Confession: Compliance, Leadership and National Identity in the Human Rights Order," *Utrecht Law Review* 10, no. 1 (2014): 104.

28 *Berrehab v Netherlands*, no. 10730/84, 28 May 1988.

29 Larson, van Rossum and Schmidt, "The Dutch Confession," 104.

30 They were fast-tracked despite the fact that the Dutch authorities had in the meantime issued a residence permit to the applicant. See Dembour, *When Humans Become Migrants*, 171.

31 Larson, van Rossum and Schmidt, "The Dutch Confession," 105–106.

32 For the rise of human rights lawyering in the Netherlands, see Larson, van Rossum and Schmidt, "The Dutch Confession," 104. See also Wibo Van Rossum, "The roots of Dutch strategic human rights litigation: comparing 'Engel' to 'SGP'," in *Equality and human rights: nothing but trouble? Liber Amicorum SIM Special 38*, eds. Titia Loenen, Marjolein van den Brink, Susanne Burri, Jenny Goldschmidt (Utrecht: SIM/ Universiteit Utrecht, 2015), 387–399.

33 Mikael Rask Madsen, "France, the UK, and the 'Boomerang' of the Internationalisation of Human Rights (1945–2000)," in *Human Rights Brought Home: Socio-Legal Perspectives on Human Rights in the National Context*, eds. Simon Halliday and Patrick Schmidt (Oxford: Hart Publishing, 2004), 74–75.

34 Madsen, "France, the UK, and the 'Boomerang' of the Internationalisation of Human Rights,"76–78. For an analysis of those social and legal developments since the 1970s, see also Liora Israel, "Rights on the Left? Social Movements, Law and Lawyers after 1968 in France," in *Rights and Courts in Pursuit of Social Change*, ed. Dia Anagnostou (Oxford: Hart Publishing, 2014), 79–103.

35 Madsen, "France, the UK, and the 'Boomerang' of the Internationalisation of Human Rights," 74–75.

36 Strasser, *Proceedings of the 2nd Colloquy on the European Court of Human Rights and the protection of refugees, asylum-seekers and displaced persons*, 49.

37 See *Cruz Varas and Others v Sweden*, no. 15576/89, 20 March 1991.

38 The applicants' nationalities are: Afghans, Albanians (nearly all of them were migrants in Greece), Moroccans, Tunisians and Algerians (many of them from France), Iranians (residing in different European countries, mostly Greece and Turkey, but also the UK, Sweden, Denmark and the Netherlands), Somalis (migrants in the Netherlands, the UK, Sweden, Italy and Greece), Turks (Netherlands, Austria, Sweden, Greece, a number of them of Kurdish origin), Iraqis and Syrians (Greece, Sweden, Turkey, Italy) and Sri Lankans (mainly from the UK, Denmark, Belgium and France).

39 *Omojudi v UK*, no. 1820/08, 24 November 2009; *A.A. v UK*, no. 8000/08, 20 September 2011; *Antwi and Others v Norway*, no. 26940/10, 14 February 2012; *Boultif v Switzerland*, no. 54273/00, 2 August 2001; *Üner v the Netherlands*, no. 46410/99, 18 October 2006; *Udeh v Switzerland*, no. 12020/09, 16 April 2013.

40 *Dougoz v Greece*, no. 40907/98, 6 June 2001; *S.D. v Greece*, no. 53541/07, 11 June 2009; *A.A. v Greece*, no. 12186/08, 22 July 2010; *R U v Greece*, no. 2237/08, 7 June 2011; *A.F. v Greece*, no. 53709/11, 13 June 2013; *Horshill v Greece*, no. 70427/11, 1 August 2013; *Mahammad and Others v Greece*, no. 48352/12, 15 January 2015.

41 *Siladin v France*, no. 73316/01, 26 July 2005; *Bigaeva v Greece*, no. 26713/05, 28 May 2009; *Gaygusuz v Austria*, no. 17371/90, 16 September 1996; *Koua Poirrez v France*, no. 40892/98, 30 September 2003.

42 *Twalib v Greece*, no. 24294/94, 9 June 1998; *Biba v Greece*, no. 33170/96, 26 September 2000; *Sajtos v Greece*, no. 53478/99, 21 March 2002; *Papa v Greece*, no. 21091/04, 6 July 2006; *G.R. v Netherlands*, no. 22251/07, 10 January 2012; *I.M. v France*, no. 9152/09, 2 February 2012; *A.C. and Others v Spain*, no. 6528/11, 22 April 2014.

43 *Mannai v Italy*, no. 9961/10, 27 March 2012; *Makhmudzhan Ergashev v Russia*, no. 49747/11, 16 October 2012; *M.E. v France*, no. 50094/10, 6 June 2013; *S.F. and Others v Sweden*, no. 52077/10, 15 May 2012; *Sufi and Elmi v UK*, nos. 8319/07 and 11449/07, 28 June 2011; *Ammari v Sweden*, no. 60959/00, 22 October 2002; *D.N.M. v Sweden*, no. 28379/11 and *S.A. v Sweden*, no. 66523/10, 27 June 2013, among many others.

44   *Alsayed Allaham v Greece*, no. 25771/03, 18 January 2007; *Zontul v Greece*, no. 12294/07, 17 January 2012.

45   *T.I. v UK* (dec.), no. 43844/98, 7 March 2000; *K.R.S. v UK* (dec.), no. 32733/08, 2 December 2008; *M.S.S. v Greece and Belgium*, no. 30696/09, 21 January 2011; *Mohammed v Austria*, no. 2283/12, 6 June 2013; *Tarakhel v Switzerland*, no. 29217/12, 4 November 2014; *Halimi v Austria and Italy* (dec.), no. 53852/11, 18 June 2013.

46   *Rantsev v Cyprus and Russia*, no. 25965/04, 7 January 2010; *Siladin v France*, no. 73316/01, 26 July 2005; *Omweynyeke v Germany* (dec.), no. 44294/04, 20 November 2007; *Sharifi and Others v Greece and Italy*, no. 16643/09, 21 October 2014; *Alibaks and Others v Netherlands* (dec.), no. 14209/88, 16 December 1988.

47   European Legal Network on Asylum (ELENA) and European Council on Refugees and Exiles (ECRE), *Research of Rule 39 ECHR Interim Measures* (April 2012), 8.

48   See Dembour, *When Humans Become Migrants*, 232.

49   About 45% (429) of the total number of petitions against the UK (955), which were rejected as inadmissible in 2011, were brought by non-nationals challenging their deportation or removal from the United Kingdom. See Paul Harvey, "Is Strasbourg obsessively interventionist? A view from the Court" *UK Human Rights Blog* (blog), 24 January 2012, http://ukhumanrightsblog.com/2012/01/24/is-strasbourg-ob sessively-interventionist-a-view-from-the-court-paul-harvey/.

50   Grigori Dikov, "The ones that lost: Russian cases rejected at the European Court," *Open Democracy* (blog), 7 December 2009, https://www.opendemocracy.net/ od-russia/grigory-dikov/ones-that-lost-russian-cases-rejected-at-european-court; Lubo-mir Majercik, "The Invisible Majority: The Unsuccessful Applications Against the Czech Republic Before the ECtHR," *CYIL* 1 (2010): 217–222.

51   *Nnyanzi v UK*, no. 21878/06, 8 April 2008; *S.H.H. v UK*, no. 60367/2010, 29 January 2013; *Basnet v UK* (dec.), no. 43136/02, 24 June 2008.

52   *Onur v UK*, no. 27319/07, 17 February 2009; *Balogun v UK*, no. 60286/09, 10 April 2012.

53   *Herman and Serazadishvili v Greece*, Nos. 26418/11 and 45884/11, 24 April 2014.

54   *Khlaifia and others v Italy*, no. 16483/12, 15 December 2016.

55   *Selmouni v France*, no. 25803/94, 28 July 1999.

56   *Nunez v Norway*, no. 55597/09, 28 June 2011; *Rodrigues da Silva and Hoogkamer v Netherlands*, no. 50435/99, 31 January 2006.

57   *Mehemi v France*, no. 25017/94, 26 September 1997.

58   *Siliadin v France*, no. 73316/01, 26 October 2005.

59   *D v United Kingdom*, no. 30240/96, 2 May 1997.

60   *Riad and Idiab v Belgium*, nos. 29787/03 29810/03, 24 January 2008.

61   Passalacqua, "Legal Mobilization and the Judicial Construction of EU Migration Law," 115.

62   Passalacqua, "Legal Mobilization and the Judicial Construction of EU Migration Law," 114.

63   Indicative examples are the lawyers in cases like *Turan Cakir v Belgium*, no. 44256/ 06, 10 March 2009; *Selmouni v France*, no. 25803/94, 28 July 1999; *Dougoz v Greece*, no. 40907/98, 6 March 2001.

64   See Maillet, "Exclusion From Rights Through Extra-Territoriality at Home," 75–79.

65   See Maillet, "Exclusion From Rights Through Extra-Territoriality at Home," 24–26.

66   It stands for "Association national d'assistance aux frontières pour les étrangers", which is made up of NGOs and trade union organizations, and it seeks to provide legal and humanitarian assistance to non-nationals in difficulty at French borders.

67   Passalacqua, "Legal Mobilization and the Judicial Construction of EU Migration Law," 166.

68   European Council on Refugees and Exiles (ECRE) and European Legal Network on Asylum (ELENA), *Survey on Legal Aid for Asylum Seekers* (October 2010), 9–10.

69 European Union Agency for Fundamental Rights, *Legal Aid for Returnees Deprived of Liberty* (Luxembourg: Publications Office of the European Union, 2021), 8.

70 See European Council on Refugees and Exiles (ECRE) and European Legal Network on Asylum (ELENA), *Legal Note on Access to Legal Aid in Europe* (November 2017).

71 European Union Agency for Fundamental Rights, *Legal Aid for Returnees Deprived of Liberty*, 18–20.

72 European Union Agency for Fundamental Rights, *Legal Aid for Returnees Deprived of Liberty*, 20.

73 See Gaëtan Cliquennois and Brice Champetier, "The Economic, Judicial and Political Influence Exerted by Private Foundations on Cases Taken by NGOs to the European Court of Human Rights: Inklings of a New Cold War?" *European Law Journal* 22, no. 1 (2016): 92–126. See also Laura Van den Eynde, "An Empirical Look at the Amicus Curiae Practice of Human Rights NGOs before the European Court of Human Rights," *Netherlands Quarterly of Human Rights* 31, no. 3 (2013): 286.

74 Andrew Geddes, "Lobbying for migrant inclusion in the European Union: new opportunities for transnational advocacy?" *Journal of European Public Policy* 7, no. 4 (2000): 632–649.

75 Amnesty International, AIRE Centre, Greek Helsinki Monitor, Liberty, Justice, Interrights, Open Society Justice Initiative, Human Rights Watch, Greek Helsinki Monitor, International Commission of Jurists (ICJ), International Federation of Human Rights, Jordanian National Centre for Human Rights, International Center for the Legal Protection of Human Rights, Helsinki Foundation for Human Rights, Ligue Francaise des Droits de l' Homme et du Citoyen (LDH), and others.

76 Joint Council for the Welfare of Immigrants, National Association for Assisting Aliens at Borders (ANAFE), European Council on Refugees and Exiles (ECRE), Groupe d'Information et de Soutien des Immigrés (GISTI), CIMADE - Service Ecuménique d'entraide, Reseau pour le soutien social des refugies et immigrés, Association of Movement for Human Rights and the Solidarity of Refugees, Service d' Aide Juridique aux Exiles (SAJE).

77 These are the Columbia Law School Human Rights Clinic, the Human Rights Centre of Ghent University, and the European Social Research Unit, and the Center for Justice and Accountability.

78 European Council on Refugees and Exiles (ECRE) and European Legal Network on Asylum (ELENA), *Survey on Legal Aid for Asylum Seekers*.

79 See Jeff Walsh, "Strategic Litigation at a European Level – What is strategic litigation and why it is important?" *European Database of Asylum Law* (blog), 14 February 2017, https://www.asylumlawdatabase.eu/en/journal/strategic-litigation-european-level.

80 See Andrea Kämpf, *National Human Rights Institutions and their work on migrants' human rights* (Berlin: German Institute for Human Rights, 2018).

81 Interview with a lawyer to Anagnostou (Athens, 24 April 2020, over Skype) who was from the *Omada Dikigoron gia ta Dikaiomata ton Prosfygon kai ton Metanaston* [Lawyers Group for the Rights of Refugees and Migrants].

82 *Horshill v Greece*, no. 70427/11, 1 August 2013, § 7–8.

83 See European Council on Refugees and Exiles (ECRE) and European Legal Network on Asylum (ELENA), *Celebrating 30 years of the ELENA Network: 1985–2015*, October 2015, https://www.ecre.org/wp-content/uploads/2016/05/ELENA-Celebration.26.10.2015.final_.pdf.

84 See European Council on Refugees and Exiles (ECRE) and European Legal Network on Asylum (ELENA), "Celebrating 30 years of the ELENA Network: 1985–2015".

85 Loveday Hodson, *NGOs and the Struggle for Human Rights in Europe* (Oxford: Hart Publishing, 2011), 82.

86 See Katayoun C. Sadeghi, "The ECtHR: the Problematic Nature of the Court's Reliance on Secondary Sources for Fact-Finding," *Connecticut Journal of International Law* 25, no.1 (2009): 127–152.

87   For example, in *Said v Netherlands*, no. 2345/02, 5 July 2005, an Amnesty International specialist provided a letter about the situation in the Eritrean military to substantiate the challenge of his deportation on non-refoulement grounds. In *Salah Sheekh v Netherlands*, no. 1948/04, 11 January 2007, Amnesty, the Dutch Refugee Council and Medecins sans Frontieres challenged the Dutch Foreign Ministry's country report regarding the situation in Somalia.

88   See Walsh, "What is strategic litigation and why it is important?".

89   Interview with a former director of JUSTICE, London, 27 June 2012.

90   See Walsh, "What is strategic litigation and why it is important?".

91   Interview with an Immigration lawyer and former Vice-Chair of the Institute of Race Relations, London, 28 March 2012.

92   NGOs were applicants in only three cases in our data set, and they were all religious organizations of Muslim immigrants.

93   Lisa McIntosh Sundstrom, "Russian NGOs and the ECtHR: A Spectrum of Approaches to Litigation", *Human Rights Quarterly* 36, no.4 (2014): 850.

94   Some of the cases that the AIRE Center litigated are: *Jaramillo v UK* (dec.), no. 24865/94, 23 October 1995; *Sorabjee v UK* (dec.), no. 23938/94, 23 October 1995; *Olachea Cahuas v Spain*, no. 24668/03, 10 August 2006; *Omwenyeke v Germany* (dec.), no. 44294/04, 20 November 2007; *A.A. v UK*, no. 8000/08, 20 September 2011; *Sufi and Elmi v UK*, nos. 8319/07 and 11449/07, 28 June 2011.

95   The Greek Helsinki Monitor litigated the cases of *Zelilof v Greece*, no. 17060/03, 24 May 2007 and *Celniku v Greece*, no. 21449/04, 5 July 2007, among other cases; SAJE in Lausanne represented the applicant in *Jusic v Switzerland*, no. 4691/06 2 December 2010; the London-based Redress brought to the ECtHR the case of *Zontul v Greece*, no. 12294/07, 17 January 2012; and Liberty litigated the case of *Alder v UK*, no. 42078/02, 22 November 2011.

96   Hodson, *NGOs and the Struggle for Human Rights in Europe*, 52.

97   Heidi Nichols Haddad, *The Hidden Hands of Justice. NGOs, Human Rights and International Courts* (Cambridge University Press, 2018), 68. See also Van den Eynde, "An Empirical Look at the Amicus Curiae Practice of Human Rights NGOs," 279–280.

98   Interview with a former director of JUSTICE, London, 27 June 2012; Interview with director of human rights organization in London, UK, 28 March 2012.

99   Hodson, *NGOs and the Struggle for Human Rights in Europe*, 51–52.

100 *Saadi v UK*, no. 13229/03, 29 January 2008, § 58–60.

101 *Hendrin Ali Said and Aras Ali Said v Hungary*, no. 13457/11, 23 October 2012, § 35.

102 *Rantsev v Cyprus and Russia*, no. 25965/04, 7 January 2010.

103 *Gebremedhin v France*, no. 25389/05, 26 April 2007.

104 *A. v Netherlands*, no. 4900/06, 20 July 2010, § 131–140; *Othman v UK*, no. 8139/09, 17 January 2012.

105 *De Souza Ribeiro v France*, no. 22689/07, 13 December 2012, § 70–75.

106 If anything, this underestimates actual NGO involvement, which in some cases is not visible, i.e. when a NGO selects and funds a case but relies upon external applicants to file the application and represent the petitioner.

107 Interview with legal officer, Amnesty International, London, 27 March 2012.

108 Interview with a former director of JUSTICE, London, 27 June 2012.

109 Hodson, *NGOs and the Struggle for Human Rights in Europe*, 57; Cliquennois and Champetier, "The Economic, Judicial and Political Influence Exerted by Private Foundations on Cases Taken by NGOs to the European Court of Human Rights: Inklings of a New Cold War?" 97–98.

110 Haddad, *The Hidden Hands of Justice*, 68.

111 See Van den Eynde, "An Empirical Look at the Amicus Curiae Practice of Human Rights NGOs," 292–3.

112   The ECtHR classifies all judgments and decisions in three levels of importance. Judgments and decisions of *high importance* make a significant contribution to the development, clarification or modification of the Court's case-law, either generally or in relation to a particular State (Level 1). Some of these judgments and decisions since the inception of the new Court in 1998 have been published or selected for publication in the Court's official Reports of Judgments and Decisions (Case Reports). Judgments and decisions of *medium-importance* (Level 2) do not make a significant contribution to the case-law, but go beyond merely applying existing case-law. Judgments and decisions of *low importance* simply apply existing case-law, and also include friendly settlements and strikeouts (Level 3).

113   Hodson, *NGOs and the Struggle for Human Rights in Europe*, 81.

114   On Italy, see Mario Savino, "The Refugee Crisis as a Challenge for Public Law: The Italian Case", *German Law Journal* 17, no. 6 (2016): 982. On Greece, see Dia Anagnostou and Danai Angeli, "A shortfall of rights and justice: Institutional design and judicial review of immigration detention in Greece," *European Journal of Legal Studies* (2022), forthcoming.

115   *Khlaifia and others v Italy*, no. 16483/12, 15 December 2016. For an analysis of Italian reception, detention and push-back practices, see Savino, "The Refugee Crisis as a Challenge for Public Law: The Italian Case".

116   *Hirsi Jamaa and Others v Italy*, no. 27765/09, 23 February 2012; *Sharifi and Others v Italy and Greece*, no. 16643/09, 21 October 2014.

117   See Savino, "The Refugee Crisis as a Challenge for Public Law: The Italian Case," 998–9.

118   According to the EU's Dublin Regulation, asylum claimants must be returned to the state through which they made their first entry that is primarily responsible for processing their claim for international protection. See European Union, Regulation (EU) No 604/2013 [2013] OJ L180/31(Dublin III Regulation).

119   Violeta Moreno-Lax, "Dismantling the Dublin System: M.S.S. v Belgium and Greece," *European Journal of Migration and Law* 14, no. 1 (2012): 8–9.

120   The European Court of Human Rights may, under Rule 39 of its Rules of Court, indicate interim measures to any State party to the ECHR. They are urgent measures that apply only where there is an imminent risk of irreparable harm, and until court proceedings are concluded. In most cases, the applicant requests the suspension of an expulsion order. In the period 2006–2010, the Court saw an increase of over 4,000% in the number of requests for interim measures. See ECRE and ELENA, *Research on ECHR Rule 39 Interim Measures*, 15.

121   *K.R.S. v the United Kingdom* (dec.), no. 32733/08, 2 December 2008. See also *T.I. v the United Kingdom* (dec.), no. 43844/98, 7 March 2000.

122   Evangelia Psychogiopoulou, "European Courts and the Rights of Migrants and Asylum Seekers in Greece," in *Rights and Courts in Pursuit of Social Change*, ed. Dia Anagnostou (Oxford: Hart Publishing, 2014), 140.

123   Interview with director of human rights organization in London, UK, 28 March 2012.

124   Moreno-Lax, "Dismantling the Dublin System," 12.

125   Interview with solicitor, Islington Law Centre, London, UK, 27 March 2012.

Part II

Judgment implementation and domestic reform

DOI: 10.4324/9781003256489-7

6 Tackling Roma segregation in education

A significant amount of ECHR litigation related to minorities has sought to challenge structural human rights problems that mar entire sectors of state activity. This chapter shifts attention to the implementation of ECtHR rulings that expose such problems and necessitate substantial and complex domestic reforms, far beyond the individual litigants. Rulings that condemned institutional forms of racism and discrimination against the Roma are a case in point, and they are far from unique or exceptional. Over the past twenty years, the ECtHR has dealt with a wide array of cases that bring to light systemic deficiencies – related to the delivery of justice, prison conditions, the criminal justice system, asylum management, and gender-based violence, among others. International courts' intervention in cases that require reforms in domestic law, policy and administrative practice is a highly controversial facet of international judicial rights review. It is strongly criticized for intruding into the realm of national governments and legislators.[1]

Since the 2000s, ECtHR judgments condemned the segregation of Roma in primary schools in Greece, Croatia, Hungary and the Czech Republic, as a form of ethnic discrimination that violates the right to education. The domestic implementation of these judgments took place under the supervisory mechanism of the ECHR – comprising, as it is well-known, the Committee of Ministers (CoM), a political body of state delegates, assisted by the Council of Europe Department of Execution of Judgments (hereby DExJ). This chapter closely traces the general measures and reforms that national authorities adopted to tackle Roma segregation in schools. It argues that the increasing participation of non-governmental actors, alongside state governments in the ECHR supervision over judgment implementation both reflects and further reinforces the transformation of the ECHR – at least important parts of it – into a regime of transnational experimentalist governance.

Roma children in various countries in Central-East and Southeast Europe (CESE) are subject to systematic exclusion in primary education. Their segregation in public schools is a common phenomenon in countries like Hungary, Romania, Bulgaria, Slovakia, the Czech Republic, Greece and elsewhere. Insidious but widespread societal prejudice and well-entrenched administrative practices systematically push away Roma children from mainstream schools and classes and place them in separate and inferior ones. In turn, low levels of Roma enrolment and educational achievement, reinforce their pervasive social marginalization from

DOI: 10.4324/9781003256489-8

an early age. Failure to include Roma pupils in schools on an equal footing with the majority undercuts their ability to become equal members of society, and to achieve integration in it.

Courts have for a long time considered legal challenges concerning the segregation of ethnic and racial minorities in schools and grappled with institutional racism as a breach of human rights. A historical milestone was the *Brown v Board of Education of Topeka* (1954) in the USA, where African Americans were by law placed in separate and inferior public schools. The US Supreme Court had ruled that separating children in schools on the basis of race was against the constitution and the principle of equality, overturning its earlier doctrine of "separate but equal".[2] Following this landmark ruling, US courts issued decisions with specific instructions on how local-national school authorities should put to practice the equality principle and end segregation in education. Unlike in the USA of the 1950s though, contemporary forms of minority disadvantage in the educational system and other areas of state activity in Europe, are often insidious, even imperceptible. Indeed, they are entrenched in a broader milieu that exhibits an ostensible and principled commitment to equality.

Structural or institutional racism is a complex system that confers social advantages on some groups and imposes burdens on others, leading to segregation, poverty, and denial of opportunity.[3] Deep and systemic inequalities shape and restrict minority access to public goods and services, such as education, housing and health. In most CESE countries, Roma discrimination in education is prohibited and it is in breach of the EU Race Equality Directive (2000/43/EC). Nonetheless, it widely persists and is reproduced not through law, but through ingrained social prejudices based on race and ethnicity, often intersecting with gender differences. The exclusion of the Roma in Europe, even if blatant, is not necessarily traceable to the intentional and discreet actions of particular actors. In this contemporary form of "second" or "third" generation discrimination, inequality emanates from deeply held, often unconscious, biases that are demeaning for minority members, and that permeate administrative and educational practices.[4]

In the second half of the 1990s and in the 2000s, NGOs began to challenge Roma discrimination in education before national courts and equality bodies in Bulgaria, Hungary and elsewhere in CESE.[5] In some countries, those legal actions continued at the European level, where the NGO European Roma Rights Center (ERRC) systematically pursued litigation in the Strasbourg Court. The preparation of a case to challenge Roma discrimination in educational structures and practices – a demanding and resource-intensive undertaking – would have hardly been possible without multi-actor coordination and NGO organizational support. The first part of this chapter explores the mobilization of lawyers and NGOs to bring Roma school segregation claims before the ECtHR, and to frame it as a form of ethnic discrimination in breach of human rights. In response to legal challenges of Roma segregation, the ECtHR issued six judgments that pronounced illegitimate and discriminatory the segregation of Roma in special schools and classes.

In the judgments under study, the Court, as it is its usual practice, did not indicate general measures and reforms that national authorities should adopt to eradicate Roma segregation in schools. National authorities, as it is well-known, have wide discretion regarding the measures and domestic reforms to remedy the violations found in the ECtHR judgments. In cases involving structural human rights problems, implementation is shaped by strong contestation but also by a high level of uncertainty as to what measures work to undo phenomena as complex as ethnic segregation in education. Eradicating the sources of violations in Roma school segregation rulings amounts to no less than transforming entire administrative systems and domains of state action.

The respondent states' governments in the Roma segregation judgments laid out various measures in their action plans to the ECHR bodies overseeing implementation. The Council of Europe Department for the Execution of Judgments and the Committee of Ministers (CoM) periodically reviewed those measures and made recommendations for revision and further action. Importantly, the cases under study had a high level of NGO engagement in judgment implementation, which was made possible by a 2006 change in the working rules of the CoM (discussed in chapter 3). The second part of this chapter examines the domestic implementation of school segregation rulings and the measures and the reforms that national authorities in the Czech Republic, Greece, Croatia and Hungary enacted to redress Roma school segregation.

This chapter argues that the systematic engagement of non-governmental actors, alongside respondent states profoundly transform the Council of Europe (CoE) supervision over judgment implementation – at least in areas of structural violations. Such supervision in part shifts from compliance with single judgments to overseeing reform in entire areas of state action and public administration. Non-governmental actors increasingly engage in it as part of broader social and legal mobilization campaigns and struggles for Roma rights. Remedial measures are defined, assessed and revised through recurrent exchanges between state authorities, non-governmental actors and the CoE supervisory bodies. Judgment implementation becomes deliberative and participatory, and the ECHR akin to a regime of transnational experimentalist governance. While not eliminating structural discrimination, experimentalism is better suited and more effective in promoting rights-enhancing reform. It also prompts us to rethink the notion of compliance as a basis for understanding the domestic impact and effectiveness of international human rights rulings.

1 Human rights litigation to challenge Roma school segregation

In Central East and Southeast Europe (CESE), Roma school segregation has a long pedigree. It persists despite its prohibition by statute or ministerial order in Bulgaria, Hungary, Slovakia, and Romania. Historical context, different policies and educational structures, including their degree of (de)centralization, variably shape school segregation in each country.[6] In the Czech Republic and Slovakia, Roma pupils are predominantly placed in special schools for children with mental disability, which receive more state funding per capita than ordinary schools.[7] In Hungary, Bulgaria and Romania, segregation primarily takes place through separate and presumably temporary classes that are professedly intended to help Roma children catch up with the rest of the students.[8]

In Greece, on the other hand, Roma segregation was not as entrenched as in the other countries, and students with special needs (including those with disabilities) were mostly placed in mainstream classrooms. Still, segregation surfaced in the 1990s, when the existence of temporary, separate classes intended to "smooth the integration of Roma into the mainstream" were considered permissible and tolerated.[9] Across Central, East and Southeast Europe, segregation also occurs informally when standard schools become labelled as "Roma" schools due to the flight of non-Roma children, whose parents enroll them in other schools and choose to live in other areas. While "Roma" schools are officially classified as standard schools, they deliver a substandard kind of education.[10]

Until well into the 2000s, legal opportunities to challenge minority segregation in education as a form of ethnic discrimination before the ECtHR, were not favorable. For most of its lifetime, the ECHR system provided weak protection against discrimination to minorities and vulnerable groups. The Convention, as it is well-known, contains a weak anti-discrimination provision (Article 14 ECHR) that is of a subsidiary nature – it is only invoked in connection with one of the other substantive rights of the Convention.[11] The ECtHR had traditionally applied a restrictive approach in its case law and it was apparently reluctant to review claims raised under Article 14 ECHR, as shown by the data presented in chapter 4.[12]

In the relatively small number of cases in which the Court had examined Article 14 claims on the merits, its approach was premised on a formal view of equality. It only recognized instances of direct discrimination and required a high standard of proof ("beyond reasonable doubt") to conclude that a particular action or behavior was motivated by prejudice on racial/ethnic grounds.[13] Indirect discrimination, on the other hand, cannot be traced in the intentions and actions of specific individuals. The emphasis must shift to the effects of legal and institutional structures that perpetuate disadvantage, exclusion and an inferior social position.[14] Cases of indirect discrimination are concerned not with differential treatment between persons in similar situations, but with the effects of neutral rules and practices and how they work to the detriment of specific minority communities.[15]

In the 1990s, the ECtHR's case law on Gypsy Travelers made incremental but significant advances in its understanding of equality and discrimination in regard to vulnerable minorities. In 1996 in *Buckley*, the Court found that the UK environmental planning policies interfered with the right to a traditional family life (Article 8 ECHR) but saw the interference as necessary in a democratic society. Three dissenting judges though had forcefully argued that the multiplicity and superimposition of administrative rules excluded Gypsies from living in particular areas, leading to unequal treatment in breach of Article 14 ECHR.[16] Their dissent for the first time raised the point that indirect discrimination can ensue from a failure to recognize social, cultural and ethnic differences.[17] In 2001 in *Chapman v UK*, the Court did not see as a breach of the Convention the failure of state authorities to give special consideration to the needs and different lifestyle of Gypsy Travelers as a vulnerable group.[18] Seven judges though dissented, invoking the obligation to take into account an emerging consensus around the prohibition of discrimination. The latter posited that national authorities must not only refrain from policies and practices that discriminate against minorities. They also have a positive duty to adopt legislation, programs and special measures to improve their situation.[19]

The legal challenges of Roma segregation in schools were products of mobilization and strategic action by NGOs that selected the cases under study, and prepared and filled the relevant complaints before the ECtHR. Individual victims and lawyers alone would likely not have been able to mount such complex and resource-demanding legal challenges. In the early 2000s, the NGO European Roma Rights Center (ERRC) began to pursue the issue of school segregation in its ECtHR litigation strategy aimed at combatting ethnic discrimination against the Roma. From its inception in 1997, the Centre had taken up strategic litigation in various (quasi)judicial bodies at the national and international levels. It opted for litigation as its main form of action to promote Roma rights, and to push for advancements in human rights case law, allocating substantial resources to it. The ERRC would support and intervene in a large number of Roma-related complaints over the next twenty years, principally in the Strasbourg Court, but also before national courts. It also strategically invoked Court rulings to advocate and pressure governments in different countries to undertake legal and policy reforms to redress Roma marginalization.[20]

At the outset, the ERRC made a strategic decision to depict and frame the gross social disparities affecting the Roma as forms of ethnic-racial discrimination. It set out to press relevant claims upon the ECtHR, despite its traditionally restrictive approach, in the light also of the intra-Court divisions and incremental shifts in its case law on discrimination against Travelers in the UK described above. The ERRC lawyers were inspired by US anti-discrimination law and by advances in equality law in other jurisdictions like in various United Nations conventions, and in national high courts. They were further emboldened by the European Union's (EU) rapidly evolving anti-discrimination standards, which Member States and the candidate states (at the time) of Central East and Southeast Europe (CESE) had to transpose at the national level.[21] In the ERRC's discussions and consultations with lawyers and NGOs in CESE in the second half of the 1990s, a crucial concern was how to document structural discrimination against the Roma in the criminal justice system in claims before the ECtHR. The US lawyers propounded the collection of statistics as a means to document practices of racial discrimination and to convince courts about it.[22]

In seeking to advance racial discrimination claims related to Roma, the ERRC shifted attention away from the issue of cultural identity, on which the UK Travelers' cases had focused. It did not address discrimination in access to public places and employment, or residential exclusion – issues that were also being litigated before domestic courts in the 1990s and early 2000s.[23] Instead, the ERRC decided to pursue litigation on segregation in education, taking into account legal opportunities in the ECHR system. In the first place, the Convention guarantees the right to education (nothing equivalent in regard to cultural identity, or social rights), thus providing a solid basis for raising a claim.[24] The ERRC's interest in education also drew inspiration from the landmark US Supreme Court case of *Brown v Board of Education* described earlier.[25] Equal access to education was viewed of pivotal significance as it could unleash an impetus for broader social-economic integration and political empowerment of the Roma.

In pursuing the issue of school segregation, the ERRC initially selected the Czech Republic as the respondent state for test case litigation in the ECtHR. Similar cases were also being litigated before domestic courts in other countries like Hungary and Bulgaria. However, they were filed by NGOs whose lack of standing in the ECtHR (or rather their restricted standing), preempted the continuation of domestic litigation in the Strasbourg Court.[26] The ERRC also had excellent contacts with individual lawyers and activists in the Czech Republic, who had collected local-level documentation attesting to a pattern of minority disadvantage. Last but not least, it was considered more straightforward to challenge the specific form that Roma segregation took in the Czech Republic – namely, their disproportionate share in special schools for children with mental difficulties.[27] The challenge for litigators was how to specifically link exclusionary educational practices to ethnic discrimination.[28]

To be sure, the ERRC was far from being the only organization in the Roma rights field in CESE. Nonetheless, it had a pivotal position in the transnational networks of lawyers and NGOs that emerged from the 1990s onwards to mobilize and pressure governments to redress Roma marginalization in the region.[29] In order to build complex court cases about systemic racism and ethnic discrimination, the ERRC mobilized a wide network of local and national level NGOs, lawyers and activists in different countries (Bulgaria, Hungary, Romania, Greece, Croatia, Slovakia and others). It relied on them to identify suitable test cases, to find minority families willing to cooperate as petitioners, and to sustain their interest through lengthy processes of case preparation and court proceedings.[30] Volunteers and activists in different regions and countries, followed the local press for incidents of death of Roma persons while in police custody.[31]

The ERRC and its collaborators at the local and national level dedicated substantial time and resources to collect evidence that would bring to light and document patterns of discrimination against the Roma. A survey that they conducted in the Czech Republic found a widespread practice of placing Roma in special schools for children with mild mental disabilities. This documentation was essential to building the claim about the existence of systemic and prejudicial practices that disadvantaged Roma children. It was particularly important in a system like the ECHR that does not formally recognize class actions or group remedies.[32] Extensive data collected in the region of Ostrava was the evidential basis upon which the ERRC built the case of *D.H. and Others v. Czech Republic* that challenged the disproportionate placement of Roma students in special schools. The data showed that a Romani child was 27 times more likely to be in a special school than a non-Romani, and that more than 75% of Romani children were in schools for children with mental disabilities. It enabled the ERRC to make a case of prima facie discrimination and to persuade the Court to reverse the burden of proof to the state.[33]

The *D.H.* case framed an innovative argument about indirect discrimination stemming from diffused ethnic prejudice – the first time that such an argument was advanced before the ECtHR. The applicants (18 Romani children) submitted that the seemingly neutral school placement tests administered by the Czech authorities did not take into account the special needs of disadvantaged Roma children. They also claimed that the placement of a disproportionate number of Roma in special schools with an inferior curriculum contravened their right to education (Art. 2 of Protocol No. 1) and amounted to racial discrimination (Art. 14 ECHR). The racial segregation to which the applicants had been subjected, was so egregious and humiliating that it arguably amounted to inhuman and degrading treatment in violation of the Convention (Article 3). Notably, in reference to the ECtHR pilot judgments, the applicants underlined that the violation of their rights was not prompted by isolated and individual incidents. Instead, they argued that it was "the consequence of administrative and regulatory conduct on the part of the authorities towards an identifiable class of citizens".[34]

The second section of the Court initially upheld the government's argument that the special school system was established for children with learning difficulties irrespective of ethnic or racial background. Subsequently though, the Grand Chamber's final judgment in *D.H. v Czech Republic* thoroughly reversed the Section judgment and marked a milestone. For the first time, the ECtHR conceded that the presented statistics disclosed a prima facie case of differential treatment of Romani students that was not objectively justified and shifted the burden of proof to the respondent state. The Czech government argued that parental consent to placing their children in special schools was a sufficient safeguard. The Court though countered that the parents were not in a position to make an informed decision, nor were they aware of the consequences that their consent to separate school placement would have for their children's futures. Significantly, the ECtHR made an enquiry into the broader societal context behind the facts. It also took note of the authorities' failure to consider the special needs of Romani children as members of a disadvantaged group.

Dubbed as a European "*Brown* moment", the *D.H.* Grand Chamber's judgment marked a breakthrough in finding a situation of "structural and systemic discrimination" in breach of the Convention. It found the disproportionate placement of Roma in special schools to breach their right to education (Article 2 Protocol 1 ECHR) and to amount to ethnic discrimination in breach of Article 14 ECHR.[35] In the *D.H.* judgment (and in subsequent ones), the ECtHR also recognized the positive duty of states to tackle invidious discrimination and to redress past discriminatory practices concerning access to education.[36] Four dissenting judges vehemently criticized the Court's decision not to examine separately the situation of each individual applicant, and instead treat the discrimination claim as a structural problem.[37] In adopting a systemic approach to indirect discrimination, the ECtHR aligned its equality case law with that in other jurisdictions, like the European Union, the United Nations bodies, the U.S. Supreme Court, and other national courts.[38]

Before the ECtHR, the *D.H.* case attracted unprecedented mobilization by NGOs and Council of Europe bodies who acted as third-party interveners – impressively twelve in total. In reaching its decision, the ECtHR Grand Chamber took thorough account of their amicus briefs. The *D.H.* judgment relayed the views of the independent Council of Europe bodies[39] that had expressed doubts about the adequacy of the psychological placement tests.[40] The Court also placed substantial weight on the views of NGOs specializing on Roma rights, the rights of children, education, minorities, and human rights – no less than nine – who intervened as third parties.[41] They expounded the inferior quality of education that children received in special schools and the detrimental consequences for the pupils' subsequent personal development; the cultural-social bias embedded in the seemingly objective placement tests; and the problematic nature of parental consent as a basis for waiving rights.[42]

Transnational networks, domestic NGOs and lawyers further mobilized in other countries to develop human rights litigation on Roma school segregation. In Croatia, the ERRC collaborated with the Croatian Helsinki Committee and its lawyer Ms. Lovorka Kusan to file the case of *Oršuš and Others v. Croatia* in the ECtHR. The case had already been examined by the Ombudsperson domestically, who found discrimination, and by the country's Constitutional Court. In *Oršuš and Others v. Croatia*, the applicants (15 Roma children) claimed before the ECtHR that their placement in separate classes, on grounds that their knowledge of Croatian language was deficient, was an instance of indirect discrimination on ethnic grounds.[43] Their separation, they argued, had such a harmful impact on their self-esteem and personality development that amounted to inhuman and degrading treatment. Reversing the First Section's judgment, the Grand Chamber conceded that the fact that only Roma children were placed in separate classes gave rise to a reasonable suspicion that language deficiency was used as a pretext for race. It found a violation of the prohibition of discrimination (Art. 14 ECHR) taken together with the right to education (Article 2, P-1 ECHR).[44]

In 2005 the Greek Helsinki Monitor (GHM), a member of the International Helsinki Foundation and well-connected with the ERRC, brought more cases before the ECtHR to challenge Roma school segregation in Greece.[45] Greek law and policy tolerated the possibility of separate education for Roma. The *Sampanis* case involved 11 applicants who were Greek nationals of Roma origin living in the area of Psari in Aspropyrgos (Attika region). In that region, the efforts of national authorities, the GHM and the Association for coordination of organizations and communities for human rights of Roma in Greece (SOKARDE), to enroll Roma children in primary schools for 2005–2006 failed due to protests by non-Roma parents. The children were subsequently placed into preparatory, Roma-only classes held in a building separate and away from the school. The applicants claimed that they had been subjected to different and less favorable treatment in comparison to non-Roma children. In the *Sampanis* and in two more similar judgments, the ECtHR found that the failure of Greek authorities to recognize the special needs of Roma students, and to justify their separate placement, obstructed their transition into ordinary classes. It reinforced their separation, led to discrimination, and violated their right to education (Article 2 Protocol 2 and Article 14 ECHR).[46]

The ECtHR rulings that denounced Roma segregation in schools as insidious discrimination powerfully unsettled the status quo at the national level: they established without dispute that separate educational arrangements were not acceptable and must be changed. In the first place, they set in a process of state reform under the ECHR oversight. The respondent states' authorities took measures that were periodically reviewed by the Convention supervisory bodies (the Committee of Ministers, CoM, and the Department of Execution of Judgments), and they were subsequently developed further or revised. The ECtHR Roma segregation judgments further triggered follow-on litigation before national, European and international courts and quasi-judicial bodies. NGO mobilization was a driving force in ongoing litigation and human rights enforcement. By condemning Roma school segregation, the ECtHR rulings did not conclude but rather catalyzed ongoing efforts for human rights reform, to which we turn in the next section.

2 Implementing ECtHR judgments

The ECtHR rulings described in the previous section brought pressure on state authorities in the Czech Republic, Croatia, Greece and Hungary to take positive action to combat Roma segregation in primary schools. They also called attention to the special needs of this vulnerable, culturally distinct and profoundly disadvantaged minority. Apart from such broad influence, they contained little direction regarding practical measures and policies on how to render the educational system more equitable. Roma school segregation takes different forms and poses diverse challenges in each country. Besides being rooted in entrenched societal attitudes, and in administrative and educational practices, separation in schools is also tied up with structures of economic marginalization and residential segregation of the Roma.[47] The school segregation judgments, involving as they did structural violations, were placed under the enhanced supervision track by the Committee of Ministers (CoM). It involved government reporting on domestic reforms, iterative cycles of assessment by the CoM and the DExJ and reformulation of implementing measures by state authorities, a high level of NGO engagement, and follow-on action within and beyond the ECHR frame.

The content and depth of domestic implementation of the ECtHR judgments that found segregation to be a form of ethnic discrimination varied widely in Greece, Croatia, Hungary and the Czech Republic. In all four countries, national authorities introduced at least some measures and changes (legislative, administrative or other) over a period of time to redress ethnic segregation in primary schools. In no country did implementation eliminate Roma school segregation – far from it. In Greece and Croatia, the adopted measures were limited to the cases at hand and to the specific locales where the violations occurred. In the Czech

Republic and in Hungary, on the other hand, judgment implementation had a more substantive impact, even as domestic resistance to restructuring the system was apparently strongest. Over time, implementation pushed forward significant educational reforms and helped sustain progressive changes in the face of political backsliding.

2.1 The limits of school reform in Croatia and Greece

In *Oršuš and others v Croatia,* the ECtHR Grand Chamber found the disproportionate placement of Roma in separate classes in the Medimurje County, where a substantial Roma population lives, to be a form of indirect discrimination. It did not condemn those classes as a general policy and nationwide practice. The Croatian government had justified their existence as "benevolent segregation": they were purportedly intended to assist those students with poor command of Croatian language. More than any other related case, the *Oršuš* ruling raised the intricate issue of how law and policy can draw the line between differential treatment in the form of special assistance to a vulnerable and marginalized group on the one hand (a kind of positive measures, as the First Section judgment had ruled[48]); and separate class structures that reinforce a position of inferiority and marginalization, and are contrary to human rights, on the other. The Grand Chamber was strongly divided in advancing the latter interpretation in *Oršuš.* No less than eight judges dissented (8/9) in what they saw as the Court's intrusion into a matter of social and educational policy that was squarely a competence of national decision-makers.

In the frame of implementing the *Oršuš* and the *Sampanis* and *Lavida* judgments, Croatian and Greek authorities, respectively, enacted a number of measures to tackle Roma segregation. In Croatia, the *Oršuš* judgment prompted national authorities to put in place a legal frame for the existence of separate classes, to develop objective criteria and standardized tests for the assessment of pupils' language skills, and to monitor their progress. In its final judgment against Croatia, the Grand Chamber had indicated a set of safeguards that could clearly delimit the temporary nature of language improvement classes.[49] In an early submission to the CoM, Amnesty International further called on the Croatian authorities to set clear criteria and objectives, and to strengthen safeguards against arbitrary placement decisions of experts and educators.[50]

Legal reforms in Croatia stipulated the obligation of schools to provide special assistance to pupils with insufficient knowledge of Croatian language, but also to integrate them into mainstream classes as soon as possible. An electronic system was also established to monitor the implementation of measures, to assess the situation and identify problems. The government submitted to the CoM that the goal was "to achieve complete integration of pupils with insufficient knowledge of Croatian language into regular classes..." It also reported an increase in the number of Roma enrolled in elementary school.[51] The new legal provisions enacted in the frame of implementing the *Oršuš* judgment were positively assessed by the CoM in 2012 that transferred its supervision from enhanced to standard procedure – essentially minimizing its oversight of the respondent state.[52]

Over the next years, Croatian authorities reported a series of soft measures in the Medimurje area, to tackle the broader and inter-related problem of high school drop-out rate among Roma pupils, which the ECtHR judgment had noted as critical. Measures such as free textbooks and meals, provision of social services to Roma, and various training and awareness raising activities targeting parents and communities, sought to promote Roma children's attendance of preschool education. They also sought to facilitate pupils' transfer in mainstream classes and to increase Roma enrolment in primary schools in the Medimurje area. In 2014, Croatian authorities reported that the majority of Roma students attending language classes advanced to the next grade, but they also acknowledged high drop-out rates and irregular school attendance among Roma pupils.[53] Following the government's action report in 2017, which provided data showing improvement in Roma access and retention to schools, the CoM decided to end its supervision of the case.[54]

In sum, in implementing the *Oršuš* judgment, Croatia importantly adopted a legal frame for students' placement in, and the functioning of special classes. This, however, did not put an end to those practices that reproduced the disproportionate placement of Roma in those.[55] Educational outcomes improved in some locales, but segregation and limited Roma access to schools persisted in others due to many factors, including the inability or unwillingness of local authorities to provide resources for busing.[56] While the judgment was a product of strategic litigation supported by NGOs, NGOs sparsely mobilized in the implementation phase before the CoM. With the exception of Amnesty International that made a submission, mobilization at the European level was limited, with NGOs being absent from the review process of government measures by the CoM.[57]

In Greece, Roma segregation in schools emerged in the 1980s and 1990s, alongside, and perhaps because of, an official policy to integrate Roma in the education system. From the 1990s onwards, Greek authorities made efforts to promote the enrolment and attendance of Roma children in schools, making use of EU funds.[58] Segregation of Roma children though occurred at the local level in response to pressure from non-Roma parents who protested their admission in integrated classes. Local school authorities informally established various kinds of separate structures. While not provided for in Greek law, those were permitted or at least tolerated by the Ministry of Education, even as the official policy was to educate all Roma in mainstream schools.[59] Large numbers of Roma children ended up in separate classes with a lower quality curriculum, professedly as a temporary arrangement to prepare them for transfer in ordinary classes. The three ECtHR judgments against Greece all condemned such kinds of separate Roma school arrangements in two locals – in Aspropyrgos (Attika region) and Sofades (Thessaly, central Greece). In *Sampanis and Others v Greece*, the ECtHR concluded that the placement of Roma children in an annex to the main school building resulted in ethnic discrimination and violated their right to education.[60]

While the ECtHR judgment in *Sampanis* had suggested a possible course of action to tackle Roma segregation, the Greek government pursued a different one. The Court had specifically censured the lack of any test or objective assessment of learning abilities, in the placement of Roma in special classes and their transfer into ordinary classes. As in the *Oršuš* case, it acknowledged that as a vulnerable minority, the Roma may require special measures to redress discrimination and facilitate their inclusion into mainstream classes. Greek authorities though did not seek to establish a system of special assistance with necessary guarantees in place (as authorities did in Croatia).[61] Instead, they reported the closing down of the school annex with Roma-only classes, and the transfer of those pupils to an ordinary school in the area. Greek authorities also issued a number of circulars with instructions to the school administrations to facilitate the enrolment of Roma children and monitor their regular attendance of classes – this had been the official state policy since the 1990s. In addition, the government implemented soft measures, such as a program to train Romani mediators, inter-cultural courses for educators, and provided social services to assist Roma families with education of their children.[62]

Prematurely, the CoM decided to terminate its supervision of *Sampanis* in 2011 on the basis of the above reported measures. It did so, despite detailed information provided by NGOs, the Greek Helsinki Monitor (GHM, counsel to the applicants), the Minority Rights Group – Greece (MRG-G), the ERRC, and Coordinated Organizations and Communities for Roma Human Rights in Greece (SOKADRE), that Roma pupils continued to be assigned to a Roma-only primary school – the same one as before, only renamed – rather than attending mainstream classes in the nearest school.[63] Their separation persisted, despite the ministerial circulars sent to local and regional authorities, on site visits by Ministry of Education officials and meetings with various stakeholders. The Ministry of Education apparently was willing to close the Roma-only school that was condemned in the *Sampanis* case (Aspropyrgos). Yet, it bent to pressure by local government and school authorities and by non-Roma parents in the area who opposed the integration of Roma in regular classes. Meanwhile, joint research by the ERRC, GHM and MRG-G in 2010 in 28 Romani communities revealed that Romani children across Greece were still not being enrolled in school. Where they did attend school, they were often segregated.[64]

In the light of ongoing and widespread Roma segregation in the country, the Greek Helsinki Monitor (GHM) successfully utilized follow-on litigation to re-open the case. It brought two more complaints in the ECtHR in 2009–2010 to generate fresh pressure for the government to implement the *Sampanis and Others v Greece* judgment and to redress Roma school segregation. The follow-on case of *Sampani and Others v Greece* concerned the same area of Aspropyrgos, where Greek authorities had failed to transfer Roma pupils in mainstream schools – contrary to what they had reported to the CoM in the initial *Sampanis* case. Additionally, the case of *Lavida and Others v Greece* was lodged on behalf of 23 Romani schoolchildren from the Greek town of Sofades.[65] They complained of being assigned to attend an all-Roma school in a district away from their place of residence (thus contrary to the basic rule in Greece that assigns children to schools near where they live). In both cases, the ECtHR anew condemned Greece for failure to take measures to dismantle continued segregation that amounted to ethnic discrimination and a breach of the right to education. This time, it also recommended (under Article 46 ECHR) measures that the Greek state ought to take, specifically to transfer school age applicants to another state school.

While reviving pressure on state officials, the new judgments of *Sampani* (no.2) and *Lavida* did not prompt any further legislative or policy reform in Greece. Government authorities remained focused on the overarching policy goal to enroll Roma children in schools. They insisted that these judgments did not require any structural measures beyond remedial action in the locales, in which the relevant complaints arose. To implement the new judgments, the Greek Ministry of Education this time pursued more resolute administrative action to enroll and integrate Roma children in mainstream schools in these two areas.[66] From 2013 and onwards, it issued circulars instructing local and regional school authorities to simplify the process of Roma school enrolment and to transfer pupils to non-segregated schools. Special reception classes were introduced for students whose native language was not Greek, and school principals were instructed to admit Roma children, and to take action against school absenteeism.[67] Officials from the Ministry of Education reportedly sought to smooth over strong local reactions through informal talks with local-regional authorities, and various stakeholders – the Roma Mediators, the Ombudsman for Roma, school principals, and parents' associations – with varying success.

The lukewarm attitude of the government in pushing ahead with Roma school integration at the local level, and the weak CoM oversight – possibly yielding to government resistance – circumscribed the remit of domestic structural and policy reform.[68] Even as the Greek government reaffirmed its commitment to Roma school integration, recurring opposition from non-Roma parents undermined any efforts to achieve it. It took years for the Roma-only school in Aspropyrgos (*Sampani* case) to close down (in 2015–16), and desegregation in Sofades (*Lavida* case) was only partially achieved, raising doubts about the sustainability of the implemented changes. The Roma school situation in other areas of the country was not known or monitored. In 2016, a Special Secretariat for Roma Inclusion was established within the Ministry of Labor, Social Insurance and Social Solidarity. In 2017, having the government's reassurance that this Special Secretariat would intervene in local areas where segregation would emerge, the CoM terminated its supervision of the judgments.[69] The implemented measures fell far short of a comprehensive school integration plan that NGOs had proposed in an early intervention to the CoM (in 2010).[70]

Despite the above limitations, the Roma school segregation judgments in Croatia and Greece firmly delegitimized the status quo. They obliged governments to justify any separate arrangements and prompted significant legislative changes (Croatia) and limited administrative action (Greece). A critical impediment was the lack of sustained engagement on the part of NGOs and other stakeholders, which is subsequently analyzed in section four of this chapter. It deprived the CoE supervisory bodies from essential information and feedback to continue their monitoring and to add rigor to their review of the enacted measures. While some NGO mobilization was evident in the first years following the first *Sampanis* judgment, it did not continue after 2010, not least due to the limited experience of the NGOs active in the cases at the time, as well as the lack of resources.[71] The Greek Helsinki Monitor (GHM), counsel in the Greek cases, successfully used follow on litigation to the ECtHR to redress the implementation gap. Other stakeholders (i.e. educators' associations, NGOs, human rights bodies) though did not become actively involved in the implementation process before the Council of Europe bodies, while their engagement at the domestic level also remained limited.

2.2 Resistance and policy reform in the Czech Republic

In *D.H v Czech Republic* (2007) and in *Horvath and Kiss v Hungary* (2013), the ECtHR found the disproportionate placement of Roma in special schools for pupils with mild mental disabilities to be a form of ethnic discrimination and a breach of their right to education. Roma children received an inferior education that obstructed their social integration. In both cases, the Court argued that the diagnostic tests that were used to place pupils in special schools lacked the necessary safeguards. They were designed for the majority population without taking due account of the specific conditions of Roma as a disadvantaged group. The Court underlined the positive obligations of the state to redress their disadvantage and "to undo a history of racial segregation in special schools".[72] While it provided some directions for general measures, it did not elaborate on what kind of educational structure would promote inclusiveness while also take into account the special needs of Roma minorities.[73] The implementation of the *D.H v Czech Republic* (2007) and the *Horvath and Kiss v Hungary* (2013) was more protracted than in Croatia and Greece and it involved a high level of sustained mobilization by non-governmental actors.[74]

Being a milestone in human rights case law, the *D.H.* judgment has attracted enormous scholarly attention. It is commonplace to contend that the judgment failed to eradicate Roma discrimination in the Czech primary school system. While true, this view is premised on unrealistic expectations placed on the ECtHR (and on all courts for that matter). Administrative reforms and changes in mentality and practice of such a scale, as required to put an end to minority segregation in an entire education system, are unlikely to occur as a result of judicial ordinance.

The *D.H.* implementation has been a protracted process. Between 2008 and 2020, the Czech government submitted at least nine updates and revisions of its action plan, and many memoranda and responses (at least fifteen) to the CoM decisions. In addition, a range of NGOs and public bodies like the Public Defender of Rights (a National Human Rights Institution), made at least 25 submissions in 2010–2020 to the CoM.[75] A large number of NGO submissions relayed information, research data and recommendations contained in reports of other organizations and international bodies that had mobilized around the issue of Roma school segregation.[76]

Through successive iterations and exchanges between the supervisory bodies, state authorities and non-governmental actors, the *D.H.* implementation process led to incremental, nonetheless important legislative, administrative and policy changes, as this section shows. Implementing measures and reforms took place in two directions: first, attempts to eliminate the entire segment of special education for pupils with mild mental disabilities, in which the Roma were predominantly placed; and secondly, changes to strengthen safeguards in the existing system that would prevent Roma children without disabilities from being placed (often without objective reason) in special schools.[77]

In the years preceding and following the *D.H.* judgment, government-introduced reforms to render national or local school systems more inclusive and non-discriminatory were inherently provisional, and intentionally shallow. They were set on preserving the segregationist status quo in Czech primary schools. In 2004, the Education Act had replaced most special schools with practical schools. Practical schools were mainstream primary schools for children with special educational needs (SEN), which, however still offered a modified curriculum of inferior quality. They also occupied the same premises as the abolished special schools.[78] Thus, separate schools continued to exist in all but name, with Roma children being disproportionately placed in those and receiving a second-class education. Following the issuing of the *D.H.* judgment, the Czech government submitted to the CoM in 2009 a National Action Plan for Inclusive Education (NAPIV). It included reference to the abovementioned 2004 Education Act as a reform implementing the *D.H.* judgment even though it was adopted well before the release of the *D.H.* by the Grand Chamber. While the action plan defined some general goals (to transform special schools into ordinary primary schools, to end segregation of Roma), it did not indicate concretely how to achieve them.[79]

In the frame of the *D.H.* implementation, NGOs, the Ombudsperson, and the Czech Human Rights Commissioner sought to leverage the judgment to pressure the Ministry of Education to undertake reforms that would eliminate separate Roma schools and classes. NGOs and human rights bodies advocated an inclusive and culturally sensitive educational system, and the application of positive action measures, in contrast to the Czech government's emphasis on an individual-based and color-blind approach.[80] Even for these officials and activists though, who genuinely strove for an inclusive school system, it was highly uncertain as to what could work in practice in view of the complexity of the educational reform task.

Attempts to change the segregationist status quo in Czech schools – a long-standing, nationwide and thoroughly institutionalized phenomenon – were met with strong resistance domestically. Opposition to desegregation mostly emanated from key stakeholders in the education system: headmasters of elementary and non-mainstream schools, special educational and elementary school teachers (i.e. Association of Special Educators), and by non-Roma but also some Roma parents.[81] Educators strongly criticized the application of inclusion-related reforms and defended the segregationist status quo in a country where public opinion was also in support of ongoing segregation.[82] The reluctance and opposition from key stakeholders and from the society at large was reflected in the half-hearted and ineffective measures introduced by the Ministry of Education in the first years following the *D.H.* ruling.

Human rights NGOs actively engaged in the implementation process and pointed out the strong limitations of the first action plan put forth by the Czech government (NAPIV). In their submissions to the CoM, they depicted it as a "plan to create a plan" that failed to embrace the fundamental principle of inclusive education, to define concrete targets and to allocate resources to it.[83] The ERRC, the Greek Helsinki Monitor and Open Society Justice Initiative (OSJI) highlighted the lack of political will to abolish special-renamed-practical schools. They also pointed to the lack of provisions for collecting data disaggregated by ethnicity, gender and disability, on the basis of which to assess the practical impact of the legislative amendments.[84] In the light of NGOs' reports, the CoM questioned whether NAPIV was put into practice, lacking as it did concrete timelines, indicators and transparent numerical targets for achieving desegregation.[85] Concerned about the lack of progress on the ground, the CoM called upon national authorities to achieve "concrete results."[86] It noted the provisional character of the action plan, and suggested that "where the desired results are not achieved, there [should be] a system for speedy and effective identification of any problems and adaptation of the relevant measures."[87]

Over the next years, the Czech authorities undertook modest legislative reforms, all in the direction of improving safeguards *within* the existing special school system. Reforms sought to limit the incidence of misdiagnosis, and the discriminatory placement of Roma pupils in practical schools: they strengthened procedural guarantees for parental consent, revised diagnostic tests as to render them culturally neutral and objective, instituted annual reassessment of pupils with mental disabilities, and prohibited the placement of children with health or social disadvantages in classes for those with mental disabilities. In its review in 2015, the CoM and NGOs welcomed the reforms of 2011–14 but expressed concerns about their effectiveness, as only a small number of Roma pupils were actually transferred from special to mainstream schools. The CoM urged the Czech authorities to create effective monitoring mechanisms domestically, and to engage in regular data collection.[88] The Czech Republic was slow to respond due to strong domestic resistance to reforming the special school system. Establishing an inclusive education was not a political priority for the government. Still, the *D.H.* judgment remained a powerful source of pressure for the NGOs and human rights bodies advocating its reform.[89]

Despite the protracted and minimalist government measures in the first seven years following the issuing of the *D.H.* judgment, the ongoing CoM supervision kept the reform impetus alive. The CoM and the Department of Execution of Judgments took an incremental approach that gave time and space to domestic actors to engage in dialogue and to reach a level of consensus. They did not impose unrealistic expectations as to the pace and scope of the changes.[90] By maintaining international oversight, the CoM and the DExJ provided venues where the Czech government had to report its actions, and where advocates of inclusive education could bring pressure to bear upon it. The drive and advocacy for reform on the part of NGOs and human rights bodies remained potent and did not subside.[91]

Sustained NGO mobilization and stakeholder engagement over time bore fruits as they paved the way for a degree of consensus to be forged. Domestically, the *D. H.* judgment spun a broader debate about inclusive education, and not just of Roma. As it is aptly described, "those resisting implementation [of the *D.H.* judgment] have at certain periods dominated public discourse and obstructed particular reforms; yet, over time, a broad alliance has emerged which has been instrumental in fostering reform that exceeds what the judgment strictly requires".[92] What critically enabled the domestic pro-implementation officials and reformers to overcome the earlier impasse was a new framing of the issue of Roma segregation that made it possible to garner wider appeal and support. They depicted segregation as part of a broader failure to establish an inclusive education system, leading to the marginalization not only of Roma but also of non-Roma pupils from other socially vulnerable groups.[93]

By incorporating this re-framing, the new reform package that the Czech government presented to the CoM in 2015–16 conveyed a significant shift in policy approach and legal change. While it continued to strengthen safeguards and checks in the diagnosis and placement of children with mild mental disabilities, it also introduced a new strategic objective, which the NGOs had long been advocating, namely, the creation of an inclusive education system. To this end, an important 2016 amendment of the Education Act abolished the educational program for children with mild mental disabilities. It provided for its gradual replacement by a unified curriculum for all primary school pupils.[94] Children with special needs would be principally educated in mainstream schools and assisted with individualized support measures to facilitate their integration. Strengthened domestic monitoring mechanisms would oversee the work of school centers that assessed the cognitive ability of pupils. Legislative reforms also made it compulsory for all children to attend a year of pre-school education to ensure their successful beginning of basic education.[95]

While the CoM welcomed the important 2016 reform of Czech education law, it did not end its supervision of the case but continued its review further to examine how the legal changes were applied in practice. It regularly reviewed the government-submitted data on the distribution of Roma in mainstream schools, and on Roma enrolment in compulsory pre-school education. Taking into consideration the submissions of non-governmental actors, it urged the Czech authorities to channel sufficient resources, to put to practice the announced inclusive education measures and to provide evidence of their effectiveness.[96]

Two years after the announcement of the policy shift towards inclusive education, NGOs submitted data to the CoM showing that the share of Roma children diagnosed with MMD remained high, which was corroborated in reports by the Czech Ombudsperson (Public Defender of Rights). They urged the government to push forward with the reforms, to allocate more resources, and to make public the officially collected data.[97] Submissions by NGOs and the Council of Europe Commissioner for Human Rights noted that segregation appeared to re-emerge in ordinary schools in Roma-inhabited areas, where mainstream schools remained predominantly Roma. In those areas, Roma children were not being diagnosed with mental disabilities but disproportionately as pupils with special learning needs or behavioral disorders.[98] In its latest review of such data in December 2020, the CoM noted a slow and small but visible improvement as regards the integration of Roma pupils in mainstream schools. It still urged the authorities to continue efforts to improve diagnostic tools, to engage stakeholders and NGOs, and to continue monitoring the results of inclusive education reforms.[99]

2.3 Desegregation reform and political backsliding in Hungary

In the early 2000s, Hungarian government authorities acknowledged the existence of Roma school segregation. They sought to tackle it as part of a broader progressive agenda to establish an inclusive education system for all, including for Roma and for persons with disabilities. A number of reforms were introduced to prevent the wrongful placement of children in special schools designed for pupils with mild mental disabilities. They sought to improve the diagnostic tests and the examination procedure, on the basis of which the placement of pupils was decided. A broad range of policies also sought to dismantle separate educational structures, which were intended to help pupils of disadvantaged background "catch up". Such structures had always been a key driver of ethnic segregation in Hungarian education.[100]

Throughout the 2000s, in the struggle for an inclusive education, litigation was systematically used by a few active NGOs – most prominently the Chance for Children Foundation (CFCF) – as a lever of pressure on the government to implement reforms in this area. Strategic litigation was facilitated by the possibility that Hungarian law gives to a third party to bring a lawsuit in the public interest (actio popularis).[101] The CFCF, in some cases in collaboration with the ERRC, lodged complaints before domestic courts to challenge Roma school segregation in various areas, as in the city of Nyíregyháza and in Heves county. In the course of 2000s, human rights bodies (like the Ombudsman) and domestic courts found Roma school segregation to violate equal treatment and to be a form of ethnic discrimination.[102]

In this national context, the ECtHR condemnation of Roma segregation in schools in the *Horvath and Kiss v Hungary* judgment in 2013 certainly "did not arrive as a revolutionary idea".[103] The case was pursued as a follow-on to the *D.H. v Czech Republic* case that served as a model of strategic legal action for the Hungarian activists and lawyers who initiated *Horvath and Kiss*. Unlike in the Czech Republic though, Roma segregation litigation in the ECtHR was a product of home-grown legal activism launched with the goal of pushing ahead with domestic reforms.[104] The CFCF initiated and prepared the case that was litigated before national courts. In 2011, when domestic remedies were exhausted, the case of *Horvath and Kiss* was lodged in the ECtHR, at which point the ERRC also became involved. By the time that the ECtHR issued its final judgment in 2013, legal and policy change towards inclusive education in Hungary had already substantially advanced. Still, the legal and policy changes that had been adopted by the government were a far cry from the situation on the ground, where Roma school segregation persisted in many parts of the country.

Minority segregation in education had already been denounced in Hungarian national law, policy and judicial interpretation in the preceding years. The significance of the 2013 *Horvath and Kiss* judgment though was elevated by a dramatically changed political milieu that had in the meantime ensued with the advent to government power of the conservative Fidesz party in 2010. The new government sought to reverse the progressive policies towards inclusive education, and in 2013, it nationalized control and management of all schools. The responsible central authority though did not take any desegregation measures and took the position that it is not its duty to promote minority integration in schools.[105] Government officials publicly supported the discredited "catch up" special classes, and they introduced legislative changes that threatened to restore the segregationist status quo.[106] This regressive trend was also affirmed in some decisions issued by domestic courts, which paved the way for provisions allowing minority segregation in religious schools.[107] In this shifting political landscape, the release of the *Horvath and Kiss* judgment critically reaffirmed the impermissibility of Roma segregation in the face of political attempts to roll back measures aimed at dismantling it. It also helped generate leverage in ongoing domestic litigation against Roma segregation.

Following its release in 2013, the *Horvath and Kiss* judgment provided a source of external pressure and the frame for continuing domestic reforms towards desegregation despite the adverse shifts in government approach. In response to *Horvath and Kiss*, the Hungarian government submitted six action plans and reports that the CoM reviewed in four rounds of assessment with regular input, analysis and independent documentation from civil society actors. Implementation involved an iterative process of domestic measures reported by state authorities and reviewed by the CoM that in turn advised further action. In its first Action Plan (AP) in 2014, the Hungarian government reported several measures. Many of those had already been adopted in the preceding years prior to the issuing of *Horvath and Kiss*, such as reform of the assessment procedure to render pupils' placement in special schools, objective and non-discriminatory. In the frame of implementing *Horvath and Kiss*, the government presented a few legislative amendments that arguably improved safeguards in the use of diagnostic tests and in the expert examination procedure. It also consulted with NGOs and experts to develop an inclusive education policy for children with special education needs.[108]

By 2015–16, Hungary had in place the legal frame for placement procedures that in principle provided for an objective assessment of a child's learning abilities. The *Horvath and Kiss* judgment possibly was not the single cause of it. The judgment's implementation though provided a frame for the CoM and the DExJ to delve into the application of the new legislation and its effects on the ground as regards the number of Roma children assigned to special schools or classes. The CoM acknowledged that the process for assessing children's learning abilities improved. Taking into account the critical assessment of NGOs though, it requested more information from the Hungarian government about the practical application of the diagnostic tests.[109] In their revised Action Plan in 2017, the Hungarian authorities provided information on the use of diagnostic tests, and on other measures adopted to ensure wider access to public schools and to promote inclusive education, such as making it compulsory for younger children to go to kindergarten.[110] In their 2019 update of the Action Plan, the Hungarian government claimed that there was no longer any systematic misdiagnoses of mental disability among Roma. It also clarified to the CoM that the placement decisions of expert committees could be challenged before administrative authorities and domestic courts.[111]

As in the *D.H.* case, the engagement of NGOs in the implementation of *Horvath and Kiss* was critical in enabling the CoM and the DExJ to apply a rigorous kind of supervision over domestic reforms. The latter would not have been possible without the independent factual information by NGOs. The ERRC and the CFCF provided data showing persistently high overrepresentation of Roma pupils among children in special classes and schools and challenged the Hungarian government's report. They also showed that the new diagnostic tools were not used on a wide scale in Hungary, that the discredited and culturally biased tests were still in use nationwide, and that there was not effective monitoring of expert panels.[112] The Hungarian government countered that the over-representation of Roma in special schools was due to the fact that they were socio-culturally disadvantaged, rather than a result of ethnic discrimination – an argument that it had already advanced before the ECtHR.

Appraisal of the actual effects of the new legislation on ethnic school segregation was linked to the highly contested issue of ethnic data collection, on which the NGOs feedback focused. Far from being a bureaucratic matter, the need to collect and publicly release ethnic data was considered as essential for policy advocacy and change. Without such data, the application and effectiveness of the adopted measures on Roma school placement could not be properly monitored, as NGOs explained in their 2015 report. Hungarian authorities continued to raise strong objections. They insisted that legal guarantees of personal data protection prevented the state from collecting ethnic data, and that the Roma families were highly reluctant to voluntarily declare their ethnicity. In view of these alleged constraints, the CoM urged the Hungarian authorities to use alternative methods, other than voluntary self-declaration, for collecting ethnically disaggregated data, similar to those used by European and international organizations. It reiterated that without such data, "it is difficult to assess whether the measures taken have had an impact and contributed to solving the problem of overrepresentation of Roma children in special schools due to their misdiagnosis as mentally or intellectually disabled".[113]

In the CoM periodic reviews of the *Horváth and Kiss* implementation until the time of this writing (April 2021), the contentious issue of ethnic data collection remained unresolved. The CoM expressed grave concern about the lack of progress in demonstrating the actual impact of the adopted measures on the over-representation of Roma children in special schools. Pointing to the collection of ethnic data in national censuses and through surveys by research institutes, the CoM urged national authorities to provide relevant statistical data.[114] It also made reference to the European Commission's launching in 2016 of infringement proceedings against Hungary on account of Roma school segregation, as a breach of the Race Equality Directive. European Commission, Fundamental Rights Agency and NGO data relayed in CoM review showed a deteriorating trend – the segregation of disadvantaged pupils, including Roma, accelerated in Hungary in the last decade.[115] The CoM asked for further information on the application of the diagnostic tests, the reformed examination system, and the actions that the government took in response to the European Commission's infringement proceedings.[116] Consultations between the CoM and the Hungarian authorities on *Horváth and Kiss* were ongoing in 2021.

3 The variable effects of human rights rulings

In seeking to give effect to the relevant rulings, national authorities in Greece, Croatia, the Czech Republic and Hungary enacted measures that variably affected domestic law and policy. The ECtHR landmark rulings may have disappointed the hopes of those who anticipated that these could end Roma segregation and transform the primary school system into a truly inclusive one. Court judgments though rarely bring fundamental social and policy change, as studies time and again have shown. Yet, in the countries under study, the domestic effects of school segregation judgments were far from negligible. Their implementation triggered significant changes in law, policy and practice, and introduced more transparency and accountability mechanisms in the educational system. The adopted measures made Roma segregation and more broadly the restrictions of minority access to education more difficult to justify and perpetuate as usual.

Reflecting comparatively on the four country cases, the implementation of Roma school segregation judgments had a limited scope in Greece, where the professed, overarching aim of government policy was to enroll all Roma children in schools. It was confined to the closing down of the two segregated schools in the two areas that were the site of the cases (and only partly so in one of the two areas). The Greek judgments were characterized by limited engagement of non-governmental actors and stakeholders before the CoE supervisory bodies and at the national level. This withered the potential of judgments to exert any structural impact, despite the seeming willingness of government authorities to desegregate Roma-only schools. In Croatia, the *Oršuš* judgment prompted legislative changes and the adoption of criteria and rules to ensure an objective process of placing children in special preparatory classes. The CoM supervision of the implementation of *Oršuš* though did not extend to an assessment of the impact of the reforms on the ground. Instead, the CoM terminated its supervision in the absence of follow-on information and feedback by stakeholders and NGOs.

On the other hand, in the Czech Republic and in Hungary, the CoM oversight over judgment implementation was more rigorous, it lasted longer and exerted sustained pressure on national authorities. Proactive and sustained NGO engagement in implementation before the CoE supervisory bodies in the Czech Republic and Hungary decisively contributed to different outcomes: the *D.H.* and the *Horvath and Kiss* judgments remained under external supervision, even though state authorities possibly implemented actions well beyond what was required from the judgment (in the *D.H.* case at least). On the other hand, the CoM prematurely terminated its supervision over the *Orsus* and the *Sampanis, Sampani* and *Lavida* judgments, in which NGO involvement was limited. It did not extend its supervision over the application of new legal provisions (Croatia) and administrative decisions (Greece) in practice.

Domestically, judgment implementation was significantly more impactful in the Czech Republic and in Hungary, even if in very different ways in the two countries, where it is still ongoing (as of December 2021). In the *D.H.* and *Horvath and Kiss* judgments, what was at stake was structural reform – amounting to no less than the establishment of an inclusive model of education. In the *D.H.* case, the structural implications were already apparent in the Court's judgment that found the legislation applicable in primary education at the time to have a prejudicial effect on Roma pupils. In *Horvath and Kiss* on the other hand, the pronounced violations strictly concerned the two individual applicants. It was at the implementation stage that the CoM supervision placed an emphasis on domestic structural reform.

In the Czech Republic, the *D.H.* judgment spurred important legislative reforms to reduce segregation and led to a policy shift towards inclusive education, but only over several cycles of state action and external review. A critical effect "stemmed from the judicial proclamation that the status quo was impermissible under the law".[117] How powerful this effect of the Roma education judgments was is evidenced in the way in which national and European officials firmly condemned segregation as illegitimate after their issuing by the Court – at a tone of censure markedly higher than their lukewarm disapproval in the past.[118] In the Czech Republic, the placement of children outside of mainstream schools must now be based on careful justification. Diagnostic standards improved and the counseling centers became more cautious (and they consulted parents) in school placement decisions of Roma children.[119]

The *D.H.* implementation also spurred the official collection of ethnically disaggregated data, making it possible to monitor the situation of Roma children in ordinary and special education structures, and to assess policy effectiveness. The Czech government amended its laws to allow for systematic collection of ethnic data, which became a priority for the Ministry of Education, and commissioned a number of surveys to this end.[120] The mobilization of NGOs and stakeholders continues in the frame of the *D.H.* judgment that remains under the CoM enhanced supervision.

At the domestic level, the ECtHR judgment implementation and NGO involvement motivated and empowered new stakeholders to mobilize – the so-called "stakeholder effect".[121] In the Czech Republic, reform of the educational system involved cooperation among state authorities (Ministry of Education) and various stakeholders – national human rights institutions, local authorities, schools but also families, social services, and NGOs. NGOs and their coalitions, such as the Czech Society for Inclusive Education, People in Need, Life Together, IQ Roma servis, the League of Human Rights, and the NGO coalition Together to School mobilized to promote inclusive education.[122] Many of them participated in 2017 in the Joint Education of Expert Platform, that assessed progress with the educational reforms and made recommendations.[123] Tackling Roma school segregation is a long-term process where, as an expert on Roma segregation rights points out, "change requires proactive and long-term engagement of educational institutions at all levels to eliminate the physical separation of Roma and non-Roma, to revise educational policies and consistently monitor their impact in order to exclude the possibility of segregation in the future".[124]

Through the lens of the ECHR as an experimentalist regime, the most salient impact of Court judgments is that they convey "destabilization rights": the cases under study powerfully challenged an entrenched segregationist status quo, without, however, prescribing particular remedies to state authorities. The *D.H.* case followed on the footsteps of a string of domestic-level litigation. In the years preceding it, NGOs had taken several cases on Roma school segregation in domestic courts and in Ombudsperson bodies in Romania, Hungary, Bulgaria and the Czech Republic.[125] The *D.H.* judgment marked a breakthrough as it established at the European level what a large number of Roma desegregation cases had achieved in bits and pieces before domestic courts and equality bodies, in the Czech Republic and in other CESE countries.[126] Alongside the other similar judgments issued by the Strasbourg Court, they provided highly authoritative recognition that separate educational arrangements for Roma perpetuate ethnic discrimination with profoundly harmful effects for the individuals involved. By doing so, they acted as catalysts for domestic follow-on litigation.

In Hungary the implementation of *Horvath and Kiss* appeared stagnated in September 2021 (at the time of this writing), with no progress on the key issue on which the CoE supervisory bodies focused their review – namely, the collection and release of ethnic data by Hungarian government authorities. Nonetheless, in a country where desegregation efforts stalled and widespread segregation in practice persisted, the domestic effect of the *Horvath and Kiss* judgment as a force of "destabilization rights" was instrumental and substantial. It provided a critical lever of external support and legitimization in the domestic anti-discrimination and desegregation movement to continue its struggle in a national context characterized by political backsliding. Equally importantly, it re-energized ongoing follow-on litigation: the latter was a centerpiece of NGO mobilization strategies to pressure for systemic change in the area of misdiagnoses and Roma segregation in schools, and the collection of ethnic data.[127]

Domestic litigation prior to and following the issuing of *Horváth and Kiss v Hungary* sought various kinds of remedies, such as damages for segregation and liability for failure to stem misdiagnoses, and in some cases national courts did order resounding remedies.[128] The country's Supreme Court (Curia) ruled that the courts can issue and enforce desegregation orders, including plans submitted by plaintiffs in desegregation cases.[129] In 2017, the Supreme Court upheld a lower court's ruling that ordered the closure and desegregation of an elementary school in Kaposvár.[130] In a high-profile case initiated around 2010, the CFCF challenged culturally biased diagnostic protocols leading to misdiagnosis of Romani children in the Heves county, despite alleged government efforts to prevent this.[131]

Before the domestic appeal court that reviewed the abovementioned Heves case after 2013, the *Horvath and Kiss* judgment powerfully strengthened the arguments of the litigating NGOs (the ERRC and the CFCF), as a lawyer involved in Roma rights litigation explained. They submitted to the domestic appeal court the assessments of the CoE supervisory bodies, the exchanges with the Hungarian authorities and the reports of the NGOs, which enabled the applicants to compellingly explain the issues before the domestic court.[132] In response to the Heves county litigation, the appeal court in 2020 ordered the collection of ethnic data, which the government must implement.[133] NGOs in consultation with experts proposed an alternative method of ethnic data collection by proxy, which does not rely on self-declaration (which Roma families are reluctant to make) but it does not breach the confidentiality of personal data of individuals either.[134] NGOs have pursued further litigation in the ECtHR with a new case concerning Roma school segregation against Hungary pending for review before the ECtHR.[135]

Beyond the respondent states and the ECHR implementation process, the Roma school judgments spawned further legal action before domestic courts in other countries and at the European level. Throughout the 2000s and 2010s, litigation by NGOs before domestic courts continued to challenge Roma segregation and to establish liability for misdiagnoses.[136] While Slovakia was not a target of ECtHR complaints, NGOs pursued domestic litigation inspired by *D.H.* and the other ECtHR rulings. The Centre for Civil and Human Rights (*Poradna*) challenged in domestic courts misdiagnosis, school level segregation and segregation in 'container schools' where Roma were separately placed.[137] NGOs also targeted the European Commission, submitting information on the segregation of Roma children in different countries and arguing that it violated the EU anti-discrimination law (the Race Equality Directive). Since 2014, the European Commission launched infringement proceedings against the Czech Republic (2014), Slovakia (2015) and Hungary (2016) over this issue, expressing concern over national legislation and administrative practices that bring disproportionate number of Roma in special classes.

Transformative human rights change, especially where problems are systemic and complex, is unlikely to occur in the frame of a single judgment and one-shot legal or administrative state action. Instead, it is a longer-term, dynamic and iterative process marked by contestation and resistance. As it is rightly stated, "the desired end point might not become evident for months or even years and may only emerge through the repeated participation of multiple actors in the design of reparations that are both congruent with the decision and politically realizable".[138] Whether ECtHR judgments tackle ethnic discrimination and minority segregation critically depends on sustained mobilization and pressure on governments, within but also beyond the ECtHR judgment implementation process.

4. The experimentalist shift and the limits of legalization

The implementation of Roma school segregation judgments in the four countries under study shows a profound transformation of the ECHR supervisory mechanism in an experimentalist direction. While the Court found that the school system in the four countries discriminated against the Roma, it did not order or indicate specific remedial measures or reforms that states must implement. Remedial measures on how to redress ethnic segregation were initially proposed by the respondent states in their action plans. Action plans are an expression of the principles of subsidiarity and margin of appreciation at work: they allow national authorities to formulate bottom-up, contextualized reform measures to redress human rights breaches.[139] Under the enhanced supervision, in the cases under study, they were over time determined through recuring, and often protracted and contentious exchanges between supervisory bodies (CoM and DExJ), national authorities and non-governmental actors. Non-governmental actors further engaged in follow-on action to counter evasive and delaying government tactics to obstruct reforms towards egalitarian and inclusive education.

It was above all the increasing engagement of non-governmental actors that injected an experimentalist dynamic in the judgment implementation phase. The Court rulings under study were not one-shot, individual legal actions. They were all products of social and legal mobilization by civil society actors, embedded in national and transnational campaigns to pressure governments for changes in law, policy and practice in order to end school segregation. The implementation process before the supervisory bodies provided an additional venue for their mobilization and for pressuring governments to tackle Roma school segregation.

NGOs, like the ERRC, Amnesty International, Open Society Justice Initiative, and COSIVE monitored and critically analyzed the governments' action plans. They countered government attempts to disguise reform (or the lack of it) and the tendency to take a minimalist approach to implementing general measures.[140] By providing critical assessment and data on Roma in special schools, NGOs feedback and reports both pressured and enabled the CoM to peruse the practical effects of the legal and administrative changes introduced by national authorities. Their systematic engagement in the implementation and CoM supervisory process reinforced a more rigorous and exacting kind of external review. The CoM supervision and review, as the cases of Hungary and the Czech Republic show, was not limited to acknowledging state administrative and legislative changes. It further extended to the application and effectiveness of the adopted measures. The wide discretion afforded to the state to design appropriate measures is thus countered by "a more exacting approach that demands evidence of impact and effectiveness before supervision can end".[141]

The high level of mobilization by domestic and international NGOs in the implementation of the *D.H.* judgment was untypical in the ECHR system in the years following its issuing by the ECtHR. However, since then, NGO involvement in the implementation phase has significantly grown, not only in Roma rights cases but in many other areas of strategic human rights litigation. In the last three years alone (from 2018), the human rights judgments under the CoM enhanced supervision that involve NGO participation has nearly tripled.[142] NGOs are eager to keep a case under enhanced supervision (rather than under standard supervision, in which external review is minimal) because it provides them a platform and leverage for continuing their advocacy domestically and transnationally. The

CoM and the Department for the Execution of Judgments pay close attention to well-documented NGO reports in deciding whether to continue their (enhanced) supervision of a case, as NGO experts and lawyers, who are knowledgeable of the system, affirm.[143]

An experimentalist account of the ECHR, as analyzed in the preceding section, departs from the notion of compliance as the yardstick for assessing the effectiveness of court rulings to advance rights protection domestically.[144] Compliance refers to state conformity with international rules and norms enforced from above, and to change of state conduct that conduces to the purposes of the rules.[145] Studies on compliance with international court rulings as a proxy for human rights effectiveness regard long periods of external supervision as foot-dragging that is damaging to the viability of the ECHR.[146]

ECHR experimentalism on the other hand, trades expediency and legalism for much needed pragmatism. Incrementalism, manifested in the recurrent ECHR cycles of external review and NGO monitoring, can provide the space and time for state authorities to figure out what works, and to reach politically pragmatic agreements on how to enhance human rights protection. Recent studies affirm "the dynamic and iterative nature of the implementation process, which may at times stall and at other times accelerate and which may be punctuated by extraneous developments that cause the political space for implementation to widen or narrow".[147] Over recurring cycles of interaction, the evasive implementation strategies of the Czech authorities to maintain segregation were gradually diluted and government policy changed in the direction of inclusive education. In Hungary on the other hand, implementation efforts also continued outside the CoE frame through follow-on litigation before domestic courts.

Complex and structural human rights problems like ethnic segregation in education and institutional racism are rarely amenable to change through orders by an international (or national for that matter) judicial center, legal change alone, or quick and easy remedies. Instead, they involve a great deal of experimentation – applying, assessing and revising different measures as to how effective they are to achieving this goal in different national contexts. Such problems make up an increasing and large share of the cases that the Strasbourg Court reviews, in areas as diverse as delivery of justice, Roma rights, prison conditions, gender violence, and immigration, among many others.

State compliance with international legal norms and court rulings does not necessarily result in enhanced protection, and it may even undermine rights protection.[148] In a study on EU anti-discrimination law and the Roma, Búzás argued that while EU states transposed international and EU anti-discrimination norms into national law, this did not undermine minority school segregation that continued to exist unassailed. Legal compliance with EU law took place alongside government resistance and the failure to conform with the underlying norms in domestic policy and practice. In the Czech Republic, law-norm gaps emanated from a) the domestic transposition of the EU Race Equality Directive in a way that made room for differential treatment when there is "objective and reasonable justification", and b) the restrictive approach that Czech courts took regarding the criteria for establishing a presumption of discrimination (which would trigger a shift of the burden of proof to the state). These arguably created ambiguities and a margin of judicial interpretation that enabled state authorities to perpetuate recruitment-and-placement practices that reinforced the segregation of Roma in special schools.[149]

Compliance studies overlook the inherent ambiguity, diversity and the strong contestation that often surrounds how international norms are translated into national policy and practice. They err in assuming that "there is a stable and agreed meaning to a rule, and we need merely to observe whether it is obeyed".[150] They also overlook the wide range of possible effects that international rulings and norms may have in domestic state law and policy but also in the mobilization and empowerment of rights advocates.[151] The above account on compliance with EU antidiscrimination norms discounts the critical role that civil society and other non-governmental actors can assume to pressure for the enforcement of these norms and related court rulings in domestic policy and practice.

The experimentalist approach to the ECHR supervision of judgment implementation, is observed in other areas of structural reform litigation regarding the Roma, besides school segregation. NGOs advanced claims related to police misconduct against the Roma, ethnic profiling, housing and eviction, and other issues that bring to light a broader pattern of institutional discrimination by law enforcement agents.[152] ECtHR judgments have found human rights violations in the failure of police authorities to engage in an effective investigation to assign responsibility for police violence and to uncover the racist motives of police conduct in incidents involving violence against Roma.[153] In an increasing number of cases, the ECtHR accepted that systematic practices of ethnic profiling against the Roma violated human rights. The experimentalist trend in ECHR judgment implementation is also increasingly common in other areas of structural reform and systemic human rights problems, such as prison reform, gender-based violence, homophobia and violence against LGBTQI, among others.[154]

Notes

1 Leora Bilsky, Rodger D. Citron and Natalie R. Davidson, "From Kiobel Back to Structural Reform: The Hidden Legacy of Holocaust Restitution Litigation," *Stanford Journal of Complex Litigation* 2, no. 1 (2014): 160.
2 "Separate but equal" was a legal doctrine in United States constitutional law, according to which racial segregation did not necessarily violate equal protection clause (Fourteenth Amendment) of the US Constitution, as long as the facilities provided to each "race" were equal.
3 For a compelling exposition of structural racism, see William M. Wiecek, "Structural Racism and the Law in America Today: An Introduction," *Kentucky Law Journal* 100, no. 1 (2011): 1–21.
4 Susan Sturm, "Second Generation Employment Discrimination: A Structural Approach," *Columbia Law Review* 101 (2001): 460.
5 Lilla Farkas and Dezideriu Gergely, *Racial discrimination in education and EU equality law*, European Commission, Directorate-General for Justice and Consumers (2020), 62–64.

6   Open Society Justice Initiative, *Strategic Litigation Impacts: Insights from Global Experience* (New York: Open Society Justice Foundations, 2018), 26.
7   Open Society Justice Initiative, *Strategic Litigation Impacts*, 27.
8   Open Society Justice Initiative, *Strategic Litigation Impacts*, 35.
9   Open Society Justice Initiative, *Strategic Litigation Impacts*, 34.
10 Laura Cashman, "New label no progress: institutional racism and the persistent segregation of Romani students in the Czech Republic," *Race, Ethnicity and Education* 20, no. 5 (2017): 596.
11 See Janneke Gerards, "The Discrimination Grounds of Article 14 of the ECHR," *Human Rights Law Review* 13, no. 1 (2013): 99. The weakness stemming from the subsidiary nature of the Article 14 anti-discrimination provision was overcome with the adoption of Protocol 12 in 2010 that established a freestanding non-discrimination clause.
12 Kevin Boyle, "Article 14 Bites At Last," *EHRAC Bulletin* 5 (Summer 2006): 2.
13 Rory O' Connell, "Cinderella comes to the Ball: Art. 14 and the right to non-discrimination in the ECHR," *Legal Studies* 29, no. 2 (2009): 219.
14 Rory O' Connell, "Substantive equality in the ECtHR?" *Michigan Law Review First Impressions* 107 (2009): 129–133.
15 O'Connell, "Cinderella Comes to the Ball," 212–213. See also Kristin Henrard, "The European Court of Human Rights, Ethnic and Religious Minorities and the Two Dimensions of the Right to Equal Treatment: Jurisprudence at Different Speeds?" *Nordic Journal of Human Rights* 34, no. 3 (2016): 160.
16 Ralph Sandland, "Developing a Jurisprudence of Difference: The Protection of the Human Rights of Travelling Peoples by the European Court of Human Rights," *Human Rights Law Review* 8, no. 3 (2008): 486–7.
17 Sandland, "Developing a Jurisprudence of Difference," 487. In its judgment *Thlimmenos v Greece*, no. 34369/97, 6 April 2000, the ECtHR established that identical treatment of individuals that are differently situated, if it is not objectively justified, could amount to discrimination.
18 Sandland, "Developing a Jurisprudence of Difference," 489. *Chapman v United Kingdom*, no. 27238/95, 18 January 2001.
19 Sandland, "Developing a Jurisprudence of Difference," 491.
20 Interview with co-founder of ERRC, London, 27 March 2012.
21 The EU adopted the Council Directive 2004/43/EC of June 2000, Implementing the Principle of Equal Treatment Between Persons Irrespective of Racial or Ethnic Origin (2004) OJ L113/14.
22 James Goldston, "Race discrimination impact litigation in Eastern Europe – A discussion of legal strategies to confront racial discrimination," *ERRC* (blog), 15 July 1997, http:// www.errc.org/roma-rights-journal/race-discrimination-impact-litigation-in-eastern-europe–a-discussion-of-legal-strategies-to-confront-racial-discrimination.
23 James Goldston, "Public Interest Litigation in Central and Eastern Europe: Roots, Prospects, and Challenges," *Human Rights Quarterly* 28, no. 2 (2006): 508–509, 513.
24 Lilla Farkas, "Mobilising for racial equality in Europe – Roma rights and transnational justice," (PhD Thesis, European University Institute, Department of Law, 28 February 2020), 203.
25 Morag Goodwin, "Taking on racial segregation: the European Court of Human Rights at a Brown v Board of Education moment?" *Rechtsgeleerd Magazijn Themis* 170, no. 3 (2009): 94.
26 Farkas and Gergely, *Racial discrimination in education and EU equality law*, 63–64.
27 Farkas, "Mobilising for racial equality in Europe – Roma rights and transnational justice," 180–182.
28 See Goldston, "Race discrimination impact litigation in Eastern Europe – A discussion of legal strategies to confront racial discrimination."

29 Peter Vermeersch, *The Romani Movement – Minority Politics and Ethnic Mobilization in Contemporary Central Europe* (Oxford: Berghahn Books, 2006), 201.

30 Farkas, "Mobilising for racial equality in Europe," 181–182.

31 Interview (over Skype) with a human rights lawyer from Bulgaria, 16 March 2012.

32 James Goldston, "The Struggle for Roma Rights: Arguments that Have Worked," *Human Rights Quarterly* 32, no. 2 (2010): 323.

33 Morag Goodwin, "White Knights On Chargers: Using the US Approach to Promote Roma Rights in Europe?" *German Law Journal* 5, no. 12 (2004): 1437.

34 *D.H. v Czech Republic*, no. 57325/00, 13 November 2007, § 214.

35 Goodwin, "Taking on racial segregation: the European Court of Human Rights at a *Brown v Board of Education* moment?" 99.

36 Henrard, "The European Court of Human Rights, Ethnic and Religious Minorities and the Two Dimensions of the Right to Equal Treatment," 159.

37 For a discussion of the dissenting opinions, see Goodwin, "Taking on racial segregation: the European Court of Human Rights at a *Brown v Board of Education* moment?" 100–102.

38 O' Connell, "Substantive Equality in the European Court of Human Rights?" 130.

39 The Advisory Committee on the Framework Convention for the Protection of National Minorities, the Council of Europe Commissioner for Human Rights, and the European Commission Against Racism and Intolerance (ECRI).

40 *D.H. v Czech Republic*, no. 57325/00, 13 November 2007, § 200.

41 Third party interventions were submitted by the following NGOs: the International Step by Step Association, the Roma Education Fund, the European Early Childhood Education Research Association; Interights, Human Rights Watch; Minority Rights Group International, the European Network Against Racism, the European Roma Information Office; and the International Federation for Human Rights (Fédération Internationale des Ligues des Droits de l'Homme – FIDH).

42 Mathias Möschel, "Is the European Court of Human Rights Case Law on Anti-Roma Violence 'Beyond Reasonable Doubt'?" *Human Rights Law Review* 12, no. 3 (2012): 495–496.

43 *Oršuš and Others v Croatia*, no. 15766/03, 17 July 2008.

44 *Oršuš and Others v Croatia*, no. 15766/03, 16 March 2010.

45 Farkas, "Mobilising for racial equality in Europe," 180.

46 *Sampanis and Others v Greece*, no. 32526/05, 5 June 2008; *Lavida and Others v Greece*, no. 7973/10, 30 May 2013.

47 Kalina Arabadjieva, "Challenging the school segregation of Roma children in Central and Eastern Europe," *International Journal of Human Rights* 20, no. 1 (2016): 34.

48 *Oršuš and Others v Croatia*, no. 15766/03, 17 July 2008, § 68.

49 These were: a) a clear legal basis for selection, b) an adapted curriculum remedying the supposed lack of proficiency in Croatian language, c) a transfer and monitoring procedure allowing for pupils who gained enough proficiency in Croatian language to transfer again to "normal" mixed classes, and d) an active and structural involvement on the part of the relevant social services due to large drop-out rates. See Van den Bogaert, "Roma Segregation in Education: Direct or Indirect Discrimination?" 745.

50 DExJ, DH - DD(2011)210, "Communication from a NGO in the case of Orsus and others against Croatia", 1115th DH meeting, 25 March 2011.

51 At the end of 2011, Croatia's Action Plan reported that the number of Roma children in elementary school between the 2005–2006 and 2009–2010 school years quadrupled. See DExJ, DH-DD(2011)53 "Action Plan in case of *Orsus and others against Croatia*, 26 January 2011; Secretariat of the Committee of Ministers, DH-DD(2011)544E, "Revised Action Plan", 6 July 2011.

52 Under enhanced supervision, the CoM closely follows implementation progress in a case and engages in exchanges with national authorities.

53 DExJ, DH-DD(2014)455, "Updated Action Plan concerning the case of *Orsus and others against Croatia*", 1201st meeting, 7 April 2014.
54 DExJ, DH-DD(2017)693, "Action Report concerning the case of *Orsus and others against Croatia*", 1294th meeting, 20 July 2017.
55 Barbara Matejcic, "Croatia's Schools Leave Roma Pupils in the Slow Lanes," *Balkan Insight* (blog). 18 November 2020, https://balkaninsight.com/2020/11/18/croa tias-schools-leave-roma-pupils-in-the-slow-lane/.
56 Sinisa-Senad, "Ensuring Readiness and Success for Primary School in Croatia – Integration in Medimurje County," Roma Education Fund, 2016, https://www.roma educationfund.org/ensuring-readiness-and-success-for-primary-school-in-croatia-inte gration-in-medimurje-county/.
57 DExJ, DH - DD(2011)210, "Communication from a NGO in the case of Orsus and others against Croatia", 1115th DH meeting, 25 March 2011.
58 Open Society Justice Initiative, *Strategic Litigation Impacts*, 40.
59 Open Society Justice Initiative, *Strategic Litigation Impacts*, 34.
60 *Sampanis and Others v Greece*, no. 32526/05, 5 June 2008.
61 Bodies like the Council of Europe European Commission against Racism and Intolerance (ECRI) had advocated the need to set up preparatory classes for Roma.
62 See Appendix to Resolution CM/ResDH(2011)119, adopted by the CoM on 14 September 2011.
63 DExJ, DH-DD(2011)263, "Communication from the applicants' representative in the case of *Sampanis and others against Greece*," 1115th Meeting, 14 April 2011.
64 DExJ, DH-DD(2011)263, "Communication from the applicants' representative in the case of Sampanis and others against Greece," 1115th Meeting, 14 April 2011.
65 *Sampani and Others v Greece*, no. 59608/09, 11 December 2012; *Lavida and Others v Greece*, no. 7973/10, 30 May 2013.
66 For an overview, see Minister's Deputies, "*Sampani and others group v Greece*," 1280th Meeting (Human Rights), 7–10 March 2017, CM/Notes/1280/H46–14.
67 DExJ, DH-DD(2013)1221, "Government Action Plan in the case of *Sampani and others against Greece*", 1186th Meeting, 13 November 2013.
68 Interview with representative of the Greek Helsinki Monitor, 6 March 2021.
69 See Minister's Deputies, "Sampani and others group v Greece," 1280th Meeting (Human Rights), 7–10 March 2017, CM/Notes/1280/H46–14.
70 Such a plan would include baseline data of the number of Romani children out of school, concrete enrolment targets, concrete activities to ensure enrolment, named responsible authorities, identified sources of financing, specific monitoring mechanisms and sanctions for authorities found to not meet their obligations. See Secretariat of the Committee of Ministers, DH-DD(2010)586, "Communication from NGOs in the cases of *D.H. and others against Czech Republic, Sampanis and others against Greece and Oršuš and others against Croatia*," 23 November 2010, 15.
71 Interview with representative of the Greek Helsinki Monitor, 6 March 2021.
72 *Horváth and Kiss v Hungary*, no. 11146/11, 29 January 2013, § 127.
73 In the *D.H.* judgment, the Court pointed to the need to ensure that any kind of separate structures are temporary and aimed at the inclusion of students into mainstream schools; any tests to assess the academic suitability of Roma students must be based on clear and objective criteria related to educational needs and not to ethnic origin; and ensure that parental consent to the separate placement of their children is fully informed. *D.H. and Others v Czech Republic*, no. 57325/00, 13 November 2007, § 201–207.
74 The CoM continued its supervision of both judgments at the time of this writing (February 2021).
75 The NGOs that intervened in the implementation process were the ERRC, Amnesty International, Open Society Justice Initiative (OSJI), Czech Society for Inclusive Education (COSIV), League of Human Rights, and Mental Disability Advocacy Center (MDAC).

76 DExJ, DH-DD(2010)586, "Communication from ERRC, Greek Helsinki Monitor and Open Society Justice Initiative in the cases of *D.H. and others against Czech Republic, Sampanis and others against Greece and Oršuš and others against Croatia,*" 23 November 2010, 5–6.

77 Open Society Justice Initiative, *Strategic Litigation Impacts*, 38.

78 Cashman, "New label no progress," 597.

79 A summary of the main points of the 2009 Action Plan is provided in the CoM Information documents, CM/Inf/DH(2010)47, 24 November 2010.

80 On this latter approach, see the submission of the Forum of Human Rights to the CoM in the context of implementing the *D.H.* judgment. See DExJ, DH-DD(2020) 693, "Communication from an NGO (Forum for Human Rights) concerning the case of *D.H. and others v Czech Republic,*" 12 August 2020.

81 Hubert Smekal and Katarina Sipulova, "*D.H. v Czech Republic* Six Years Later: On the Power of an International Human Rights Court to Push Through Systemic Change," *Netherlands Quarterly of Human Rights* 32, no. 3 (2014): 313–315.

82 Cashman, "New label no progress," 601.

83 DExJ, DH-DD(2010)586, "Communication from NGOs in the cases of *D.H. and others against Czech Republic, Sampanis and others against Greece and Oršuš and others against Croatia,*" 23 November 2010.

84 DExJ, DH-DD(2011)1070, "Communication from NGOs (Open Society Justice Initiative + ERRC European Roma Rights Centre) in the case of *D.H. and others against Czech Republic* (App. No. 57325/00)," 1128th Meeting, 28 November 2011.

85 DExJ, DH – DD(2012)1089, "Communication from NGOs (OSJI, COSIV, ERRC, AI and Liga Lydskych Prav), in the case of *D.H. and others v Czech Republic,*" 1157th Meeting, 22 November 2012.

86 For an overview, see Directorate General, Human Rights and Rule of Law, "Memorandum prepared by the Department for the Execution of Judgments of the European Court of Human Rights," 3 March 2015, H/Exec(2015)8, 3.

87 See CoM Information documents, CM/Inf/DH(2010)47, 24 November 2010, 5.

88 See Directorate General, Human Rights and Rule of Law, "Memorandum prepared by the Department for the Execution of Judgments of the European Court of Human Rights," 3 March 2015, H/Exec(2015)8, 4, 8.

89 Smekal and Sipulova, "*D.H. v Czech Republic* Six Years Later," 316–319.

90 Alice Donald and Anne-Katrin Speck, "The Dynamics of Domestic Human Rights Implementation: Lessons from Qualitative Research in Europe," *Journal of Human Rights Practice* 12, no. 1 (2020): 62–63.

91 Open Society Justice Initiative, *Strategic Litigation Impacts: Roma School Desegregation* (New York: Open Society Foundations, 2016), 60.

92 Donald and Speck, "The Dynamics of Domestic Human Rights Implementation," 66.

93 Donald and Speck, "The Dynamics of Domestic Human Rights Implementation," 64–65.

94 Ministers' Deputies, H46–12, "*D.H. and Others v. Czech Republic* (No. 57325/00)," 1288th Meeting, 7 June 2017.

95 Ministers' Deputies, Notes on the Agenda, "H46–11 *D.H. and others v. the Czech Republic,*" 1259th Meeting, 7–9 June 2016, CM/Notes/1259/H46–11, 2. See also "Comprehensive Evaluation of the Reform of Inclusive Education in Relation to Roma Pupils", in Secretariat of the Committee of Ministers, DH-DD(2019)391, "Communication from the authorities in the case of *D.H. and others v. Czech Republic,*" 1348 Meting, 9 April 2019.

96 Ministers' Deputies, Notes on the Agenda, "H46–12 *D.H. and Others v. Czech Republic,*" 7 June 2017, CM/Notes/1288/H46–12.

97   See DExJ, DH-DD(2018)554, "Communication from a NGO (Open Society Fund Prague and Open Society Justice Initiative) in the case of *D.H. v. Czech Republic* and reply from the authorities," 6 June 2018.

98   DExJ, DH-DD(2019) Communication from a NHRI in the case of *D.H. v. Czech Republic*, 7 June 2019.

99   Ministers' Deputies, Notes, *D.H. and Others v Czech Republic*, 3 December 2020, CM/Notes/1390/H46–8.

100   Open Society Justice Initiative, *Strategic Litigation Impacts*, 35, 42–43.

101   Actio popularis was abolished in 2012 on the occasion of a profound reform of the Hungarian constitutional system.

102   See Bernard Rorke, "Hungary: A short history of segregation," *ERRC* (blog), 16 July 2015, http://www.errc.org/news/hungary-a-short-history-of-segregation.

103   Open Society Justice Initiative, *Strategic Litigation Impacts*, 73.

104   Interview with lawyer involved in Roma school segregation litigation in Hungary, 10 March 2021.

105   European Roma Rights Center (ERRC), Written comments of the ERRC concerning Hungary, for consideration of the Human Rights Committee 122nd Session (12 March – 6 April 2018), https://tbinternet.ohchr.org/Treaties/CCPR/Shared% 20Documents/HUN/INT_CCPR_CSS_HUN_30228_E.pdf, 4.

106   Open Society Justice Initiative, *Strategic Litigation Impacts*, 73. In 2014, the Hungarian government amended the Act on Public Education to allow for church-maintained schools and for schools which are serving national minorities to have segregated classes.

107   In April 2015, in the Nyíregyháza case, the Hungarian Supreme Court overturned an earlier judgment and exempted the Greek Catholic Church from anti-discrimination provisions in law, allowing the Church to re-open and run a segregated Roma-only school. See Rorke, "Hungary: A short history of segregation."

108   DH-DD(2014)186, Action Report and Action Plan of 29 January 2014, *Horváth and Kiss v. Hungary* judgment, 7 February 2014.

109   CoM, Notes on the Agenda, "H46–9 Horváth and Kiss v. Hungary (Application No. 11146/11)," 1242nd meeting, 10 December 2015, CM/Notes/1243/H46–9CM/.

110   DExJ, DH-DD(2017)1075, "Updated Action Report and Action Plan, *Horváth and Kiss v. Hungary*," 1302nd Meeting, 28 September 2017.

111   DExJ, DH-DD(2019)384, "Action Plan - Communication from Hungary concerning the case of *Horváth and Kiss v. Hungary*," 1348th Meeting, 8 April 2019.

112   DExJ, DH-DD(2015)1292, "Communication from a NGO (CFCF and ERRC) in the case of *Horvath and Kiss v Hungary* and reply from the authorities," 1243rd Meeting, 30 November 2015.

113   CoM, Notes on the Agenda, "H46–13 Horváth and Kiss v. Hungary (Application No. 11146/11)," 1302nd Meeting, 7 December 2017, CM/Notes/1302/H46–13.

114   CoM, Notes on the Agenda, "H46–11 Horváth and Kiss v. Hungary," 1348th Meeting, 6 June 2019, CM/Notes/1348/H46–11.

115   CoM, Notes on the Agenda, "H46–11 Horváth and Kiss v. Hungary," 1348th Meeting, 6 June 2019, CM/Notes/1348/H46–11.

116   CoM, Notes on the Agenda, "H46–11 Horváth and Kiss v. Hungary," 1348th Meeting, 6 June 2019, CM/Notes/1348/H46–11.

117   Open Society Justice Initiative, *Strategic Litigation Impacts*, 71.

118   Open Society Justice Initiative, *Strategic Litigation Impacts*, 71–72.

119   Open Society Justice Initiative, *Strategic Litigation Impacts: Roma School Desegregation*, 47–48.

120   Open Society Justice Initiative, *Strategic Litigation Impacts: Roma School Desegregation*, 37–38.

121   Charles F. Sabel and William H. Simon, "Destabilization Rights: How Public Law Litigation Succeeds," *Harvard Law Review* 117, no. 4 (2004): 1077.

122 DExJ, DH-DD(2019)673, "Reply from the authorities following a communication from a NGO in the case of *D.H. and others v Czech Republic*", 1355th Meeting, 14 June 2019, 4. See also Zoltán I. Búzás, "Is the Good News About Law Compliance Good News About Norm Compliance? The Case of Racial Equality," *International Organization* 72, no. 2 (2018): 375–376.

123 CoM, "H46–12 D.H. and Others v. Czech Republic," 1318th Meeting, 5–7 June 2018, CM/Del/Dec(2017)1288/H46–12.

124 Sina Van den Bogaert, "Roma Segregation in Education: Direct or Indirect Discrimination?" *ZaöRV* 71 (2011), 753.

125 Farkas, "Mobilising for racial equality in Europe," 191–192.

126 Farkas, "Mobilising for racial equality in Europe," 191–192, 196–197.

127 See Open Society Justice Initiative, *Strategic Litigation Impacts*, 64.

128 Farkas, "Mobilising for racial equality in Europe," 197–198.

129 FXB Center for Health and Human Rights at Harvard University, *Strategies and Tactics to Combat Segregation of Roma Children in Schools* (Harvard University, 2015), 117.

130 European Roma Rights Center (ERRC), Written comments of the ERRC concerning Hungary, for consideration of the Human Rights Committee 122nd Session (12 March – 6 April 2018), https://tbinternet.ohchr.org/Treaties/CCPR/Shared%20Documents/HUN/INT_CCPR_CSS_HUN_30228_E.pdf, 4.

131 Open Society Justice Initiative, *Strategic Litigation Impacts*, 37–38.

132 Interview, lawyer involved in Roma rights litigation in Hungary, 24 March 2021.

133 NGO-driven litigation on the issue of ethnic data collection related to Roma continues not only at the national but also at the European level. For example, the ERRC took a case to the European Committee of Social Rights against the Czech Republic, which concerns ethnic data collection in child care institutions, where there is disproportionate placement of Roma children.

134 Interview, lawyer involved in Roma rights litigation in Hungary, 24 March 2021.

135 *Imre Szolcsan v Hungary*, no. 24408/16, case communicated on 9 October 2019.

136 Farkas and Gergely, *Racial discrimination in education and EU equality law*, 65–66.

137 Farkas and Gergely, *Racial discrimination in education and EU equality law*, 67.

138 Long, and Speck, "Identifying and Assessing the Implementation of Human Rights Decisions," 147.

139 Aysel Eybil Küçüksu, "Enforcing Rights Beyond Litigation: Mapping HRO Strategies in Monitoring ECtHR Judgment Implementation," iCourts Working Paper Series, no. 264 (2021): 5.

140 Küçüksu, "Enforcing Rights Beyond Litigation," 13–15; Alice Donald, Debra Long, and Anne-Katrin Speck, "Identifying and Assessing the Implementation of Human Rights Decisions," *Journal of Human Rights Practice* 12, no. 1 (2020): 128.

141 Donald, Long, and Speck, "Identifying and Assessing the Implementation of Human Rights Decisions," 137.

142 Interview with a European Implementation Network representative, 8 March 2021.

143 Interview with a European Implementation Network representative, 8 March 2021.

144 Andreas von Staden, *Strategies of Compliance with the European Court of Human Rights* (Pennsylvania: University of Pennsylvania Press, 2018).

145 Robert Howse, and Ruti Teitel, "Beyond Compliance: Rethinking Why International Law Really Matters," *Global Policy* 1, no.2 (2010): 130.

146 Darren Hawkings and Wade Jacoby Hawkings, "Partial Compliance: A Comparison of the European and Inter-American Courts for Human Rights," *Journal of International Law and International Relations* 6, no.1 (2010): 35–85.

147 Donald and Speck, "The Dynamics of Domestic Human Rights Implementation: Lessons from Qualitative Research in Europe," 48–70.

148 Búzás, "Is the Good News About Law Compliance Good News About Norm Compliance? The Case of Racial Equality," 351–385.

149 Búzás, "Is the Good News About Law Compliance Good News About Norm Compliance?", 373–377.
150 Howse and Teitel, "Beyond Compliance," 127.
151 See Alexandra Huneeus, "Compliance with Judgments and Decisions," in *The Oxford Handbook of International Adjudication*, eds. Cesare P. R. Romano, Karen J. Alter, and Yuval Shany (Oxford: Oxford University Press, 2013), 438–460.
152 Gabor Hera, "The relationship between the Roma and the police: a Roma perspective," *Policing and Society* 27, no. 4 (2017): 393–394, 396.
153 *Nachova v Bulgaria*, nos. 43577/98 and 43579/98, 6 July 2005; *Bekos and Koutropoulos v Greece*, no. 15250/02, 13 March 2006. See also Farkas, "Mobilising for racial equality in Europe," 206–208.
154 See for example, the *Identoba and Others v Georgia*, no. 73235/12, 12 May 2015. On its implementation and the role of NGOs in it, see Alice Donald, "The Power of Persistence: How NGOs can Ensure that Judgments Lead to Justice," http://bristol. ac.uk/media-library/sites/law/hric/2021-documents/8.%20Power%20of%20Persis tence_Donald_ENG.pdf.

7 Pressuring for asylum and immigration detention reform

Over the past twenty years, an increasing number of petitions prompted the Court to review systemic human rights problems related to immigration and asylum management in different countries. Structural reform litigation (SRL) involved the lodging of repeat individual claims, as well as selected test cases initiated or supported by non-governmental organizations, as we saw in chapter 5. A variety of NGOs systematically or selectively supported cases litigated in the Strasbourg Court and intervened as third parties to advance arguments in favor of migrants' protection. Civil society and legal activism sought to expose deficiencies in national asylum systems and to pressure governments for reform, often as part of broader advocacy campaigns and social struggles for migrants' rights. Over the past fifteen years, non-governmental organizations have increasingly extended their mobilization in the judgment implementation phase too. Their participation transforms the supervisory mechanism and reinforces the functioning of the ECHR as a regime of experimentalist governance.

This chapter explores the ECHR supervision and domestic implementation of Court rulings that involve complex and structural human rights problems related to immigration and asylum. Until the 2000s, adverse judgments in this area primarily targeted West European states that were longstanding immigration countries. Any violations stemmed from specific gaps and occasional failures in rights protection, which, even if serious, rarely emanated from systemic deficiencies. Rulings that challenge specific flaws in the handling of individual cases, such as expulsion orders on non-refoulement grounds, continue to make up the bulk of ECtHR judgments against West European states. In redressing violations of this nature, national authorities of the respondent state typically adopt individual measures, such as issuing a residence permit or referring a negative asylum decision back to immigration services for new proceedings.[1]

In some cases, national authorities also undertake general measures to remedy violations, such as specific legislative amendments, adjustments of administrative practice, or shifts in domestic judicial approach. For example, in the case of *Salah Sheekh*, the ECtHR found the Netherlands in violation of Article 3 ECHR on account of the applicant's imminent expulsion to Somalia, where he was at risk of inhuman treatment as a member of the Ashraf minority.[2] In response, the Dutch authorities modified their non-refoulement/expulsion policy specifically for those

DOI: 10.4324/9781003256489-9

Third Country Nationals (TCNs), who were members of vulnerable minority groups.[3] In another judgment, *Saadi v United Kingdom*, the ECtHR found the UK in violation of Article 5 ECHR (right to liberty and security) for detaining an Iraqi asylum seeker.[4] British authorities reviewed his application through a fast-track procedure but failed to promptly inform him of the reasons for his detention. In response to this judgment, state authorities instructed immigration officers responsible for filling out the relevant detention forms, to immediately inform fast-tracked asylum applicants who were detained, of the reason for their detention.[5]

Since the 2000s though, an increasing number of migration-related complaints in the ECtHR involved structural human rights breaches of greater complexity and scale than the cases described above. They brought to light substandard conditions of detention, dysfunctional asylum procedures, and unacceptable migrant reception structures, among others, that necessitated far reaching legal and structural reforms within states. A significant number of such cases targeted south European states at the external border of the EU, but also states in Central and East Europe, that lacked well-established and effective migration and asylum management systems. In the second decade of the 2000s, countries like Greece and Italy saw sharply rising numbers of migrants and refugees (mixed flows) from Asia, Africa and the Middle East crossing their borders. Their numbers peaked in 2014–15, overwhelming reception capacities and exposing the structural shortcomings of immigration management in these countries.

From the 2000s onwards, systematic and strategic legal action increasingly supported by activist lawyers and civil society actors, exposed the structural deficiencies of Greece's asylum system in the ECtHR. In response, the Court found violations of the Convention in scores of individual cases that brought to light the profound inadequacies and unlawful administrative practices related to asylum, arbitrary immigration detention and reception conditions, among others. The first part of this chapter describes the migrant-related ECtHR litigation targeting Greece and the resulting judgments finding breaches of the Convention.

The ECtHR adverse judgments against Greece set in an ongoing (at the time of this writing, January 2022) process of domestic reform, under the supervision of the Committee of Ministers (hereby CoM) supported by the Department for the Execution of Judgments (DExecJ). In applying the new working methods for complex and structural breaches, their oversight focused not on a case-by-case assessment of remedial measures, but on a few leading cases, under which a large number of repeat cases were grouped. In essence, they exercised supervision over entire areas of domestic law and executive action related to immigration and asylum management. Greek governments sought to enhance legal safeguards and conditions of detention, to (re)structure the asylum system in line with basic procedural and substantive safeguards, and to improve reception conditions. Drawing from a wealth of reports, action plans, decisions and memoranda exchanged between the ECHR supervisory bodies, Greek authorities and non-governmental actors, the second part of this chapter examines the various measures and reforms implemented to redress human rights violations.

As a EU member state, Greece's domestic asylum and migration management system is fundamentally shaped by and inextricably linked with EU asylum law and policy. Litigation in the Strasbourg Court directed at Greece also targeted key aspects of EU asylum law – the Dublin Regulation in particular. Even though the EU is not a party to the ECHR, the judgments that found Greece's asylum system seriously deficient had far reaching implications also for EU asylum law and policy. The third part of this chapter examines the ramifications of these judgments – the *M.S.S.* being the leading one – for EU asylum law and policy.

In violations of a structural nature, this chapter argues, the growing involvement of non-governmental actors in ECtHR litigation and more recently in the implementation phase, fundamentally reconfigured the nature and extent of the Convention's external oversight into an experimentalist endeavor. National authorities enacted reforms in deliberation with the supervisory bodies, and significantly, with the participation of a variety of non-governmental actors who provided regular feedback in recurring cycles of review, revision and follow-on action. This experimentalist pattern of multi-actor interaction left far-reaching discretion of national authorities, but it also reinforced external accountability and pressure for human rights reform. While domestic reforms in Greece regressed with rising immigration flows and policy shifts, leading ECtHR judgments had substantial consequences for the implementation of EU law, being as they were incorporated in proactive civil society mobilization and advocacy at the EU level.

1 Litigating for human rights of asylum seekers in Greece

Until well into the 2000s, the approach of Greek authorities to managing the increasing numbers of undocumented migrants entering the country primarily relied on arrest and internment. A properly equipped asylum service and an application procedure that met basic human rights guarantees were entirely lacking. Instead, responsibility for asylum applications was assigned to the Directorate of the Greek Police, an institution that did not have the capacity, training or expertise to carry it out. As a result, immigrants who might have been entitled to international protection faced considerable obstacles in accessing the asylum procedure. They also faced the risk of expulsion without serious consideration of their claims.[6]

While a number of individual complaints involving immigrants in Greece had been brought in the ECtHR until the early 2000s, it was not until the second half of the decade that human rights litigation became systematic in this area. At that time, a group of activist lawyers and a few NGOs like the Greek Council for Refugees (GCR) began to pursue ECtHR litigation as a strategic form of action in a loosely coordinated fashion, to promote migrants' rights.[7] From about 2005–2006 onwards, scores of migrant-related petitions were regularly brought to the ECtHR against Greece with the support of a relatively small number of immigration lawyers and a few NGOs. They raised claims about breaches related to the lawfulness and conditions of detention, and to asylum procedure – two closely interlinked areas in the country's highly deficient immigration management system at the time.

Greece's systemic deficiencies in the migration reception and asylum management system were condemned by the ECtHR in the landmark judgment of *M.S.S. v Greece and Belgium*. The *M.S.S.* case was a product of strategic litigation and transnational mobilization. It concerned an asylum seeker from Afghanistan who was returned back by Belgian authorities back to Greece, where he had made his entry into the EU, in accordance with the EU's Dublin Regulation. Before being removed to Greece, he contacted a committed human rights lawyer in Belgium, who prepared a petition for the ECtHR. The applicant's lawyer had what has been characterized as a brilliant idea to direct the complaints not only at the transferring state (Belgium), as *K.R.S.* had done earlier, but also at the receiving state (Greece).[8] The lawyer drew from the wealth of information available by human rights and international organizations to document asylum conditions in Greece, where he made contact with immigration lawyers and NGOs.

Once the case was communicated to the governments, a large number of NGOs (AIRE Center, Amnesty International, and others), the UNHCR and state governments were granted leave to intervene as third parties before the ECtHR Grand Chamber. They had different agendas and their interventions were driven by varying and adversarial motives and goals. Governments asserted the prerogative of states to control migration.[9] The Netherlands and the UK argued that deficiencies in the Greek asylum system were not of such magnitude as to render the protection afforded to asylum seekers illusory. They claimed that to refrain from transferring people there would undermine inter-state trust and the effectiveness European asylum procedures.[10] Non-governmental actors on the other hand, advocated for enhanced protection for asylum seekers in Greece and challenged the substantial disparities in levels of rights protection in different EU Member States.

Many of the NGOs intervened as third parties in the *M.S.S.* case as part of their mobilization in a broader transnational campaign to challenge the asymmetric nature of EU asylum law. They specifically criticized the highly unequal allocation of responsibility among member states that arguably worked to the detriment of human rights protection. In this regard, the *M.S.S.* case followed the trail of earlier litigation pursued at the national and European level.[11] It sought to challenge a) the assigning of primary responsibility for the management of asylum claims to the state of first entry – effectively placing a disproportionate burden on member states at the south European periphery; and b) the presumption entailed in the Dublin regulation that all EU Member States are safe (that they act in accordance with fundamental rights) for purposes of dealing with asylum applicants. Underpinning such challenges was the quest for a fairer distribution of responsibility among EU Member States in processing asylum claims that would give effect to the principle of solidarity enshrined in EU law.

The *M.S.S.* judgment that was released in early 2011 was a massive condemnation of Greece's malfunctioning asylum system. The ECtHR recognized the excessive difficulties that states at the EU's external border like Greece faced, but it also found multiple human rights violations on account of: a) poor detention conditions and degrading treatment by the police; b) the failure of Greek authorities to take into account the applicant's vulnerability, to inform him about possibilities for accommodation (stipulated in the EU's Reception Conditions Directive[12]), and to promptly examine his asylum application; and c) several other deficiencies of the asylum procedures that included a poorly functioning notification procedure and lack of information in a language understood by asylum applicants, including about legal aid and the possibility of appeal.[13] Altogether, these systemic failures increased the risk of returning a person to his/her country without a proper examination of his/her application and without having access to an effective remedy (Articles 3 and 13 ECHR).

The *M.S.S.* judgment also found that Belgium violated Article 3 and 13 ECHR for returning the applicant to Greece, even though the Belgian authorities were well aware of the country's dysfunctional asylum system. Thus, the judgment categorically challenged the presumption embedded in the Dublin system that all EU member states are "safe" regarding their level of rights protection.

International bodies like the United Nations High Commissioner for Refugees (UNHCR) and the Council of Europe Commissioner of Human Rights, and NGOs with knowledge of the national and local context were instrumental in providing the evidential basis for framing the failures of the asylum procedure and the poor living conditions as human rights breaches. Their reports and third-party submissions did not merely corroborate the evidence for alleged violations in the individual case of the *M.S.S.* Most importantly, they were critical in enabling the Court to establish the systemic deficiencies of the Greek asylum system, thus calling attention to the need for structural reform.[14] The Court concluded that "the situation described by the applicant exists on a large scale and is the everyday lot of a large number of asylum-seekers with the same profile as that of the applicant."[15]

The ECtHR extensively referred to reports by the European Committee for the Prevention of Torture (CPT) Amnesty International (AI) and Medecins sans Frontieres to determine the systematic placement of asylum seekers in detention without informing them of the reasons for their detention (*M.S.S. v Belgium and Greece*, § 226). UNHCR surveys showed that almost all first-instance decisions on asylum applications in Greece were negative and drafted in a stereotyped manner; the rate of asylum or subsidiary protection granted by Greek authorities was extremely low; and the watchdog role played by the refugee advisory committees at second instance had been removed. The Council of Europe Commissioner of Human Rights, the UNHCR, Amnesty International and the AIRE Center documented the situation of extreme poverty and destitution, which asylum seekers in Greece experienced. The evidence and information provided by these non-governmental actors prompted the Court (as it itself acknowledged) to depart from its earlier position in a similar case in 2008, the *K.R.S. v UK*[16], which it had deemed inadmissible.[17]

Meanwhile, two activist lawyers from Greece brought another case to the ECtHR that exposed the lack of an appropriate frame in Greece for dealing with the particularly precarious situation of unaccompanied minors (UMs).[18] *Rahimi v*

Greece concerned the detention of an unaccompanied minor from Afghanistan who sought asylum in Greece. In its judgment, the ECtHR stated that it was incumbent on the Greek State to protect and care for such vulnerable individuals. The applicant's conditions of detention in the same space as adult detainees and the authorities' failure to provide him with suitable care following his release, amounted to degrading treatment (Article 3 ECHR). They also breached his right to liberty and security (Article 5 ECHR) and violated Article 13 ECHR on account of the lack of an effective domestic remedy. Unlike the *M.S.S.*, the *Rahimi* case did not attract any third-party interveners. Yet, the lawyers representing the applicant relied on a large number of reports by NGOs, the UNHCR, and other bodies, to build their case and to document the situation of unaccompanied migrant children in Greece.

In sum, through test case (as in *M.S.S.*) and repeat litigation (as in *Rahimi* and in many other repetitive cases), lawyers and non-governmental actors framed the problems and conditions facing migrants and asylum seekers in Greece as breaches of the Convention – the key first phase in human rights experimentalism. By doing so, they challenged the lack of a proper and effective asylum procedure in Greece, the use of detention as a substitute for it, and the poor living conditions of asylum seekers. The resulting judgments did not prescribe any remedial measures for improving rights protection in Greece's asylum and reception system – areas that are administratively complex and surrounded by strong political contestation. The release of the *M.S.S.* and *Rahimi* judgments marked the onset of a long implementation process in Greece under the supervision of the Committee of Ministers (CoM) and the Department for the Execution of judgments (DExJ), to which we turn the next section.

2 Judgment implementation and domestic asylum reform

The implementation of *M.S.S.* and *Rahimi* – leading cases for over thirty repetitive ECtHR judgments against Greece (see Table 7.1) – set a frame of external supervision over continuing, and often evasive, efforts of national authorities to reform immigration detention and asylum structures. Seeking to bring these areas into conformity with ECHR standards, they pursued legislative, administrative and other changes related to asylum procedure, reception and living conditions of asylum seekers, and unaccompanied minors (UM). Domestically, various ministries and administrative bodies have competencies in the fields of migration and asylum.[19] We can discern three key phases in the responses of Greek authorities: a) the 2011–13 phase, following the release of the *M.S.S* and the *Rahimi*, when key legislative reforms and amendments were promulgated, b) the 2014–16 phase that was marked by slow progress in implementation and administrative practice and new pressures created by the sharp rise of mass migrant inflows, and c) the 2017–19 phase when the increased numbers of migrants overburdened the capacity of the new reception and asylum system, and the conditions that ensued after the EU-Turkey statement raised new human rights issues.

Table 7.1 ECtHR judgments related to asylum system in Greece

Leading cases	Repetitive cases	Cause of human rights breaches	ECHR Articles violated	Non-governmental stakeholders involved (directly or indirectly)	Implementation status
M.S.S. v Greece and Belgium (2011) and 16 other cases	*Tabesh v Greece* (8256/07, 2010); *A.F. v Greece* (2013); *B.M. v Greece* (2014); *Bygylashvili* (2012); *Chkhartishvili* (2013); *De Los Santos and De La Cruz* (2014); *F.H. Horshill* (2014); *Kaja* (2013); *Tatishvili* (2006); *A.L.K.* (2014); *H.H.* (2015); *Chazaryan and Others* (2015); *A.Y.* (2016); *Tenko* (2016); *S.G.* (2017); *A.E.A.* (2018)	- Lack of an effective remedy against expulsion due to deficiencies in the registration and examination of asylum applications (i.e. lack of thorough and timely examination of asylum claim and the risks incurred in case of expulsion to countries of origin)	Article 3 ECHR Article 13 ECHR	Litigation: As TPIs, Centre for Advice on Individual Rights (AIRE Centre); Amnesty International (AI); CoE Commissioner of Human Rights; UNHCR; Greek Helsinki Monitor (GHM). Reports by CPT, Human Rights Watch (HRW), AI, Cimade, CoE Commissioner of Human Rights, Medecins sans Frontieres Implementation: Greek Council for Refugees, GHM, Refugee Rights Europe, Open Society Justice Initiative (OSJI), AI, International Commission of Jurists (ICJ), European Council on Refugees and Exiles (ECRE), Hellenic League for Human Rights; UNHCR	Closed (2009)
M.S.S. v Greece and Belgium (2011)	*A.L.K.* (2015); *H.H.* (2015); *F.H.* (2014); *S.G.* (2017);	- Degrading treatment due to living conditions of asylum seekers	Article 3 ECHR	Litigation: see above	Open
Rahimi v Greece (2011)	*Barjamaj* (2013); *Housein* (2014); *H. A. and Others* (2019); *Sh.D. and Others* (2019)	- Degrading treatment due to living conditions of asylum seekers, with special attention to the needs of unaccompanied minors	-Article 3 ECHR	- Implementation: Greek Helsinki Monitor; Refugee Rights Europe; Greek Council for Refugees	Partially closed and partially open[20]

Asylum reform had already been on the agenda of the Greek government when the ECtHR issued the *M.S.S.* and the *Rahimi* judgments in 2011. The EU had put pressure on Greece – occupying a critical position in the Schengen zone as a state of first entry – to put in place an effective system to manage and stem the flow of irregular migrants. Greece was also its weak link, being the entry point of most irregular migrants in the EU. The EU had been deeply concerned about the lack of a proper asylum system, which was out of line with minimum standards for receiving and processing asylum applications, and it pledged financial and logistical support for setting up such a system. In 2010, Greek authorities presented the Greek Action Plan on Migration Management to the EU Justice and Home Affairs Council that outlined strategic priorities for migration management and reception, and institutional restructuring.[21] The EU Council of Ministers was already monitoring progress with the reform of the Greek asylum system.[22]

The release of the *M.S.S.* and *Rahimi* judgments in 2011 provided a strong impetus for pushing forward a domestic reform process that had not yet taken off the ground, despite EU pressure.[23] In 2011, the Greek government submitted to the CoM the abovementioned Greek Action Plan on Migration Management, a comprehensive program for the establishment of a modern asylum system.[24] More importantly, it passed a law that established an Asylum and First Reception Service, including an Appeals Authority to examine appeals at second level.[25] It provided for a full-fledged and independent asylum service with regional offices, staffed with trained civil servants, and furnished with all essential mechanisms (for notification, interpretation, legal assistance, etc.) The new law also provided for the establishment of the First Reception Centers (FRC) to screen newly arriving migrants and direct them to the Regional Asylum Office and to appropriate accommodation facilities. Until the new Asylum Service became operational, a transitional procedure was foreseen to clear a sizeable backlog of asylum claims.[26] The new Asylum Service would function in line with the EU Qualification Directive, establishing minimum qualifications about granting and withdrawing the status of refugee.[27]

The implementation of the *M.S.S.* and *Rahimi* groups of judgments established a vital frame for the continuous reform of Greece's asylum system under the oversight of the CoM and the Department for the Execution of Judgments (DExJ). Greek authorities submitted to the CoM that the proposed reforms described above would facilitate access to asylum and the processing of applications.[28] The implementing measures were discussed with the CoM and the DExJ in iterative rounds of external assessment and state response over a period of ten years. NGOs and other stakeholders (national and international) regularly intervened before the CoE supervisory bodies. They monitored and critically appraised government measures, supplied independent information, and suggested alternative courses of action. From 2011 and until the time of this writing (December 2021), Greek authorities submitted to the CoM thirteen reports and other communications (letters, memos, draft laws, etc.), the UNHCR submitted 5 and NGOs twenty-two reports and letters.[29]

The new Asylum Service became operational in 2013 and put in place in Greece a basic infrastructure for processing asylum claims. The CoM acknowledged it as a milestone of progress, yet, it did not end their supervision of domestic reforms in connection with the *M.S.S.* and *Rahimi* judgments. It continued its oversight over the application of the legislated measures into practice. In assessing the capacity and effectiveness of the new Asylum Service, the CoM invited Greek authorities to intensify their efforts and to provide concrete information on its functioning: recruitment and training of staff, the operation of the new Asylum Offices; data on the applications registered and processed; the evaluation procedure for vulnerable persons, and the number of arrested and deported migrants.[30]

The engagement of several non-governmental actors in the implementation phase was instrumental in providing the factual information for the CoM and the DExJ to both continue and deepen its oversight in successive rounds of assessment over the next eight years. NGOs active in the migration field and with knowledge of the local and national situation, as well as international bodies such as the United Nations High Commissioner for Refugees (UNHCR) monitored the operation of the nascent asylum structures and provided their own documentation. In their submissions to the CoM in 2012–13, they identified persistent shortcomings that continued to endanger migrants' human rights in Greece. The International Commission of Jurists (ICJ), the European Council on Refugees and Exiles (ECRE), and the Open Society Institute (OSI) reported substantial delays in setting up the Asylum Service and the Appeals Authority, that constrained access to the asylum procedure. The ICJ, the ECRE and the Hellenic League for Human Rights (HLHR) pointed to shortcomings in interpretation, information and legal aid, that placed asylum seekers at risk of being deported without filling an application.[31]

The documentation and critical analyses of implementing measures that NGOs and other stakeholders submitted to the CoM strengthened external control and accountability of Greek government actions. In response to the CoM review in 2015, Greek authorities reported the creation of ten more Asylum Service units, staff increases, the streamlining of information to migrants, and provision of free legal aid to appeal asylum decisions.[32] The Director of the Asylum Service, the Ministry of Public Order and the Ministry of Interior and Administrative Reform in Greece responded to the UNHCR and NGOs' claims that hurdles in accessing the asylum procedure undermined effective guarantees against non-refoulement.[33] They submitted to the CoM a variety of data (number of applications, decisions granting or rejecting international protection, etc.) to counter their claims, and to demonstrate the effectiveness of the new Asylum Service.[34] A legal officer at the Legal Council of the State (the body responsible to coordinate domestic implementation of ECtHR judgments in Greece) affirmed that the government now has to reckon with the views of non-governmental stakeholders in the process before the CoM.[35] This was in marked contrast to the past when judgment implementation was a completely bureaucratic and opaque affair.

The domestic implementation of the leading *M.S.S.* and *Rahimi* judgments under the CoM supervision described above, brings to light an experimentalist approach rather than a top-down enforcement of international and judicially pre-scribed rules. National authorities proposed and enacted various reform mea-sures that were reviewed by the CoM and independently monitored and critically assessed by a range of non-governmental actors. Seeking to secure access to an effective asylum procedure in a country that was lacking a proper asylum system, was an enormously complex task that entailed changes in large sections of the public administration. Ensuring basic human rights standards in a fragmented structure of under-resourced reception and accommodation facilities, managed by a variety of state, public, private and international actors, could not be achieved through legal change alone and through one-off action.[36] The complexity of the reform, political resistance, or plain uncertainty as to what would work, all rendered state responses provisional and subject to ongoing modification.

Unpredictable and dramatic shifts in levels and pathways of migration into Greece rapidly changed conditions on the ground. They further underscored the need to extend and intensify state efforts in order to ensure basic rights guarantees. In 2015–16, more than 1.1 million migrants and refugees from Syria, Iraq, Afghanistan and African countries crossed the Aegean Sea and came in the Greek islands of Samos, Chios and Mytilene. Most of them con-tinued through the so-called "Balkan corridor" in central and north European countries until March 2016 when many of those countries closed their borders.

The unprecedented rise in migration flows put tremendous strain on Gree-ce's fledgling asylum infrastructure and resulted in conditions that marked a serious set-back for domestic human rights protection. Over 50,000 migrants remained in Greece, and more entered in the following years, leading to an increase in the number of asylum applications that the Asylum Service was unable to handle. It was not yet fully functional, with only seven out of the 13 planned Regional Asylum Offices being operational in May 2016, as the NGO Greek Council for Refugees (GCR) reported to the CoE supervisory bodies. The GCR also disputed the Greek government's claim that legal aid was provided to asylum seekers, as stipulated in EU asylum law.[37] Over-whelmed by large numbers of migrants, these deficiencies anew restricted access to the asylum procedure and led to long delays in processing claims.[38] The reluctance of member states to take in migrants through the EU's emer-gency relocation scheme, exacerbated the pressure on Greece's reception and asylum system.

In a climate of urgency and with a strong anti-immigration public opinion across Europe, the EU's response led to a restrictive shift in Greek and EU policy and to a serious set-back for domestic human rights implementation. It put the emphasis on effective border control to curtail the entry of migrants at the expense of human rights protection. Concluded in March 2016, the EU-Turkey statement provided for the return of TCNs arriving through the Aegean islands, who were not eligible for international protection, back to Turkey. To implement the EU-Turkey statement, the Greek government passed new legislation in April 2016 that transposed the EU's recast Qualification Directive.[39] At the same time, it also established a highly restrictive, fast-track screening and asylum procedure (tight deadlines for newly arriving TCNs to be concluded in two weeks, no time between each step of the process, etc.) Before the CoM, NGOs and the UN Special Rapporteur criticized the new legislation for undermining basic rights safeguards, which was also admitted by the Head of Greece's Asylum Service.[40]

The EU-Turkey statement led to a drastic reduction of migrant flows through the Aegean Sea. At the same time, it also created a situation in which basic rights guarantees established in the preceding years were compromised. The Greek government, under pressure by the EU too, introduced provisions that prevented newly arriving TCNs from traveling to the mainland; they had to remain in the hotspots and other facilities in the islands until a final decision on their asylum claim was made. Intended to facilitate swift returns to Turkey, this policy led to severe overcrowding of the First Reception Centers (FRC, or hotspots) in the islands. In the mainland, asylum seekers stayed in several temporary accommodation facilities around the country and in leased apartments, set up in cooperation with the European Commission and the UNHCR. NGOs reported a lack of access to an asylum procedure for those TCNs staying outside of official migrant camps, due to continued staff and capacity limitations of the Asylum Service.[41]

Throughout this period of crisis and restrictive policy responses, the CoM continued its oversight and formed an external accountability mechanism, with which Greek governments had to reckon. In response to the CoM 2015 and 2017 assessments, national authorities proceeded to enact long-overdue measures for dealing with the situation of unaccompanied minors (UMs), who entered Greece in increasing numbers in 2015–16. Greek authorities had not tackled the dire predicament of this highly vulnerable group seven years after the issuing of the *M. S.S.* and the *Rahimi* judgments, despite CoM recommendations and pressure by NGOs.[42] In their revised action plan in 2015, they presented a comprehensive strategy for an effective guardianship system, that included family reunification and the prevention of trafficking. The UNHCR strongly recommended the establishment of a Best Interest Determination procedure for all UMs, and the allocation of responsibility for it to a single administrative authority.[43] At last, in 2018, a new guardianship law (Law 4554/2018) set out the terms of appointment and the responsibilities of guardians for UMs. The CoM welcomed it and urged the authorities to swiftly implement it, and to increase suitable accommodation for UMs.[44]

The *M.S.S.* and the *Rahimi* groups of judgments were part of a broader campaign to pressure Greece to establish a proper and effective asylum system, and to challenge EU asylum policy (we turn to this in section 6). Above all, they were powerful catalysts in pushing forward wholesale domestic reform: the establishment of an asylum service; the creation of reception and accommodation facilities for asylum seekers, and a policy and appropriate structures for unaccompanied minors and vulnerable persons. Their implementation took place in a distinctive experimentalist mode: the ECHR supervisory bodies reviewed provisional measures enacted by national authorities in recurrent cycles of assessment, taking on board information and analyses by a host of non-governmental actors, and national authorities subsequently expanded or revised them.

Non-governmental actors reinforced their advocacy and pressure by taking further action outside of and beyond the formal supervision and judgment implementation process. They engaged in follow-on legal action before domestic courts and in the ECtHR to challenge evolving conditions, policies and practices in the aftermath of the 2015 migration crisis. NGOs like the AIRE Center, Greek Council for Refugees, the European Council on Refugees and Exiles and others that regularly monitored the implementation of *M.S.S.* and *Rahimi,* supported fresh complaints in the ECtHR and intervened as third parties. In *J.B. v Greece,* for instance, they disputed before the Strasbourg Court the assumption of Turkey as a safe country for the return of Syrians on non-refoulement grounds, which was embedded in the EU-Turkey statement.[45] Follow-on action legal action was also taken to challenge the dire and overcrowded living conditions in camps, despite the increase in accommodation capacity after 2016.[46]

In 2019, the Strasbourg Court found Greece in violation of the ECHR on account of the deplorable living conditions for families and undocumented UMs in the Idomeni camp (near the border with North Macedonia) (Article 3 ECHR).[47] More related complaints targeting the camp in Moria (in the island of Lesvos) and elsewhere, were pending for review before the ECtHR at the time of this writing (December 2021).[48] In view of all these, the CoM called the authorities to step up their efforts, and to improve provision of accommodation, health care and access to education for refugee and migrant children.[49]

In sum, the CoM periodic review of asylum and related reforms with regular and critical feedback from non-governmental actors, alongside continuous civil society mobilization before domestic and European courts – all typical of an experimentalist setting – sustained considerable pressure on the Greek government. They provided a frame for long-term reform that was still ongoing at the time of this writing (January 2022). Despite the serious regress in human rights protection after 2015, domestic reforms did not stall but continued in less controversial areas such as the situation of vulnerable migrants and unaccompanied minors (UMs). By 2019, a full-fledged structure of 12 Regional Asylum Offices and 11 autonomous asylum units were in operation in the country, and basic reception and accommodation structures. At the same time, in 2019–2020, legislative reforms introduced stringent procedural standards for asylum seekers, which NGOs and the UNHCR argued, may lead to a denial of rights and violations of non-refoulement.[50] Throughout this period, follow-on litigation has instilled fresh pressure and exposed new problems from a human rights perspective.

In 2019–2020, Greek authorities unsuccessfully argued that the situation on the ground went beyond the one existing at the time of the *M.S.S.* and *Rahimi* groups of judgments and exceeded the remit of their implementation. In the light of ongoing deficiencies in the asylum system, as reported by NGOs, the Greek Ombudsman and the UNHCR, the CoM and the DExJ continued their supervision of these judgments. They urged Greek authorities to cooperate with other stakeholders and international organizations, and to elaborate a revised plan for the registration and processing of asylum applications to improve the system's overall efficiency and fairness.[51]

3 Challenging arbitrary immigration detention through litigation

Linked to the systemic deficiencies of Greece's asylum system was the widespread use of immigration detention, to which irregular migrants and asylum seekers were especially vulnerable.[52] The *M.S.S.* judgment shed light to the close connection between unlawful detention practices and a highly defective asylum procedure. It also exposed detention conditions that were thoroughly unsuitable for vulnerable individuals, unaccompanied minors and families with children. Greek authorities widely used detention as a way of managing the large number of undocumented migrants.[53] A generalized practice existed of the police detaining illegally entering migrants with a view to their deportation, and as a means of preventive control, often with the justification that they posed a threat to public order.[54]

According to the ECHR, states can control the liberty of non-nationals in an immigration context, however, under certain conditions and limits. Arrest and detention are lawful when states seek to prevent an unauthorized entry into a country or in the case of a person against whom action is being taken with a view to deportation.[55] In the latter case, deprivation of liberty is justified for as long as pre-deportation proceedings are pursued with due diligence.[56] In any case, detention must be in accordance with the procedural and substantive rules prescribed by national law (Article 5(1) ECHR). Its length should not exceed what is reasonably required for the purpose pursued. The place and conditions of detention should be appropriate "bearing in mind that the measure [of detention] is applicable not to those who have committed criminal offences but to aliens, who, often fearing for their lives, have fled from their own country".[57] Detainees must be able to take proceedings to challenge the lawfulness of their detention before a court, and they must be released if detention is deemed unlawful.[58]

Widespread resort to immigration detention undermined legal guarantees related to the liberty of asylum seekers and of migrants. It also restricted access to the procedure of applying for asylum and international protection (already difficult due to the lack of a proper asylum service up until 2013). Many persons in need of international protection were arrested and detained before being able to submit an application. Even after they initiated the procedure, national authorities often still detained asylum applicants (who can lawfully reside in a country until their application is fully examined[59]), by treating them as being in a pre-deportation phase, or on grounds of having made an unauthorized entry in the country.[60]

From the 2000s onwards, repeat litigation with scores of individual complaints brought to the attention of the ECtHR the systematic and arbitrary use of immigration detention in the country. Greece has the largest number of adverse ECtHR judgments in this issue area. The institutional design of domestic judicial review, specifically the lack of a right to appeal the decisions of first-instance administrative courts related to immigration detention, made it easy to exhaust domestic remedies. It rendered the ECtHR the only alternative judicial venue to appeal the decisions of Greek courts.[61] Before the Strasbourg Court, applicants were represented by activist Greek lawyers, in most cases without support by an NGO. This, for example was the case in *Dougoz*, the first judgment against Greece in 2001 concerning the detention of a Syrian national.[62] The Court found violation of the Convention on account of the conditions and unlawfulness of detention, as well as lack of judicial review of the latter (Articles 3 and 5 ECHR). The Committee of Ministers (CoM) prematurely closed its examination of the case, even though no remedial measures had been reported by the Greek authorities.[63]

Recurring litigation and adverse judgments over the next fifteen years provided the frame for the CoM and the DExJ to continue to oversee and monitor Greece's reforms in this area. Human rights were violated on account of poor detention conditions, as well as due to the lack of an effective remedy to challenge the conditions and the lawfulness of detention (Article 5 § 2, and Article 3 and 13 EHCR).[64] Greek law did not provide for direct judicial review of the lawfulness and conditions of migrants' detention, depriving applicants from a basic safeguard against arbitrary detention (violation of Article 5 § 4 ECHR). *Kaja v Greece* (2006) involved an Albanian immigrant detained in a police station cell, with a view to expulsion. The Court found that detention conditions were not suitable for long-term but only for short term internment, thus in violation of Article 3 ECHR.[65] In many other cases, it found conditions in various detention facilities in Greece (police stations, premises of authorities in charge of immigration and foreign nationals, border posts or the special holding facility at the Athens international airport) to be inhuman and contrary to Article 3 ECHR.[66]

ECtHR judgments also challenged the lawfulness of detention of migrants and asylum seekers on various grounds. In the leading case of *S.D. v Greece*, the applicant, who had fled from Turkey, was detained for a long time in a holding center at a border post and was only able to have his asylum application registered by the authorities at the third attempt. He was still arrested and detained for deportation even after being formally granted asylum applicant status. In 2009, the ECtHR found unlawful his arrest and detention, in violation of the right to liberty and security (Article 5 ECHR), and the conditions of detention to be degrading, contrary to Article 3 ECHR.[67] *Efremidze* concerned detention of irregular migrants for whom Greek authorities did not take steps to execute the deportation orders[68]; in *Lica*, detention continued even though the deportation had been stayed by judicial decision[69]; and in *Ahmade*, the ECtHR found at fault the detention of an asylum seeker with a view to deportation, even though his asylum claim was still pending.[70] In *J.R. and Others*, the Court condemned the lack of information concerning the available remedies to challenge detention before a court in a simple language accessible to the applicants, and the lack of legal assistance to pursue these remedies (violation of Article 5§4 ECHR).[71]

While individual lawyers brought most of the cases of immigration detention to the ECtHR, international bodies and non-governmental organizations were widely, even if indirectly involved in litigation.[72] Nearly in all cases, the applicants substantively referred to reports by the Committee for the Prevention of Torture (CPT), the National Human Rights Commission (NGRC) in Greece and NGOs, to buttress their claims.[73] Reports and letters by the UNHCR, the Greek Ombudsman, the Council of Europe Committee for the Prevention of Torture (CPT), the Council of Europe Human Rights Commissioner, Human Rights Watch and Amnesty International supplied critical evidence about the defective state of detention conditions (i.e. in the Soufli border crossing point, in Rhodope in northeast of Greece, and elsewhere).[74] The ECtHR heavily relied on these reports to document and condemn poor detention conditions, often against contradictory but unsubstantiated information provided by the Greek government.[75]

4 Reforming the legality and conditions of detention

Greece's lack of a legal frame for regulating the internment of undocumented migrants and asylum seekers was a yawning gap for human rights protection. Filling it was essential for ensuring the legality of detention and indirectly, for tackling poor detention conditions. And yet, Greek authorities did not pursue any reforms to this end until after the ECtHR issued its second major condemnation in *Kaja* in 2006. For overseeing domestic implementation, the CoM, grouped the large number of adverse rulings related to immigration detention in Greece under a small number of leading cases – *Dougoz* (2000), *Kaja, S.D.,* and eventually *M.S.S.* too (see Table 7.2). The ECtHR judgments issued in the 2000s (*Kaja, S.D., A.A., Tabesh, R.U.*) provided the impetus for the Greek government to put in place a legal frame to regulate the detention of TCNs, in line with relevant EU law.

It was for the first time in 2008 that the Greek government established a legal basis for the detention of asylum seekers (Presidential Decree 90/2008) and transposed the EU Asylum Procedures Directive (2005/85/EC). The 2011 law that provided for an asylum service, discussed in the previous section, stipulated that asylum applicants should be kept in pre-removal detention centers and not in police holding cells or border guard stations, where conditions were generally worse. In line with the ECHR, it determined that detention could be ordered for undocumented TCNs, for whom deportation was pending[76], when there was a risk of absconding, the TCN hampered the removal process, or s/he posed a threat to national security.[77] In 2013, national legislation that transposed EU asylum law further strengthened guarantees against the arbitrary detention of those seeking international protection (they could only be held for specific reasons provided for by law). It also placed a maximum limit of 18 months on the detention of all TCNs (asylum seekers and undocumented migrants).[78]

National legislative reforms also provided for a domestic remedy to challenge the lawfulness and conditions of detention. The absence of such a remedy had been a principle source of human rights violations in the large number of adverse ECtHR judgments against Greece. Law 3900/2010 amended earlier legislation, making it possible to challenge the lawfulness of detention before administrative courts.[81] It also obliged the police director ordering detention with a view to deportation to automatically review its lawfulness every three months.[82] Following this new legislation, the ECtHR over the next years recorded fewer cases in which violations arose from the lack of a domestic remedy.

Table 7.2 ECtHR judgments related to immigration detention in Greece

Leading cases	Repetitive cases	Issues	Human rights violations found	Non-governmental stakeholders involved (directly or indirectly) in litigation and implementation	Implementation status
Dougoz v Greece (2001)	N/A (judgment execution prior to P-14 changes)	• Detention conditions • Unlawfulness of detention • Lack of judicial review of detention	Article 3 ECHR Article 5 §1 and 5§ 4 ECHR	CPT report on conditions of detention	Closed (2009)
Kaja v Greece (2006), *A.F. v Greece* (2013)[79], and 15 other cases	*B.M. v Greece* (2014); *Bygylashvili* (2012); *Chkhartishvili* (2013); *De Los Santos and De La Cruz* (2014); *F.H.* (2014); *Horshill* (2013); *Tatishvili* (2014); *A.L.K.* (2015); *H.H.* (2015); *Chazaryan and Others* (2015); *A.Y.* (2016); *Tenko* (2016); *S.G.* (2017); *Barjamaj* (2013); *Housein* (2014)	• Detention conditions • Unlawfulness of detention • Lack of judicial review of detention	-Article 3 ECHR -Article 5 §§1 and 4 ECHR	Litigation: CPT (reports on detention conditions in Greece); NGO "Metadrasi", Greek Council for Refugees, UNHCR, Greek Ombudsman, National Human Rights Commission, ProAsyl	Closed (2019)[80] but not implemented in their general measures; ongoing CoM supervision under the leading *M.S.S.* case
S.D. v Greece (2009) and 15 other cases	*A.A.* (2010); *Efremidze* (2011); *Rahimi* (2011); *Tabesh* (2010); *R.U.* (2011); *Ahmade* (2012); *Mahmundi and Others* (2012); *C.D. and Others* (2014); *Lin* (2013); *Khuroshvili* (2014); *Lica* (2012); *Herman and Sherazadishvili* (2014); *A.E.* (2015); *MD* (2015); *Mohamad* (2015); *Mahammad and Others* (2015); *E.A.* (2015); *R.T.* (2016); *O.S. A. and Others* 39065/16 (2019); *Amadou* (2016);	• Detention conditions • Unlawfulness of detention • Lack of domestic judicial review of migrants' detention	• Article 3 ECHR • Article 5§4 ECHR • Article 5 §1	Litigation: UNHCR report; Greek Ombudsman; Committee for the Prevention of Torture (CPT); Human Rights Commissioner of the Council of Europe; Human Rights Watch report; Amnesty International report; National Human Rights Commission	** Since September 2016, CoM supervision continued under the *M.S.S* judgment

Leading cases	Repetitive cases	Issues	Human rights violations found	Non-governmental stakeholders involved (directly or indirectly) in litigation and implementation	Implementation status
M.S.S. v Greece and Belgium (2011)	*Chkhartishvili* (2013); *Horshill* (2013); *B.M. v Greece* (2014);	• Detention conditions • Lack of domestic remedy to challenge the lawfulness and conditions of detention	• Article 3 ECHR • Article 13 ECHR	Litigation: CPT reports on detention conditions; Amnesty International	Open ** Closed only in regard to domestic remedy to challenge lawfulness and conditions of detention (June 2019)
	A.F. v Greece (2013); *Bugy-lashvili* (2012); *De Los Santos and De La Cruz* (2014); *F.H.* (2014); *Kaja* (2006); *Tatishvili* (2014); *AI.K.* (2015); *H.H.* (2015); *Chazaryan and Others* (2015); *A.Y.* (2016); *Tenko* (2016); *S.G.* (2017); *A.E.A.* (2018); *Sh.D. and Others* (2019)	–		Litigation: As TPIs, Centre for Advice on Individual Rights (AIRE Centre); Amnesty International (AI); CoE Commissioner of Human Rights; UNHCR; Greek Helsinki Monitor (GHM). Reports by CPT, Human Rights Watch (HRW), AI, Cimade, CoE Commissioner of Human Rights, Medecins sans Frontieres Implementation: Greek Council for Refugees, GHM, Refugee Rights Europe, Open Society Justice Initiative (OSJI), AI, International Commission of Jurists (ICJ), European Council on Refugees and Exiles (ECRE), Hellenic League for Human Rights,	

The legislative reforms of 2010–2013 were an important step forward in allowing migrants to be held in accordance with domestic law and basic legal safeguards, as the ECtHR acknowledged in relevant judgments that it issued.[83] In its review of the *S.D. group of cases*, the CoM noted the Court's approval, but it also expressed doubts as to whether provisions, such as the automatic review of detention by the police director ordering it, were an effective remedy.[84] Submissions by non-governmental actors to the CoM and more complaints in the Court intensified concerns about the application of the enacted legislative reforms against arbitrary detention, in practice. Applicants referred to information by NGOs, like Pro Asyl, that regional administrative courts routinely assessed migrants' claims regarding detention conditions as ill-founded and unjustifiable.[85]

Recurrent complaints in the ECtHR and repetitive violations suggested that the source of the problem was not solely one of legal rules but also of bad administrative and judicial practice.[86] Greek courts, as affirmed in repetitive cases adjudicated by the Court, did not effectively apply the new rules related to judicial review of the lawfulness and conditions of detention, and their approach remained contradictory.[87] The NGO Hellenic League of Human Rights reported that administrative judges in Greece refused to consider overwhelming evidence by international organizations about substandard conditions in detention centers, and only considered proof strictly in the individual case at hand.[88] In the light of this feedback, the CoM remained concerned about how domestic courts applied the new legislation.[89]

For nearly ten years after the relevant legislative reforms, the CoM maintained its supervision over this issue in the implementation of the *S.D.* line of cases (in 2016 it was transferred in the *M.S.S.* group, see Table 7.2). Throughout this time, the Greek government insisted that the 2010 legal reform, mentioned earlier, provided an effective remedy. It appears that some first instance administrative courts began to review executive action in line with ECHR guarantees, yet, their overall approach remained contradictory, absent the possibility of appeal to and review by higher courts.[90] This latter aspect undermined the existence of an effective remedy in practice. An effective remedy would require far-reaching changes in the judicial approach and culture of first instance administrative courts – changes of a vast scope, for which domestic support was entirely lacking. In its review of June 2019, the CoM nonetheless acknowledged that an effective remedy to challenge the lawfulness and conditions of detention now existed, and thus closed its supervision of this issue.

For over ten years, the CoM also exercised its supervision over reforms to improve conditions of immigration detention in the frame of implementing the *S.D.* and *M.S.S.* groups of judgments (see Table 7.2). Improvements in detention conditions in line with human rights guarantees is an enormously complex task engaging public administration on a large scale and entailing far more than legal reform. Immigration detention is shaped by the basic policy orientation of a government, it is closely linked to accommodation capacity, and it is strongly affected by the size of migrant inflows. Initially, Greek authorities claimed that the First Reception Centers (FRC), introduced with the 2011 law that created the new Asylum Service (discussed earlier in this chapter), would tackle detention-related problems. Following the screening, registration and identification in these centers, incoming TCNs would be directed to procedures according to their status and international protection needs.[91] In its review of 2012, the CoM considered the First Reception Service to be a positive development. Yet, it inquired how Greek authorities would abolish the widely documented and systematic practices of detaining asylum seekers.[92]

During the first years of the CoM supervision (2009–2014), the political and economic conditions in Greece were highly unfavorable to rights-enhancing reforms regarding immigration detention. The country was in the midst of deep economic recession and fiscal austerity. Strong anti-immigrant sentiment was diffused in the society, primarily being directed at undocumented migrants, many of them with asylum claims that had been pending for years (due to the lack of an asylum system at the time). The center right government that came to power in 2012 used large scale arrest and detention of migrants in the large cities, which overwhelmed capacity in existing detention facilities.

Regarding detention conditions, NGOs, the CPT, the UNHCR and the Greek Ombudsman thoroughly disputed the government's report to the CoM that refurbishments and better health care provision had improved these conditions.[93] They provided documentation that asylum seekers and irregular migrants were detained for prolonged periods in unsuitable and overcrowded establishments (i.e. in police stations) and pre-return centers with insufficient means of subsistence.[94] Repeat litigation in the ECtHR also directed scrutiny to specific detention facilities, like the one next to Athens International Airport and the notorious Petrou Ralli facility (center of Athens).[95] The absence of special measures or policies for the detention of vulnerable groups, such as unaccompanied minors (UMs) and families with small children, was of particular concern to the CoM. UMs were detained together with adults, as reported by the Greek Ombudsman and the CPT, including in the notorious pre-return center of Amygdaleza.[96] The CoM asked for further information and urged Greek authorities to develop a comprehensive strategy to improve detention conditions in line with the recommendations of non-governmental actors, and fully utilizing the resources available from EU funds.

A change in government in early 2015 brought to power a left-dominated government that reversed the immigration detention policy of its center-right predecessor. It abolished the closed detention centers, introduced measures that drastically reduced the use of immigration detention and placed a 6-month limit to it.[97] This policy shift had been a pre-election commitment of the governing party. Yet, it drew its justification from ECtHR rulings against Greece that exposed the dire and overcrowded conditions in closed detention centers. Along with the creation of First Reception Centers (FRCs) that streamlined the placement of TCNs in appropriate facilities, the new policy led to temporary improvements in detention conditions, which were acknowledged by the CPT.[98] In their

2016 Action Plan, Greek authorities were quick to report that the detention of asylum seekers and undocumented migrants occurred as an exception under existing national and EU law.[99] The decongestion of detention centers though was short-lived. As large numbers of newcomers arrived in 2015–16, conditions in the First Reception Centers (FRC) and in pre-returns centers in the islands rapidly deteriorated anew.

In the context of the 2015–16 immigration surge and its aftermath, the left government anew overturned its policy of reducing detention under pressure from increasing numbers of migrants, public opinion and the EU. The legislation that it passed in 2016 to implement the EU-Turkey statement partly enhanced legal safeguards, but it also reinforced anew resort to detention.[100] In fact, it provided for potentially continuous detention during the initial processing of identity verification and asylum claims, and then pre-removal.[101] All newly arrived TCNs were automatically and indiscriminately detained in hotspots in the islands that transformed into closed reception facilities, as the Greek Council of Refugees reported to the CoM in the frame of implementing the *M.S.S.* judgment.[102] Administrative detention was also systematically imposed on TCNs apprehended at the land border with Turkey, and less so in pre-return centers in mainland Greece.[103] Thus, conditions in the various reception and detention facilities in the islands and in the border point of Evros became overcrowded and deteriorated.[104]

In the post-2016 period, detention did not only increase as a means of immigration control in Greece, but it also acquired new forms that fell outside existing legal safeguards. The detention and living conditions of asylum seekers and irregular migrants deteriorated, especially in the islands, as the UNHCR, CPT and NGOs like the Greek Council of Refugees (GCR) massively documented in their submissions to the CoM. Throughout 2017 and 2018, the CoM and the DExJ renewed their call to Greek authorities to improve such conditions and service provision (especially health). They placed particular emphasis on the continued detention of children and UMs in unsuitable facilities and urged Greek authorities to provide further information about establishing alternatives to their detention.[105] The CoM continued its supervision in this area at the time of this writing (December 2021). By providing independent and up to date information about detention conditions in different regions and locales, the engagement of civil society and international bodies in the implementation process was critical for maintaining the CoM oversight of Greek reforms over the past decade.

For over ten years, the CoM supervision over judgment implementation provided a frame of periodic review for Greek government action to remedy the conditions of immigration detention. Besides temporary improvements in capacity, and an effective lever of pressure for measures to protect UMs and the most vulnerable migrants, ECtHR judgment implementation brought little rights-protecting change on the ground. The sharp rise of migrant flows in 2015–16 and its aftermath prompted a highly restrictive policy shift and created conditions that systematically breached the human rights of migrants and asylum seekers. In response, civil society, lawyers and other non-governmental actors mobilized to pursue further domestic and ECHR litigation, paving the way for new cycles of international judicial review, domestic implementation and external supervision. They brought and supported more complaints in the ECtHR to challenge the newly imposed restrictions in the freedom of movement of migrants in the hotspots in the islands[106], the detention and living conditions of UMs in camps[107] and of Syrian, Afghan and Palestinian and other nationals, both adults and children, in various detention facilities.[108]

5 The strength, limits and pitfalls of human rights experimentalism

Focusing on the case of Greece, the preceding sections shed light to the shifting nature of ECHR supervision and judgment implementation in areas marred by complex and structural problems. Domestic implementation of judgments related to asylum and immigration detention in Greece, was a process that had little semblance to the notion of compliance as conformity with specific legal rules and remedies prescribed by an international court. Adverse ECtHR rulings condemned the lawfulness and conditions of detention, and different aspects of the asylum and reception system in Greece but they did not indicate specific measures on how to enhance rights protection.

Judgment implementation in the cases under study can more accurately be depicted as an experimentalist endeavor. It involved recurring exchanges between the CoM (and the DExJ) with national authorities and a host of non-governmental organizations, in the course of which domestic reforms to establish fair and effective asylum and immigration management were reported, contested assessed and modified. A recent study that focuses on immigration describes the issuing and implementation of a ECtHR ruling as "a collectively negotiated achievement," supporting the experimentalist account of the present study:

> The DExJ assists the CoM in supervising execution through review of state action plans, and research and consultation with applicants, policy makers, and human rights experts, such as the CoE Commissioner for Human Rights. Within these parameters, states experiment with what execution looks like in practice. Civil society groups weigh in with formal communications to the CoM, via the DExJ and domestic advocacy campaigns. The execution process is where states learn how to balance the exercise of national sovereignty with internationally acceptable implementation of human rights protections.[109]

For over ten years, ECHR supervision over judgment implementation in Greece provided an important frame of external accountability. It channeled sustained pressure for asylum reform to improve rights protection, despite dramatic shifts in migration flows and trying conditions on the ground. Such pressure for enhanced rights protection would not have been fomented through ordinary electoral politics or government policy. Through recurring exchanges and periodic assessments by the CoM, Greek authorities incrementally and provisionally enacted several legislative changes and established and put into operation a full-fledged and country-wide asylum system. The surge in migration flows in 2015–16 thoroughly changed the situation on the ground, rendered inadequate the measures that

Greek authorities had adopted until that time and undermined anew the protection of migrants' rights.

Asylum protection is influenced by many factors that are dynamic and fluctuate: the government approach and policy, variable state and sub-national capacities and conditions, the financial and administrative support from international organizations and the EU, and the ebbs and flows (often unpredictable) of migration, among others.[110] The complexity of structural reform makes it difficult for any international court or body to infer in abstract terms what changes are appropriate and practicable to enhance human rights protection on the ground. The indeterminacy of human rights rulings allowed for flexibility and far-reaching discretion to national authorities who are best placed to understand and tackle local problems. At the same time, such state voluntarism also made for procrastination and evasive responses, prolonging reform and external review, as the Greek case study shows.

In the shifting ECHR supervisory system, this state voluntarism is countered by the systematic engagement of non-governmental actors – both key and twin features of an experimentalist setting. By providing national level information and critical analyses, non-governmental participation enabled external supervision over domestic reforms to become more thorough and substantive than in the past. Enhanced supervision of the *M.S.S.* and the *Rahimi* cases unsettled the previously lax approach of Greek authorities: they were accustomed to handling ECtHR judgment implementation as a non-priority. The engagement of non-governmental actors heightened a sense of concern and restraint among authorities, as officials in the Greek Council of State confirmed. Apart from ad hoc contacts, cooperation with NGOs had not developed on a regular and institutionalized basis at the national level.[111]

Experimentalism is better suited to redressing administratively complex human rights problems. Yet, it is not necessarily effective in securing a higher level of rights protection especially in areas that interface with control of state borders, security issues, and public perceptions of crisis. In the post-2015 period in Greece, as we saw, a restrictive policy shift (national and EU) prioritized border control at the expense of migrants' rights protection. Following the advent of a right government of New Democracy in 2019, new legislation expanded the use of accelerated border procedure for asylum claims and introduced stringent procedures that made it more difficult to apply for asylum status.[112] It also drastically scaled back emergency support and integration programs, increasing the risk of destitution among asylum seekers and refugees. There have been repeated allegations and mounting evidence about the increased use of pushbacks at sea, and the use of extrajudicial detention.[113] These government acts stalled earlier efforts to enhance rights protection, and starkly showed the limits of human rights experimentalism, especially in the persistent absence of EU-wide solidarity.

The experimentalist model in the ECHR supervision over domestic reforms and remedies in structural human rights problems is not unique in Greece. In the migration field, it is also evidenced in ECtHR judgments that condemned Italy for the collective expulsion of migrants without access to an asylum procedure, and for the lack of an effective remedy domestically to complain about detention conditions.[114] NGOs were actively involved not only in the respective litigation, but also in the implementation process. In the frame of the relevant judgments, Italian authorities enacted a series of legislative and other reform measures establishing procedural guarantees, various kinds of services in reception centers, and procedures for individual identification for TCNs rescued at sea.[115]

As state authorities learn to negotiate with CoE bodies and non-governmental actors acceptable terms of judgment implementation, they arguably also learn to develop practices that fall outside the limits of the law and the ECtHR jurisdiction, rendering violations invisible. Following implementation of the *Hirsi Jamaa* judgment that condemned the collective expulsion of migrants to Libya, Italian authorities shifted border control policies in ways that circumvented but were not clearly out of line with ECHR law: they made indirect "pullback deals" with Libyan authorities, and they criminalized NGOs involved in assisting migrants in distress at sea.[116] Strategic legal action launched with the support of NGOs and dedicated lawyers has recently brought fresh claims against these Italian state practices in another case currently pending before the ECtHR.[117] More cases that challenge refoulement and collective expulsion practices at land or sea borders, against different countries (Spain, Poland, Greece, Italy, and others) are also (July 2021) pending before the ECtHR.

In fact, the strength of experimentalism lies in the continuous vigilance of proactive non-governmental and civil society forces that bring to the fore new problems, and frame and initiate new human rights challenges. The extent of non-governmental actors' involvement, communication and exchange with national authorities and the CoM in the *M.S.S.* group of judgments was by all counts exceptional in ECtHR migrant-related rulings. Yet, it is no longer unique in areas of state activity and in countries with repeat violations arising in areas that are administratively complex and structurally deficient, such as prisons or justice systems.

Over the past five years, the engagement of non-governmental actors (primarily NGOs, but also the UNHCR, the Council of Europe Commissioner of Human Rights, and national human rights institutions) in the migrant-related judgment implementation before the CoM and the DExJ has rapidly grown. The case law data compiled for this study shows that out of 455 adverse ECtHR migration-related judgments (issued until 2020), non-governmental actors were involved in 27 leading cases. It must be recalled though that these leading cases mark problems and areas of state action, under which the ECHR groups a much larger number of adverse judgments (repetitive violations) for the CoM supervision of their implementation. Another 150 repetitive violations are grouped under the 27 leading judgments, in the implementation of which non-governmental actors engage and submit their input. Altogether, in 2020 non-governmental actors engaged in 38% (176/455) of all migration-related judgments that were under the supervision of the CoM and the DExJ.[118] In this regard, the *M.S.S.* and *Rahimi* judgments, while unusual ten years ago, are increasingly typical of an emerging pattern of human rights enforcement and change.

Involving recursive processes of human rights mobilization, adjudication, and judgment implementation in a multi-level system, experimentalism does not necessarily broaden the remit of migrants' protection but it may be punctuated by arrest or even regress of their rights.[119] In the past few years, the ECtHR arguably "poked a hole" in the prohibition of collective expulsion.[120] In its controversial *N.D. and N.T. v Spain* judgment, while the ECtHR affirmed the prohibition of pushbacks at sea (*Hirsi Jamaa v Italy*), it also accepted the sending back of migrants, who made an entry into Spain through force and by creating a disruptive situation. By highlighting the latter, the Grand Chamber decided that Spain had not violated the Convention (the prohibition of collective expulsion, Article 4 Protocol 4) by sending back irregular migrants to Morocco quickly and widely, without an individual assessment of their circumstances (whether they had a valid claim to international protection) and in the absence of any procedure or legal assistance.[121] Several NGOs have mobilized to contest the issues that it raised in judgments released by or currently pending before the ECtHR.[122]

6 Mobilizing the M.S.S. to pressure for EU policy change

The *M.S.S.* judgment was not only a strategic tool to push for domestic reforms in asylum and immigration detention in Greece. It was also part of a broader mobilization campaign by NGOs and international bodies to promote the rights of migrants and asylum seekers at the EU level and to pressure for a reconfiguration of the EU asylum policy. The *M.S.S.* case stood at the heart of this campaign to discredit the asymmetrical nature of the Dublin system that places disproportionate responsibility for managing asylum claims to states of first entry, like Greece.

In the *M.S.S.* case, and in a string of others that preceded and followed it, a variety of NGOs and international bodies challenged the principle of inter-state trust embedded in the EU's Dublin Regulation (DR). According to this principle, all member states are safe for transferring asylum seekers, and capable of guaranteeing a basic level of rights protection.[123] In the *M.S.S.* case that also targeted Belgium, the ECtHR for the first time comprehensively tackled the question of the responsibilities of "sending states" under the DR: it recognized that national authorities must refrain from transferring asylum seekers to states of first entry like Greece, where there are indications of systemic deficiencies that might engender human rights violations.[124] Even though the EU is not formally a party to the ECHR, thus it is not formally bound by the Court's decisions, the release of the *M.S.S.* judgment had profound consequences at the EU level. It functioned as a powerful catalyst and "destabilizer" of the assumptions regarding rights protection embedded in the Dublin system.

The *M.S.S.* banishing of the assumption that all member states are safe in terms of ensuring human rights guarantees, struck in the most unequivocal and authoritative manner at the heart of the Dublin system. It destabilized it in one stroke, even if it brought to light what all knew.[125] The release of *M.S.S.* triggered responses at the national and supranational levels, as well as further mobilization and legal action. Its impact was amplified by a similar decision issued by the Court of Justice of the European Union (CJEU) a couple of months later. Concerning two cases reviewed jointly, the *N.S./N.E.* decision also recognized the responsibility of sending states in Dublin transfers.[126]

The *N.S.* case originated from the UK, and it was a product of strategic litigation supported by a variety of actors with different agendas: human rights and international organizations (AIRE Center, Amnesty International, UNHCR) advocated on behalf of the rights of asylum seekers facing a Dublin transfer from the UK to Greece; and lawyers and agencies like the Equality and Human Rights Commission who sought to ascertain the validity of the EU's Charter of Fundamental Rights (CFR) in the UK.[127] These non-governmental and human rights actors made submissions before the CJEU, alongside twelve Member States,[128] Switzerland and the European Commission.[129] The CJEU relied on the *M.S.S.* ruling, including for making a factual assessment about conditions in Greece.[130] Its decision in *N.S./N.E.* was crucial in providing an interpretation of EU law that national courts would have had to follow. It transformed what was previously a discretionary power of member states to assume responsibility for an asylum claim, into a duty to prevent human rights violations by taking over the claim examination.[131]

The *M.S.S.* judgment, alongside *NS/NE*, also triggered immediate responses from governments and the European Commission, as well as extensive follow-on action by non-governmental actors before national and European courts. Belgium, which the *M.S.S.* judgment condemned for returning back the applicant even though the authorities were aware about the deficiencies in Greece, suspended transfers there. It also proceeded to legislative and jurisprudential changes that improved remedies for those seeking to prevent their transfer to a country with questionable human rights conditions.[132] The European Commission also suspended all Dublin transfers to Greece. In 2013, an amendment of the Dublin Regulation (Dublin III) made *rebuttable* the assumption of mutual trust. It stipulated that transfers of asylum applicants to member states of first entry shall not be carried out when there are indications of "systemic flaws" in the reception conditions that could result in inhuman and degrading treatment.[133]

Besides Belgium, the majority of member states suspended transfers to Greece in the aftermath of the *M.S.S.* judgment. Few did so as a matter of general policy (i.e. Germany), while most states relied on the individual assessment of each case (i.e. Austria, Italy, Slovakia and Switzerland, among others). Human rights concerns were especially raised in regard to states of first entry, like Greece, Italy, Malta, Bulgaria or Hungary. Widespread follow-on litigation and mobilization in several member states and at the European level, aimed to give effect to the *M.S.S.* ruling and its implications for the structure and functioning of the EU Dublin system. Domestic courts, often relying on NGOs' reports about conditions in states of first entry, issued decisions that clarified the preconditions for conducting a Dublin procedure and the right to appeal Dublin transfers.[134]

Follow-on legal action initiated or supported by non-governmental organizations also targeted European courts. In some cases, the ECtHR made similar findings as in *M.S.S.*, while in others it did not find a violation of the ECHR or deemed the claims inadmissible.[135] In 2012, the Legal Aid Service for Exiles (Service d'Aide Juridique aux Exilés – SAJE) brought the *Tarakhel* case against Switzerland, to challenge the suitability of reception and accommodation conditions for children and families in Italy. Five state governments and NGOs – Defence for Children, the AIRE Center, ECRE and Amnesty International – made third party interventions.[136] The ECtHR ruled that the Swiss authorities should have obtained guarantees from Italian authorities that the applicants (an Afghan couple with six children) would be accommodated in conditions suitable for children and the family would be kept together. NGOs continued to mobilize before Swiss courts to prevent the transfer of vulnerable asylum seekers to Italy.[137]

NGOs and the UNHCR targeted the European Commission again in 2016, when the latter sought the resumption of Dublin transfers in order to restore the functioning of the Schengen area. Noting the poor living conditions and inadequate asylum procedures, the Open Society Justice Initiative argued that the resumption of Dublin transfers to Greece would be unlawful before the CoM confirmed the positive performance of Greek authorities in human rights reform.[138] Despite reports by NGOs and the UNHCR and evidence that some of the systemic problems in Greece had not been completely resolved, the European Commission recommended the resumption of transfers to Greece as of March 2017, for most asylum seekers except vulnerable ones (such as unaccompanied minors).[139] Many states started to send again transfer requests to Greece, as legal challenges continued before domestic courts to prevent such transfers.[140]

Recent studies view the impact of the *M.S.S.* judgment as limited because it arguably failed to bring about change in the EU's Dublin asylum system towards a balanced allocation of responsibility among member states.[141] International human rights rulings though are not orders to reform national and EU law and policy. Nonetheless, the impact and effectiveness of the *M.S.S.* judgment on supranational policy and asylum practice was significant, indeed powerful. It set in an experimentalist process, this time outside of the ECHR formal implementation mechanism, of continuous mobilization and decentralized decision-making to bring member states' policy and practice into line with the judgment's main findings.

The *M.S.S.* judgment destabilized the supranational status quo and triggered follow-on litigation and social mobilization at the national and European levels over a period of more than ten years. It became a catalyst for national court rulings to review Dublin transfers on grounds of human rights protection, and for member states to refrain from such transfers. The *M.S.S.* judgment also prompted a freeze (temporary but for several years) on the application of the contentious Dublin rules, and it started to chip away at its very design. The Dublin system was not radically altered towards one of a balanced allocation of responsibility for examining asylum claims among member states. Yet, the *M.S.S.* ruling stands out as the key single factor that undermined the original Dublin architecture. It set in motion multi-level responses that over a period of ten years thoroughly delegitimized it and made its pre-existing structure unsustainable, even if politically still upheld by most member states' governments.

7 Conclusion

In examining judgment implementation in immigration and asylum management in Greece – an area of intricate legal rules and administrative practices – this chapter argued that the ECHR supervisory machinery has undergone a profound shift in an experimentalist direction. The increasing engagement of non-governmental and civil society actors providing information about the national-local context to the supervisory bodies, has transformed judgment implementation from an exclusively governmental affair to a deliberative and participatory process of human rights enforcement. Equally importantly, it has rendered the ECHR oversight more substantive and rigorous – a salutary counterbalance to the far-reaching discretion enjoyed by national governments. As a model of internationally induced, domestic change, experimentalism envisages rights-enhancing reforms at the state level taking place incrementally over time, rather than as a result of single judgments or one-off acts by the respondent states.

Under the periodic oversight of the ECHR supervisory bodies and sustained pressure, including through repeat litigation, Greek governments established a basic legislative frame and a proper asylum structure. Some positive albeit inconsistent changes also took place regarding domestic judicial review of immigration detention. Beyond these, improvements in migrants' protection were limited and since 2016 regressed with restrictive shifts in immigration policy and rising migrant flows. Outside of the ECHR enforcement mechanism, the leading *M.S.S.* judgment was a catalyst for change at the EU level. It prompted widespread follow-on legal action before domestic and European courts and strong civil society advocacy to challenge the presumption that all EU states safeguard basic rights for migrants and are thus "safe" for Dublin returns. In this way, the *M.S.S.* was critical in leading courts and state governments in several countries to suspend, even if temporarily, such returns.

Notes

1 See for example, *R.C. v Sweden*, no. 41827/07, 9 June 2010; *J.K. and Others v Sweden*, no. 59166/12, 23 August 2016.
2 *Salah Sheekh v Netherlands*, no. 1948/04, 11 January 2007.
3 See CM/ResDH(2010), Execution of the judgment of the ECtHR *Salah Sheekh against Netherlands*, 2 March 2010.
4 *Saadi v United Kingdom*, no. 13229/03, 29 January 2008.
5 Resolution CM/ResDH(2010)67, execution of the judgment of the ECtHR *Saadi against UK*.
6 See *Ahmade v Greece*, no. 50520/09, 25 September 2012; *Mohamad v Greece*, no. 70586/11, 11 December 2014; *E.A. v Greece*, no. 74308/10, 30 July 2015.
7 Interview, lawyer from Greek Council for Refugees (over skype), 11 May 2021.
8 Dembour, *When Humans Become Migrants*, 419.

9 Belgium, Germany, France, Greece, Ireland, Italy, the Netherlands, Austria, Poland, the UK and the Czech Republic. Evangelia Psychogiopoulou, "European Courts and the Rights of Migrants and Asylum Seekers in Greece," in *Rights and Courts in Pursuit of Social Change*, ed. Dia Anagnostou (Oxford: Hart Publishing, 2014), 146.

10 *M.S.S. v Belgium and Greece*, no. 30696/09, 21 January 2011, § 330–331.

11 See for instance, *T.I. v the United Kingdom* (dec.), no. 43844/98, 7 March 2000; *K. R.S. v the United Kingdom* (dec.), no. 32733/08, 2 December 2008.

12 European Union, Directive 2013/33/EU of the European Parliament and the Council of 26 June 2013 laying down standards for the reception of applicants for international protection (recast) (2013), OJ L180/96.

13 *M.S.S. v Belgium and Greece*, no. 30696/09, 21 January 2011. On the judgment's legally groundbreaking qualities, see Gina Clayton, "Asylum Seekers in Europe: M.S.S v. Belgium and Greece," *Human Rights Law Review* 11, no. 4 (2011): 758–773 and Violeta Moreno-Lax, "Dismantling the Dublin System: M.S.S. v Belgium and Greece," *European Journal of Migration and Law* 14, no. 1 (2012): 1–31.

14 See Boryana Gotsova "Rules Over Rights? Legal Aspects of the European Commission Recommendation for the Resumption of Dublin Transfers of Asylum Seekers to Greece," *German Law Journal* 20, no.5 (2019): 640.

15 *M.S.S. v Belgium and Greece*, no. 30696/09, 21 January 2011, § 244–246, 255.

16 *K.R.S. v UK*, no. 32733/08 (dec.), 2 December 2008.

17 *M.S.S. v Belgium and Greece*, no. 30696/09, 21 January 2011, § 347–348.

18 *Rahimi v Greece*, no. 8687/08, 5 April 2011.

19 These are the Ministry of Immigration, General Secretariat for Human Rights in the Ministry of Justice, Foreigners' Directorate, Ministry of Employment, Asylum Service and others.

20 The CoM closed its supervision over *Barjama* and *Housein* judgments in June 2019, while continuing its supervision over the underlying issues in the frame of two new adverse judgments that were issued in 2019, *H.A. and Others v Greece* (app. No. 19951/16, 28 May 2019) and *Sh.D. and Others v Greece* (app. No. 14165/16, 13 September 2019).

21 Commission Recommendation (EU) 2016/2256 of 8 December 2016, addressed to the Member States on the resumption of transfers to Greece under Regulation (EU) No. 604/2013 of the European Parliament and of the Council [2016] OJ L340/60.

22 Council of the European Union, Press release 7308/12, 3151st Council Meeting, Justice and Home Affairs, Brussels, 8 March 2012, 8–9.

23 Angeliki Dimitriadi, and Antonia-Maria Sarantaki, *National report on the governance of the asylum reception system in Greece*, CEASEVAL Research on the Common European Asylum System No. 20, Chemnitz, March 2019, 5.

24 DExJ, DH - DD(2011)670E, Communication from Greece in the case of *M.S.S. against Belgium and Greece* (No. 30696/09) (Greek Action Plan on Migration Management), 2 September 2011.

25 Law 3907/2011 on Establishment of Asylum and First Reception Service, and adaptation of Greek law to the provisions of Directive 2008/115/EC of the European Parliament and of the Council of 16 December 2008 on common standards and procedures in Member States for returning illegally staying third-country nationals. See *Government Gazette*, Issue 1, No. 7, 26 January 2011.

26 In the first months of 2012, Greek authorities were quick to report a decrease of the backlogged cases, and an increase in the international recognition rate from about 1% to 12.35%. Ministers' Deputies, Information Documents, CM/Inf/DH(2012)19, *M. S.S. v Belgium and Greece*, 29 May 2012, § 44–47.

27 Presidential Decree 114/2013, *Government Gazette* No. 146, 14 June 2013. It replaced Presidential Decree 113/2010 that first transposed the EU Qualification Directive 2005/85/EC.

28 DExJ, H/Exec(2014)4rev, *M.S.S. v. Belgium and Greece* group of cases, Memorandum, 6 June 2014, § 12–16.
29 See the Department of the Execution of ECtHR Judgments database in HUDOC. The supervisory bodies reviewed the measures and findings of these reports and submissions in eight memoranda and notes and issued 14 decisions and 1 resolution.
30 CoM, CM/Inf/DH(2012)19, *M.S.S. v Belgium and Greece*, 29 May 2012, § 50–52.
31 DExJ, H/Exec(2014)4rev, *M.S.S. v. Belgium and Greece* group of cases, Memorandum, 6 June 2014, § 17–21.
32 DExJ, H/Exec(2015)6rev, *M.S.S. group of cases v Greece*, "Information provided by the Greek authorities and from other sources on general measures regarding asylum procedures and conditions of detention," 27 February 2015, § 5–9.
33 DExJ, DH-DD(2015)270, Communication from NGOs in the case of *M.S.S. v Belgium and Greece*, 1222th Meeting, 10 March 2015.
34 DExJ, H/Exec(2015)6rev, *M.S.S. group of cases v Greece*, "Information provided by the Greek authorities and from other sources on general measures regarding asylum procedures and conditions of detention," 27 February 2015, § 11–18.
35 Interview with legal officer, Legal Council of the State, Athens, 28 May 2019.
36 See Dimitriadi and Sarantaki, *National report on the governance of the asylum reception system in Greece*, 13–14.
37 DExJ, DH-DD(2015)606, Communication from a Greek NGO (GCR) in the case of *M.S.S. against Greece*, 10 June 2015.
38 CM/Notes/1288/H46–15, *M.S.S. and Rahimi groups v Greece*, 1288 Meeting, 7 June 2017.
39 Law 4375/2016 on the Organization and functioning of the Asylum Service, Appeals Authority, Reception and Identification Service, establishment of General Secretariat for Reception, the transposition into Greek legislation of the provisions of EU Directive 2013/32/EU on Common Procedures for Granting and Withdrawing International Protection. Law 4375/2016 was amended in June 2016 and in March 2017.
40 DExJ, DH-DD(2016)725, Communication from a Greek NGO (GCR) in the case of *M.S.S. against Greece*, 14 June 2016.
41 DExJ, DH-DD(2017)919, Communication from a NGO (Open Society Justice Initiative) in the case of *M.S.S. v Belgium and Greece*, 1294 Meeting, 30 August 2017.
42 CM/Notes/1243/H46–8, *M.S.S. and Rahimi groups v Greece*, 1243th Meeting, 10 December 2015.
43 CM/Notes/1243/H46–8, *M.S.S. and Rahimi groups v Greece*, 1243th Meeting, 10 December 2015.
44 CM/Del/Dec(2019)1348/H46–9, *M.S.S. and Rahimi groups v Greece*, 6 June 2019.
45 See for example the TPI by the AIRE Centre, ECRE and the International Commission of Jurists (ICJ), in the case *J.B. v Greece*, no. 54796/16, communicated to the Greek government, https://www.asylumlawdatabase.eu/sites/default/files/aldfiles/Greece-JB_v_Greece-ECtHR-amicus-ICJothers-final-eng-2017.pdf
46 CM/Notes/1348/H46–9, *M.S.S. and Rahimi groups v. Greece*, 1348th meeting, 4–6 June 2019, 7.
47 *Sh.D. and others v Greece, Austria, Croatia, Hungary, Northern Macedonia, Serbia and Slovenia*, no. 14165/16, 13 June 2019.
48 *Al H. and others v Greece*, nos. 4892/18 and 4920/18; *Esraa Al Beid and others v Greece*, no. 36423/16; *A.I. and Others v Greece*, no. 13958/16; *Sedo v Greece*, no. 2080/19; all pending for review.
49 CM/Del/Dec(2019)1348/H46–9, *M.S.S. and Rahimi groups v Greece*, 1348th meeting, 6 June 2019.
50 Law 4636/2019 on international protection and other provisions, and Law 4686/2020 on Improvement of immigration legislation.

51 CM/Notes/1348/H46-9, *M.S.S. and Rahimi groups v Greece*, 1348th meeting, 4–6 June 2019, 6.

52 Cathryn Costello, *The Human Rights of Migrants and Refugees in European Law* (Oxford University Press, 2015), 280.

53 Unreturnable migrants are those who cannot be returned to their country of origin because of legal obstacles in Greece, or due to lack of cooperation with the consular authorities of the country of origin. See Eleni Koutsouraki, "The Indefinite Detention of Undesirable and Unreturnable Third-Country Nationals in Greece," *Refugee Survey Quarterly* 36, no.1 (2017): 86.

54 See *S.D. v Greece*, no. 53541/07, 11 September 2009, § 35–36.

55 ECHR, article 5 §1(f).

56 Costello, *The Human Rights of Migrants and Refugees in European Law*, 292.

57 Council of Europe/European Court of Human Rights, Research Division, *Guide to Article 5 ECHR: right to liberty and security* (Council of Europe, 2021), 11–15.

58 ECHR, article 5 §4.

59 *S.D. v Greece*, no. 53541/07, 11 September 2009; *RU v Greece*, no. 2237/08, 7 September 2011.

60 Costello, *The Human Rights of Migrants and Refugees in European Law*, 284–285. See also *Saadi v. the United Kingdom*, no. 13229/03, 29 January 2008.

61 Dia Anagnostou and Danai Angeli, "A shortfall of rights and justice: Institutional design and judicial review of immigration detention in Greece," *European Journal of Legal Studies* (forthcoming 2022).

62 *Dougoz v Greece*, no. 40907/98, 6 March 2001.

63 Resolution CM/ResDH(2009)128, Execution of the judgment of the European Court of Human Rights, *Dougoz v Greece*.

64 *Mahmundi and others v Greece*, no. 14902/10, 31 July 2012; *R.U. v Greece*, no. 2237/08, 7 June 2011; *Lica v Greece*, no. 74729/10, 17 July 2012.

65 *Kaja v Greece*, no. 32927/03, 27 July 2006, § 48.

66 *A.F. v Greece*, no. 53709/11, 13 June 2013; *B.M. v Greece*, no. 53608/11, 19 December 2013; *Bygulashvili v Greece*, no. 58164/10, 25 September 2012.

67 *S.D. v Greece*, no. 53541/07, 11 June 2009.

68 *Efremidze v Greece*, no. 33225/08, 21 June 2011.

69 *Lica v Greece*, no. 74279/10, 17 July 2012.

70 *Ahmade v Greece*, no. 50520/09, 25 September 2012.

71 *J.R. and Others v Greece*, no. 22696/16, 25 January 2018; see also *O.S.A. and Others v Greece*, no. 39065/16, 21 June 2019; and *KAAK and Others v Greece*, no. 34215/16, 3 January 2020.

72 In a few cases, as in *A.Y. v Greece*, no. 58399/11, 5 November 2015, the legal claim before the ECtHR was prepared by lawyers from the Greek Refugee Council.

73 See *R.T. v Greece*, no. 5124/11, 11 May 2016, §52.

74 For instance, see *S.D. v Greece*, Information Note on the Court's case law, No. 120, June 2009.

75 *A.Y. v Greece*, no. 58399/11, 5 November 2015, § 32–34 and § 56–57.

76 According to the ECtHR, detention for the purpose of effectuating a deportation order was lawful as long as the competent authorities were actively taking steps to execute such an order. See *Efremidze v Greece*, no. 33225/08, 21 June 2011, § 55; *H.A. v Greece*, no. 58424/11, 21 January 2016, § 53; *Herman and Sherazadishvili v Greece*, nos. 26418/11 45884/11, 24 April 2014, § 64.

77 Law 3907/2011, articles 30–31. See also CM/Notes/1265/H46-13, *S.D. group v. Greece* (Application No. 53541/07), 1265 Meeting, 22 September 2016, reference document DH-DD(2016)826.

78 Presidential Decree 113/2013 transposing Article 18 of Directive 2005/85/EC on minimum standards on procedures in Member States for granting and withdrawing refugee status.

79   *Kaja* and *A.F.* are not leading but repetitive cases. I put them in this column because the CoM treated them as a group with the remaining 15 cases.

80   Resolution CM/ResDH(2019)154 Execution of the judgments of the ECtHR, 17 cases against Greece. Adopted by the CoM on 6 June 2019 at the 1348th meeting of the Ministers' Deputies.

81   Law 3900/2010 on Rationalization of procedures and acceleration of administrative trials. It amended Law 3386/2005, article 76(3).

82   CM/Notes/1265/H46–13, *S.D. group v. Greece* (Application No. 53541/07), 1265 Meeting, 22 September 2016, reference document DH-DD(2016)826.

83   *Horshill v Greece*, no. 70427/11, 1 August 2013,§ 60; *Charkartishvili v Greece*, no. 22910/10, 2 May 2013, § 72; *A.Y. v Greece*, no. 58399/11, 5 November 2015, § 87; *R.T. v Greece*, no. 5124/11, 11 February 2016, § 98.

84   CM/Inf/DH(2012)19, *M.S.S. against Belgium and Greece*, 29 May 2012, § 33–34.

85   *B.M. v Greece*, no. 53608/11, 19 December 2013, § 72, 74.

86   CM/Notes/1265/H46–13, *S.D. group v. Greece* (Application No. 53541/07), 1265 Meeting, 22 September 2016, reference document DH-DD(2016)826.

87   *R.T. v Greece*, no. 5124/11, 11 May 2016. For a detailed analysis of the domestic remedy related to immigration detention in Greece, see Angeli and Anagnostou, "A shortfall of rights and justice: Institutional design and immigration detention in Greece."

88   DExJ, DH-DD(2013)1277, Communication from a NGO (HLHR - Hellenic League for Human Rights) (12/11/13) in the case of *M.S.S. against Belgium and Greece*, 1186th meeting, 22 November 2013, § 35.

89   CM/Notes/1265/H46–13, *S.D. group v. Greece* (Application No. 53541/07), 1265 Meeting, 22 September 2016, reference document DH-DD(2016)826.

90   See Angeli and Anagnostou, "A shortfall of rights and justice: Institutional design and immigration detention in Greece."

91   CM/Inf/DH(2012)19, *M.S.S. against Belgium and Greece*, 29 May 2012, § 20, 22.

92   CM/Inf/DH(2012)19, *M.S.S. against Belgium and Greece*, 29 May 2012, § 24.

93   DExJ, H/Exec(2015)6rev, *M.S.S. group of cases v Greece*, 27 February 2015.

94   DExJ, H/Exec(2014)4rev, *M.S.S. v. Belgium and Greece* group of cases, Memorandum, 6 June 2014.

95   CM/Inf/DH(2012)19, *M.S.S. against Belgium and Greece*, 29 May 2012, § 25–26.

96   CM/Inf/DH(2012)19, *M.S.S. against Belgium and Greece*, 29 May 2012, § 27–31.

97   Koutsouraki, "The Indefinite Detention of Undesirable and Unreturnable Third-Country Nationals in Greece," 97.

98   DExJ, DH-DD(2016)182, Communication from the authorities concerning the case of *M.S.S. v Belgium and Greece*, 1250th meeting, 23 February 2016.

99   DExJ, DH-DD(2016)826, Action report (06/07/2016), Communication from Greece in the *S.D. group of cases against Greece*, 1265th meeting, 8 July 2016.

100   Law 4375/2016. It also transposed EU Directive 2013/33.

101   Koutsouraki, "The Indefinite Detention of Undesirable and Unreturnable Third-Country Nationals in Greece," 98.

102   DExJ, DH-DD(2016)725, Communication from a Greek NGO (GCR) in the case of *M.S.S. against Greece*, 14 June 2016.

103   Koutsouraki, "The Indefinite Detention of Undesirable and Unreturnable Third-Country Nationals in Greece," 98–99.

104   CM/Del/Dec(2019)1348/H46–9, *M.S.S. and Rahimi groups v Greece*, 6 June 2019, 8.

105   Resolution, CM/ResDH(2019)154, Execution of the judgments of the ECtHR 17 cases against Greece, 1348th meeting, 6 June 2019.

106   *Sedo v Greece*, no. 2080/19; *AI v Greece*, no. 13958/16; *Al Beib v Greece*, no. 36423/16; the final decision in all is pending (as of July 2020).

107   *Sh.D v Greece*, no. 14165/16, 13 June 2019.

108 *Ali v Greece* (dec.), nos. 68951/17, 8196/18, 9 July 2020; *Kaak v Greece*, no. 34215/16, 3 October 2019; *M.A. v Greece* (dec.), no. 14222/16, 29 September 2020; *Ibram v Greece* (dec.), nos. 3934/19, 3941/19, 4463/19, 4562/19, 4581/ 19, 7312/19, 13497/19, 5 March 2020; *H.A. v Greece*, no. 19951/16, 28 February 2019.

109 Jessica Greenberg, "Counterpedagogy, Sovereignty, and Migration at the European Court of Human Rights," *Law and Social Inquiry* 46, no. 2 (2021): 521.

110 Gotsova "Rules Over Rights? Legal Aspects of the European Commission Recommendation for the Resumption of Dublin Transfers of Asylum Seekers to Greece," 647.

111 Interview with legal officer at the Council of State, Athens, 28 May 2019.

112 International Protection Act passed by Greek Parliament in November 2019.

113 Joel Hernandez, "Greece Struggles to Balance Competing Migration Demands," *The Online Journal of Migration Policy Institute* (blog), 25 September 2020.

114 See *Khlaifia and others v Italy*, no. 16483/12, 15 December 2016; *Sharifi and Others v Italy and Greece*, no. 16643/09, 21 October 2014; *Hirsi Jamaa and Others v Italy*, no. 27765/09, 23 February 2012.

115 Greenberg, "Counterpedagogy, Sovereignty, and Migration at the ECtHR," 528.

116 Greenberg, "Counterpedagogy, Sovereignty, and Migration at the ECtHR," 525–530.

117 See for instance, Moritz Baumgartel, "High Risk, High Reward: Taking the Question of Italy's Involvement in Libyan 'Pullback' Policies to the ECtHR," *European Journal of International Law* (blog), 14 May 2018.

118 Data from the case law data set compiled for this study (on file with author).

119 For a similar argument, see Gráinne De Búrca, "Human Rights Experimentalism," *American Journal of International Law* 111, no. 2 (2017): 296.

120 Nora Markard, "A Hole of Unclear Dimensions: Reading *ND and NT v Spain*," *EU Immigration and Asylum Law and Policy* (blog), 1 April 2020, https://eumigrationla wblog.eu/a-hole-of-unclear-dimensions-reading-nd-and-nt-v-spain/.

121 *N.D. and N.T. v Spain*, nos. 8675/15 and 8697/15, 13 February 2020.

122 See for example *Asady and Others v Slovakia*, no. 24917/15, 24 March 2020.

123 See Gotsova "Rules Over Rights? Legal Aspects of the European Commission Recommendation for the Resumption of Dublin Transfers of Asylum Seekers to Greece," 642.

124 Moritz Baumgärte, *Demanding Rights – Europe's Supranational Courts and the Dilemma of Migrant Vulnerability* (Cambridge University Press, 2019), 51.

125 Costello, *The Human Rights of Migrants and Refugees in European Law*, 277.

126 CJEU, C-493/10, Order of the President of the Court, *M.E. and Others v Refugee Applications Commissioner, Minister for Justice and Law Reform* (2011); CJEU, C-411/10, Order of the President of the Court (2010).

127 Interview with UK lawyer, London, 26 June 2012. See also Psychogiopoulou, "European Courts and the Rights of Migrants and Asylum Seekers in Greece," 145.

128 Belgium, Germany, France, Greece, Ireland, Italy, the Netherlands, Austria, Poland, the UK and the Czech Republic. On the positions of the different states, see Cathryn Costello, "Dublin-case NS/NE: Finally, an end to blind trust across the EU?" *Asiel-en Migrantenrecht* 2 (2012): 91–92.

129 Costello, "Dublin-case NS/ME: Finally, an end to blind trust across the EU?" 86.

130 Baumgärte, *Demanding Rights*, 58.

131 Gotsova "Rules Over Rights?," 658.

132 Baumgärte, *Demanding Rights*, 56.

133 Regulation 604/2013, of the European Parliament and of the Council of 26 June 2013 Establishing the Criteria and Mechanisms for Determining the Member State Responsible for Examining an Application for International Protection Lodged in One of the Member States by a Third-Country National or a Stateless Person [2013] OJ L180/31, art. 3(2).

134 Matiada Ngalikpima and Maria Hennessy, *Dublin Regulation – Lives on Hold*, February 2013, 267–260.
135 *Mohammed v Austria*, no. 2283/12, 6 September 2013; *A.S. v Switzerland*, no. 39350/13, 30 June 2015; *Sharifi and Others v Italy and Greece*, no. 16643/09, 21 October 2014, among many others.
136 *Tarakhel v Switzerland*, no. 29217/12, 4 November 2014.
137 Baumgärte, *Demanding Rights*, 68.
138 Gotsova "Rules Over Rights?," 650.
139 European Commission Recommendation (EU) 2016/2256 of 8 December 2016 addressed to the Member States on the resumption of transfers to Greece under Regulation (EU) No 604/2013 of the European Parliament and of the Council [2016] OJ L340/60.
140 Gotsova "Rules Over Rights?", 656–658.
141 Baumgärte, *Demanding Rights*, 79–80.

8   The ECHR as an experimentalist governance regime

Over the past twenty years, the ECtHR has developed into an international venue not only for individual disputes vis-à-vis executive action, but also for challenging state policies and practices. A rapidly growing number of rights claims since the 1990s concern ethnic discrimination in education, law enforcement practices and other areas, deficiencies in immigration and asylum management, and gross state abuses in regions of ethnic conflict, among others. The accession of former communist states of East-Central Europe and the former Soviet Union brought into the Convention newly democratized states and states with deficient rule of law standards. Large numbers of cases involving systemic human rights breaches before the Court came from these "new" countries. Cases entailing repetitive and structural violations also originated from longstanding democracies and from the "old" states of south Europe, Turkey, and West European countries. While the eastward enlargement of the ECHR set the broad context for a rapid rise in litigation, it was not in itself the main cause for the growth of minority- and migrant-related complaints.

In the preceding chapters, this book has developed two lines of argument. In the first place, it contends that the driving force behind the rise in ECtHR litigation was the proliferation of a variety of legal support structures and actors, comprising human rights lawyers and a wide range of civil society and other non-governmental actors. They played a critical role in enabling and supporting individuals from minorities and migrants to bring large numbers of complaints before the Strasbourg Court. Possessing expertise, access to resources and context-specific knowledge, they were able to frame a burgeoning set of local-national issues into human rights claims. They both seized expanding ECHR opportunities in the 1990s and in turn contributed to advances in the evolving case law. They form part of a wider constituency of legal and social actors who believe in and activate the power of an international court to bring governments to conform to international human rights law.[1]

Increased litigation diversifies and expands the issues brought to the attention of an international court. It thus creates more possibilities for it to intervene in national policy debates and to engage in incremental decision-making.[2] By invoking broad human rights principles, legal actors join forces with social activists, and they can influence the agenda of international courts on behalf of previously excluded social

DOI: 10.4324/9781003256489-10

groups.[3] Non-governmental actors mobilized in the ECtHR often as part of broader campaigns and strategies to challenge ethnic discrimination, and to condemn and pressure governments to change asylum and immigration detention policies and practices. Their strategic and systematic involvement in litigation and legal mobilization in the ECHR was instrumental in bringing to light repetitive violations of a structural nature. Systemic violations with important policy implications now form a considerable amount of the cases that reach and are dealt with in the Convention system.

This book argues that in structural and administratively complex social problems, like those mentioned above, systematic non-governmental engagement in litigation and increasingly in judgment implementation, has transformed the ECHR into a regime of transnational experimentalist governance. It has also interjected into the ECHR a strong societal and participatory dimension. Experimentalism is a theory about how broadly agreed framework goals are elaborated and implemented in a multilevel setting across different national-local contexts.[4] Through its lens, a key productive element and potential to affect rights-enhancing domestic reform lies in the sustained interactions that human rights treaties set into motion between international law bodies, state authorities and non-governmental actors. In a judicially enforced treaty like the ECHR, these multi-actor interactions take place through iterative cycles of: bottom-up rights claiming, international adjudication, external supervision and domestic implementation of judgments, as well as follow-on action.

As a governing principle in international law and treaty systems, experimentalism is premised on the idea that human rights norms are not (and cannot be) enforced from above. Instead, their scope and content are continuously (re) defined through bottom-up processes of legal framing, social-legal mobilization and judicial interpretation. Judicially pronounced norms are further "translated" into domestic policy and practice through negotiation and deliberation between governments, international treaty bodies, and a range of civil society and other interested parties. In this process, measures put forth by governments are recursively assessed by supervisory bodies with feedback from non-governmental actors knowledgeable of the national context. They are revised in the light of the consequences of their application in practice and the learning that ensues. State, non-state actors and international bodies can learn from one another and reach a pragmatic consensus on what can be done to tackle human rights violations.[5] In keeping with local and national diversity, experimentalism allows discretion and flexibility in norm implementation. While it stands opposite to the central imposition of norms, it is not a decentralized regime either: it envisions a center that does not issue top-down directives but has a facilitating and supporting role.[6]

The experimentalist account propounded in this book is closely linked to the structural turn of the ECHR and its increasing involvement in cases entailing systemic violations. The first part of this chapter examines the ECtHR's mode of intervention in reference to the pilot judgment procedure that has been applied in a few dozens of such cases. The ECHR engagement with structural violations though extends well-beyond formally designated pilot judgments. It also takes place as a result of repetitive violations of an individual kind that altogether reveal a systemic problem, the redress of which requires domestic changes of large scale and complexity. For purposes of supervision by the Committee of Ministers (CoM), they are grouped under a smaller number of leading judgments. In those cases, systematic and proactive engagement of non-governmental actors both reflects and reinforces distinctive experimentalist dynamics in the ECHR supervisory and judgment implementation process.

The second part of this chapter reviews some of the findings of the case studies examined in this book and elaborates on the ECHR as a regime of transnational experimentalist governance – a model that is consistent with a constitutive approach to international human rights law. The last part positions the experimentalist account of the ECHR in relation to the alternative models that have been put forth to depict its functioning and main purpose – the individual justice, constitutional, and pluralist models. It argues that experimentalism is best placed to address concerns related to the legitimacy of the ECtHR, and to promote the embeddedness of the Convention in the domestic legal and political systems.

1 The structural turn in the ECHR

Scholarship on the ECHR and human rights courts has identified and analyzed the rise of a new model of international rights litigation geared towards structural reform, rather than exclusively individual justice. The structural turn of these courts, namely, their growing involvement in cases entailing state policy and administrative reform, is reminiscent of the shift from private civil litigation to public law litigation in the 1950s and 1960s in the USA, infamously expounded by Abraham Chayes.[7] In the original declaratory model of international human rights review, state governments are obliged to give effect to the rulings issued by regional courts. Yet, they retain far-reaching discretion on how to redress the violations pronounced in a judgment through reform of domestic law, policy and practice. Confronted with repetitive and systemic violations though, international rights review in part shifted away from the declaratory model to a structural approach.[8] Human rights courts may explicitly require or direct respondent states to make specific changes in policy or administrative practice. The remedies may affect many others besides the applicants, and these may be involved in supervising the implementation of a remedy.[9]

In Europe, the structural turn of the Strasbourg Court is manifested and has been explored in connection with the pilot judgment procedure adopted in a few dozens of cases.[10] In a pilot judgment, the ECtHR identifies a structural problem, such as prolonged non-enforcement of domestic court decisions, inhuman conditions of detention, or deficient national legislation, that gives rise to repetitive violations. The Court prescribes to the respondent state remedial measures – even in this case in rather general terms.[11] The underlying assumption is that by indicating specific remedies in the ruling itself, the ECtHR provides clarity and reduces disagreement as to what national authorities must do to redress the recurrent violations, thereby promoting swifter and more effective domestic implementation.[12]

The pilot judgment procedure manifests a prescriptive and interventionist approach on the part of the Court to pressure recalcitrant states to undertake structural reform. To be sure, the Court has adopted it highly selectively, cautiously, and as an exception from its usual declaratory approach, usually to tackle large-scale systemic violations that are specifically attributed to defective legislation.[13] The targeted states have mostly been from Eastern Europe and the former Soviet bloc, but some pilot judgments have also addressed Western and Central Europe.[14] In dealing with repetitive violations, the Court has in a other instances issued quasi-pilot or Article 46 judgments. They highlight the obligation of the respondent state to implement general measures, but without issuing specific or binding remedial orders in the operative part of the respective judgments.[15] The Court's stipulating of specific remedies to respondent states strengthens its policymaking intervention, and arguably reinforces its con-stitutionalizing role.[16]

While analysis of the structural turn has focused on formally designated (quasi) pilot or Article 46 judgments, the Court's involvement in cases entailing repetitive violations and structural reform extends well beyond such judgments.[17] It is mani-fested in a much larger number of ordinary cases that are filed as individual claims, but which have consequences well beyond the individual petitioners. Prison condi-tions, gender-based violence, ethnic discrimination, school segregation, immigration and asylum, and state abuses in armed conflict, have all been the subject of test case litigation or repeat litigation. They expose structural human rights problems and require legal, administrative, or policy reform. Regardless of the form it takes, the ECtHR involvement in structural violations and remedies marks a departure from "a purely individualized justice limited to prescribing a just remedy to a particular victim of a violation towards a generalized justice in which a state is required to reform its law and practice."[18]

In the much larger number of cases and judgments that require and engage states in structural and policy reform without bearing the label of "(quasi)pilot", the ECtHR remains on the sidelines after it pronounces a violation of a structural nature. In the first place, the Court is highly sensitive to indicate more forcefully remedial measures, confronted as it is with increasing challenges to its legitimacy. It is reluctant to do so lest it oversteps the principle of subsidiarity; the latter has been reaffirmed and highlighted in successive high-level, inter-state conferences on Convention reform over the past ten years. Leaving aside the varying meanings of, as well as normative and judicial approaches to subsidiarity,[19] the Court's concern to avoid prescribing remedies is undoubtedly very real in the current political environment, as the negotiations leading up to the 2018 Copenhagen Declaration revealed.[20]

An equally important impediment is that the possibility for centralized and prescriptive remedial instructions by an international court is unattainable when reform of complex administrative systems like education, asylum or prison condi-tions is at stake. Translating a human rights violation into legal, administrative or other measures that can combat discrimination, establish fairer and also effective asylum procedures, or ensure humane reception and detention conditions in circumstances of immigration flux, are tasks of inherent and profound uncertainty. Such deficiencies are rarely remedied by legislative changes alone or through single shot actions.[21] In such areas, the ECtHR would be hard pressed to determine at the outset remedial measures that states must enact.[22] Mandating domestic reform seems like a "quixotic undertaking" for an international court that lacks knowledge of national-local context and enforcement mechanisms.[23] It is thus not surprising that human rights courts for most part refrain from ordering states to enact specific measures and reforms.

Scholarly analysis of the structural turn has largely focused on the ECtHR itself. Yet, the enforcement of its rulings is the work of the Committee of Ministers (CoM), a body of state delegates, supported by the Department for the Execution of Judgments (DExJ). Over the past fifteen years, this supervisory machinery has seen an expansion of its monitoring role, with the bulk of it delegated by the CoM to the DExJ, a body of legal experts. Even though it is not institutionally part of the Court, the DExJ "operates as the 'long arm' of the Court in the post-judgment peer review process."[24] It negotiates with the respondent state over what is required to implement a judgment in bilateral or multilateral meetings with national authorities, it examines the submissions by non-governmental actors, monitors and makes the substantive assessment of respondent state actions. Its proposals over whether or not to continue supervision of a case are generally endorsed by the CoM. Thus, supervision over domestic implementation involves "a hybrid form of human rights monitoring" in which state delegates and legal technocrats "jointly share competences under the shadow of a Court."[25]

2 The experimentalist turn in the ECHR

The experimentalist account developed in this book shifts the focus of analysis to the ECHR regime as a whole and how it interacts with respondent states to tackle complex and structural human rights problems. In an experimentalist governance setting, courts are important actors foremost as "destabilizers of dysfunctional arrangements"[26] and as "catalysts for reform."[27] International human rights rulings, including those issued by the ECtHR, rarely prescribe specific remedies that respondent states must enact, as explained earlier. Instead, by pronouncing a violation they produce "destabilization rights": they signal that the status quo in an area is illegitimate and cannot continue intact. They delegitimize in the most authoritative manner established structures and practices of state administration that engender rights abuses. By doing so, adverse human rights rulings trigger a reform process, and become "focal points" around which legal, non-legal, private and governmental actors mobilize (NGOs, professional associations, advocacy groups, etc.)[28] By activating external supervision, these rulings obligate, encourage but also pressure decision-makers and administrators to justify and reformulate their policies for compatibility with the pronounced norms.

Over the past fifteen years, the ECHR increasingly resembles a regime of transnational experimentalist governance. A variety of legal and civil society actors frame and bring numerous claims related to ethnic discrimination and dysfunctional immigration and asylum systems before the Strasbourg Court. In many cases, recourse to the Court is a strategic form of action, variably linked to broader mobilization campaigns. Following the finding of a violation involving structural and complex problems, the respondent state authorities propose and enact measures to redress it under the enhanced supervision of the CoM and the DExJ. The Convention leaves "a very wide margin of appreciation to States in finding legislative and other solutions adapted to national circumstances; [w]hat counts is that the result is achieved: no more similar violations."[29]

In the experimentalist mode, the ECHR supervision involves recurrent exchanges between state authorities, the Council of Europe (CoE) supervisory bodies and non-governmental actors. Implementing measures aimed to tackle structural and complex shortcomings, are proposed, discussed, assessed and revised over a few or several cycles of assessment, with the participation of and feedback from non-governmental actors. Studies affirm the growing importance of institutionalized dialogue and bilateral exchanges between the DExJ and respondent state authorities. Implementing measures in complex cases are negotiated until an agreement is reached – an approach that breaks with the prescription of remedial orders from above that underpins the pilot judgments.[30] The experimentalist shift in the ECHR, partial and incomplete to be sure, is an institutional adaptation to the growth and diversification of litigation that greatly extended the remit of the Court's review into systemic violations and areas of administrative complexity. It has been critically driven by the expanded participation of non-governmental actors in the ECHR system.

The cases of a) Roma segregation in education, and b) immigration detention and asylum in Greece and the EU, closely resemble the experimentalist functioning of the ECHR as described above. In both areas, ECtHR litigation was launched and supported by civil society organizations (CSOs), or by individual lawyers, in connection with their strategies and commitment to advance Roma and migrants' rights. The ECtHR rulings on the Roma brought to light and condemned an entrenched phenomenon of school segregation that takes different forms in the Czech Republic, Hungary, Greece and Croatia. The mobilization of CSOs continued in the judgment implementation phase, albeit in variable degrees in the different countries. It provided to the supervisory bodies documentation and critical analyses of the measures enacted by national authorities to redress segregation. CSOs also engaged in follow-on advocacy and litigation before domestic and European courts, bringing similar claims to counter evasive state responses and exercise pressure for policy change in the respondent states and beyond.

In the Roma segregation cases, the degree of CSO engagement in implementation, both before the CoE supervisory bodies and at the national level, was critical for the potential of rulings to influence positive change. In the judgments against the Czech Republic and Hungary, CSOs systematically brought to the supervisory bodies detailed information related to the practical implementation of remedial measures and continuously monitored their effects. They were thus able to keep the cases under enhanced supervision[31] against government efforts to portray violations as isolated incidents and implementation as complete.[32] CSOs active participation decisively influenced the rigor and depth of external review and accountability by the supervisory bodies. These bodies exercised their oversight not only over the adoption but also over the application of national legislative and policy measures in practice. CSOs leveraged their participation in the supervision process to exercise pressure at the national level too. Largely due to the more limited CSO engagement in the cases against Greece and Croatia on the other hand, the CoE bodies prematurely ended their supervision in these countries without assessing the practical application of the legislative changes.

Judgment implementation did not eradicate Roma segregation in schools in any of the countries under study – far from it. Yet, over recurrent cycles of external review, ECtHR rulings promoted significant legislative and administrative changes (Czech Republic, Croatia), enhanced safeguards in school placement procedures (Czech Republic, Hungary, Croatia), effectively pressured for the collection of ethnically disaggregated data (Czech Republic, less so in Hungary), and provided a significant counterpoint to government efforts to roll back progressive policies related to Roma and education (Hungary). The effectiveness of judgment implementation must be understood in reference to the the specific challenges in each national context. Where violations are systemic and their redress requires large-scale structural and administrative change, as in ethnic discrimination in education, it is more appropriate to evaluate effectiveness "in relation to improving institutional capacity to identify, prevent, and redress exclusion, bias, and abuse."[33]

In Greece, ECtHR rulings powerfully condemned the serious deficiencies of the asylum system, as well as immigration detention conditions and practices, in response to strategic and repeat litigation. Supervision over their implementation established an external frame for periodic evaluation of far-reaching structural reforms that took place over the past ten years – the establishment and functioning of a proper and full-fledged asylum system that was lacking until 2011. This is not to argue that human rights rulings singlehandedly led to this reform. Yet, implementation provided sustained pressure for the government to take human rights into account, and to continue the reforms in the face of austerity, sharp rise in migration flows, and overwhelming pressure on existing reception and accommodation capacities. Throughout this process, NGOs, international bodies and national human rights institutions regularly submitted to the supervisory bodies analyses of the effects of government reforms on the ground in prodigious detail.

A broader policy shift in Greece and in the EU towards more restrictive immigration and asylum policies, and the strong and unfavorable effects of the 2015–2016 mass migration at various levels, severely circumscribed further change towards rights enhancing reforms. Regarding immigration detention, conditions during some periods improved, but they overall remained poor. On the positive side, the numerous ECtHR adverse rulings condemning the lack of safeguards against the lawfulness of immigration detention promoted a more substantive review by first instance administrative courts, albeit not consistently – a problem closely linked to the lack of a right to appeal their decisions in the Greek legal system.[34] Last but not least, the most important leading judgment of *M.S.S. v Greece and Belgium* (2011) prompted considerable follow-on litigation at the national but also at the European level. Various non-governmental organizations actively mobilized the M.S.S. ruling in their advocacy campaigns. Their mobilization had far-reaching consequences for the application of EU asylum law by different states and the EU itself – most notably the suspension of Dublin transfers to Greece and other countries with deficient asylum systems.

Beyond the supervisory mechanism of judgment implementation, the ECHR regime as a whole increasingly functions as one that is akin to transnational experimentalist governance since the 2000s – at least in areas of structural human rights problems. This transformation has been driven by bottom-up and decentralized processes of social and legal mobilization in the ECHR regime. Deployed strategically, international litigation is embedded in, and in turn helps advance broader struggles about minorities and other vulnerable groups. It seeks to make broad normative principles like equality, non-discrimination and the right to education, relevant and enforceable in particular domains of state action and in different national contexts. Non-governmental actors systematically mobilize in ECHR litigation, judgment implementation, and follow-on action to renew pressure on state authorities, and to continue to make human rights law relevant for various social groups and local-national problems. By doing so, they strengthen the possibility to embed human rights protection in state policy and practice.

The experimentalist account of the ECHR in this book is corroborated in recent studies focusing on systemic discrimination against sexual minorities in law enforcement in Georgia.[35] ECtHR rulings condemning such discrimination and active civil society mobilization in litigation and in judgment implementation opened up an ongoing process of domestic reform to tackle hate crime under international scrutiny. This would not have occurred as a matter of course in domestic politics and it is a significant outcome in itself, regardless of the persistent failure of the Georgian government to enact effective structural reform. Civil society actors supplied invaluable documentation that corrected official government accounts of the situation, and critically contributed to defining the benchmark for implementation before the ECHR supervisory bodies.[36] Recurrent assessment and deliberation may last for years, depending on the complexity of the problems, input from civil society and other non-governmental actors, government will, as well as political and other conditions.

This study does not suggest that the experimentalist functioning of the ECHR supervisory system is a panacea for promoting rights-expansive reforms domestically – it is not. It does, however, point to the need to take a longer-term perspective in assessing human rights change. The continuous interaction between supervisory bodies, states and non-governmental actors over implementation can over time lead to progressive reforms domestically, particularly if Court rulings are incorporated into broader mobilization strategies to promote human rights change.[37] From an experimentalist perspective, implementation is a dynamic, iterative and open-ended process: "the desired end point might not become evident for months or even years and may only emerge through the repeated participation of multiple actors in the design of reparations that are both congruent with the decision and politically realizable."[38]

Experimentalism does not foresee a constant progression to ever expansive rights conceptions and practices – on the contrary. Litigation may indeed reverse precedents, resulting in regression, as we saw in the immigration field, while progressive decisions may trigger state resistance and backlash.[39] International human rights law cannot do miracles domestically. It cannot eradicate problems such as institutional racism and discrimination, inhuman prison conditions, or structural failures of national justice systems. Such problems can only be contained through constant vigilance and systematic monitoring. They can only be fully eradicated in the long-term, with transformative social or institutional change, or a fundamental restructuring of the international system.

The ability of Court rulings to effectively advance rights protection presupposes a minimum level of good political and executive will, and a reasonably independent judiciary. Experimentalism is unlikely to work and promote productive exchanges and deliberation over human rights reform, absent a degree of political liberalization in a state and the existence of a domestic civil society that actively engages in human rights advocacy.[40] This is especially unlikely in areas involving egregious human rights violations linked to actions of security forces and to conflicts over state territory and national sovereignty.

The experimentalist account of the ECHR advanced in this book is consistent with a constitutive approach to international human rights law. A constitutive perspective departs from strict legalism, namely, the assumption that legal rules, once codified (through international treaties or case law) are naturally or automatically obeyed by governments.[41] It is also at odds with a regulative model that conceives of international law as a set of rules (assumed to have a stable and agreed meaning) that are primarily meant to regulate, constrain, or directly alter the behavior of state decision-makers. While similarly sceptical of legalism, the regulative model views the effective enforcement of international legal rules to require a centralized authority and the political backing of those who wield power, which human rights law usually lacks.[42]

From a constitutive perspective, on the other hand, international human rights law is primarily productive by virtue of the diffused effects that it has in reconstituting social and political relations. Preeminent among these are the decentralized processes of social and legal mobilization through which human rights law acquires content and meaning, and its ability to empower marginalized groups and to align with social movements' goals more broadly.[43] These can have powerful political consequences in state policies and practices, despite the absence of authoritative interpretation and centralized enforcement.[44]

Far from prescribing clear and uniformly interpreted rules, human rights are broad and abstract principles that are continuously framed, contested and judicially (re)interpreted through claims that arise from local-national contexts. From a constitutive perspective, the notion of compliance as state observance of particular rules that presumably directly follow from a ruling of an international court, is a narrow ground for understanding the effects of human rights rulings. It is especially so in systemic and administratively complex problems such as ethnic discrimination, in which it is simply impossible to determine "a causal relationship between the contents of judicial decisions and state practice, leading to a congruence between the two."[45] While acknowledging that political support and a degree of centralized authority are necessary, experimentalism views effective human rights implementation as primarily occurring through iterative and decentralized processes of legal and social mobilization.

3 An alternative model of the ECHR?

The transnational experimentalist governance account of the ECHR developed in this book moves beyond the classical debate of whether the Strasbourg Court provides individual or constitutional justice.[46] The Court has clearly gone beyond the individual justice model that views the ECtHR as a court that primarily reviews claims for the benefit of every individual applicant. This paradigm continues to be widely espoused and to animate the functioning of the ECtHR. Yet, consistent and systematic delivery of individual justice is for all intents and purposes untenable and illusory, as it is attested by the large portion of individual complaints that are rejected as inadmissible (around 95%).[47]

At the antipode of the individual justice model, scholars argue that the ECtHR increasing involvement in cases that expose systemic violations and have public policy consequences (such as pilot judgments), and its prioritizing of the more serious cases, have effectively put it on a constitutionalization track.[48] Without going here into any detail about the particular characteristics that render a court constitutional (and leaving aside the strong aversion of states to the latter), the constitutional vision evokes the existence of a hierarchical and unitary legal order, from which the ECHR with its contracting states is very far.

Building precisely on the large heterogeneity of national legal systems, scholars have posited an alternative paradigm, that of pluralism, as predominantly defining the relationship of the ECtHR with the contracting states. It views the ECHR as a heterarchical and highly decentralized enforcement system that is the perfect embodiment of the subsidiarity principle. Through this lens, ECHR norms are variably interpreted across national legal orders based on different political, legal and cultural traditions, and these interpretations occasionally deviate from the ECtHR case. The overall tendency for the contracting states though is to strike a fair balance between national specificities and European human rights in a climate of mutual acceptance and respect. By and large, states converge upon support for the Convention and this is achieved through well-intentioned and constructive dialogue between national and European judges.[49]

This book argues that the ECtHR is not part of a constitutionalizing or pluralist order. Instead, it can more accurately be depicted as the central pillar of a transnational experimentalist governance regime. The Court is the authoritative interpreter of Convention norms, but their enforcement into domestic law, policy and practice is critically aided by the Council of Europe's political and legal expert bodies. They supervise the implementation of Court rulings and are pivotal parts of the ECHR as a transnational experimentalist governance regime. The nature and functioning of this regime fundamentally differ from the constitutionalist paradigm with its connotations of unity and hierarchy, but it also diverges from the pluralist notion of a decentralized system that relies on state voluntarism.

In transnational human rights experimentalism, enforcement of broad rights principles across diverse national contexts is accomplished through the active engagement of a variety of non-state and non-governmental actors in international legal institutions and treaty bodies. They frame local and national issues as legal human rights claims and provide context-specific input and a critical counterpoint to governments' minimalist approach to judgment implementation. By providing context-specific information and independent documentation, they also strengthen the quality and depth of international supervision and external accountability. Civil society and non-governmental stakeholders' participation provides a critical, and previously missing, link in the continuous exchanges between national governments, the ECtHR and CoE supervisory bodies. In these multi-actor recursive interactions, far-reaching state discretion in implementing measures is counterbalanced by sustained and rigorous international scrutiny that is applied in complex cases under enhanced supervision.

The review of claims entailing structural human rights problems is a vital function of the Court but it is also strongly contested on grounds of legitimacy. The perception of unelected judges, pronouncing violations and prescribing structural and policy changes to states, fuels into narratives of "creeping constitutionalization" of international judiciaries, as well as into opposition to international law more broadly. International human rights courts are especially prone to criticisms for trespassing their legitimate mandate in cases that touch upon highly sensitive issues of immigration, national identity and border control. The ECtHR's engagement with rights claims related to how states deal with minorities and immigrants has triggered contestation over the Court's perceived intrusion into the realm of national-level democratic decision-making. It struck a sensitive chord among governments, prompting challenges to the legitimacy of international rights review.[50] In response, state governments have strongly advocated for expanding the margin of appreciation and deference to national decision-makers.

In reflecting how to address the issues of ECHR legitimacy and effectiveness, the notion of embeddedness is a promising principle as a guide to redesigning the ECtHR, and the work of its political and legal expert bodies.[51] It is based on the idea that "compliance with international law can increase when international institutions – including tribunals – can penetrate the surface of the state to interact with government decision-makers and private actors to influence domestic politics."[52] The notion of embeddedness is advanced both as a counterweight but also as a supplement to subsidiarity. It recognizes that legal, political and cultural diversity across states can engender divergent but not necessarily incompatible approaches to common legal problems. This is the foundation for the substantial discretion afforded to states to abide with their treaty obligations.[53] At the same time, embeddedness calls for a more interventionist, presumably temporarily, stance when national institutions are not in a position to defend human rights and thus to justify subsidiarity and deference. On this point, Helfer's analysis suggests a degree of flexibility and differentiation in how the ECtHR deals with different state governments,[54] or what other studies have dubbed "variable geometry".[55]

International human rights courts constantly straddle the line between being intrusive and allowing wide state discretion. Experimentalism provides a way for treading on this middle ground. If its potential is fully exploited, the experimentalist dynamic described above can powerfully promote the diffused embeddedness of the ECHR domestically over time. In practice, the embeddedness principle calls for promoting regular exchanges between the ECtHR, the CoE supervisory bodies, and national institutions (courts, parliaments, executive agents) in order to incentivize, persuade, and at times demand authorities to act in conformity with human rights.[56] Helfer's analysis focuses on recurring interactions of the ECtHR with formal institutions and state officials. These are arguably strongly consequential in promoting gradual changes in state behavior, even through partial compliance with the Court's judgments, as other studies also argue.[57]

Mobilization by civil society and other human rights institutions and stakeholders to pressure for rights-enhancing domestic reforms can further penetrate the surface of the state. This is especially feasible if engagement of civil society and non-governmental actors before the CoE supervisory bodies is matched by advocacy and alliance building domestically and transnationally. It can promote "the skillful use of persuasion, advocacy and multi-actor deliberations", increase dialogue between civil society and the state, and "realign the interests and incentives of decision-makers" in favor of implementing actions that would give effect to the Court's judgments.[58] Litigation before domestic courts and recourse to national human rights institutions are particularly fruitful and potentially effective examples of follow-on action pursued by civil society in order to pressure and persuade for implementing Court rulings, as we saw in the case study on Roma school segregation.

Understanding the ECHR as an experimentalist regime directly speaks to debates regarding the continuing reform of the Court and the Convention system.[59] Experimentalist practices are compatible with subsidiarity that seeks to allay concerns about international institutions presumably dictating intrusively to state governments how they should protect human rights. This book shows that while international judiciaries and treaty bodies engage more extensively and actively in domestic policy reforms, this does not amount to the imposition of state laws and practices "from afar." Neither does it signal the incursion of the international judicial role into the national legislator's turf. The ECHR operates in a far more decentered, deliberative and potentially effective way, which its vocal critics (and sometimes its proponents) misconstrue. Experimentalism is also consistent with conceptions of subsidiarity advanced in the 2018 Copenhagen Declaration. These move beyond a state-centric view of subsidiarity to support the initiatives of various state and non-governmental actors in human rights protection.[60]

State parties and the ECHR must explicitly acknowledge and seek to strengthen the experimentalist features of the Convention. They must further promote the engagement of non-state actors in the Convention, both at the national and European level, and strengthen their capacity to engage in the litigation and judgment implementation. Strengthening the central remedial role of the ECtHR and the CoM, or, conversely, the states' margin of appreciation, are unlikely to address the challenges currently facing the Convention system. Instead, harnessing participatory and experimentalist features in the ECHR supervisory mechanism but also in the Convention regime more broadly will both ensure subsidiarity and bring rigor and substance to external review, simultaneously bolstering its effectiveness and legitimacy. Strengthening the interaction and dialogue of civil society with the Court and the CoE supervisory bodies "may anchor the development of human rights more solidly in European democracies."[61]

Notes

1 Mikael Rask Madsen, "The Challenging Authority of the European Court of Human Rights: From Cold War Legal Diplomacy to the Brighton Declaration and Backlash," *Law and Contemporary Problems* 79, no. 1 (2016), 164.
2 Robert Keohane, Andrew Moravscik and A.-M. Slaughter, "Legalized Dispute Resolution: Interstate and Transnational", *International Organization*, Vol. 54, No. 3 (2000) pp.457–488.
3 Rachel A. Cichowski, *The European Court and Civil Society – Litigation, Mobilization and Governance* (Cambridge University Press, 2007).
4 Gráinne De Búrca, "Human Rights Experimentalism", *American Journal of International Law*, Vol. 111, No. 2 (2017): 277–316.
5 Gráinne De Búrca, "Human Rights Experimentalism," *American Journal of International Law* 111, no. 2 (2017): 282.
6 Charles F. Sabel and William H. Simon, "Democratic Experimentalism", *Searching for Contemporary Legal Thought*, edited by Justin Desautels-Stein and Christopher Tomlins (Cambridge University Press, 2017), 479, 484.
7 Alexandra Huneeus, "Reforming the State from Afar: Structural Reform Litigation at the Human Rights Courts", *Yale Journal of International Law*, Vol. 40, No. 1 (2015), 15. This shift was first analyzed in Abraham Chayes, "The Role of the Judge in Public Law Litigation", *Harvard Law Review* 89, no. 7 (1976): 1281–1316
8 Huneeus, "Reforming the State from Afar", 1–40.
9 Huneeus, "Reforming the State from Afar", 3.
10 Lize R. Glaz, "The Execution Process of Pilot Judgments before the Committee of Ministers." *Human Rights and International Legal Discourse* 13, no. 2 (2019), 76.
11 Glaz, "The Execution Process of Pilot Judgments", 80, 88–89.
12 Philip Leach "No longer offering fine mantras to a parched child? The European Court's developing approach to remedies", *Constituting Europe – The European Court of Human Rights in a National, European and Global Context*, edited by Andreas Føllesdal, Birgit Peters and Geir Ulfstein (Cambridge University Press, 2013), 160, 179.
13 Leach "No longer offering fine mantras to a parched child?", 160; Başak Cali and Anne Koch, "Foxes Guarding the Foxes – The Peer Review of Human Rights Judgments by the Committee of Ministers of the Council of Europe", *Human Rights Law Review* 14 (2014), 310.
14 Leach "No longer offering fine mantras to a parched child?", 162–163.
15 Leach "No longer offering fine mantras to a parched child?", 166.
16 Sadurski, "Partnering with Strasbourg", 402.
17 Antoine Buyse, "The Pilot Judgment Procedure at the European Court of Human Rights: Possibilities and Challenges." *European Court of Human Rights – 50 Years* (Athens: Athens Bar Association, 2010): 78–90; Dilek Kurban, "Forsaking Individual Justice: The Implications of the European Court of Human Rights' Pilot Judgment

Procedure for Victims of Gross and Systematic Violations." *Human Rights Law Review* 16 (2016): 739–741.

18 Wojciech Sadurski, "Partnering with Strasbourg: Constitutionalisation of the European Court of Human Rights, the Accession of Central and East European States to the Council of Europe, and the Idea of Pilot Judgments." *Human Rights Law Review* 9, no. 3 (2009), 426.

19 Robert Spano, "The Future of the European Court of Human Rights – Subsidiarity, Process-Based Review and the Rule of Law." *Human Rights Law Review* 18 (2018): 473–494; Andreas Føllesdal, "Subsidiarity and International Human Rights Courts: Respective Self-Governance and Protecting Human Rights – or Neither?" *Law and Contemporary Problems* 79 (2016): 147–163.

20 See Alice Donald and Philip Leach, "A Wolf in Sheep's Clothing: Why the Draft Copenhagen Declaration Must be Rewritten." *Blog of the European Journal of International Law*, 21 February 2018.

21 Kurban, "Forsaking Individual Justice," 768.

22 Huneeus, "Reforming the State from Afar," 21.

23 Huneeus, "Reforming the State from Afar," 4.

24 Cali and Anne Koch, "Foxes Guarding the Foxes", 314.

25 Cali and Anne Koch, "Foxes Guarding the Foxes", 315–319.

26 Charles F. Sabel and William H. Simon, "Destabilization Rights: How Public Law Litigation Succeeds," *Harvard Law Review* 117, no. 4 (2004): 1015–1101.

27 Joanne Scott and Susan Sturm, "Courts as Catalysts: Re-thinking the Judicial Role in New Governance," *Columbia Journal of European Law* 13 (2006): 565–594.

28 Susan Sturm, "Second Generation Employment Discrimination: A Structural Approach," *Columbia Law Review* 101 (2001): 557.

29 Committee of Ministers, *Annual Report 2017* (Strasbourg: Council of Europe, 2018), 12.

30 Elisabeth Lambert Abdelgawad, "Dialogue and the Implementation of the European Court of Human Rights Judgments," *Netherlands Quarterly of Human Rights* 34, no.4 (2016): 345–350.

31 Aysel Eybil Küçüksu, "In the Aftermath of a Judgment: Why Human Rights Organisations Should Harness the Potential of Rule 9", *Strasbourg Observers*, 3 March 2021.

32 Alice Donald, Debra Long, and Anne-Katrin Speck, "Identifying and Assessing the Implementation of Human Rights Decisions." *Journal of Human Rights Practice* 12, no. 1 (2020), 128.

33 Sturm, "Second Generation Employment Discrimination", 463.

34 See Danai Angeli and Dia Anagnostou, "A shortfall of rights and justice: Institutional design and judicial review of immigration detention in Greece", *European Journal of Legal Studies* (2022), forthcoming.

35 *Identoba and others v Georgia*, no. 73235/12, 12 May 2015.

36 Alice Donald, "The Power of Persistence: How NGOs can Ensure that Judgments Lead to Justice". *Implementing Human Rights Decisions: Reflections, Successes and New Directions*. University of Bristol, Human Rights Law Implementation Project, 2021.

37 For a similar argument, see Gráinne De Búrca, *Reframing Human Rights in a Turbulent Era* (Oxford: Oxford University Press, 2021), 24.

38 Donald, Debra Long, and Anne-Katrin Speck, "Identifying and Assessing the Implementation of Human Rights Decisions", 145.

39 Philip Leach, "The Continuing Utility of International Human Rights Mechanisms?" *Blog of the European Journal of International Law*. 1 November 2017. Available at ejiltalk.org/the-continuing-utility-of-international-human-rights-mechanisms/

40 De Burca, "Human Rights Experimentalism", 279.

41 Geoff Dancy and Christopher J. Fariss. "Rescuing Human Rights Law from International Legalism and its Critics." *Human Rights Quarterly* 39, no. 1 (2017): 12–13.

42 Dancy and Fariss. "Rescuing Human Rights Law", 8.

43 See for instance Beth A. Simmons, *Mobilizing for Human Rights – International Law in Domestic Politics* (New York: Cambridge University Press, 2009).

44 Dancy and Fariss. "Rescuing Human Rights Law", 13–16; Douglas Cassel, "Does International Human Rights Law Make a Difference?" *Chicago Journal of International Law* 2, no. 1 (2001): 121–135; Robert Howse and Ruti Teitel. "Beyond Compliance: Rethinking Why International Law Really Matters." *Global Policy* 1, no.2 (2010): 127–136.

45 Huneeus, "Reforming the State from Afar," 5.

46 Steven Greer and Luzius Wildhaber, "Revisiting the Debate about 'constitutionalising' the European Court of Human Rights," *Human Rights Law Review* 12, no. 4 (2012): 655–687.

47 Greer and Wildhaber, "Revisiting the Debate about 'constitutionalising' the ECtHR," 659.

48 Greer and Wildhaber, "Revisiting the Debate about 'constitutionalising' the ECtHR," 670–674; Sadurski, "Partnering with Strasbourg".

49 Greer and Wildhaber, "Revisiting the Debate about 'constitutionalising' the ECtHR," 680–682. See also Nico Krisch, *Beyond Constitutionalism: The Pluralist Structure of Post-national Law* (Oxford University Press, 2010), chapter 4.

50 Mikael Rask Madsen, "Two-level politics and the backlash against international courts: Evidence from the politicisation of the European court of human rights," *British Journal of Politics and International Relations* 22, no. 4 (2020): 728–738.

51 Lawrence Helfer, "Redesigning the European Court of Human Rights: Embeddedness as a Deep Structural Principle of the European Human Rights Regime", *European Journal of International Law* 19, no. 1 (2008): 130.

52 Helfer, "Redesigning the European Court of Human Rights," 131.

53 Helfer, "Redesigning the European Court of Human Rights," 134.

54 Helfer, "Redesigning the European Court of Human Rights", 147–8.

55 Başak Cali, "Coping with Crisis: Whither the Variable Geometry in the Jurisprudence of the European Court of Human Rights", *Wisconsin International Law Journal* 35, no. 2 (2018).

56 Helfer, "Redesigning the European Court of Human Rights", 150–1.

57 Daren Hawkings and Wade Jacoby, "Partial Compliance: A Comparison of the European and Inter-American Courts for Human Rights," *Journal of International Law and International Relations* 6, no.1 (2010–2011): 85.

58 Helfer, "Redesigning the European Court of Human Rights", 135.

59 See the debate around the Copenhagen Declaration in Leach and Donald, "Copenhagen: Keeping on Keeping on. A Reply to Mikael Rask Madsen and Jonas Christoffersen on the Draft Copenhagen Declaration," *EJIL* (blog).

60 See Geir Ulfstein and Andreas Follesdal, "Copenhagen – much ado about little?" *EJIL Talk* (blog), 14 April 2018, https://www.ejiltalk.org/copenhagen-much-ado-about-little/.

61 Copenhagen Declaration, § 33.

Annex: A note on methodology and data collection

In exploring the growth of minority- and migrant-related litigation in the ECHR, this book draws on a large body of quantitative and qualitative data. It combines analysis of a large-N ECHR case law dataset compiled for this study, with focused case study research. The case law data set comprises two sections, a) 491 minority-related decisions and judgments issued by the ECHR bodies in 1960–2012, and b) 605 ECtHR migrant-related judgments issued in 1960–2020. The dataset includes judgments and decisions, rather than petitions. Data on all petitions to the ECtHR is not publicized and it is not possible to collect it. The bulk of the petitions are rejected as inadmissible and unmeritorious in the first stage. A portion of inadmissibility decisions are published in the Court's case law database of HUDOC, and some of those were included in the minority-related data set compiled for this study. Given the lack of available data on petitions to the ECtHR, data on judgments and decisions is used as a proxy for assessing trends in the evolution of ECHR migrant and minority-related litigation. The large size of the data set in the two categories of cases ensures that we can draw a fairly comprehensive picture of ECHR litigation trends.

The cases included in the dataset do not for most part raise issues or advance demands that are commonly recognized as minority rights, such as cultural rights, or to immigrants' rights as such. The Convention, as it is well-known, guarantees individual rights and not rights that are collectively asserted by minority or migrant groups. At the same time, individuals from minorities raise claims that are closely linked to the public participation of the minority, to which they belong (for example, the banning of, or restrictions imposed upon a minority party or association) or they allege discrimination on ethnic grounds. The case law data also includes petitions related to violations in contexts of inter-communal and armed conflict linked to ethnic, national or religious divisions; these are not about minority rights per se, but about state abuses against individuals who are affected because of their belonging to a certain national-ethnic group.

Regarding immigrants, the cases in the dataset include cases that raise issues and involve disputes directly linked to the conditions and problems of contemporary immigration in Europe. It excludes cases in which the foreign status of the applicant is merely incidental and unrelated to immigration issues (as for instance, in the *Bouamar v Belgium*, no. 9106/80, 29 February 1988 which is about juvenile detention, or as in *Sahin v Germany*, no.30943/96, 10 November 2001 that is about parental visitation rights).

The case law data sets were compiled by utilizing the ECtHR official data base HUDOC, and by consulting specialized handbooks, case law portals and reports of ECtHR case law. They record detailed information on the state against which each case was brought, dates, outcome of the case, level of importance, issue area, legal actors involved, extent and nature of civil society involvement, and participation of third-party interveners (TPI), among others. On the basis of this data set, detailed descriptive information and aggregate data can be generated on patterns of litigation and legal mobilization across countries, over time and in different issue areas, the states against which violations are claimed, the litigants, the judicial outcome of petitions, and the involvement of lawyers and third-party interveners. The case law data also shows the level of civil society involvement in different kinds of cases.

Besides descriptive analysis of aggregate case law data, this book relies on qualitative research generated through two case studies: school segregation of Roma as a form of ethnic discrimination, and immigration detention and asylum management. These case studies explore whether and how experimentalist practices emerge as a variety of state and non-governmental actors engage in litigation and judgment implementation. Case study research involves a wealth of legal documents and reports issued by the government, NGOs and international organizations that are directly related to judgment implementation. These are made available by the Committee of Ministers and the HUDOC database of the Council of Europe Department of the Execution of Judgments. Case study research also draws from 30 interviews that were conducted with lawyers, NGO representatives, state and Council of Europe officials, minority, migrant rights and human rights activists from different European countries, who were involved in ECHR litigation and judgment implementation. It also draws from reports issued by human rights organizations and from public law organizations that monitor and report on the situation of Roma, migrants and asylum seekers in different countries.

References

Albiston, Catherine R. and Laura Beth Nielsen. "Funding the Cause: How Public Interest Law Organizations Fund their Activities and Why it Matters for Social Change." *Law and Social Inquiry* 39, no. 1 (2014): 62–96.

Alter, Karen. *The New Terrain of International Law – Courts, Politics, Rights.* Princeton: Princeton University Press, 2014.

Alter, Karen. "The EU's Legal System and Domestic Policy: Spillover or Backlash?" *International Organization* 54, no. 3 (2000): 489–518.

Alter, Karen J., and Jeannette Vargas. "Explaining Variation in the Use of European Litigation Strategies." *Comparative Political Studies* 33, no. 4 (2000): 452–482.

Alter, Karen J., Laurence R. Helfer and Mikael Rask Madsen. "How Context Shapes the Authority of International Courts." *Law and Contemporary Problems* 79, no. 1 (2016): 1–36.

Amnesty International. *Joint Response to the Proposals to Ensure the Future Effectiveness of the European Court of Human Rights.* 1 December2003.

Anagnostou, Dia. "From Belfast to Diyarbakir and Grozny via Strasbourg: Transnational Legal Mobilisation Against State Violations in Contexts of Armed Conflict." In *Rights in Pursuit of Social Change – Legal Mobilisation in the European Multi-level System*, edited by Dia Anagnostou, 157–180. Oxford: Hart Publishing, 2014.

Anagnostou, Dia. "Untangling the domestic impact of the European Court of Human Rights: Institutional make-up, conceptual issues and mediating factors." In *The European Court of Human Rights: Implementing the Strasbourg's Judgments into Domestic Policy*, edited by Dia Anagnostou, 1–25. Edinburgh: Edinburgh University Press, 2013.

Anagnostou, Dia and Alina Mungiu-Pippidi. "Domestic Implementation of Human Rights Judgments in Europe: Legal Infrastructure and Government Effectiveness Matter." *European Journal of International Law* 25, no.1 (2014): 205–227.

Anagnostou, Dia and Yonko Grozev. "Human rights litigation and restrictive state implementation of Strasbourg Court judgments: The case of ethnic minorities from Southeast Europe." *European Public Law* 16, no. 3 (2010): 401–418.

Anagnostou, Dia and Evangelia Psychogiopoulou. "Under what conditions can ECtHR rulings promote rights-expansive policy change? Religious and ethnic minorities in Greece." In *The European Court of Human Rights: Implementing the Strasbourg's Judgments into Domestic Policy*, edited by Dia Anagnostou, 143–165. Edinburgh: Edinburgh University Press, 2013.

Andersen, Ellen Ann. *Out of the Closets and Into the Courts – Legal Opportunity Structure and Gay Rights Litigation.* Ann Arbor: The University of Michigan Press, 2006.

Angeli, Danai and Dia Anagnostou, "A shortfall of rights and justice: Institutional design and judicial review of immigration detention in Greece", *European Journal of Legal Studies* (2022), forthcoming.

Arabadjieva, Kalina. "Challenging the school segregation of Roma children in Central and Eastern Europe." *International Journal of Human Rights* 20, no. 1 (2016): 33–54.

Baird, Vanessa and Tonja Jacobi. "Judicial Agenda Setting Through Signaling and Strategic Litigant Responses." *Journal of Law and Policy* 29 (2009): 215–239.

Bartholomeusz, Lance. "The Amicus Curiae before International Courts and Tribunals." *Non-State Actors and International Law* 5, no. 3 (2005): 209–286.

Bates, Ed. *The Evolution of the ECHR*. Oxford: Oxford University Press, 2010.

Bates, Ed. "Supervising the Execution of Judgments Delivered by the ECtHR: The Challenges Facing the Committee of Ministers." In *European Court of Human Rights Remedies and Execution of Judgments*, edited by Theodora Christou and Juan Pablo Raymond, 49–106. London: The British Institute of International and Comparative Law, 2005.

Battjes, Hemme. "Landmarks: Soering's Legacy." *Amsterdam Law Forum* 1, no. 1 (2008): 139–149.

Baumgärte, Moritz. *Demanding Rights – Europe's Supranational Courts and the Dilemma of Migrant Vulnerability*. Cambridge: Cambridge University Press, 2019.

Beernaert, Marie-Aude. "Protocol 14 and New Strasbourg Procedures: Towards Greater Efficiency? And at What Price?" *European Human Rights Law Review* 5 (2004): 544–557.

Benford, Robert D. and David A. Snow. "Framing Processes and Social Movements: An Overview and Assessment." *Annual Review of Sociology* 26 (2000): 611–639.

Benoit-Rohmer, Florence. *The Minority Question in Europe – Texts and Commentary*. Strasbourg: Council of Europe publishing, 1996.

Bernhardt, Rudolf. "Reform of the Control Machinery under the European Convention on Human Rights: Protocol No. 11." *American Journal of International Law* 89, no. 1 (1995): 145–154.

Bilsky, Leora, Rodger D. Citron and Natalie R. Davidson. "From *Kiobel* Back to Structural Reform: The Hidden Legacy of Holocaust Restitution Litigation." *Stanford Journal of Complex Litigation* 2, no. 1 (2014): 138–184.

Boon, Andrew. "Cause Lawyers in a Cold Climate." In *Cause Lawyering and the State in a Global Era*, edited by Austin Sarat and Stuart Scheingold, 144–185. Oxford: Oxford University Press, 2001.

Boyle, Kevin. "Article 14 Bites At Last." *EHRAC Bulletin* 5 (Summer 2006): 1–4.

Boyle, Kevin. "Human Rights and Political Resolution in Northern Ireland." *Yale Journal of International Law* 9, no. 1 (1982): 156–177.

Börzel, Tanja A. "Participation Through Law Enforcement The Case of the European Union." *Comparative Political Studies* 39, no. 1 (2006): 128–152.

Buckley, Carla. "The European Convention on Human Rights and the Right to Life in Turkey." *Human Rights Law Review* 1, no. 1 (2001): 35–65.

Buckley, Carla. *Turkey and the ECHR – A Report on the Litigation Programme of the Kurdish Human Rights Project*. London: KHRP, 2000.

Bumiller, Kristin. "Victims in the Shadow of the Law: A Critique of the Model of Legal Protection." *Signs* 12, no. 3 (Spring 1987): 421–439.

Buyse, Antoine. "The Pilot Judgment Procedure at the European Court of Human Rights: Possibilities and Challenges." In *European Court of Human Rights – 50 Years*, 78–90. Athens: Athens Bar Association, 2010.

Búzás, Zoltán I. "Is the Good News About Law Compliance Good News About Norm Compliance? The Case of Racial Equality." *International Organization* 72, no. 2 (Spring 2018): 351–385.

Cali, Başak. "Explaining variation in the intrusiveness of regional human rights remedies in domestic orders." *International Journal of Constitutional Law* 16, no. 1 (2018a): 214–234.

Cali, Başak. "Coping with Crisis: Whither the Variable Geometry in the Jurisprudence of the European Court of Human Rights." *Wisconsin International Law Journal* 35, no. 2 (2018b): 237–276.

Cali, Başak and Anne Koch. "Foxes Guarding the Foxes – The Peer Review of Human Rights Judgments by the Committee of Ministers of the Council of Europe." *Human Rights Law Review* 14 (2014): 301–325.

Cançado Trindade, Antônio Augusto. *The Access of Individuals to International Justice.* Oxford: Oxford University Press, 2015.

Cashman, Laura. "New label no progress: institutional racism and the persistent segregation of Romani students in the Czech Republic." *Race, Ethnicity and Education* 20, no. 5 (2017): 595–608.

Cassel, Douglas. "Does International Human Rights Law Make a Difference?" *Chicago Journal of International Law* 2, no. 1 (2001): 121–135.

Cassidy, Frank, ed. *Aboriginal Title in British Columbia: Delgamuukw v The Queen – Proceedings of a conference held September 1991.* Lantzville, BC: Oolichan Books, 1992.

Cavallaro, James and Stephanie Erin Brewer. "Re-evaluating Regional Human Rights Litigation in the Twenty-First Century: The Case of the Inter-American Court." *American Journal of International Law* 102, no. 4 (2008): 768–827.

Chayes, Abraham. "The Role of the Judge in Public Law Litigation." *Harvard Law Review* 89, no. 7 (1976): 1281–1316.

Chevalier-Watts, Juliet. "Has human rights law become *lex specialis* for the European Court of Human Rights in right to life cases arising from internal armed conflicts?" *International Journal of Human Rights* 14, no. 4 (2010): 584–602.

Cichowski, Rachel A. "The European Court of Human Rights, Amicus Curiae, and Violence against Women." *Law and Society Review* 50, no. 4 (2016): 890–919.

Cichowski, Rachel A. "Civil Society and the ECtHR." In *The ECtHR between Law and Politics*, edited by Jans Christoffersen and Mikael Rask Madsen, 77–97. Oxford: Oxford University Press, 2011.

Cichowski, Rachel A. *The European Court and Civil Society – Litigation, Mobilization and Governance.* Cambridge: Cambridge University Press, 2007.

Cichowski, Rachel A. "Introduction: Courts, Democracy, and Governance." *Comparative Political Studies* 39, no. 1 (2006a): 3–21.

Cichowski, Rachel A. "Courts, Rights and Democratic Participation." *Comparative Political Studies* 39, no. 1 (2006b): 50–75.

Clark, Ann Marie. *Diplomacy of Conscience – Amnesty International and Changing Human Rights Norms.* Princeton: Princeton University Press, 2001.

Clayton, Gina. "Asylum Seekers in Europe: M.S.S v. Belgium and Greece." *Human Rights Law Review* 11, no. 4 (2011): 758–773.

Clements, Luke, Philip A. Thomas and Robert Thomas. "The Rights of Minorities – A Romany Perspective." *OSCE Office for Democratic Institutions and Human Rights Bulletin* 4, no. 4 (1996): 4–16.

Cliquennois, Gaëtan and Brice Champetier. "The Economic, Judicial and Political Influence Exerted by Private Foundations on Cases Taken by NGOs to the European Court of Human Rights: Inklings of a New Cold War?" *European Law Journal* 22, no. 1 (2016): 92–126.

Conant, Lisa. "Who Files Suit? Legal Mobilization and Torture Violations in Europe." *Law and Policy* 38, no. 4 (2016): 280–303.

Conant, Lisa. "Individuals, Courts and the Development of European Social Rights." *Comparative Political Studies* 39, no. 1 (2006): 76–100.

Conant, Lisa. *Justice Contained*. Ithaca: Cornell University Press, 2002.

Costello, Cathryn. *The Human Rights of Migrants and Refugees in European Law*. Oxford: Oxford University Press, 2015.

Council of Europe. *Environment and the ECHR*. European Court of Human Rights Fact Sheet, 21 July2021. https://www.echr.coe.int/documents/fs_environment_eng.pdf.

Council of Europe. *Report on an additional protocol on the rights of minorities to the ECHR*. Parliamentary Assembly, Doc. No. 6742, 19 January1993. https://assembly. coe.int/nw/xml/XRef/X2H-XrefViewHTML.asp?FileID=6772&lang=E N.

Council of Europe. *Practical Guide on Admissibility Criteria*. Strasbourg: Council of Europe, 2014.

Council of Europe. *Yearbook of the ECHR 1965*. The Hague: Martinus Nijhoff, 1967.

Dancy, Geoff and Christopher J. Fariss. "Rescuing Human Rights Law from International Legalism and its Critics." *Human Rights Quarterly* 39, no. 1 (2017): 1–36.

Dawson, Mark and Elise Muir. "Individual, Institutional and Collective Vigilance in Protecting Fundamental Rights in the EU: Lessons from the Roma." *Common Market Law Review* 48, no. 3 (2011): 751–775.

De Búrca, Gráinne. *Reframing Human Rights in a Turbulent Era*. Oxford: Oxford University Press, 2021.

De Búrca, Gráinne. "Human Rights Experimentalism." *American Journal of International Law* 111, no. 2 (2017a): 277–316.

De Búrca, Gráinne. "Global Experimentalist Governance and Human Rights." *ESIL Reflections* 6, no. 8 (2017b): 1–6.

De Búrca, Gráinne. "Stumbling into Experimentalism: The EU Anti-Discrimination Regime." In *Experimentalist Governance in the European Union: Towards a New Architecture*, edited by Charles F. Sabel and Jonathan Zeitlin, 215–235. Oxford: Oxford University Press, 2010.

De Búrca, Gráinne, Robert O. Keohane and Charles Sabel. "Global Experimentalist Governance." *British Journal of Political Science* 44, no. 3 (2014): 477–486.

De Búrca, Gráinne, Robert O. Keohane and Charles Sabel. "New Modes of Pluralist Global Governance." *International Law and Politics* 45 (2013): 723–786.

De Fazio, Gianluca. "Legal opportunity structure and social movement strategy in Northern Ireland and the United States." *International Journal of Comparative Sociology* 53, no. 3 (2012): 3–22.

Dembour, Marie-Benedicte. *When Humans Become Migrants: Study of the European Court of Human Rights with an Inter-American Counterpoint*. Oxford: Oxford University Press, 2015.

Dezalay, Yves and Bryant Garth. "From the Cold War to Kosovo: The Rise and Renewal of the Field of International Human Rights." *Annual Review of Law and Social Science* 2 (2006): 231–255.

Di Rattalma, Marco Frigessi. "NGOs before the ECtHR: Beyond Amicus Curiae Participation?" In *Civil Society, International Courts and Compliance Bodies*, edited by Tullio Treves, Marco Frigessi di Rattalma, Attila Tanzi, Alessandro Fodella, Cesare Pitea, and Chiara Ragni, 57–66. The Hague: Asser Press, 2005.

Dickson, Brice. *The ECHR and the Conflict in Northern Ireland*. Oxford: Oxford University Press, 2010.

Dickson, Brice. "Miscarriages of Justice in Northern Ireland." In *Miscarriages of Justice – A Review of Justice in Error*, edited by Clive Walker and Keir Starmer, 287–303. Oxford: Oxford University Press, 1999.

Dikov, Grigory. "The ones that lost: Russian cases rejected at the European Court." *Open Democracy*. 7 December2009. https://www.opendemocracy.net/od-russia/grigory-dikov/ones-that-lost-russian-cases-rejected-at-european-court.

Dimitriadi, Angeliki and Antonia-Maria Sarantaki. *National report on the governance of the asylum reception system in Greece*. CEASEVAL Research on the Common European Asylum System No. 20, Chemnitz, March2019.

Dolidze, Anna. "Bridging Comparative and International Law: Amicus Curiae Participation as a Vertical Legal Transplant." *European Journal of International Law* 26, no. 4 (2015): 851–880.

Donald, Alice. "The Power of Persistence: How NGOs can Ensure that Judgments Lead to Justice". *Implementing Human Rights Decisions: Reflections, Successes and New Directions*. University of Bristol, Human Rights Law Implementation Project, 2021. Available at http://bristol.ac.uk/media-library/sites/law/hric/2021-documents/8.%20Power%20of%20Persistence_Donald_ENG.pdf.

Donald, Alice and Anne-Katrin Speck. "The Dynamics of Domestic Human Rights Implementation: Lessons from Qualitative Research in Europe." *Journal of Human Rights Practice* 12, no. 1 (2020): 48–70.

Donald, Alice and Anne-Katrin Speck. "The European Court of Human Rights' Remedial Practice and its Impact on the Execution of Judgments." *Human Rights Law Review* 19, no. 1 (2019): 83–117.

Donald, Alice, Debra Long and Anne-Katrin Speck. "Identifying and Assessing the Implementation of Human Rights Decisions." *Journal of Human Rights Practice* 12, no. 1 (2020): 125–148.

Donald, Alice and Philip Leach. "A Wolf in Sheep's Clothing: Why the Draft Copenhagen Declaration Must be Rewritten." *European Journal of International Law* (blog), 21 February2018. https://www.ejiltalk.org/a-wolf-in-sheeps-clothing-why-the-draft-copenhagen-declaration-must-be-rewritten/.

Edel, Frederic. *The prohibition of discrimination under the ECHR*. Human Rights files no. 22, Strasbourg: Council of Europe Publishing, 2010.

Epp, Charles. *The Rights Revolution*. Chicago: The University of Chicago Press, 1998.

Eskridge, William N., Jr. "Some Effects of Identity-Based Social Movements on Constitutional Law in the Twentieth Century." *Michigan Law Review* 100, no. 8 (2002): 2062–2407.

European Council on Refugees and Exiles and European Legal Network on Asylum (ELENA). *Survey on Legal Aid for Asylum Seekers in Europe*. October2010.

European Union Agency for Fundamental Rights. *Legal Aid for Returnees Deprived of Liberty*. Luxembourg: Publications Office of the European Union, 2021.

Evans Case, Rhonda and Terri E. Givens. "Re-engineering Legal Opportunity Structures in the European Union? The Starting Line Group and the Politics of the Racial Equality Directive." *Journal of Common Market Studies* 48, no. 2 (2010): 221–241.

Farkas, Lilla. *"Mobilising for racial equality in Europe – Roma rights and transnational justice."* PhD Thesis, European University Institute, Department of Law, 28 February2020.

Farkas, Lilla and Gergely Dezideriu. *Racial discrimination in education and EU equality law*. European Commission, Directorate-General for Justice and Consumers, 2020.

Føllesdal, Andreas. "Subsidiarity and International Human-Rights Courts: Respecting Self-Governance and Protecting Human Rights – Or Neither?", *Law and Contemporary Problems* 79 (2016): 147–163.

Føllesdal, Andreas and Geir Ulfstein. "The Draft Copenhagen Declaration: Whose Responsibility and Dialogue?" *EJIL Talk* (22 February2018). Accessed 27 December 2020. ejiltalk. org/the-draft-copenhagen-declaration-whose-responsibility-and-dialogue/.

Forst, Déborah. "The Execution of Judgments of the European Court of Human Rights." *Vienna Journal of International Constitutional Law* 7, no. 3 (2013), 1–51.

Fuchs, Gesine. "Strategic Litigation for Gender Equality in the Workplace and Legal Opportunity Structures in Four European Countries." *Canadian Journal of Law and Society* 28, no. 2 (2013): 189–208.

Galanter, Marc. "Why the 'Haves' Come out Ahead: Speculations on the Limits of Legal Change." *Law and Society Review: Litigation and Dispute Processing: Part One* 9, no. 1, (Autumn 1974): 95–160.

Gamson, William A. and David S. Meyer. "Framing political opportunity." In *Comparative Perspectives on Social Movements*, edited by Doug McAdam, John D. McCarthy and Mayer N. Zald, 275–290. Cambridge: Cambridge University Press, 1996.

Georgetti, Chiara. "What Happens after a Judgment is Given? Judgment Compliance and the Performance of International Courts and Tribunals." In *The Performance of International Courts and Tribunals*, edited by Theresa Squatrito, Oran R. Young, Andreas Follesdal and Geir Ulfstein, 324–350. Cambridge: Cambridge University Press, 2018.

Gerards, Janneke. "The Discrimination Grounds of Article 14 of the ECHR." *Human Rights Law Review* 13, no. 1 (2013): 99–124.

Gerards, Janneke and Lize R. Glas. "Access to justice in the European Convention on Human Rights system." *Netherlands Quarterly of Human Rights* 35, no. 1 (2017): 11–30.

Gilligan, Emma. *Terror in Chechnya: Russia and the Tragedy of Civilians in War*. Princeton: Princeton University Press, 2010.

Glaz, Lize R. "The Execution Process of Pilot Judgments before the Committee of Ministers." *Human Rights and International Legal Discourse* 13, no. 2 (2019): 73–98.

Goldston, James. "The Struggle for Roma Rights: Arguments that Have Worked." *Human Rights Quarterly* 32, no. 2 (2010): 311–325.

Goldston, James. "Public Interest Litigation in Central and Eastern Europe: Roots, Prospects, and Challenges." *Human Rights Quarterly* 28, no. 2 (2006): 492–527.

Goldston, James. "Race discrimination impact litigation in Eastern Europe – A discussion of legal strategies to confront racial discrimination," *ERRC* (blog), 15 July1997, http://www.errc.org/roma-rights-journal/race-discrimination-impact-litigation-in-ea stern-europe–a-discussion-of-legal-strategies-to-confront-racial-discrimination.

Goodwin, Morag. "Taking on racial segregation: the European Court of Human Rights at a Brown v Board of Education moment?" *Rechtsgeleerd Magazijn Themis* 170, no. 3 (2009): 93–105.

Goodwin, Morag. "White Knights On Chargers: Using the US Approach to Promote Roma Rights in Europe?" *German Law Journal* 5, no. 12 (2004): 1431–1447.

Gordon, Anthony and Paul Mageean. "Habits of Mind and "Truth Telling": Article 2 ECHR in Post-Conflict Northern Ireland." In *Judges, Transition, and Human Rights*, edited by John Morison, KieranMcEvoy and Gordon Anthony, 181–200. Oxford: Oxford University Press, 2007.

Gotsova, Boryana. "Rules Over Rights? Legal Aspects of the European Commission Recommendation for the Resumption of Dublin Transfers of Asylum Seekers to Greece." *German Law Journal* 20, no. 5 (2019): 637–659.

Green, Leslie C. "Derogations of Human Rights in Emergency Situations." *Canadian Yearbook of International Law* 16 (1978): 92–115.

Greenberg, Jessica. "Counterpedagogy, Sovereignty, and Migration at the European Court of Human Rights." *Law and Social Inquiry* 46, no. 2 (2021): 518–539.

Greer, Steven. *The European Convention of Human Rights – Achievements, Problems and Prospects.* Cambridge: Cambridge University Press, 2006.

Greer, Steven and Luzius Wildhaber. "Revisiting the Debate about 'constitutionalising' the European Court of Human Rights." *Human Rights Law Review* 12, no. 4 (2012): 655–687.

Grossman, Joel and Austin Sarat. "Litigation in the Federal Courts: A Comparative Perspective." *Law and Society Review* 9, no. 2 (1975): 321–346.

Guarnieri, Carlo. "Courts and marginalized groups: Perspectives from Continental Europe." *International Journal of Constitutional Law* 5, no. 2 (2007): 187–210.

Guasti, Petra, David S. Siroky and Daniel Stockemer. "Judgment without justice: on the efficacy of the European human rights regime." *Democratization* 24, no. 2 (2016): 226–243.

Guerrero, Marion. *Strategic Litigation in EU Gender Equality Law.* Luxembourg: Publications Office of the European Union, 2020.

Guerrero, Marion. "Activating the Courtrooms: Opportunities for Strategic Same Sex Rights Litigation before the European Court of Human Rights and the Court of Justice of the European Union." Presentation, LSE Conference on Social Justice in the Next Century, 2014.

Harlow, Carol and Richard Rawlings. *Pressure Through Law.* London: Routledge1992.

Harmsen, Robert. "The Reform of the Convention System: Institutional Restructuring and the (Geo-)Politics of Human Rights." In *The ECtHR between Law and Politics*, edited by Jans Christoffersen and Mikael Rask Madsen, 119–143. Oxford: Oxford University Press, 2011.

Hartman, Joan F. "Derogations from human rights treaties in public emergencies." *Harvard International Law Journal* 22, no. 1 (1981): 1–52.

Harvey, Colin J. "Dissident Voices: Refugees, Human Rights and Asylum in Europe." *Social and Legal Studies* 9, no. 3 (2000): 367–396.

Harvey, Colin J. and Stephen Livingstone. "Protecting the Marginalised: The Role of the ECHR." *Northern Irish Legal Quarterly* 51, no. 3 (2000): 445–465.

Harvey, Paul. "Is Strasbourg obsessively interventionist? A view from the Court" *UK Human Rights Blog* (blog). 24 January2012. http://ukhumanrightsblog.com/2012/01/24/is-strasbourg-obsessively-interventionist-a-view-from-the-court-paul-harvey/.

Hawkings, Darren and Wade Jacoby. "Partial Compliance: A Comparison of the European and Inter-American Courts for Human Rights." *Journal of International Law and International Relations* 6, no. 1 (2010–2011):35–85.

Heger Boyle, Elizabeth and Melissa Thompson. "National Politics and Resort to the European Commission on Human Rights." *Law & Society Review* 35, no. 2 (2001): 321–344.

Helfer, Laurence R. and Erik Voeten. "International Courts as Agents of Legal Change: Evidence from LGBT Rights in Europe." *International Organization* 68, no. 1 (2014): 77–110.

Henrard, Kristin. "The European Court of Human Rights, Ethnic and Religious Minorities and the Two Dimensions of the Right to Equal Treatment: Jurisprudence at Different Speeds?" *Nordic Journal of Human Rights* 34, no. 3 (2016): 157–177.

Hera, Gabor. "The relationship between the Roma and the police: a Roma perspective." *Policing and Society* 27, no. 4 (2017): 393–407.

Hersant, Jeanne. "Mobilizations for Western Thrace and Cyprus in Contemporary Turkey." In *Social Movements, Mobilization and Contestation in the Middle East and North Africa*, edited by Joel Beinin and Frédéric Vairel, 167–182. Stanford: Stanford University Press, 2013.

Hillebrecht, Courtney. *Domestic Politics and International Human Rights Tribunals.* Cambridge: Cambridge University Press, 2015.

Hilson, Chris. "New social movements: the role of legal opportunity." *Journal of European Public Policy* 9, no. 2 (2002): 238–255.

Hioureas, Christina G. "Behind the Scenes of Protocol No. 14: Politics in Reforming the European Court of Human Rights." *Berkeley Journal of International Law* 24, no. 2 (2006): 718–757.

Hodson, Loveday. *NGOs and the Struggle for Human Rights in Europe.* Oxford: Hart Publishing, 2011.

Howse, Robert and Ruti Teitel. "Beyond Compliance: Rethinking Why International Law Really Matters." *Global Policy* 1, no. 2 (2010): 127–136.

Huneeus, Alexandra. "Reforming the State from Afar: Structural Reform Litigation at the Human Rights Courts." *Yale Journal of International Law* 40, no. 1 (2015): 1–40.

Huneeus, Alexandra. "Compliance with Judgments and Decisions." In *The Oxford Handbook of International Adjudication*, edited by Cesare P.R. Romano, Karen J. Alter, and Yuval Shany, 438–460. Oxford: Oxford University Press, 2013.

Israel, Liora. "Rights on the Left? Social Movements, Law and Lawyers after 1968 in France." In *Rights and Courts in Pursuit of Social Change*, edited by Dia Anagnostou, 79–103. Oxford: Hart Publishing, 2014.

Jacquot, Sophie and Tommaso Vitale. "Law as a weapon of the weak? A comparative analysis of legal mobilization by Roma and women's groups at the European level." *Journal of European Public Policy* 21, no. 4 (2014): 587–604.

Jones, Ben. "European Court of Human Rights: is the admissions system transparent enough?" *UK Human Rights Blog* (Blog). 27 January 2012. http://ukhumanrights blog.com/2012/01/27/european-court-of-human-rights-is-the-admissions-system-tra nsparent-enough-ben-jones/.

Kawar, Leila. *Contesting Immigration Policy in Court – Legal Activism and Its Radiating Efects in the United States and France.* Cambridge: Cambridge University Press, 2015.

Keck, Margaret and Kathryn Sikkink. *Activists Beyond Border – Advocacy Networks in International Politics.* Ithaca: Cornell University Press, 1998.

Keller, Helen and Cedric Marti. "Reconceptualizing Implementation: The Judicialization of the Execution of the European Court of Human Rights' Judgments." *European Journal of International Law* 26, no. 4 (2016): 829–850.

Keohane, Robert, Andrew Moravscik and A.-M. Slaughter. "Legalized Dispute Resolution: Interstate and Transnational." *International Organization* 54, no. 3 (2000): 457–488.

Kocak, Mustafa and Esin Orucu. "Dissolution of Political Parties in the Name of Democracy: Cases from Turkey and the ECtHR." *European Public Law* 9, no. 3 (2003): 399–420.

Koivurova, Timo. "Jurisprudence of the European Court of Human Rights Regarding Indigenous Peoples: Retrospect and Prospects." *International Journal on Minority and Group Rights* 18, no. 1 (2011): 1–37.

Koopmans, Ruud. "Political. Opportunity. Structure. Some Splitting to Balance the Lumping." *Sociological Forum* 14, no. 1 (1999): 93–105.

Koutsouraki, Eleni. "The Indefinite Detention of Undesirable and Unreturnable Third-Country Nationals in Greece." *Refugee Survey Quarterly* 36, no. 1 (2017): 85–106.

Krisch, Nico. *Beyond Constitutionalism: The Pluralist Structure of Post-national Law.* Oxford: Oxford University Press, 2010.

Küçüksu, Aysel Eybil. "In the Aftermath of a Judgment: Why Human Rights Organisations Should Harness the Potential of Rule 9." *Strasbourg Observers* (Blog), 3 March2021, https://strasbourgobservers.com/2021/03/03/in-the-aftermath-of-a-judgment-why-human-rights-organisations-should-harness-the-potential-of-rule-9/?subscribe=pending#504.

Küçüksu, Aysel Eybil. "Enforcing Rights Beyond Litigation: Mapping HRO Strategies in Monitoring ECtHR Judgment Implementation", iCourts Working Paper Series, no. 264 (2021), 5.

Kurban, Dilek. *Limits of Supranational Justice – The European Court of Human Rights and Turkey's Kurdish Conflict.* Cambridge: Cambridge University Press, 2020.

Kurban, Dilek. *"The Limits of Transnational Justice: The ECtHR, Turkey and the Kurdish Conflict."* PhD Thesis, Maastricht University Faculty of Law, August2017.

Kurban, Dilek. "Forsaking Individual Justice: The Implications of the European Court of Human Rights' Pilot Judgment Procedure for Victims of Gross and Systematic Violations." *Human Rights Law Review* 16 (2016): 731–769.

Lambert Abdelgawad, Elisabeth. "Dialogue and the Implementation of the European Court of Human Rights Judgments." *Netherlands Quarterly of Human Rights* 34, no. 4 (2016): 340–363.

Lambert-Abdelgawad, Elisabeth. *The Execution of Judgments of the European Court of Human Rights.* Strasbourg: Council of Europe Publishing, 2008.

Larson, Erik, Wibo van Rossum and Patrick Schmidt. "The Dutch Confession: Compliance, Leadership and National Identity in the Human Rights Order." *Utrecht Law Review* 10, no. 1 (2014): 96–112.

Leach, Philip and Alice Donald. "Copenhagen: Keeping on Keeping on. A Reply to Mikael Rask Madsen and Jonas Christoffersen on the Draft Copenhagen Declaration." *European Journal of International Law* (blog), 24 February2018, https://www.ejiltalk.org/copenhagen-keeping-on-keeping-on-a-reply-to-mikael-rask-madsen-and-jonas-christoffersen-on-the-draft-copenhagen-declaration.

Leach, Philip. "The Continuing Utility of International Human Rights Mechanisms?" *European Journal of International Law* (blog), 1 November2017, ejiltalk.org/the-conti nuing-utility-of-international-human-rights-mechanisms/.

Leach, Philip. "No longer offering fine mantras to a parched child? The European Court's developing approach to remedies." In *Constituting Europe – The European Court of Human Rights in a National, European and Global Context*, edited by Andreas Føllesdal, Birgit Peters and Geir Ulfstein, 142–180. Cambridge: Cambridge University Press, 2013.

Leach, Philip. "The Chechen Conflict: Analysing the Oversight of the ECtHR." *European Human Rights Law Review* 6 (2008): 732–761.

Lester, Anthony. "30 Years On." In *30 At the Turning of the Tide*, edited by Mayerlene Engineer, Julius Honnor, Louis Mackay, Olivia Skinner and Alice Trouncer. London: Commission for Racial Equality, 2006.

Lindblom, Anna-Karin. *Non-Governmental Organisations in International Law.* Cambridge: Cambridge University Press, 2005.

Madsen, Mikael Rask. "The Challenging Authority of the European Court of Human Rights: From Cold War Legal Diplomacy to the Brighton Declaration and Backlash." *Law and Contemporary Problems* 79, no. 1 (2016): 141–178.

Madsen, Mikael Rask. "The Protracted Institutionalization of the Strasbourg Court: From Legal Diplomacy to Integrationist Jurisprudence." In *The ECtHR between Law and*

Politics, edited by Jans Christoffersen and Mikael Rask Madsen, 43–60. Oxford: Oxford University Press, 2011.

Madsen, Mikael Rask. "France, the UK, and the 'Boomerang' of the Internationalisation of Human Rights (1945–2000)." In *Human Rights Brought Home: Socio-Legal Perspectives on Human Rights in the National Context*, edited by Simon Halliday and Patrick Schmidt, 57–87. Oxford: Hart Publishing, 2004.

Madsen, Mikael Rask. "From Cold War Instrument to Supreme European Court: The ECtHR at the Crossroads of International and National Law and Politics." *Law and Social Inquiry* 32, no. 1 (Winter 1997): 137–159.

Madsen, Mikael Rask. "Two-level politics and the backlash against international courts: Evidence from the politicisation of the European court of human rights." *British Journal of Politics and International Relations* 22, no. 4 (2020): 728–738.

Majercik, Lubomir. "The Invisible Majority: The Unsuccessful Applications Against the Czech Republic Before the ECtHR." *CYIL* 1 (2010): 217–222.

Marks, Susan. "Civil Liberties at the Margin: the UK Derogation and the European Court of Human Rights." *Oxford Journal of Legal Studies* 15, no. 1 (1995): 69–95.

Martens, S.K. "Commentary," in *Compliance with Judgments of International Courts*, edited by M.K. Bulterman and M. Kuijer, 47–79, The Hague: Martinus Nijhoff, 1996.

Martin, Lisa. "Against Compliance." In *International Law and International Relations: Interdisciplinary-perspectives-international-law-and-international-relations*, edited by Jeffrey L. Dunoff and Mark A. Pollack, 591–612. New York: Cambridge University Press2012.

Massicard, Elise. "Variations in the Judicialisation of the Alevi Issue – From Turkey to Europe." *Revue française de science politique* 64, no. 4 (2014): 711–733.

Matejcic, Barbara. "*Croatia's Schools Leave Roma Pupils in the Slow Lanes.*" Balkan Insight (blog). 18 November2020. https://balkaninsight.com/2020/11/18/croatias-school s-leave-roma-pupils-in-the-slow-lane/.

Mayer, Lloyd Hitoshi. "NGO Standing and Influence in Regional Human Rights Courts and Commissions." *Brookings Journal of International Law* 36, no. 3 (2011): 911–940.

McAdam, Doug, John D. McCarthy and Mayer N. Zald. "Introduction: Opportunities, mobilizing structures, and framing processes – toward a synthetic, comparative perspective on social movements." In *Comparative perspectives on social movements*, edited by Doug McAdam, John D. McCarthy and Mayer N. Zald, 1–20. Cambridge: Cambridge University Press, 1996.

McCammon, Holly J. and Allison R. McGrath. "Litigating Change? Social Movements and the Court System." *Sociology Compass* 92, no. 2 (2015): 128–139.

McCarthy, John D. "The Globalization of Social Movement Theory." In *Transnational Social Movements and Global Politics*, edited by Jackie Smith, Charles Chatfield and Ron Pagnucco, 243–259. Syracuse: Syracuse University Press, 1997.

McCrudden, Christopher and Brendan O'Leary. *Courts and Consociations: Human Rights versus Power-Sharing*. Oxford: Oxford University Press, 2013.

McIntosh Sundstrom, Lisa. "Russian NGOs and the European Court of Human Rights: A Spectrum of Approaches to Litigation." *Human Rights Quarterly* 36, no. 4 (2014): 844–868.

McIntosh Sundstrom, Lisa. "Advocacy beyond litigation: Examining Russian NGO efforts on implementation of European Court of Human Rights judgments." *Communist and Post-Communist Studies* 45, no. 3–4 (2012): 255–268.

Miara, Lucja and Victoria Prais. "The role of civil society in the execution of judgments of the ECtHR." *European Human Rights Law Review* 5 (2012): 528–539.

Miller, Vaughne. *Protocol 11 and the New European Court of Human Rights.* House of Commons Library, Research Paper 98/109, 4 December1998.

Mohamed, Abdelsalam. "Individual and NGO Participation in Human Rights Litigation before the African Court of Human and People's Rights." *MSU-DCL Journal of International Law* 8 (1999): 377–396.

Mole, Nuala and Catherine Meredith. *Asylum and the ECHR.* Human Rights files No. 9, Strasbourg: Council of Europe Publishing, 2010.

Moreno-Lax, Violeta, "Dismantling the Dublin System: M.S.S. v Belgium and Greece", *European Journal of Migration and Law* 14, no. 1 (2012): 1–31.

Mowbray, Alastair. "An Examination of the European Court of Human Rights' Approach to Overruling its Previous Case Law." *Human Rights Law Review* 9, no. 2 (2009): 179–201.

Mowbray, Alastair. "The Creativity of the European Court of Human Rights." *Human Rights Law Review* 5, no. 1 (2005): 57–79.

Möschel, Mathias. "Is the European Court of Human Rights Case Law on Anti-Roma Violence 'Beyond Reasonable Doubt'?" *Human Rights Law Review* 12, no. 3 (2012): 479–507.

Murray, Rachel. "Addressing the Implementation Crisis: Securing Reparation and Righting Wrongs." *Journal of Human Rights Practice* 12, no. 1 (2020): 1–21.

Murray, Rachel and Clara Sandoval. "Balancing Specificity of Reparation Measures and States' Discretion to Enhance Implementation." *Journal of Human Rights Practice* 12, no. 1 (2020): 101–124.

Music, Sinisa-Senad. "Ensuring Readiness and Success for Primary School in Croatia – Integration in Medimurje County." Roma Education Fund, 2016. https://www.roma educationfund.org/ensuring-readiness-and-success-for-primary-school-in-croatia-integration-in-medimurje-county/.

Neier, Aryeh. *International Human Rights Movement – A History.* Princeton: Princeton University Press, 2012.

NeJaime, Douglas. "Winning Through Losing." *Iowa Law Review* 96 (2011): 941–1011.

Nichols Haddad, Heidi. *The Hidden Hands of Justice. NGOs, Human Rights and International Courts.* Cambridge: Cambridge University Press, 2018.

Neukirch, Claus, Katrin Simhandl, Wolfgang Zellner. "Implementing Minority Rights in the Framework of the CSCE/OSCE." In *Mechanisms for the Implementation of Minority Rights Standards, Minority Issues Handbook Vol. 2*, 159–181. Strasbourg: Council of Europe Publishing, 2005.

Newman, Gerald L. "Bi-Level Remedies for Human Rights Violations." *Harvard International Law Journal* 55, no. 2 (2014): 323–360.

Nielsen, Laura Beth, Robert L. Nelson and Ryon Lancaster. "Individual Justice or Collective Legal Mobilization? Employment Discrimination Litigation in the Post-Civil Rights United States." *Journal of Empirical Legal Studies* 7, no. 2 (2010): 175–201.

O' Boyle, Michael. "On Reforming the Operation of the European Court of Human Rights." *European Human Rights Law Review* 1 (2008): 1–11.

O'Boyle, Michael, David Harris, Ed Bates and Carla Buckley. *Law of the European Convention of Human Rights.* Oxford: Oxford University Press, 2009.

O' Connell, Rory. "Substantive equality in the ECtHR?" *Michigan Law Review First Impressions* 107 (2009a): 129–133.

O' Connell, Rory. "Cinderella comes to the Ball: Art. 14 and the right to non-discrimination in the ECHR." *Legal Studies* 29, no. 2 (2009b): 211–229.

O' Meara, Noreen. *Reforming the European Court of Human Rights: The Impacts of Protocols 15 and 16 to the ECHR*. The Danish National Research Foundation's Centre of Excellence for International Courts, Working Paper Series, No. 31, 2015.

Open Society Justice Initiative. *The Application of the 'Significant Disadvantage' Criterion by the European Court of Human Rights*. New York: Open Society Justice Initiative, November 2015.

Ovey, Clare and Robin White. *The European Convention of Human Rights*. Oxford: Oxford University Press, 2006.

Overdevest, Christine and Jonathan Zeitlin. "Experimentalism in transnational forest governance: Implementing European Union Forest Law Enforcement, Governance and Trade (FLEGT) Voluntary Partnership Agreements in Indonesia and Ghana." *Regulation & Governance* 12, no. 1 (2018): 64–87.

Pentassuglia. Gaetano. "The Strasbourg Court and Minority Groups: Shooting in the Dark or a New Interpretive Ethos?" *International Journal of Minority and Group Rights* 19, no. 1 (2012): 1–23.

Peroni, Lourdes. "Minorities before the European Court of Human Rights." In *International Approaches to Governing Ethnic Diversity*, edited by Jane Boulden and Will Kymlicka, 26–50. Oxford: Oxford University Press, 2015.

Portillo, Shannon. "Social Equality and the Mobilization of the Law." *Sociology Compass* 5, no. 11 (2011): 949–956.

Psychogiopoulou, Evangelia, "European Courts and the Rights of Migrants and Asylum Seekers in Greece." In *Rights and Courts in Pursuit of Social Change*, edited by Dia Anagnostou, 129–155. Oxford: Hart Publishing, 2014.

Raustiala, Kal and Anne-Marie Slaughter. "International Law, International Relations and Compliance." In *Handbook of International Relations*, edited by Walter Carlsnaes, Thomas Risse and Beth A. Simmons, 538–558. London: Sage Publications, 2002.

Ringelheim, Julie. *Diversite culturelle et droits de l' homme: La protection des minorities par la Convention Européenne*. Brussels: Bruylant, 2006.

Rorke, Bernard. "Hungary: A short history of segregation," *ERRC* (blog), 16 July2015, http://www.errc.org/news/hungary-a-short-history-of-segregation.

Rosenberg, Gerald. *The Hollow Hope: Can Courts Bring About Social Change?*Chicago: University of Chicago Press, 1991.

Sabel, Charles F. and Jonathan Zeitlin. "Experimentalist Governance." In *The Oxford Handbook of Governance*, edited by David Levi-Faur, 170–182. Oxford: Oxford University Press, 2012.

Sabel, Charles F. and Jonathan Zeitlin. "Learning From Difference: The New Architecture of Experimentalist Governance in the EU." In *Experimentalist Governance in the European Union: Towards a New Architecture*, edited by Charles F. Sabel, and Jonathan Zeitlin, 1–28. Oxford: Oxford University Press, 2010.

Sabel, Charles F. and William H. Simon. "Democratic Experimentalism." *Searching for Contemporary Legal Thought*, edited by Justin Desautels-Stein and Christopher Tomlins, 477–498. Cambridge: Cambridge University Press, 2017.

Sabel, Charles F. and William H.Simon. "Destabilization Rights: How Public Law Litigation Succeeds." *Harvard Law Review* 117, no. 4 (2004): 1015–1101.

Sadurski, Wojciech. "Partnering with Strasbourg: Constitutionalisation of the European Court of Human Rights, the Accession of Central and East European States to the Council of Europe, and the Idea of Pilot Judgments." *Human Rights Law Review* 9, no. 3 (2009): 397–453.

Sandland, Ralph. "Developing a Jurisprudence of Difference: The Protection of the Human Rights of Travelling Peoples by the European Court of Human Rights." *Human Rights Law Review* 8, no. 3 (2008): 475–516.

Sarat, Austin and Stuart Scheingold, eds. *Cause Lawyers and Social Movements.* Stanford: Stanford University Press, 2006.

Savino, Mario. "The Refugee Crisis as a Challenge for Public Law: The Italian Case." *German Law Journal* 17, no. 6 (2016): 981–1004.

Scheingold, Stuart A. *The Politics of Rights – Lawyers, Public Policy and Political Change,* Ann Arbor: The University of Michigan Press, 2007.

Schermers, Henry G. *The Merger of the Commission and Court of Human Rights (Protocol 11 to the European Convention on Human Rights).* Saarbrucken: Europa-Institut Universitat des Saarlades, 1994.

Schmidt, Susanne K. "Who cares about nationality? The path-dependent case law of the ECJ from goods to citizens." *Journal of European Public Policy* 19, no. 1 (2012): 8–24.

Scott, Joanne and Susan Sturm. "Courts as Catalysts: Rethinking the Judicial Role in New Governance." *Columbia Journal of European Law* 13 (2007): 565–594.

Shelton, Dinah. "Performance of Regional Human Rights Courts." In *The Performance of International Courts and Tribunals,* edited by Theresa Squatrito, Oran R.Young, AndreasFollesdal, GeirUlfstein, 114–153. Cambridge: Cambridge University Press, 2018.

Shelton, Dinah. "Law, Non-Law and the Problem of 'Soft Law'". In *Commitment and Compliance – The Role of Non-Binding Norms in the International Legal System,* edited by Dinah Shelton, 1–18. Oxford: Oxford University Press2000.

Shelton, Dinah. "The Participation of NGOs in International Judicial Proceedings." *American Journal of International Law* 88 (1994): 611–642.

Sikkink, Kathryn. "Patterns of Dynamic Multilevel Governance and the Insider-Outsider Coalition." In *Transnational Protest and Global Activism,* edited by Donatella della Porta and Sidney Tarrow, 151–174. Oxford: Rowman & Littlefield Publishers, Inc., 2005.

Simmons, Beth A. *Mobilizing for Human Rights – International Law in Domestic Politics.* New York: Cambridge University Press, 2009.

Sitaropoulos, Nikolaos. "Supervising Execution of ECtHR Judgments Concerning Minorities – The Committee of Ministers Potentials and Constraints", *III Annuaire International des Droits de l' Homme* 3 (2008): 523–550.

Smekal, Hubert and Katarina Sipulova, "*D.H. v Czech Republic* Six Years Later: On the Power of an International Human Rights Court to Push Through Systemic Change," *Netherlands Quarterly of Human Rights* 32, no. 3 (2014): 288–321.

Spano, Robert. "The Future of the European Court of Human Rights – Subsidiarity, Process-Based Review and the Rule of Law." *Human Rights Law Review* 18 (2018): 473–494.

Squatrito, Theresa. "Conditions of democracy-enhancing multilateralism: expansion of rights protections in Europe?" *Review of International Studies* 38, no. 4 (2012): 707–733.

Strasser, Wolfgang. "Intervention by Mr. Wolfgang Strasser." In *Proceedings of the 2nd Colloquy on the European Court of Human Rights and the protection of refugees, asylum-seekers and displaced persons,* 47–60. Strasbourg: Council of Europe Publishing, 19–20 May2000.

Sturm, Susan. "Second Generation Employment Discrimination: A Structural Approach." *Columbia Law Review* 101 (2001): 458–568.

Sullivan, John L. *ETA and Basque Nationalism – The Fight for Euskadi 1890–1986.* London: Routledge, 2015.

Susi, Mart. "The Definition of a 'Structural Problem' in the Case-Law of the European Court of Human Rights Since 2010." *German Yearbook of International Law* 55 (2012): 385–418.

Swaak, Leo F. and Therese Cachia. "The European Court of Human Rights: A Success Story?" *Human Rights Brief* 11, no. 3 (2004): 32–35.

Taqi, Irum. "Adjudicating Disappearance Cases in Turkey: An Argument for Adopting the Inter-American Court of Human Rights' Approach." *Fordham International Law Journal* 24, no. 3 (2001): 940–987.

Tarrow, Sydney. "States and opportunities: The political structuring of social movements." In *Comparative perspectives on social movements*, edited by Doug McAdam, John D. McCarthy and Mayer N. Zald, 41–61. Cambridge: Cambridge University Press, 1996.

Thornberry, Patrick and Maria Amor Martin Estebanez. *Minority rights in Europe: A review of the work and standards of the Council of Europe.* Strasbourg: Council of Europe Publishing, 2004.

Tickell, Andrew. "Radical but risky changes afoot at the European Court of Human Rights." *UK Human Rights Blog* (blog). 9 July 2013. https://ukhumanrightsblog. com/2013/07/09/radical-but-risky-changes-afoot-at-the-european-court-of-human-rights-andrew-tickell/.

Tickell, Andrew. "Dismantling the Iron-Cage: the Discursive Persistence and Legal Failure of a 'Bureaucratic Rational' Construction of the Admissibility Decision-Making of the ECtHR." *German Law Journal* 12, no. 10 (2011): 1786–1812.

Tsereleli, Nino. "The Role of the European Court of Human Rights in Facilitating Legislative Change in Cases of Long-Term Delays in Implementation." In *The International Human Rights Judiciary and National Parliaments*, edited by Matthew Saul, Andreas Follesdal, Geir Ulfstein, 223–247. Cambridge: Cambridge University Press, 2017.

Tsitselikis, Konstantinos. "Minority Mobilisation in Greece and Litigation in Strasbourg" *International Journal on Minority and Group Rights* 16, no. 1 (2008): 24–48.

Ulfstein, Geir, and Andreas Follesdal. "Copenhagen – much ado about little?" *EJIL Talk* (blog). 14 April 2018. https://www.ejiltalk.org/copenhagen-much-ado-about-little/.

Van Bossuyt, Anneleen. "Fit for Purpose or Faulty Design? Analysis of the Jurisprudence of the European Court of Human Rights and the European Court of Justice on the Legal Protection of Minorities." *Journal on Ethnopolitics and Minority Issues in Europe* 6 (2007): 1–20.

Van den Bogaert, Sina. "Roma Segregation in Education: Direct or Indirect Discrimination?" *ZaöRV* 71 (2011): 719–753.

Van den Eynde, Laura. "An Empirical Look at the Amicus Curiae Practice of Human Rights NGOs before the European Court of Human Rights." *Netherlands Quarterly of Human Rights* 31, no. 3 (2013): 271–313.

Van den Eynde, Laura. *"Litigation Practices of Non-Governmental Organisations before the European Court of Human Rights."* European Master's Degree in Human Rights and Democratisation: Awarded Theses of the Academic Year 2009/2011. Marsilio Editori, 2011.

Van der Vet, Freek. "Seeking Life, Finding Justice: Russian NGO Litigation and Chechen Disappearances before the ECtHR." *Human Rights Review* 13, no. 3 (2012): 303–325.

Van Rossum, Wibo. "The roots of Dutch strategic human rights litigation: comparing 'Engel' to 'SGP'." In *Equality and human rights: nothing but trouble? Liber Amicorum*

SIM Special 38, edited by Titia Loenen, Marjolein van den Brink, Susanne Burri, Jenny Goldschmidt, 387–399. Utrecht: SIM/Universiteit Utrecht, 2015.

Vanhala, Lisa. *Making Rights a Reality? Disability Rights Activists and Legal Mobilization.* Cambridge: Cambridge University Press, 2011.

Vanhala, Lisa. "Anti-discrimination policy actors and their use of litigation strategies: the influence of identity politics." *Journal of European Public Policy* 16, no. 5 (2009): 738–754.

Vermeersch, Peter. *The Romani Movement – Minority Politics and Ethnic Mobilization in Contemporary Central Europe.* Oxford: Berghahn Books, 2006.

Voeten, Erik. "The Impartiality of International Judges: Evidence from the ECtHR." *American Political Science Review* 102, no. 4 (2008): 417–433.

Von Staden, Andreas. *Strategies of Compliance with the European Court of Human Rights.* Pennsylvania: University of Pennsylvania Press, 2018.

Vogiatzis, Nikos. "The Admissibility Criterion under Article 35(3)(b) ECHR: A 'Significant Disadvantage' to Human Rights Protection?" *International and Comparative Law Quarterly* 65, no. 1 (2016): 185–211.

Walsh, Jeff. "*What is strategic litigation and why is it important?*" Blog article in the European Database of Asylum Law. 14 February 2018. Available at https://www.asylumlawdatabase. eu/en/journal/strategic-litigation-european-level.

Weiss, Adam. "*What is Strategic Litigation.*" ERRC (blog). 1 June 2015. http://www. errc.org/blog/what-is-strategic-litigation/62.

Wiecek, William M. "Structural Racism and the Law in America Today: An Introduction." *Kentucky Law Journal* 100, no. 1 (2011): 1–21.

Yargiç, Sinem. "The Need to Amend Turkish Legislation to Ensure Political Participation in Turkey." *Yönetim Bilimleri Dergisi* 21, no. 11 (2013): 205–224.

Zemans, Frances Kahn. "Legal Mobilization: The Neglected Role of the Law in the Political System." *American Political Science Review* 77, no. 3 (1983): 690–703.

Index

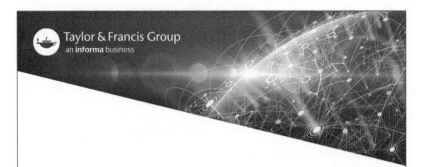